KU-795-475

1978-79 EDITION

GREECE
ON $10 & $15 A DAY

By JOHN WILCOCK

Published by
ARTHUR FROMMER, INC.
380 Madison Avenue
New York, New York 10017

Distributed by
SIMON AND SCHUSTER
A GULF+WESTERN COMPANY
1230 Avenue of the Americas
New York, New York 10020
0-671-24188-5

Distributed outside the USA and Canada by
FLEETBOOKS
c/o Feffer and Simons, Inc.
100 Park Avenue
New York, New York 10017

Distributed in Canada by
P J PAPERBACKS LTD.
330 Steelcase Road East
Markham, Ontario L3R2M1

Cover photograph courtesy of the Greek National Tourist Organization

Manufactured in the United States of America

CONTENTS

MAPS

"Other countries offer you discoveries in manners of lore or landscape; Greece offers you something harder—the discovery of yourself."

—Lawrence Durrell

"The tourist eagerly packs his bags, anticipating the pleasurable indulgence of his body under an ever unclouded sun, but is astonished to find that whether he wants it or not, he is being subtly coerced in one form or another to reinvestigate what he thought were his native principles, to understand their origins fully, to explore the meaning of his life and thought, to come to terms with himself. Greece is not a landscape alone; it is a state of mind that is perpetually renewing itself."

—Kimon Friar

Chapter I

GREECE ON $10 & $15 A DAY

The Reason Why

SINCE THIS BOOK was first written, Greece has seen many dramatic changes—political, social and economic. Oddly enough, the tourist has been little affected in any area except that of the pocketbook. Despite wide fluctuations in the political climate, life in most of the Greek islands—where the vast majority of tourists head for—goes on pretty much unchanged. From that point of view Greece is still one of the most peaceful, away-from-it-all places in the world—and may it always remain so.

But the price structure has been a different story with increases of as much as 100 per cent on restaurant meals over the past three or four years, and a commensurate increase in other areas. Greece is still just possible on $10 a day, based on that being the figure for one person's bed and meals. But in many places you will have to stay in rooms in private homes (just as comfortable) rather than hotels. On $15, it is entirely possible.

And now, before getting into the facts and figures, a few opening comments.

PAST vs. PRESENT: Before I went to Greece, nothing I had heard or read had prepared me for the fact that here was a country that had entered the 20th century. For some totally inexplicable reason, there seems to be a conspiracy among tourist bureaus, travel writers, and other guides to keep this knowledge securely buried. It's as if they felt that once the word got around that Greece might have something to offer besides ruins, tourists would desert the country in droves because they felt it might be like any other country.

Well, Greece is *not* like any other country—but neither does its sole attraction lie in its history.

I should say right at the outset that I am about as interested in history as any thoughtful human being can be. The events of the past have much to tell us about the present, and even more to teach us about the future if we choose to learn.

But history is something written after the fact, usually by people who weren't there, and a lively sense of what life means here and now is worth more than any museum or ancient site can possibly reveal. I find myself entirely in agreement with those who favor life over inanimate art (if it ever comes to a choice), and to back my point I would venture to suggest that anything that is being created today—whatever the objective standards of "good" or "bad" by which we judge it—will find its place in the museums of the future merely because it *existed* today.

And so I arrived in Greece with a prejudice—with a belief that monuments and ruins were going to be the sum total of what I would find, and that to display an ignorance about them, or (heaven forbid!) boredom with too many of them, would mark me as an illiterate ignoramus. And—being among tourists of a certain type (the type who boast of the number of tours they have taken)—that is precisely what happened.

Increasingly, I found myself forced into adopting extreme attitudes (i.e., that ruins were "dull") as a reaction to their complete intolerance for any suggestion that something might possibly have happened in the world, even in Greece, since the ancient civilizations died out.

THE UNEXPECTED GREECE: Greece surprised me, as I say, because it is a country that does not live in the past, and any visitor who fails to notice this, because of a preoccupation with history, is missing a lot of good things about life.

Some of the things I had read about the country had puzzled me. The light is brighter, they wrote, or the water is better, and the air is clearer and the sea is . . . well, more like a sea should be. How can you make head or tail of comments like that? Everybody knows that light is just light and water doesn't taste at all, and as for sea—it's that familiar salty stuff that you can find anywhere in the world.

But, astonishingly enough, I have to report that the things they wrote were true. The light is somehow different, the water—always ice cold but never iced—is the purest and richest and most satisfying drink I have ever tasted, and the sea . . . well, the sea made Greece and Greeks what they are.

It's a rugged, mountainous country, washed by the sparkling sea along more than 9,000 miles of coastline, from the breathtaking cliffs of Mount Athos in the north to the beaches of its magnificent islands, scattered for hundreds of miles across the Aegean Sea. In earlier times, the sea provided the only access to many parts of the country, and the Greeks have expended uncountable numbers of lifetimes trying to master it. Almost seven million out of Greece's total population of nine million inhabit either islands or coastal areas.

They have traveled the world learning the ways of the sea, and the ways of other lands, too, and there is hardly a town in Greece where somebody hasn't been to America and where somebody else doesn't speak French and German and Italian and all the international tongues that give the world its diversity.

THE ELEMENTAL LAND: Greece is a country of basic things, however trite a comment like that might sound. One learns the way some things always have been and always will be. I can't explain exactly why it is, but since I first arrived in Greece, I found myself constantly thinking about how man survived in the days when there was nothing to help him but his native intelligence. How, in fact, he might one day have to survive again.

What do I know, with my British and American "civilization," about building a home for myself in a wilderness, and making tools and creating fire and catching food and learning medicine and even devising a system by which order and meaning can be brought from chaos? Well, the Greeks did all that once—in a civilization so long ago that our Christian calendar is almost yester-

GREECE

Filippi

THESSALONIKI

Kastoria

Karial
AGION OROS

Ioannina

Meteora

Kalampaka

KERKIRA

Arta

Nea Anchialos

Nikopolis

Delfi

Ossios Loukas

KIOS

KEFALLINIA

Egosthena

Dafni

ATHENS

Vravrona

ZAKINTHOS

Korinthos

SALAMIS

Epidauros

Ermioni

PATMOS

Olympia

Kranidi

PAROS

Mistra

Sparta

MILOS

Monemvasia

Rodos

Lindos

Apolakia

CRETE

Iraklion

Potamies

Kritsa

Gortis

LASSITHION

day by comparison. Other peoples and civilizations have done it too, of course,
but somehow in Greece you are constantly being reminded of it in the little
day-to-day encounters with life.

The Greeks love figures, for example. Every storekeeper, every newsdealer, every waiter, will jump at the opportunity to write down prices for you on the back of an envelope or cigarette box. The waiters, in fact, all carry blank pads on which they scrawl the figures for each item, checking it along with you with a soft, thick pencil. Then, a quick calculation for 15 per cent of the bill is added, a neat line ruled underneath, and the addition checked lovingly and meticulously.

Do they ever think, these modern Greek mathematicians, of the heritage given them by their ancestor Pythagoras, who believed that numbers were "the secret soul of the universe," and who wrote: "Numbers take man by the hand and conduct him unerringly along the paths of reason"?

Greece is a country (many writers have said, including Henry Miller and Lawrence Durrell) that makes you examine yourself more closely. It is a country that it is difficult to define or to categorize, because the terms by which we are accustomed to evaluate things no longer seem to apply. It is a country where, for the first time in my 20 years of writing for a living, I felt inadequate to convey my impressions—and still do.

I know that I have become more aware of the subtle merger of day into night and have pondered, as never before, the stars and the moon and the age-old science of astronomy through which thousands of generations have tried to make sense out of the unfathomable. Astronomy and astrology are not fads, I mused, but arts—or at least systems. Like their modern-day cousin, psychology, they give their practitioners a working hypothesis until more evidence comes in.

And I have spent hours in old ruins—when more academically minded visitors were checking off the landmarks in their guidebooks—just watching ants. It may be true, as has been suggested, that ants have the organizational ability to one day take over the world, but before that day comes, they are just as much at the mercy of fate as the rest of us.

GRECIAN IMAGES: It is doubtful that you will have the same thoughts about Greece that I have, but it is even more doubtful that Greece will do nothing to your thought processes. In some hardly definable way, you will leave the country a different person than when you came. And you can scarcely fail to carry back the memories of evenings spent dining on the wide steps in Plaka to the bittersweet music of the groups from a dozen tavernas around you . . . or of the innumerable cats (have you ever noticed the way people express their own feelings in the way they handle a cat?) in every doorway . . . of the movie stars' pictures on bicycle seats . . . of the open-air movies with the illuminated view of the majestic Acropolis catching your eye at dull moments in the action . . . of the way the man who gave you directions ingeniously turned over his hand to indicate you wanted the next street over . . . of the smells of souvlaki cooking on street corners . . . of the sponge men, covered with their wares, in Syntagma Square (do they run for cover when it rains or just squelch along?) . . . of the shoeshine man who sits down while you stand . . . of the slender young girls in bright shift dresses, and bearded boys in grubby jeans from a score of countries.

Least of all can you forget the boats. To travel around the Greek islands by boat is a strangely sobering experience, but strangely satisfying, too. Deck class is not exactly comfortable. It involves struggling on board in competition with hordes of other people carrying beds, blankets, sleeping bags, air mattresses, boxes, bags, and suitcases; fighting for a place to sit; surveying rough seas, lack of interesting food, and often people being sick all around you.

But to compensate is the usually calm blue sea . . . the rippling waves . . . the sun . . . the moon . . . the rhythm of the ship's engine . . . the sound of the anchor sliding into the depths, and the whipped cream of the water as the boat docks . . . the passengers who fish with wire and hook while the boat waits for the launch bringing the new travelers out from the harbor. There is plenty of action on boats if you look for it.

THE BOOK ITSELF: But enough of these rambling thoughts, induced by the spell of Greece, and back to business.

The aim of this book, as in all the other $10-a-Day Books, is to show you how to keep basic living costs (room and three meals) down to $10 or $15 a day, per person. And there's nothing fantastic or gimmicky about that goal. Admittedly, with the cost of living rising rapidly over the past two years, it is not nearly as easy as it once was to find hotel rooms for less than $5 and meals for $2—and that's why we think you will find this book your most helpful traveling companion. Particularly in Athens, the impact of greater numbers of foreign travelers each year has forced prices up; and many hotels and restaurants recommended in the previous edition are, regretfully, no longer included. But for the traveler who really wants to see Greece itself, and not just other tourists, there are amazing values waiting.

The bulk of our recommendations are aimed at $5-6 per person hotel rooms and $3 meals. The hotels are clean and comfortable establishments that can be used with confidence by persons of all ages and both sexes. For those of our readers, students particularly, who want to travel in more spartan style, the book includes "starvation budget" suggestions that can reduce the daily tariff as much as possible. Equally, for those who wish to spend more, there are "big splurge" recommendations, including some rather elegant hotels and restaurants that are still moderately priced by American standards.

Finally, there are a few general recommendations that I want to make at this point, since they can save you a great deal of money.

WHEN TO TRAVEL: Greece is wonderful for a summer vacation, but so many people are finding this out that if you come during the high season you will not only pay more, you will see and enjoy less. During July and August many hotels require you to pay for a continental breakfast (whether you eat it or not) and some require demi- or full-pension, lunch and/or dinner, at around 200 drs ($5.66) each. This is about twice what these meals would cost you at a decent restaurant.

During the off season, most hotels offer discounts on room rates up to 30%, as well as eliminating the meal requirement. In the summer, rooms are rented at the daily rate no matter how long you stay or how large your party. Other seasons, there may be discounts for stays of three days or longer, and for parties of more than ten.

It is always difficult to make firm reservations at other than luxury hotels; if you arrive during the rush you will often find your first three choices of lodging booked solid, whereas rooms are readily available almost everywhere without reservations during the rest of the year.

Finally, if you are traveling alone and find all single rooms booked, your only recourse in summer is to pay for a double. During any other season, the manager will probably offer you a large double room for the cost of a single.

Note: The prices given in this book are based on summer one-day rates, since that seems to be the information most people want; but a spring or fall vacation in Greece is, to my mind, much to be preferred.

There are plenty of reasons other than cost to visit Greece in the off seasons. In April, though the Aegean is too cold for comfortable swimming, you will be able to see Greece at its most beautiful. After winter rains and a month of sunshine, the land is carpeted with lush green grass and more wildflowers than in all the lands of Oz. Almond and peach trees are in blossom, the days are warm and sunny, the nights cool. Orthodox Easter is the biggest holiday of the year (just one week after Western Christianity's Easter), and there are no words to do justice to the candlelight processions of Good Friday, or the frenzy of fireworks that bursts at midnight on Saturday.

In May the Aegean is warm enough for swimming, and whole fields are crimson with poppies. Olympia and Mycenae, crowded with tour buses during the summer, are nearly deserted. Orchards are heavy with lemons, and seaside tavernas are serving the big shrimp that run in the spring. In June, the sea bathing is beautiful, the tavernas and discotheques on the beaches are opening, jasmine fills the air . . . and the great migration is just beginning. By July, the famous Greek sun has burned up flowers and grass to produce those harsh yet strangely beautiful landscapes that so many people think of as "characteristically Greek," and the better-known resort towns—Hydra and Mykonos, for example—have become so Westernized that you can sit in a waterfront cafe for hours without even hearing a word of Greek.

Eventually September rolls around, the flood of visitors begins to ebb, and Greece starts to become itself again. The marvelous hospitality of the people, sorely tried in the summer, blossoms again when the grapes are pressed and the cool nights return. And there is still good swimming through October. The first rains refresh the land and a whole new crop of flowers begins to bloom as the oranges blossom. Try it some time.

September to May is the Greek's Greece, June to August is the tourist's Greece. They are two distinct places with one common denominator—beauty.

WHERE TO TRAVEL: Not very long ago, large chunks of Greece were inaccessible to all but the hardiest traveler. Mountain areas in the north and even parts of the Peloponnese had few roads and fewer hotels acceptable by Western standards. But times have changed. The problem now is how to decide—among thousands of classical and Byzantine sites, overwhelming landscapes, quaint villages, and sophisticated resorts spread over 40,000 square miles of mainland and more than a thousand islands—just how much you can see. If you are interested in classical Greece, Olympia and Delphi are absolutely a must. If pre-classic archaeology is your bag, Mycenae and Knossos are just as mandatory. If church history turns you on, Mystras, Meteora, and Mount Athos will be required stops. And if, like most of us, you just want a perfect place to relax, you may have to choose between the charms of green Corfu, white Mykonos, golden Skiathos, and a hundred other lovely islands.

One of the most frustrating and delightful things about a Greek vacation is the way the country can turn you on to pleasures you never knew you cared about. Like the professor in "Never on Sunday" you may come to see the ruins and find the real Greece while dancing in a taverna. On the other hand, you may visit Delphi for the view, and spend the rest of your vacation searching out classical ruins. So my first piece of advice is: don't pre-plan a hard and fast itinerary. Settle on a starting point where you can take a few days to get the

GREECE:
DISTANCES

Distances in Kilometers (1.6Km=1 Mile)

feel of Greece, and leave the rest of your time as open as possible. Most information and reservations are much easier to handle in person and on the spot, and very few places require reservations—at least not yet.

For most visitors, the first stop is Athens. This can be good or bad, depending on how Athens strikes you—which is why I have devoted so much space to it. On the positive side, the city is centrally located, contains all the information and facilities to help you discover the rest of Greece, has enough "must" sightseeing to occupy at least a few days, and is both more modern and more Western than the rest of Greece, which can ease the transition to a foreign culture. On the other hand, it is *so* Western—with noisy traffic, shoving crowds, pollution, and big buildings—that it can't really give you much idea of the rest of Greece.

There are two solutions. You can either start somewhere else (Corfu, for example, as this book does), or you can carefully seek out one of the neighborhoods of Athens off the tourist track, and get to know your neighbors. Either way, you will soon accumulate a lot of advice on where to go. (Warning: everyone's home island or village is the most beautiful in Greece.) Only when you've gotten to know the Greeks can you know Greece. So the second piece of advice is: don't isolate yourself in the circuit of planned tours, centrally located hotels, and tourist restaurants . . . unless you want to spend your time talking to people from Cleveland.

The gist of all this advice is: get off the beaten track and do some exploring. A great deal of exploration went into the research for this book, but I would never claim that it covers Greece. Guidebooks tend to tell you not only what you must see, but what you should feel when you see it. There's another sort of pleasure altogether in finding that little taverna with good food and a fantastic view that isn't mentioned in the books. Public transport, both bus and train, is inexpensive, safe, and regular. The people are just like people anywhere . . . though perhaps more hospitable than most, especially off the tourist routes. Even in little villages, someone will be able to speak English, and everyone else seems to be happy to play charades. At the worst, you might waste some time . . . but one of the most important lessons Greece can teach us harried, hurried Westerners is the pleasure of wasting time.

HOW TO TRAVEL: Two brief points: solo and simply. By "solo" I don't mean all by yourself—a traveling companion or three can make any trip more enjoyable. I mean that you can save a great deal of money and keep your options open to dally and change course if you don't rely on package tours. There are a few exceptions to this, mentioned later on; but by and large, group tours (1) cost more because they deal with hotels and restaurants catering to tourists, and because the operators have a profit margin; (2) maintain a rigid schedule, and (3) insulate you from contact with anyone but other tourists. They are popular because so many people are too timid or too lazy to make their own arrangements. But equipped with a little courage and this book you can easily match and surpass their itineraries for much less money.

Traveling "simply" refers to understanding the Greek hotel system and taking advantage of it. Hotels in Greece are assigned a category (A, B, C or D) by the government, and may not charge more than the standard rates for that category. The government-authorized price list is posted in the lobby and in each room, and the Tourist Police will actually close any business that violates the rates or is proved to have cheated tourists. In other words, your interests are fully protected and you can safely assume that you will receive exact value.

That value—the price variation for each category—is determined by the facilities offered. These include the presence of a bar, restaurant, and lounges as well as the size of the rooms and other amenities that may affect you more

TOURING GREECE

directly—like whether the bed has an inner-spring mattress. You are, of course, entitled to inspect the room (and the bed) before handing over your passport for sign-in. The greatest factor in price differential, however, is the presence in the room of a private bath. Americans tend to say "with bath" automatically when presented with the choice and by doing so they nearly double the cost of their room. "Without bath" does not mean that you have to go around dirty. Normally there will be a separate shower room and toilet just a few steps from your room, serving from two to seven rooms. These are typically clean and functional facilities . . . and I have made a point of recommending only hotels where that is the case. If you take a bathless room, a hot shower may cost you 14 drs extra, or it may be included in the price of the room.

Looked at another way, the older hotels tend to have rooms without baths as well as limited public facilities, while the newer ones have been built with tourists in mind. For a room with character and charm, a fabulous view, and perhaps a grand staircase or ancient courtyard, you will pay less than for a room that looks like a motel, in a concrete and glass box with a bar and restaurant you won't want to use. The final choice is up to you, but I will try to make clear just what your choices are.

MONEY IN GREECE: The unit of Greek currency is the drachma. At this writing, for one U.S. dollar you receive approximately 35 drachmas in exchange. That makes each drachma worth a little less than 3¢. Exchange rates vary a bit day by day. See the Appendix for a currency conversion chart.

The drachma is subdivided into 100 leptas, which come in denominations of 10, 20, and 50. The lepta coins are, by U.S. standards, worth very little.

Keep in mind that the drachma prices themselves, like prices in any currency in any country, can and do change in the course of time. The prices quoted throughout this book are those that were quoted to me at the time this book was researched. There is no guarantee they will remain the same as the months pass, nor should you expect them to remain the same. Still, the establishments mentioned in this book, whether their prices rise or not, ought to remain the best relative values.

THE FUTURE OF THIS BOOK: As with the other books in this series, we'd appreciate hearing about your own finds in Greece. Readers of $10-a-Day Books have one major thing in common, and that is to see as much as possible with as little expense as possible. In this, we can all help each other. If you have suggestions, corrections, additions that you have discovered and would like to share with all of us, please send them to Arthur Frommer, Inc., 380 Madison Avenue, New York, N.Y. 10017. Readers whose suggestions are printed as "Readers' Selections" in the next edition of *Greece on $10 & $15 a Day* will receive a free copy of that new, revised book.

THE $10-A-DAY TRAVEL CLUB: In just a few paragraphs you'll begin your explorations of the low-cost attractions of Greece. But before you do, you may want to learn about a device for saving money on all your trips and travels; we refer, of course, to the now widely known $10-a-Day Travel Club, which has gone into its 14th successful year of operation.

The Club was formed at the urging of numerous readers of the $10-a-Day Books, who felt that the organization of a $10-a-Day Travel Club could bring financial benefits, continuing travel information, and a sense of community to budget-minded travelers in all parts of the world. We thought—and have since learned—that the idea had merit. For by combining the purchasing power of thousands of $10-a-day'ers, it has proved possible to obtain a wide range of exciting travel benefits—including, on occasion, substantial discounts to members from auto rental agencies, restaurants, sightseeing operators, hotels, and other purveyors of tourist services throughout the United States and abroad.

In order to make membership in the Club as attractive as possible—and thus build a Club large enough to achieve the above goals—we have agreed to offer members immediate benefits whose value exceeds the cost of the membership fee, which is $10 a year.

And thus, upon receipt of that sum, we shall send all new members, by return mail, the following items:

(1) The latest edition of any *two* of the following books (please designate in your letter which two you wish to receive):

Europe on $10 a Day
Australia on $15 a Day
England on $15 a Day
Greece on $10 & $15 a Day
Hawaii on $15 & $20 a Day
Ireland on $10 a Day
Israel on $15 a Day
Mexico and Guatemala on $10 a Day
New Zealand on $10 & $15 a Day
Scandinavia on $15 & $20 a Day
South America on $10 & $15 a Day
Spain and Morocco (plus the Canary Is.) on $10 & $15 a Day

Turkey on $10 & $15 a Day
Washington, D.C. on $15 a Day

Dollar-Wise Guide to England
Dollar-Wise Guide to France
Dollar-Wise Guide to Germany
Dollar-Wise Guide to Italy
Dollar-Wise Guide to Portugal
Dollar-Wise Guide to California and Las Vegas
Dollar-Wise Guide to New England
Dollar-Wise Guide to the Southeast and New Orleans
(Dollar-Wise Guides discuss accommodations and facilities in all price
categories, with special emphasis on the medium-priced.)

Whole World Handbook
(Prepared by the prestigious Council on International Educational Exchange, the *Whole World Handbook* deals with more than 1,000 programs of student travel, study, and employment in Europe, the Near East,
Africa, Asia, Australia, and Latin America.)

Where to Stay U.S.A.
(By the Council on International Educational Exchange, this extraordinary guide is the first ever to list accommodations in all 50 states that cost
anywhere from 50¢ to $12 per night.)

(2) A copy of **Arthur Frommer's Guide to New York**—a pocket-size guide
to the hotels, restaurants, night spots, and sightseeing attractions throughout
the New York area.
(3) A copy of **Surprising Amsterdam and Happy Holland**—A pocket-size
guide by Ian Keown.
(4) A one-year subscription to the quarterly Club newsletter—**The Wonderful World of Budget Travel**—which keeps members up-to-date on fast-
breaking developments in low-cost travel to all areas of the world.
(5) A voucher entitling you to a $5 discount on any Arthur Frommer
International Inc. tour booked by you through travel agents in the United
States and Canada.
(6) Your personal membership card, which once received entitles you to
purchase through the Club all Arthur Frommer Publications for a third to a
half off their regular retail prices during the term of your membership.

Those are the immediate and definite benefits we can assure members of
the Club. But even more exciting are the further and more substantial benefits
which it is our continuing aim to procure. These are announced at frequent
intervals throughout the year and can be obtained by presentation of your
membership card. Equally valuable is the Club's eight-page newsletter, *The
Wonderful World of Budget Travel,* which carries such features as "The Travelers' Directory," a list of members worldwide willing to provide hospitality to
fellow members passing through their area, and "Share-a-Trip," budget travelers looking for share-cost companions. Also included: advance news of individual and group tour programs operated by Arthur Frommer International,
Inc.; information on freighter travel; tips on other travel clubs (air travel clubs,
home and apartment exchanges, pen pals, etc.) and on travel opportunities and
money-saving travel methods.

If you would like to join this hardy band of international budgeteers and participate in its exchange of information and hospitality, simply send $10, along with your name and address, to: $10-a-Day Travel Club, Inc., 380 Madison Avenue, New York, N.Y. 10017. Remember to specify which *two* of the books in section (1) above you wish to receive in your initial package of members' benefits.

PLEASE KEEP IN MIND: Throughout the following chapters are, obviously, names upon names of hotels, restaurants, towns, sightseeing attractions, people, etc. etc. etc. The trouble with all these names is that they've been snatched from the Greek alphabet and sort of translated into something more familiar to the English-speaker's eye. Unfortunately, there is little agreement on the English equivalents, phonetic or otherwise, for Greek letters and their sounds. So when you're trekking through Greece, looking for a particular town, say, and you come upon a sign written in Greek and "English," that English may just be somebody's very private phonetic rendition—and not quite the version (as haphazard a system as any other, I suppose) that appears in this book. It's really not all that confusing if you keep some frequent "inconsistencies" in mind:

The Alphabet

Aα	álfa	Nν	ní
Bβ	víta	Ξξ	xí
Γγ	gáma	Oo	ómikron
Δδ	thèlta	Ππ	pí
Eε	èpsilón	Pρ	ró
Zζ	zíta	Σσ	sígma
Hη	íta	Tτ	táf
Θθ	thíta	Yυ	ipsilón
Iι	yóta	Φφ	fí
Kκ	kápa	Xχ	hí
Λλ	làmtha	Ψψ	psí
Mμ	mí	Ωω	oméga

In the Roman (our alphabet is called Roman—now why is that? They didn't invent it) phonetic transliteration of the Greek, the following letters are sometimes confusingly interchangeable: C and K (Chania is also spelled as Khania); I and E; GH and G (Agios and Aghios); U and N; Y and I; V and B; O and U; I and A; AE and E. Actually, the list becomes somewhat interminable, and you may be better off paying attention to the sound the names are trying to convey, not the spelling.

Now that I've gotten that over with, I might as well mention that there are places throughout Greece that don't even bother with the English version. Those of you who had to learn the Greek alphabet for the old fratty lodge, or whatever, may be in luck. If you know the alphabet, you can puzzle out the sounds. A Gamma sounds like a G, a Theta like a TH, a Delta like a D, a Pi like a P, and so on. Except when you've finally figured out what the street sign says, your bus stop is long past. When in doubt, ask (in Greece it can be very entertaining getting where you're going). A sometimes reliable method is to ask whoever's running the desk at your hotel to write out your destination in Greek, so you can show it to the bus or taxi driver or somebody. That is, if you can communicate with whoever's running the desk. . . .

As for dusting off your ancient Greek and trying to communicate thereby —many happy returns. Nobody but a patriarch or two will understand you. It's like conversing with an Italian taxi driver in Latin.

Problems in communicating? Yes, but no problems with the people with whom you are trying to communicate. If a Greek can't help you, he'll take you to somebody who can. And good feelings come across in any language.

Chapter II

GETTING THERE

1. By Air
2. By Train, Ship, or Bus from Europe
3.-4. Stops on the Way:
   Corfu and Patras

FOR MOST PEOPLE, a trip to Greece includes a trip to other European destinations. Your first consideration, then, in flying yourself across the Atlantic, is where else you are planning to go. Since the fall of 1977, there are four new and extraordinarily cheap transatlantic fare categories—but three of them apply exclusively to London, and only one to Athens. In order to determine which of all possible fares is best for you, get yourself a pad, pencil, and pocket calculator and read on.

1. By Air

PLANE ECONOMICS: The basic premise from which you begin is that all the *major* international airlines charge exactly the same fares. All these lines—American and foreign—belong to the International Air Transport Association (IATA), an airline industry self-regulating body that prescribes fares, and periodically revises them, on a uniform basis for all its members (the fares must then be approved by the various governments involved, however). This means, essentially, that no IATA member can undercut another—IATA members compete for passengers in other ways. But not every airline belongs to IATA. Laker Airways, for one, whose London-New York Skytrain service is at this writing the cheapest way to get to Europe ($236 round trip), is not an IATA member. The reason that Laker is flying passengers so cheaply is that the airline received fare approval from both the American and British governments—and so did the IATA airlines once they came up with *two* competitive plans for that same New York-London run. Then all the other IATA carriers wanted in on the act to their other destinations, so now there is the Super-APEX fare—the cheapest way to get to Athens, among other places.

In this section, all the existing transatlantic fares (with the exception, of course, of first class) will be examined in descending price order, ending up with the cut-rate fares and the youth and charter options. Note that all the fares presented below are valid only as of this writing (fall, 1977). Double-check before you set your plans—with all the fares atumbling down, you never know what will happen tomorrow.

"REGULAR" FARES: Prices in each of the four following fare classifications are broken down in basic season and peak season. Basic season is September 15th to May 14th eastbound, October 15th to June 14th westbound. Peak season is May 15th to September 14th eastbound, June 15th to October 14th westbound. (The seasons are slightly different for the APEX excursions—see below.)

All the fares set forth in this section are valid through March 31, 1978. In each case the figure represents the *round-trip* rate from New York, on, of course, a jet aircraft. (The prices will, of course, be different from other U.S. cities with international service.)

Economy-Class Fares

The fares presented here are those you would pay if you could not avail yourself of any of the decidedly cheaper plans—an unlikely possibility. They do, however, include *free* stopovers at *any* of the European cities on the way to and from your destination—consult the airline you are choosing or a travel agent for details. Also, children between the ages of two and 12 travel at half price, infants under two at 90% off.

	Basic Season	Peak Season		Basic Season	Peak Season
Amsterdam	$ 650	$ 822	London	$ 626	$ 764
Athens	978	1132	Madrid	650	822
Barcelona	660	848	Munich	706	892
Berlin	706	892	Nice	762	916
Brussels	650	822	Oslo	694	878
Copenhagen	694	878	Paris	650	822
Frankfurt	694	878	Rome	826	966
Hamburg	694	878	Stockholm	748	932
Helsinki	782	970	Vienna	762	946
Istanbul	1008	1166	Zurich	694	878

14- to 21-Day Excursions

The first way to cut the cost of your air transportation to Europe is to take a 14- to 21-day "excursion"—which simply means that you plan a trip of 14 to 21 days' duration. If, under this plan, you go for a minimum of 14 days, but return no later than midnight of the 21st day following your day of departure, you'll save yourself, in basic season, 21% of the economy-class fare from New York to Athens. And the ticket includes five (maximum) air stopovers.

Note that these fares are available for Monday-through-Thursday departures only; if you fly on a weekend, you'll pay a $15 supplement (Friday and Saturday eastbound, Saturday and Sunday westbound).

	Basic Season	Peak Season		Basic Season	Peak Season
Amsterdam	$ 587	$ 681	London	$ 541	$ 631
Athens	769	875	Madrid	587	681
Barcelona	618	711	Munich	643	736
Berlin	643	736	Nice	666	758
Brussels	587	681	Oslo	634	725
Copenhagen	634	725	Paris	587	681
Frankfurt	634	725	Rome	717	807
Hamburg	634	725	Stockholm	704	797
Helsinki	747	838	Vienna	678	770
Istanbul	785	895	Zurich	634	725

22- to 45-Day Excursions

You're entitled to this even-cheaper fare if you travel a minimum of 22 days and a maximum of 45 days. You may purchase your reserved-seat ticket at any time—but if you can purchase it 45 days or more before you leave, the APEX fare (see below) is the better deal. Still, with the 22- to 45-day excursion, (basic season) you'll be saving 39% of the economy-class price. Weekend supplements apply, and there are no air stopovers included.

	Basic Season	Peak Season		Basic Season	Peak Season
Amsterdam	$ 487	$ 601	London	$ 467	$ 587
Athens	594	724	Madrid	487	601
Barcelona	502	617	Munich	526	644
Berlin	526	644	Nice	534	644
Brussels	487	601	Oslo	511	628
Copenhagen	511	628	Paris	487	601
Frankfurt	511	628	Rome	565	689
Hamburg	511	628	Stockholm	548	665
Helsinki	564	681	Vienna	551	665
Istanbul	615	754	Zurich	511	628

Apex Excursions

Meaning advance purchase excursions, the APEX fares allow you to fly to and from Athens at a savings of 47% of the economy-class price in basic season. All you have to do to qualify is purchase your ticket *more than* 45 days prior to your departure, and you must stay abroad a minimum of 14 days and a maximum of 45 days.

There is one disadvantage to the APEX fares that you should consider before you buy such a ticket: cancellation, no matter what the reason, entails a penalty charge of 10% of the fare or $50, whichever is higher.

As mentioned earlier, the duration of the "seasons" differs with the APEX fares. APEX basic season is September through May, eastbound or westbound. Peak season is June, July, and August, either direction. An additional difference: eastbound in July, westbound in August, you will be required to pay a "peak of peak" surcharge: $20 one way, $40 round trip. And, as with all excursion fares, there is a $15 supplement for eastbound travel on Fridays and Saturdays, the same for westbound crossings on Saturdays and Sundays—the chart below does not reflect these particular charges. (The cheaper super-APEX category is explained in the next section.)

	Basic Season	Peak Season		Basic Season	Peak Season
Amsterdam	$ 376	$ 477	London	$ 350	$ 440
Athens	515	622	Madrid	355	445
Barcelona	373	463	Munich	407	518
Berlin	407	518	Nice	422	529
Brussels	376	477	Oslo	392	498
Copenhagen	392	498	Paris	376	477
Frankfurt	392	498	Rome	459	571
Hamburg	392	498	Stockholm	419	525
Helsinki	426	530	Vienna	435	554
Istanbul	532	647	Zurich	392	492

THE NEW CUT-RATE FARES: As mentioned at the beginning of this chapter, there are *four* new fare categories for the transatlantic trip to Europe and they are spectacularly low. Although each of them is rife with conditions and restrictions, and although three of the four apply only between New York and London, most people (who might otherwise not travel) will be able to accommodate themselves to at least one of them—they're worth it.

Note: Each of the four fare categories, in effect since late September, 1977, has been instituted for a trial period only. Laker's Skytrain is approved through July, 1978; the other three, through March, 1978—but it is unlikely that they will be eliminated after those dates. The prices, limitations, regulations, etc., may change; the fare categories, if they prove successful, are expected to be around for a long while. By all means, check with a travel agent or the air carriers themselves, for all these fares are newly instituted as of this writing, and some of the details are bound to change.

We'll reverse our order of discussion in this section, beginning with the lowest of the cut-rate fares and moving upward.

Laker's London Skytrain ($236 round trip)

Requiring the most flexibility (and patience) of the prospective passenger, Skytrain service—between New York and London only—is also referred to as a "no frills standby" fare. Which means that it is nothing more (or less) than a shuttle service between London and New York, one flight a day each way. Tickets are sold one way only, and they may be purchased on the day the flight departs—first-come, first-served. As soon as the 345 seats are sold, the ticket desk closes; remaining customers must come back and try again the next day.

The cost from New York to London is $135. From London to New York it is £59—about $101, depending on the rate of exchange that particular day (so the round-trip $236 is really an approximation).

Planes leave JFK Airport in New York at 11 p.m. Tickets go on sale at 4 a.m. that day, and they must be purchased at the Laker sales office (see below). Cash, travelers checks, and select credit cards are taken. A travel agent may *not* write your ticket. You may purchase tickets for yourself, members of your immediate family, and *one* friend—have all the passports, please. The tickets may not be used on any other flight.

No free meals are included in the ticket price. You may, however, purchase them: a hot dinner for $3, hot breakfast for $2, continental breakfast or a snack for $1.25. You're welcome to bring your own food.

In New York, tickets for Skytrain are sold only at the Laker Travel Center, 9525 Queens Blvd., Rego Park, Queens—about halfway between Manhattan and JFK. After tickets are purchased, Laker will bus you to the airport.

The London airport from and to which Laker flies is Gatwick (not the more convenient Heathrow). Frequent trains run directly from Gatwick to Victoria Station, about a 35-minute ride. You must repeat the same ticket-purchase process at Gatwick when you're set to come home—there is no minimum or maximum stay required.

Laker Airways maintains two telephone numbers in New York with recorded messages about Skytrain. Call (212) 995-2113 for all the necessary rules and regulations, such as those just presented (call anyway—as we keep saying, such specifics tend to change), and including instructions on how to get to the Laker Travel Center by public transportation. Telephone (212) 459-7323 and you'll find out about seat availability for that day.

IATA London Standby Fare ($256 round trip)

Similar to the Skytrain plan, the standby fare—again, New York-London only—does have some advantages for its additional $20. Available on all scheduled New York-London flights of six major airlines (see below), it is also a same-day-only, one-way, first-come, first-served arrangement.

A limited number of seats that have not been sold at higher prices become available—at JFK—at various times (consult each individual airline) on the day of departure. Although you may purchase your ticket in advance, it is not confirmed until the day the seat becomes available, and it does not guarantee a seat.

The price is, actually, $146 to London, $110 from London. The following six airlines offer the standby fare: Pan Am, TWA, British Airways, El Al, Air India, and Iran Air—all of which use Heathrow Airport in London, and offer their usual free food during the flight.

IATA London Budget Fare ($256 round trip)

Offered by the same six airlines mentioned above, this identically priced fare has the advantage of a guaranteed seat. But for that privilege, you must notify the airline of the *week* in which you wish to depart, and you must do so at least three weeks in advance. In other words, you cannot request a specific flight on a particular day—just the particular week. The airline will assign you a flight and a day during that week, and they will notify you at least a week before the day of departure. You'll have to repeat the process in London. But since these tickets are also sold one way only ($146 to London, $110 to New York), you have the flexibility to choose another airline and another fare plan if you wish.

Planes serve Heathrow Airport in London, and all the usual free "frills" are yours on these flights.

GETTING TO ATHENS

IATA Super-APEX

This fare category—the only one of the new cut-raters applicable to Athens—is almost the same as the APEX fare detailed above . . . except that it's cheaper. From New York to Athens, the super-APEX is $473, bringing your savings up to 52% for the economy-class fare in basic season. The same length-of-stay and advance-booking requirements apply as with the regular APEX, and the ticket is sold on a round-trip basis only. Other than price, the major difference between this fare category and the regular APEX is that it is available from the following cities only: New York, Boston, Philadelphia, Washington, D.C., Chicago, Detroit, and Los Angeles.

Originally devised for the New York-London carriers (at $290), the super-APEX at this writing has not received official government sanction to other European destinations. Olympic Airways has applied for the $473 fare mentioned above, and it is expected to be approved. Call and check. What the super-APEX fares to other destinations will be is as yet uncertain. Ask about these too.

YOUTH FARE AND CHARTER PLANS: There are other ways to fly across the ocean. Young people between the ages of 12 and 24 qualify for youth fare tickets, which currently sell for $604 round trip between New York and Athens and are valid for an entire year. Available to everybody is a whole alphabet worth of charter and package plans: ABCs, GITs, OTCs, TGCs, etc. These are often run on a short-term basis (one to three weeks), some require purchase of land arrangements, and each has its own complicated set of regulations and restrictions. They are worth checking into, however: those with hotels and such included may well prove cheaper, all totaled, than buying your own cut-rate ticket and paying for your own hotels; and some of those plans not including land arrangements *are* cheaper, in fact, than the super-APEX fares. Your travel agent is the best source of information on all of these.

2. By Train, Ship, or Bus from Europe

BY TRAIN AND/OR SHIP: Daily trains leave **Rome** at 7:30 a.m. and 2:30 p.m. for **Brindisi**, a small and not particularly interesting town on Italy's east coast. It is not necessary to spend any time in Brindisi, because the trains arrive (in exactly seven hours) just in time to connect with the Hellenic Mediterranean Lines' *Egnatia* or *Appia,* waiting at the dock.

The ships offer many opportunities of traveling in style. First stop is the Greek island of **Corfu,** nine hours away, and to travel there in the cheapest fashion, it is necessary to buy only a $32 ticket, which offers use of a reclining, aircraft-type seat in a comfortable lounge, with no restrictions about roaming into all other parts of the one-class ships. There's a big lounge with television sets blaring, a small bar for coffee and snacks, a sundeck complete with swimming pool, which isn't filled with water until after the ship has left Corfu the following morning—so wait before you jump.

From Corfu, the ships head to the mainland of Greece. Athens-bound passengers will eventually debark at **Patras,** which is reached at 7 p.m. at night, and there a special bus transports them the remaining five hours' drive into Athens. This costs an additional $6 on the basic fare.

From Brindisi to Patras in the cheapest seat is about $35 and, assuming you don't eat or have brought food along with you, there need be no additional expense because use of lounge, pool and all decks is free to all. For about $60 you can have a comfortable bunk in a four-passenger cabin with wash basin, towels and closet to hang your jacket or dress. A cabin for two costs about $130.

The reclining seats don't actually recline very far, and the decision about whether to settle for one night's "sleep" of approximately the same comfort as you would get in a train or plane must be entirely up to you. If it were possible to stay up all night in the lounge or bar, matters might be different, but both close down at 1 a.m., so the additional charge for a bunk is worth it, in my view.

Schedules change slightly each year, but in the 1977 season there was daily service from Brindisi from mid-March through October.

It is possible, as I have said, to leave Rome the same day as you plan to catch the overnight boat. Second-class train fare from Rome to Brindisi is about $25.

The ferries from Brindisi to Greece also carry cars at a cost, depending on size, of $38 upwards. Further information is available from Hellenic Mediterranean Lines' office (Ufficio Passegeri de l'Adriatica S.P.A.N.), 11 Via Regina Margherita, Rome (tel: 23825). In Athens, the office is at Leoforos Amalias 28 (tel: 236-333). American Express and other tourist offices in both countries also carry schedules.

Fragline's car ferry *Georgios,* which operates between Brindisi and Patras three times weekly in summer, is a couple of dollars cheaper than HML. Check schedules at their Brindisi office: Corso Garibaldi 49, tel: 27667.

If you have a car, then DFDS Seaways is the cheapest. They operate from Bari in Italy at 3 p.m. every Thursday, arriving in Patras 17 hours later. The cost is about $50 per person for the cheapest bunk in a four-berth cabin. The trick is to take four in the car and then you don't pay for the vehicle at all. The ships are classy Danish types with sundeck, swimming pool, coffee shop, casino and duty-free stores, etc. DFDS also operates these boats from Genoa at 6 p.m every Monday, heading round the toe of Italy and arriving in Patras 44 hours later. Cheapest bunk in a four-berth cabin on this trip is about $75, with the same deal (free) for a car with four passengers. These rates are slightly cheaper in non-summer months. DFDS agents are **Morfimare,** L&G Morrfini, 38 Corso A de Tulio, Bari (tel: 221204); **W. Morphy & Son,** Votsi & Othonos at Amalia Street, Patras (tel: 77329); **G. E. Alevizos,** 14 Xenofontos St., Athens (tel: 3234-292), and **DFDS,** Ponte Calvi, Genoa (tel: 205807).

Hellenic Mediterranean Lines operates the *Cynthia* between Marseilles and Piraeus with stops at Genoa and Naples. It takes three or four days, depending on where you board, has stop-off time in port, fairly good (if monotonous) meals, and relaxation in an old-fashioned lounge or beside the seldom-filled pool.

It's an old and not too comfortable ship but the trip can be quite relaxing, and if you can afford it, better to take a double-bunked exterior cabin (B-1 class). Even then, the cabins are very small. The *Cynthia* runs every two weeks (it's a small ship, so it can go through the Corinth Canal), and bookings can be made via HML's agents, **Barry Rogliano and Co.,** at 14 Rue Beauvau, P.O.B. 843, Marseilles; or at **Mediterranean & Overseas Shipping,** Via XX September 29/7, Genoa, or Via S. Nicola alla Dogana 15, Naples. The ship also goes in to Alexandria, Cyprus and Beirut—and, of course, returns the same way via Piraeus.

In all, there are many ships making the trip from European ports to Greece—but my advice is to know that which you are boarding. In other words, not all the ships offer the same level of comfort or cleanliness. Reader Mary Ellen Kitler of Basel, Switzerland wrote me that the ship *Kalokodronis* of the New Epirotiki Lines (it runs from Brindisi to Piraeus) was, in her opinion, not up to snuff.

BY BUS: Half a dozen lines are now operating buses direct from London to Athens and back, usually with three overnight hotel stops en route. **Pimlico Travel** at 36 Ebury Street, London SW 1 (tel: 01/730-5231) are agents for Economy Holidays of 18 Panepistimiou Street, Athens (tel: 634-045) and their fares are around $120 round trip. Route is via Munich, Zagreb and Belgrade, and trips are made weekly.

Cheaper is Greg Williams' famous **Magic Bus,** a gaily painted vehicle with reclining seats, tapes of rock music and a hostess. Bus leaves Athens each Wednesday morning, takes four days to London with stops for camping "near rivers or beaches." (If you lack camping equipment you sleep on the bus.) Fare is about $60 each way. Write to Greg Williams, Middenstraat 11a, Rumpt, Holland, or check with Bill outside American Express in Athens any morning. (Other times you can find him at Mano's Rest House, 16 Kidathineon Street, tel: 3220-336.)

3. Corfu

Corfu (or **Kerkira,** as the Greeks call it) is a beautiful island rich with almost every kind of vegetation, including cactus and palm trees. There are said to be more than three million olive trees alone on the island, and certainly it is luxuriously green wherever on it you may happen to travel. Oranges, lemons, sugar cane, and vines also grow in profusion, and one of its native products is a wine made from kumquats.

The visitor's first sight, from the boat as it traverses the narrow channel between the island and the Greek and Albanian coasts, is of tall, brown buildings and the town partly nestled between a pair of old forts. The forts are called the "old" and the "new" forts, but both were built by the Venetians at least four centuries ago.

The Venetians were only one of many foreign armies that occupied the island at different times: the Romans and the Goths were in control before them, the Turks invaded in the 16th and 18th centuries, the French (under Napoleon) and the Russians later occupied the island. After the fall of Napoleon, the British became the island's protector and would have probably owned the island still, but for the machinations of a brilliant Greek politician, Ioannis Capodistrias, who arranged for its union with Greece from 1864 onwards.

AROUND THE TOWN: Narrow streets winding between the tall old buildings give a fascinating flavor to the old town, around which it is very satisfying

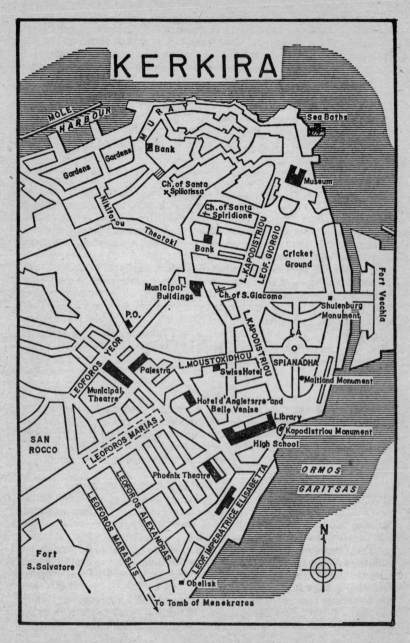

to wander, peeping through shuttered windows, and stepping into the doorways of shops and homes, sometimes almost into the laps of working tailors, cobblers, or carpenters to avoid passing cars and motorcycles.

Barber shops are on almost every street: it's an event in itself to have a shave or a haircut while watching the passing action in the barber's big, clean mirror, with the strains of Greek pop songs from the jukebox of a nearby cafe, a fitting accompaniment.

The **"new" fortress,** built in the 1550s, overlooks the port, just off the square on the harbor. It is necessary to obtain military permission to go inside, but this can usually be arranged through the tourist office. The **"old" fort** overlooks the Esplanade, or main square, and is also occupied by the military, although you will be allowed inside if you wait at the entrance gate for a few minutes, until the authorities consider that enough people have gathered to make it worthwhile sending along a guide.

At another side of the square sits the impressive **Royal Palace,** illuminated at night with the royal coat-of-arms, and housing the public library, small art gallery (including some Chinese and Japanese art), and archaeological museum. It was built by the British (other traces of the British on Corfu: occasional cricket matches and ginger beer) in the early 19th century and used as a royal residence until 1939.

Just off the square, on Voulgareos Street, is the **town hall.** This was built in 1690 as a Venetian naval officers' club, and converted into a theater in the following century. It has been used as a town hall since the beginning of this century.

Among the numerous churches in the capital, that of **Saint Sypridon** —Corfu's patron saint—is probably the most interesting. Sypridon, born on Corfu, became a bishop, and when he died his body was buried on the island. His presence there is popularly believed to have saved the island from a plague in the 17th century and defeat by the Turks in the 18th. The church (two blocks back into town from Kapodistriou Street) celebrates its heritage with great festivity four times a year; each time the remains of the beloved saint are carried around the island. The dates: Palm Sunday, the Saturday before Easter, August the 11th, and the first Sunday in November.

CORFU'S BUDGET HOTELS:

CORFU'S BUDGET HOTELS: The boat docks at the far end of the harbor, a walk of about two or three hundred yards from the main part of town. There's one hotel down here, the **Ionion** (Stratigou St., tel: 29915) which costs around 230 drs single, 360 drs double without bath. It's cheap but pleasant enough with airy rooms opening onto balconies with a view across the water.

A short walk along the harbor past a score or so of small fishing boats will bring you to Plateia Georgiou, a tree-filled square behind which sit three D-class hotels, the **Acropole** (K. Zavitsianou St. 19, tel: 29569); the **Konstantinoupolis** (tel: 29826) and the **New York** (Ypapartis St., tel: 29922), all okay if a bit spartan—and cheap: around 215 drs single, 250 drs double.

There's a classier hotel here, too—the **Hotel Astron** (7 Donzelot Street, tel: 29505)—just past the New York Hotel, but it's pretty expensive: about 700 drs double.

The area behind this pleasant square on the harbor is a jumble of narrow streets and alleyways lined with crumbling old buildings. At first it seems like a maze without rhyme or reason, but if you locate the street called Nikiphoros Theotokis, just behind "the building with a street through it," you'll see that, starting in a small way, it makes almost a right angle turn and becomes a comparatively broad main street off to the left.

Follow Nikiphoros Theotokis to its inevitable end, and you'll be in a vast, park-like square called the Esplanade, or Kato Plateia. The last street that crosses Theotokis before the Esplanade is Kapodistriou.

An ideal place to stay is the lovely **Hotel Arcadion** (tel: 22671), a cheerful place overlooking the Esplanade (main square) and built in traditional Corfu style. Note the wrought-iron work above the entrance, the brass chandeliers in the dining room, the wood on the lounge ceiling, imported from India. Rooms here have that "extra touch": wood dressing tables with red velvet cushioned stools, music, hand-embroidered pictures done by Mrs. Moschou, the charming English-speaking manager. All in all, more like an elegant home than a hotel. Most rooms have showers: singles 250 drs without bath; doubles around 425 drs without bath, 485 drs with.

Especially friendly to our readers is the 40-room **Hermes** (Markora 14, tel: 29268), which is just off San Rocco Square, a good place to stay if you plan on catching a lot of buses to the beach, and convenient to restaurants and the Esplanade. The young owner, who speaks English, has a modern, clean, and attractive place with marble lobby and stairs, tiled floors covered with red carpeting, and minuscule balconies. Also a pleasant little bar (breakfast available but no other meals). Single rooms cost 230 drs without shower, 300 drs with; doubles, 350 and 425 drs respectively. Directly on the same busy San Rocco Square is the **San Rocco** (tel: 28170), a D-class hotel, with rooms from 200 drs single and 250 drs double, all without bath.

The **Hotel Bretagne** (Nat. Stadiou 27, tel: 28-724129) is a comfortable and (according to a reader) "immaculate" place with modern furniture and balconies: about 425 drs double.

Numerous small, cheap hotels are scattered around the island, at beaches and inland. North of the town, at Ipsos, is the **Hotel Mega** (tel: 93208); south at Gastouri is the **Achilleon** (230 drs single, 350 drs double). Also at Ipsis is the slightly less expensive **Hotel Kostas,** 230 drs single, 320 drs double. Some of these small hotels usually insist on full board, but the Mega will let you have room without meals but with bath for 425 drs double, 350 drs single. The Achilleon is a friendly spot. Patrons are encouraged to dine outside in their swim suits. There are **car-camping sites** at Kondokali (7 kms), Ipsos (15 kms), and Dassia (13 kms)—35 drs daily, plus 35 drs for the car, and 35 drs for the tent—with all facilities and a bar. All over the island are **houses to rent** (the tourist office will recommend a good real estate agent and also help you find a room), and in many villages **rooms** are available in private homes for about 150 drs per person. The **youth hostel** charges 60 drs nightly.

Further down from Kaiser's Bridge—on the seaside—is the **Hotel Potamaki,** (demi-pension only, for about 1000 drs double). In the same area, which is a beautiful place for swimming, there are also **private houses** for accommodation and cheap tavernas. The area is called Moraitika and can be reached by bus from San Rocco.

There is no youth hostel in Corfu town itself but there are **hostels** at Kondokali and at Aghia Iohannis, about nine kms away. Another inexpensive alternative to the hotels in the increasingly crowded town is to pitch a tent under the olive and orange trees at **Pyrgi Village,** on the beach about eight miles away. This camping site has showers and telephone. And for about 100 drs per day you can rent a bicycle or for 150 drs a scooter, and thus be independent of public transport. Taxis are still relatively inexpensive. Cars cost a fortune to rent but aren't really needed because the island is well served by buses.

READER'S SELECTION: "The **Hotel Bretagne,** Nat. Stadiou St. 27, is kept in immaculate condition and was one of the most comfortable of our European tour (about 350 drs double with breakfast)" (Chas. Woollams, Terrigal, Australia).

. . . AND RESTAURANTS, ETC.: No shortage of restaurants in town, of course; try the **Akteon** (tel: 22894) if you want the best view while you dine. At night there are two new discos to reconnoiter: the **Bora Bora** and the **Coucouvaya,** both about one kilometer from the new port. In Dassia, eat at the **Dionysos** taverna, where you can get wine straight from the barrel.

THE ACTION: The big event of the day is to go to **Pelekas** (after mid-July) to see the sun set. Don't knock it until you've tried it. The bus leaves from San Rocco Square and jogs its way along a beautiful slice of countryside past women leading donkeys, and through semi-tropical terrain. Soon the climb begins up the range of hills that fringe the west coast of the island, and the driver swings the bus giddily around one hairpin turn after another. It's a big bus, and its unwieldiness sometimes necessitates considerable maneuvering on a particularly sharp corner.

By the time the small mountain village of Pelekas, with its pink houses, comes into view, there are tantalizing glimpses, through the trees, of the coast and the limitless seas beyond. But there is more to come. The bus swings round and round until, at the peak of the hill, it draws up beside a small cafe, just as the sun begins its last lap down the western sky.

This bus is a special one, laid on at 6 p.m. each day for tourists, but there are other people up here, too; rugged German or English hikers, camera bugs, an Italian family with food and wine, wealthy Greeks in big American cars. The sunset performance draws a mixed audience.

At one end of the hill, stone steps lead up to a circular viewing point that looks like a small bandstand, and it is already filled with people looking like plums bursting out of a Christmas cake. The platform is at the highest point of the hill, and from it there is a panoramic view of 360 degrees. It would be a spectacular point from which to stage a fireworks display.

Right on time, the sun goes down. For a while, it sits as though suspended, a glowing, deep-bronze disc half-submerged in puffy, translucent fibre. With a pair of sugar tongs, it seems, you could manage to pull it out again before it completely disappears.

The performance is over about 8 p.m. and, up on this mountain, there is a definite chill in the air. The bus driver, who has seen the show many times before, briefly honks his horn and the audience reclaims its seats for the ride back to town.

AROUND THE ISLAND: North of Corfu town, the area around **Ipsos** is inundated with new hotels and is beginning to look like Miami Beach. Once past there though the view gets increasingly spectacular as the road rises higher and higher offering tantalizing glimpses of pretty coves far below, and of the Albanian hills constantly changing color and getting closer, then further away as the highway curves in away from the coast. The cliffs at **Nissaki** are a good spot to stop and admire the view.

At **Koulouri** turn off and head downhill to the **White House Restaurant,** and pause for a look at the house where Lawrence Durrell lived for three years and where his book *Prospero's Cell* was written. From here to Kassiopi the road is lined with lush olive groves, often studded with massive gray boulders. **Kassiopi** itself is a charming seaside village on a gorgeous bay, populated like most other parts of Corfu by garrulous Germans and Britons on package tours. The **Kassiopi Taverna** and the **Oasis** have rooms. The cheapest place to eat is **To Kyma,** which commands a fine view of the harbor.

A big, new hotel complex was rumored for this stretch of coast but a wealthy Rothschild bought the land and prevented it being built.

Heading south from Corfu town, following the signs to Lefkimi, you'll first reach **Achillion** where a kitsch palace sits amid a lush, tropical garden with gorgeous views of the bay of Corfu and the green inland hills. The palace is now a casino/hotel where you can examine the memorabilia of the Empress of Austria.

Next continue down the coast to **Benitses,** once a charming fishing village, now jammed with tourists, most of whom seem to spend their time swarming down the highway from one town to the next comparing prices in the tourist shops. For accommodations, there are two C-class hotels, the **Spinule** and the **Benitsa;** and for eating, the restaurant **Trata.** Also plenty of rooms for rent.

For those wishing to combine urban living with proximity to the sea this stretch of coast—Benitses/Miramare/Moraitka/Messonghi—is a better base than crowded Corfu town. Easily accessible by bus it abounds in hotels, tavernas, restaurants and gift shops—also swarms of tourists who easily outnumber the natives. At **Paleokatstritsas** you can sometimes get a room at the cafe/bar to the left of the hotel Zephyros for around 200 drs single, 330 drs double including breakfast.

More likely is **Pelekas** where, somehow despite the never-ending caravans that plow through the tiny town the locals manage to pretend tourists don't exist and, to the few that stay, offer fantastic hospitality: rooms for about 120 drs single, 200 drs double. There's a beautiful beach not far away which has been discovered by the international backpack crowd, and music and partying continues into the early hours all week.

Corfu's best beaches, by the way, are at **Sidari** and **Glyfada,** both reachable by bus. Others are at **Ag. Gordis** (south of Glyfada); **Ag. Georgios** (southern tip of island); **Ag. Stephanos** and **Angiou** (northwest corner of island). By the way, the mountain villages are great to visit because tourists mostly want to be on the beach and so tend to avoid the high places.

Three lovely coves, **Nissaki, Kalami** and **Koukoura,** mentioned by Durrell in his book, are strung out in the north of the island, where you'll also find Corfu's highest mountain, **Mount Pantocrator** (3,000 feet).

BUS TRANSPORTATION: The National Tourist Office has bus schedules available. Buses do run almost everywhere with green buses (mostly heading north) leaving from the old port (near the new fortress square) and blue buses (mostly southern routes) leaving from San Rocco square. Twice a week there's a long-distance bus leaving Corfu for Paris and London, via Rome, Milan and Geneva. Best place for information on this, and almost anything else, is the **Corfu Travel agency** (Kapodistriou 18, tel: 29596) whose owner, Marie Aspioti, is the author of a book about the island.

BOATS FROM CORFU: There are boats to Brindisi (Italy) at 9 a.m. every day but Wednesday. The trip takes eight hours. The *Egnatia, Poseidonia* and *Appia,* all operated by Hellenic Mediterranean Lines, are luxury boats with bars, swimming pools, etc. and ply between Patras and Italy, calling at Corfu on the way there and back. Of a similar class is Fragline's *Georgios* which follows the same route three times each week. A Russian-operated hydrofoil, the *Kometa,* does the same trip faster for around the same rates but lacks the luxury trimmings. This makes the trip between Corfu and Brindisi daily.

There's a daily boat from Corfu at 2:30 p.m. (except Sundays) to the lovely island of **Paxos,** and the *Chrysovalandou* and the *Oinoussai* ply between Corfu and Patras daily leaving Corfu at 9:45 a.m., arriving at Patras at 6:30 p.m., and returning to Corfu at 8 a.m. en route to Brindisi.

The *Mediterranean Sky* leaves at 10 p.m. nightly for Bari. There's a boat to Dubrovnik every Thursday at 8 p.m., and a Yugoslav boat, the *Slavija,* departs for Dubrovnik and Rijeka every Tuesday at 3:30 p.m. "A lot of people find it economical as well as relaxing to take a ferry boat from Rijeka down to Corfu," my adventurous friend Jovanka says, "and thus avoid all the tiresome hassle of traveling night and day overland by train."

MISCELLANEOUS: Long distance **phone calls** take hours and can be arranged from hotels or from the phone company office at Mantijarou Street. But if you simply want to call Athens, dial 021 and then the Athens number. **Telegrams,** same address. . . . Main **post office** is at Paleologhu Street. . . . **Tourist police,** tel: 303. . . . Coldest months of the year are January and February, when the temperature drops to 40-50 degrees; in September and October, it's 65-75 degrees. . . . Best bookstore (plenty of paperbacks, most foreign papers) is **Boura's** near the Corfu Bar on the Esplanade. . . . There are five open-air cinemas (**Phoenix, Oasis, Alsos, Nafsika,** and **Orpheus**). . . . Best place to find a **taxi** at night is right across from the Hotel Arcadion on the Esplanade. . . . Eat fruit in Corfu, it's delicious. . . . **Tennis** available for tourists. Ask the tourist office to arrange guest membership. . . . Public library has books in English. . . . The **tourist office** (open 8 a.m.-1 p.m., 5-7 p.m. daily; Sundays 9:30-11 a.m.) is situated in the new Government Building (Diikitirion) next to the post office on Samara Street, tel: 229-730. There is a **port information office** where the boat docks, open mid-March through October—7-9 a.m.—for arrival and departure of Italy-Greece ferry boats (tel: 229-298).

BY AIR: There are three flights daily to Athens (Corfu office: Kapodistriou 20, tel: 23694), with extra flights on Saturdays—about one hour and $30 each way.

READERS' SELECTIONS: "For handwoven Greek material, the shop of **Raphail Bacolas** at Paleologou 84 has the best buys in Greece" (Virginia Hughes, Ft. Mitchell, Ky.). . . . "There is an ancient **synagogue** in Corfu dating from the 16th century, used by the survivors of a Jewish community which was shipped to concentration camps in WWII. It is an emotional and interesting experience to visit it. Contact Moisse Soussis of the King Alkinas Hotel for details" (Carl Hopfinger, Canoga Park, Calif.).

CRUISING FROM CORFU: One of the pleasantest ways to spend a week off Corfu is to take a cruise in the 85-foot yacht now operated by **Viking's Tours,** with visits to Kefalonia, Lefkas, Paxi, Parga, Ithaki and Scorpios. This is cruising on a charmingly small scale with plenty of stops for bathing and sightseeing and an average of five hours per day at sea. There are six double berths aboard, but most passengers are accommodated in comfortable rooms at the various island ports of call. (In spring and fall this cruise switches to a Cyclades route instead.)

The cruise leaves Athens (bus to Patras, ferry to Kefalonia) every Thursday, and the price per person of $265 (1978) includes everything except lunch, dinner and shore excursions.

What follows is a brief diary kept by this writer on a recent Viking cruise:

Wednesday: Up at 7 a.m. to catch the bus to Patras via the Corinth canal where a stop is made for lunch. At 1:30 we're at Patras and boarding the ferry for the four-hour ride to the port of **Sami** on **Kefalonia** where the Viking boat awaits us, the rest of our party already aboard. Viking's allows the cruise to be joined on both Wednesdays (at Sami) and Saturdays (Corfu) so there is always an overlap—and a welcome influx of new passengers in the middle of everybody's cruise. **Kefalonia,** our first stop, is the island of wonders: a stone said to move of its own accord, snakes who visit a certain church every August, fascinating underground caverns. Sami, where the ferry from Patras docks, is pleasantly nondescript, but a walk west along the shore passes a series of tiny rocky beaches and a small seaside lake where the water is almost fresh, having traversed the island via some subterranean channel after entering on the island's northern shore near Argostolion. Here is an ancient mill wheel which once provided power from the onrush of the sea entering the channel. An amazingly picturesque spot.

Argostolion, the island's capital, is connected to Sami, 23 kms away, by bus. Its harbor is a broad channel on which can often be seen seaplanes landing to scoop up sea water, which is then dropped onto the late summer fires which break out on the surrounding hills. One of the island's loveliest beaches, **Plati Yialos,** is not far away, in an area seriously damaged by the 1953 earthquake. The countryside is still dotted with ruined houses although one hilltop community has been rebuilt as a model village—lovely homes and bougainvillea-filled gardens—by a wealthy local shipowner. In the island's center are other sleepy villages: **Mataxata,** for example, where Lord Byron wrote, and **Travijata,** with its ruined Venetian castle nearby. The unpaved road to the monastery of **Aghios Andreas** winds past the vineyards where grow the sweet grapes which produce the island's famous Rombola wine. When the harvesting is on passersby will be offered handfuls of the grapes to sample. The road is lined with limestone kilns where intense burning of the stone mixed with wood produces the chalk to whitewash local homes.

Thursday: Today we're at **Ithaca.** "When you start on your journey to Ithaca," Homer wrote, "then pray that the road is long, full of adventure full of knowledge. . . . Always keep Ithaca fixed in your mind/To arrive there is your ultimate goal/But do not hurry the voyage at all." The island, its tranquil capital of **Vathi** dominating the most sheltered of natural harbors, "undoubtedly echoes the name of the island's mythical hero Ithacus," wrote the noted archaeologist Heinrich Schliemann. Homer speaks of it in the Odyssey, says Schliemann, and after the days of Ulysses "the island vanishes from the pages of history and the writers who came after Homer mention Ithaca only in importance in the heroic age." Today, reached by thrice-weekly ferry from Patras, it is as rewarding a destination as when Homer mentioned it 2,500 years ago. The lights of the **Katharon monastery** high atop **Mount Anoge** (Homer's Mount Neriton) look like a burning fire in the hills when seen from Vathi's harbour, thousands of feet below. So it's hardly surprising to find that the view of the town from the monastery is magnificent. It is only by ascending the hill (one hour by taxi over a precipitous, rocky path) that one gets Ithaca into perspective and realizes that it is almost two islands of equal size, connected by a narrow isthmus of land on which was located—according to local tradition—the ancient palace of Ulysses.

Friday: If anyone ever asks you what you'd like for a very special birthday present, say: "A fireworks display over the harbor from the ramparts of **Parga castle.**" The site of this Venetian fortress, overlooking the capital of the tiny island of **Lefkas,** is spectacular: the culmination of a steep climb through the town's winding back streets and up through the pines and cypress which have reclaimed the castle grounds. There's a magnificent view of tree-clad mountains sloping down to a glorious bay whose sandy beaches nudge clear coral waters. Parga snuggles between this bay and the town's harbor, the 17th-century castle on a promontory overlooking both. From the harbor an excursion can be made to one of the most famous sites of classical times: the **Acheron Necromaanteion** or Oracle of the Dead, at **Ephyra,** which (according to Homer's *Odyssey*) Odysseus was advised to visit by the magician Circe. For centuries after Homer's time, the famous oracle was consulted by kings and commoners, who took a guided tour around the subterranean labyrinth, just as visitors tour its ruins today. The sanctuary was abandoned after 167 A.D., when the Romans destroyed it.

Saturday: Most people love Corfu and there was some disquiet among the passengers when they learned our stop here would be only for a day. But by the time everybody was back aboard it was obvious from their comments that it was the shopping that had appealed the most. Dresses, T-shirts, tie-dyed outfits were almost all anybody had to talk about, although there were a few scattered comments about the attractive narrow streets of Corfu's old town and the availability of horse-drawn buggy rides (150 drs for ten minutes!). None of the cruise party, it transpired, had time to visit the **Achilleon,** the fabulous palace built by Elizabeth of Austria two centuries ago, part of which is now a gambling casino. The few members of the party who became bored with window-shopping took the 30-minute bus ride across the island to **Paleokas-tritsa,** where a pebbly beach in a lovely cove is thronged with vacationists staying at the adjoining pensions. There are prettier bays en route but the danger of alighting at any of them is that the return buses are too full to stop. At 9:30 p.m., four nights a week, the **Sound & Light** show in Corfu's Venetian Palace is in English—but tonight it rained.

Sunday: Now we're on the return leg, heading south, and today's stop—at the charming island of **Paxos**—may be one of the nicest of all. There's really nothing much to do here except lie in the sun, so, after the obligatory coffee in one of the harbor cafes, almost everybody headed for the sea-splashed rocks just outside the port and did just that.

Monday: Though an island, **Lefkas** is joined by a narrow causeway to the Greek mainland, and a peaceful lagoon forms part of the harbor of its capital on the island's northern tip. The one main street seems to stretch interminably, its major landmark an unusual clock atop what looks like a Meccano-set metal tower. Behind the stores, in the side streets, donkeys graze on vacant lots and bright blue morning glory hangs languidly over crumbling walls. From the middle to the end of August, Lefkas stages an annual folk-dance festival with international groups from many countries. There was once a shrine to Apollo here on the island with annual games that took place in the god's honor, so nothing much has changed.

Tuesday: After our usual stop for swimming today (at some point the boat always anchors offshore and lets down the ladder), we sailed right into the bay of **Scorpios** island where the Onassis family keeps a cruiser moored. Everybody craned their necks to see but there was not a sign of life on the island. Most of the day was spent exchanging names and addresses. We've all made new friends and seen places we could never have reached under our own steam. "Ithaca has given you the beautiful voyage," Homer wrote. "Without her you would never have taken the road/But she has nothing more to give you. . . . With the great wisdom you have gained, with so much experience? You must surely have understood by then what Ithaca means."

4. Patras

For some people, Patras is their first taste of Greece, and it's a pleasant place to begin. A busy port, it commands the western entrance to the Peloponnese, and a ferry at Rion, seven miles away, offers access to Northern Greece. Most of the town ascends a hill from the port—several streets end in steps—and the view from the top is worth the climb.

Although a bustling town (pop. 100,000), Patras prides itself on being less frenetic than Athens, but the numerous new apartment buildings that are still going up show that it shares in the current prosperity.

Strolling the streets is pleasant, and sitting along the harbor or at the end of the pier, watching men fish or do calisthenics near the wall of the breakwater, is even more pleasant.

On the spacious Plateia George I, in the heart of the city, is a magnificent fountain: gryphons spouting water and all presided over by a pipe-playing Pan. Sit at the open-air tables of the **Sweet Palace** cafe, which competes for business with the garish Texas Fried Chicken Inc.

ORIENTATION AND HOTELS: Whether you get off the bus from Athens or the boat from Piraeus or Brindisi, you'll be in what at first glance appears to be a rather drab harbor with plenty of hotels, all within walking distance. The Majestic faces right onto the little square. The Mediterranee is just up the street. Three others—the Cecil, the Angleterre, and the Splendid—are just to the left, along the front, and three more are two blocks off to the right along St. Andrew's Street (the one *behind* the harbor). Except for the Mediterranee, which is new, they all are badly in need of paint jobs and some sprucing up.

The 63-room **Majestic** (tel: 272002) has rooms with balconies (mostly with a view of the harbor), and charges about 350 drs single, 450 drs double for its few rooms without bath. The **Hotel Mediterranee,** at St. Nikolas 18 (tel: 279602), is up the street from the Majestic. All rooms and hallways are fully carpeted; shower in every room, as well as balconies with tables and chairs; telephones; elevators whose doors light up when they arrive at your floor. A first-class hotel in style but C-class in price, due to a slight oversight on the size of a couple of the singles and doubles, which cost 400 drs and 500 drs respectively. The attached restaurant has an exceptionally clean and well-kept kitchen.

A six-minute walk to the left of the Majestic as you face the water is the **El Greco** (tel: 272931) a compact 30-room hotel charging 390 drs for double with bath, 300 drs for a single with bath. A few rooms without bath are available. Breakfast is 30 drs.

You might also consider walking along Ag. Andreon or Ag. Nikolaon and looking for a cheap hotel that suits your taste. There are several, including the following:

On Ag. Andreon—**Delphi** (tel: 273050), **Kentrikon** (tel: 277276), **Olympia** (tel: 277512). On Ag. Nikolaon—**Hellas** (tel: 273352), and **Ilion** (tel: 273161).

If you are uncertain about choosing a place to stay, remember that it is quite acceptable to ask to see the room the desk clerk offers, before registering.

RESTAURANTS IN PATRAS: Aghiou Nikolaon (St. Nicholas) Street, the one that leads off the harbor at right angles between the Majestic and Delphi hotels, houses half a dozen restaurants—their tables spread around the side-

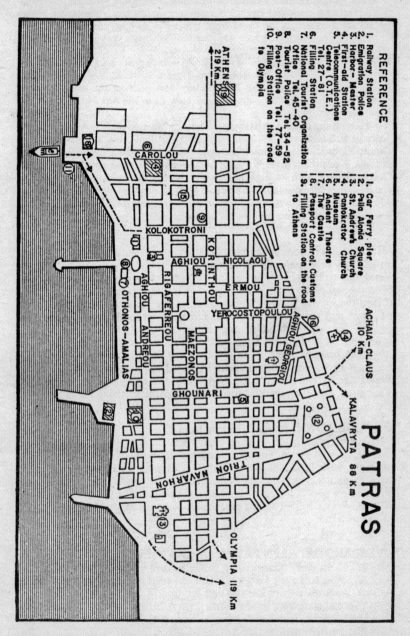

walk. Best plan is to walk the block inspecting diners' plates to see if there's anything you want; in general, the further you go up St. Nicholas Street, the cheaper the restaurants get and the less variety they offer.

The gleaming modern espresso cafe called **Vossinakis** (46 Dimitri Gounari Street) is a good spot for sandwiches and snacks; upstairs is a new roof garden restaurant. Just across the street from the bar is an open souvlaki stand.

SOME WALKS AROUND TOWN:
A walk up St. Nicholas Street will eventually bring you to 193 stone steps ascending the hillside, at the top of which are the remains of the **13th-century fort** built on the remains of the former Acropolis. There's a magnificent view from the top which makes the climb well worthwhile.

Keep going to the left past the Plateia 25 Martion and down through the peaceful streets as you descend, and you'll eventually hit the main street of Dimitri Gounari, from which other major streets head back towards the center of town. Korinthon Street, for example, passes through the magnificent **King George Square,** with its stone lion fountains, mouths gushing water, and several buildings surmounted with classical statues. From one point of the square, you can stand and watch the outdoor movie being projected at first-floor level—just too far away to hear the dialogue clearly.

MISCELLANY:
Several churches here have clocks *painted* on their belfries, an arbitrary time confusing the unwary. . . . The best of many pastry shops is **Karabites,** at 23 Aghiou Nikolaon. . . . **Boat tickets** to Corfu are obtainable from the shipping agent's office at 55 Amalias Street, just down to the right (facing the square) from the tourist office on the harbor. . . . There are clean toilets in that tourist office. . . . Illuminated bright red, green, and yellow-paneled "kiosks," with advertising matter on them, lend a bright touch to several streets at night. . . . Sit at the cafe at the end of the pier and watch the sun set. A beautiful sight. . . . If you have any problems in Patras, you'll find Leonidas Paparodopoulos extremely helpful. He's manager of the **Olympias Travel Agency** (Amalias 37, tel: 275495) in town and his agency is the local Viking rep. (See Chapter VIII for all the good things about Viking's.)

OUTSIDE TOWN:
A short bus ride from Patras is the beach and hotel at **Petaloudes** ("Butterflies"), 16 kms from town. It has simple, good food served at tables under the trees. There are also rooms upstairs for about 250 drs double per night. After lunch you can stroll down to a tiny beach, sit under the shade trees, or saunter over to the nearby fence and, while standing among yellow and blue flowers, peer at the olives growing and the sprouting young vines. On the hillside, slender, softly pointing pines shade off up a gently curving, precipitous profile of a hill.

OVERLAND BETWEEN PATRAS AND ATHENS:
Buses leave Patras for Athens at least every hour between 5:30 a.m. and 5:30 p.m., then again at 6, 8:15, and 9 p.m. The trip lasts five hours and costs about 250 drs one way. In Athens, buses leave from Kavalas and Kifisson Streets (tel: 5124-914).

A second-class train seat to Patras from Athens costs a few drachmas less than the bus fare. Trains, unfortunately, don't run as often. In Athens, call 3624-402 for information.

You might want to consider renting a car in Patras and driving to Athens, where you can leave it off either the same day or later. **Hellascars** and **Retca** are two car rental agencies that have offices in both places.

BOATS BETWEEN PATRAS, ITALY AND ATHENS: Hellenic Mediterranean Lines operates the *Egnatia* and the *Appia* between Patras and Brindisi on alternate days. Both are plush ships, with TV lounges, dining room, bar and swimming pool; they take about 24 hours for the complete trip from Athens to Brindisi, stopping en route at Corfu and Igoumenitsa. HML also operates a connecting bus service between Athens and Patras (bus takes five hours). An aircraft-type seat on any of the boats costs about $40 between Brindisi and Patras.

READERS' SELECTIONS: "There is a hotel, the **Delphini,** in Patras right where you get off the boat from Brindisi. Great idea for those who do not wish to arrive in Athens late at night or for those who need a rest after the hot ride from Athens. Good service, and a swimming pool being built"—now about 400 drs double (Donald Viney, Virginia Beach, Va.). . . . "The bus from Patras takes almost four hours so if you'll arrive in Athens late at night it's better to stay in Patras and make the trip in the morning unless you're familiar with Athens and have been before" (R. P. Smart, Toronto, Canada). . . . "When the airport bus lets you off in Athens at the so-called downtown air terminal (a booth with a canopy) don't panic; walk about 25 feet to the right to the newsstand whose owner speaks English. He'll let you use his phone and give instructions to your cab driver to get the right hotel" (Raymond Holbrook, Dallas, Texas). . . . "A marvelously inexpensive (comparatively) way to get up into northern Italy from Greece is to go by **Danish Seaways:** 44 hours from Patras to Genova on the best ships in the Mediterranean. Car is free with four paying passengers. Athens address: G E Alevizos, 14 Xenofontos Street, tel: 3234-292" (Mildred D. Meeh, Canterbury, N.H.).

Chapter III

ATHENS

1. Getting Oriented
2. Some Walks Around Town

THE CITY OF ATHENS has grown from a town of a few thousand people to a metropolis of more than a million in the lifetime of some of the people who live in it—and it is still growing at a feverish pace. In many ways, a traveler feels the growth pains. Jackhammers tear up sidewalks (and eardrums); pedestrians and motorists compete defiantly for the available road space, which is often inadequate; buses start from a score of terminal points in obscure parts of town, and bureaucratic red tape strangles all but the simplest of official transactions. Moreover, large tracts of the sprawling modern city are covered by unimaginative concrete office and apartment blocks.

But Athens does have a unique flavor, if you know where to look for it. In the older part of town, tiny Byzantine churches still squat defiantly in the middle of busy streets and under the shadow of smart stores; large parks break up the monotony of concrete and the roar of traffic, and that view from Lycabettus also includes the magnificent Acropolis. Athens' particular excitement is a blend of East and West, and of city and village. Sponge-sellers hawk their wares in front of the steel and glass TWA building with its American Snack Bar; a gypsy cranks out old tunes on a hurdy-gurdy by a kiosk that sells all the major magazines and newspapers of Europe and the United States. Athenians have a brisk businesslike air when dealing with customers . . . but they still find plenty of time each day to sit in the sidewalk cafes that dot each street, sipping coffee or lemonade and watching the passing parade. There is probably no better way for a visitor to decelerate to the casual pace of Greece than to find a shady table near the fountain in Syntagma Square, order a drink (don't expect to get it right away), and spend an hour contemplating the hectic comings and goings of tourists from a dozen countries.

Unfortunately, if you intend to *see* Athens, you can't spend all your time merely watching it. But before you join the parade, an idea of where you are and where you're going may help.

1. Getting Oriented

As the "Athens at a Glance" map on page 35 shows, most of the tourist attractions of Athens lie within a square that is approximately a mile on each side. The Acropolis marks the southwest corner of this square, and Mount Lycabettus the northeast corner. At least one of these two landmarks is visible from most parts of the city. Running between them, Stadiou and Venizelou

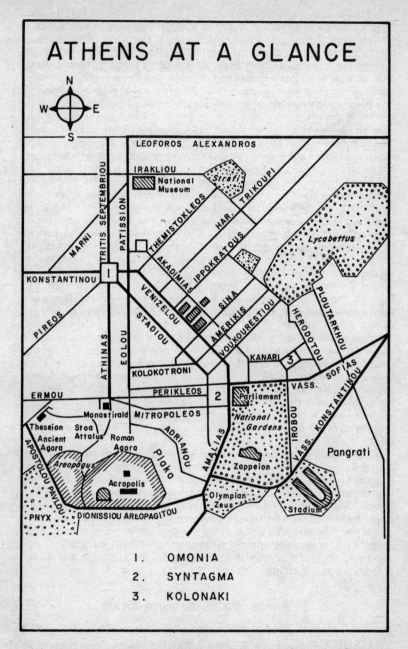

ATHENS AT A GLANCE

1. OMONIA
2. SYNTAGMA
3. KOLONAKI

streets connect the two major squares: Omonia in the northwest, and Syntagma near the center. The National Gardens extend from Syntagma to the Stadium, which marks the southeast corner of "tourist territory."

The remains of ancient Athens lie along the southern edge of this square, from the temple of Olympian Zeus and Hadrian's Arch on Amalias, west to the Acropolis, Areopagus, Agora, and Theseion. Just north of this archaeologist's paradise are two areas that invariably delight the ordinary visitor: Plaka, between the Acropolis and Adrianou, with its sleepy village air by day and the wild nightlife of its discotheques and tavernas; and the souvenir and antique bazaar along the narrow streets east of the Monastiraki subway station.

North of Monastiraki, along Athinas street toward Omonia Square, is the heart of the city's market district: a crude but colorful area including huge open-air meat markets and wholesale warehouses containing sacks of fragrant foodstuffs from around the world. Omonia itself is a noisy shopping area of big department stores and hole-in-the-wall enterprises side by side with hotels and restaurants.

Further north, on Patission (called also 28 Oktobriou), is the National Archaeological Museum, one of the finest of its kind in the world. A few blocks south, and one block east of Patission, lies Kaningos Square, a major bus terminal and the beginning of Akadimias street. Along Akadimias are the many bookstores and private schools of the University district, centered between Ippokratous and Sina, where the National Library, University, and Academy stand in a row facing Venizelou. Uphill, the lower slopes of Lycabettus are covered with modern apartments, culminating in the posh residential district around Kolonaki Square, and "Embassy Row," along Vassilissis Sofias. Further east, Sofias joins with Vassileos Konstantinou at the Athens Hilton, near the American Embassy. South lies the residential district of Pangrati, bringing us back to the Stadium.

It is possible to get a fast overview of most of these locations by signing up for the three-hour standard morning **tour,** operated by almost all the tour companies. A bus with an English-speaking guide will take you past the Temple of Zeus and Hadrian's Arch, the Stadium, the Royal Palace (on Irodou Attikou opposite the National Gardens), and give you an hour at either the Archaeological Museum or the sites in the Acropolis area. Another way to literally get an "overview" is to take the **funicular** up Lycabettus for a panorama that includes all of Athens and, on clear days, Piraeus and the Aegean Sea, six miles away.

But the best way to discover Athens is the same as in any strange city: just get off the main avenues and wander at random, letting your intuition and happenstance guide you. The casual stroller reaps unexpected rewards: tiny twisting streets that lead to quiet shady squares, shops that sell everything from second-hand trousers to beaten gold ikons, a cat seated on the whitewashed steps of a church, ears cocked attentively to the baritone voices inside.

If you remember that you can't get lost (because all you need to do is hop aboard a bus, or ask a cab driver to take you to one of the major squares), you'll enjoy your random rambles with less trepidation. But just to get you started, here are a few suggestions.

2. Some Walks Around Town

SYNTAGMA: Plateia Syntagma, or **Constitution Square,** lies at the intersection of seven major streets near the center of downtown Athens. As the government, business, and hospitality center of Greece, it is the logical place to start your explorations of the capital city.

The Square is bounded on the east (upper) side by the **Hellenic Parliament Building,** once the Royal Palace. Directly in front of it is the **Tomb of the Unknown Soldier,** guarded by evzones. These handsome young soldiers wear the traditional fez, ruffed skirt, and pom-poms, and attract a lot of attention from camera bugs. At the height of the tourist season, it looks as though the guards need guards. A formal **Changing of the Guard** takes place here on Sunday mornings between 8 and 10.

To the right of the Parliament Building are the rather formal **National Gardens,** containing a small zoo, an open-air theater, the **Zappeion Exhibition Hall,** and hundreds of cafe tables, crowded in the evening with people listening to free concerts. At the southern end of the Gardens (along Leoforos Olgas) is a large children's playground. There are plenty of winding paths through the heavy shrubbery, which effectively cuts off the roar of nearby traffic.

Along Georgiou Avenue on the northern side of the Square stand the King George II and the Grande Bretagne, venerable and sedate luxury hotels, which maintain vast areas of cafe tables in the center of the square. The King George has a rooftop restaurant—a sky-high place to start your explorations of the capital city.

Further down, where Georgiou becomes Karageorgi Street, at the northwest corner of the square, is a branch of the National Bank of Greece. Inside at the front is a **tourist information center** that provides free maps of the city and country, folders on all parts of Greece, up-to-date interisland ship schedules, bus and train information, and a hotel information and reservation service.

The western (lower) side of the square features two buildings of outstanding importance to the traveler: **American Express,** with the usual banking, mail, and tour services located on the third and fourth floors and entered from Ermou street; and a branch **post office** open from 8 a.m. straight through to 11:30 p.m. On the broad walk in front of these buildings are three newsstands which seem to stock every magazine known to the civilized world, newspapers from a dozen countries, and several hundred paperback books. The kiosks of Greece are famous for their stock of items: razor blades, soap, string, postcards, transistor radios, batteries, pens, thumbtacks, soft drinks, candy, combs—you name it. Most also have telephones and the standard procedure is to dial the number you want, and pay one drachma on completion of a local call.

In front of American Express is an outdoor cafe which has to be one of the best people-watching spots in Greece. The cafe serves only expensive snacks, but the parade is endlessly fascinating: not only girls in everything from backpacks to party dresses, but itinerant sponge sellers covered with their wares, lottery ticket vendors, and a mod-clad gaggle of local boys on the lookout for unaccompanied females.

Like most businesses in Greece, American Express closes in the afternoon (mail section at 1, offices at 2) and re-opens from 4 to 7 in the evening. Since mail delivery is at 4:30, the busiest traffic is just after that. There's also a peak hour at noon when anyone floating around town drops by to see what's going on. Two or three people will be sure to be displaying signs: "Want a good VW Bus?" or "Room for two going to Turkey." The groups sitting in front of American Express and those across the traffic served by the Grande Bretagne regard each other with mutual amusement. Shops of different types re-open at different times during the week. All times are listed week by week in the *Athens News.*

Along the south side of the square on Othonos and Mitropoleos are the offices of several world airlines as well as three eating places we'll consider in a later chapter. Just around the corner on Filellinon are several good travel services. Unfortunately, the tall buildings have blocked out the view of the Acropolis, but St. George's chapel on Mount Lycabettus, illuminated at night, can be seen from most of the square. And in the middle of all this activity a fountain (also illuminated in the evenings) refreshes the eyes and ears of the weary table-sitters. Now that you're familiar with home base, let's get out a little.

ATHENS IN PERSPECTIVE—THE VIEW FROM THE MOUNTAIN:

As early as possible in your visit you should take time to climb **Lycabettus**. In the early morning, sunlight from behind you lights up every detail of the city and caresses the Acropolis; at dusk, the city fades slowly away, the Parthenon last of all . . . and then begins to twinkle with a myriad of lights. For either (or both) of these sights, leave Syntagma on Vassilissis Sofias, and walk past the left end of the Parliament Building and the National Gardens, where the flower sellers display their giant bouquets. At the corner of Irodou Attikou you will pass the Benaki Museum on your left (see Chapter VI). Five more blocks along the Embassy Row section of Sofias will bring you to the Byzantine Museum on your right. At the next street, Ploutarkhou, turn left and start the long slow climb which ends at the funicular station. The cable cars run from 10 a.m. until midnight, and cost 30 drs round trip. You'll emerge on the terrace of a restaurant with a very respectable view—but don't stop yet. A few steps more will bring you to the chapel of St. George and the lookout point by the belltower. A perspective map scratched in marble alerts you to the major recognizable sites. If you look carefully, you can even see the white spume of the fountain in Omonia Square, rising above the buildings that surround it. No matter how sultry the streets of the town, there's almost always a breeze up here. Occasionally an erratic wind will bring you a snatch of music from a radio far below.

The restaurant just below the chapel is twice as expensive as equally good places down below—but if it's not the best or cheapest place in town, it's certainly the highest. For a big romantic evening the view may justify the expense. The sea shimmers dully far off to the south, a flare flickers over the airport, Mount Hymettus broods over the eastern suburbs.

Since the funicular is enclosed, you may decide to walk down. The path (starting just under the chapel from the lower restaurant terrace) will take you past two small cafes with a different view at every turn, and bring you finally to **Dexamenee reservoir.** This is a small park on the lower slope originally built by the Emperor Hadrian. If you leave the lower end of the park and after a block or so turn right, you'll come to **Kolonaki Square.** It is surrounded by pleasant cafes whose prices reflect the affluence of their clientele. But don't let this scare you off: within reasonable limits it's safe to say that "expensive" in Greece is relatively inexpensive by American standards. And the square is certainly a pleasant spot to recuperate from your hike, especially if you're a connoisseur of pretty clothes. The cafes are open all day, but cater largely to nannies keeping an eye on small children; the fashion parade begins after dark, as in most squares. The British Council stands at one corner of Kolonaki, and often posts announcements of plays and concerts in English.

You might leave the square on Kanari and turn right on Akadimias for two blocks. A left down Amerikis will take you past two English-language bookstores which feature a wide variety of paperbacks about Greece. Before you load up, be prepared for the import tax on books, which nearly doubles their price. Another left on Venizelou will bring you back to Syntagma Square.

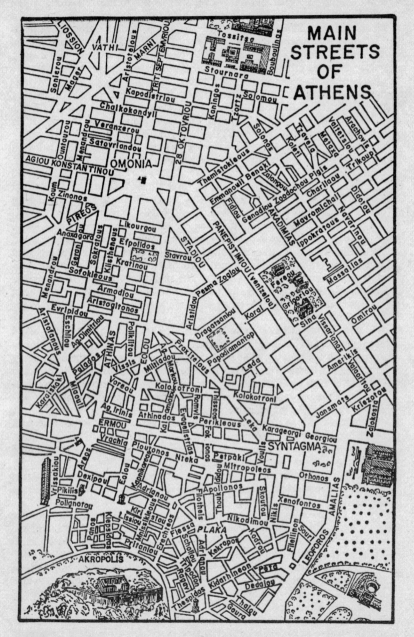

MAIN
STREETS
OF
ATHENS

THE OLD TOWN: Now that you've seen something of modern Athens, try a stroll through the older sections. Right after breakfast is a good time to head for the antique and bric-a-brac shops of Pandrossou Street. Leave Syntagma at the southwest corner and walk down Mitropoleos to the Cathedral. On the way you'll pass a tiny Byzantine church tucked between the columns of a modern office building—a contrast like that of the modern Cathedral with **St. Elefterious,** the original church of this parish, which still sits next to its gigantic offspring. (Athenians have a saying about a tall person walking with a short one, which means that they look like the Cathedral and St. Elefterious.) Inside the Cathedral are some beautifully colored windows (no pictures, just windows), and hundreds of "afieromata": more little silvered plates in the form of people or parts of the body, with which invalids draw the attention of saints to their particular ailment. Inside the tiny ancient church next door are some intriguing stone carvings, particularly that of the fighting animals, separated by the cross at the front. There are often cherry or peach sellers on the Cathedral steps, and over to one side is a statue of a bishop killed by the Turks in the last century.

From the lower end of the square, three streets lead to the **Monastiraki Square.** Each street is crowded with tiny stores offering a happy melange of old furniture, copper pots and oil pitchers, sandals, souvenir statues, jewelry, flokati (goatskin rugs), and knitted, handwoven, or embroidered goods. Many of the shops carry signs indicating that several languages are spoken . . . and the salesmen are sharp traders in all of them. No posted price is to be regarded as final: you are likely to be scorned if you *don't* do some melodramatic haggling. Check out **Dimitris Zoumas,** whose shop at Adrianou 50B specializes in colorful national costumes and also *tamata* (votive offerings), the thin metal replicas of arms, legs, breasts, etc. that grateful worshippers deposit in churches for ailments cured.

Beyond the subway station, Iphestou Street is loud with the music of old phonographs, and old men thumb through stacks of almost prehistoric records. People from the country villages do their shopping here, and the ugly, heavy shoes are a testament to a way of life that demands durability rather than elegance or even comfort. By way of contrast, there are also white buckskins and bright plastic wedgies with enormous cork soles hanging in plastic packages in front of the innumerable shoestores.

Things from the country are here, too—brightly colored woven bags with tassels, and carved wooden wool holders known as roka on which shepherds hang the wool before weaving it. Here and there the sound of a heavy hammer on an anvil splits the air, and tiny bells tinkle as a pony tosses his neck to drive off the flies that hover around the colored beads and plastic roses decorating his harness. The cart he pulls holds strips of metal for one of the smithies along the block.

At the lower end of Iphestou, a left turn will bring you to the entrance of the ancient **Agora.** If it's Thursday or Sunday, you can wander among the ruins for free; on other days a ticket for 10 drs will admit you to the so-called **Theseion** (actually a temple to Hephaestus, god of the forge: hence "Iphestou" and its smithies nearby), the best preserved of the ancient temples; and the **Stoa of Attalos,** a reconstruction of one of the ancient market buildings which houses the archaeological finds from the Agora.

Back at Monastiraki, a right turn up Areos will take you past the remains of **Hadrian's Library** and the **Roman Agora,** as well as the booths of the flea market, where second-hand dealers hawk everything from army trousers to Polish paperbacks.

At the busiest side of the Agora is the octagonal **Tower of the Winds** and beyond it the popular square known as **Plateia Pallias Agoras,** which is always crowded with young people from nearby rooming houses eating at the shaded tables of the Poseidon restaurant.

The Tower of the Winds, a beautifully preserved building, is worth a little attention. It was erected during the reign of Julius Caesar and by its elaborate mechanism visitors to the Agora could tell the time of day. No ordinary clock, it is correctly known as the **Horologion of Andronikos Kyrrhestes** (meaning "the clock of Andronikos from Kyrrhos," a town in either Syria or Macedonia —experts disagree about which), and served as combination sundial, weather-vane, and hydraulic clock, elaborately operated by water flowing from an upper cistern into a lower tank at a controlled rate. A float on the water surface of the lower cistern was attached to a thin bronze chain, which adjusted the mechanism and recorded the time according to how much water remained. This device, similar in principle to an hour glass, was a familiar one in ancient times and was called a *klepsydra*. In fact the well atop the Acropolis from which the water flowed to Andronikos' clock in the Agora, was called the Klepsydra spring.

The exact date of the tower's construction is not known, but it is mentioned in the writings of both Varro (116-27 B.C.) and Vitruvius, the Roman military engineer famous for his treatise *De Architectura*, written about 36 B.C. According to Vitruvius, the tower was surmounted by a revolving bronze figure of Triton, the mythological merman, who held a wand which pointed in the direction of the prevailing wind. There is no trace of Triton today, but on each of the tower's eight sides can be seen carved representations of the ancient "Gods of the Wind"—eight in all—and it is for this reason that the 2,000-year-old building is most commonly known as The Tower of the Winds.

The figures are: Boreas, the god of the north wind, his mantle blowing in the air, tooting on a twisted shell; Kaikias, northeast wind, emptying hailstones from a shield; Apeliotes, east wind, displaying fruit and flowers; Euros, south-east wind, threatening a hurricane; Notos, south wind, causing a shower by emptying an urn; Lipos, southwest wind, blowing a ship before him to indicate a rapid voyage; Zephyros, west wind, tossing flowers from his lap into the air; and Skirion, northwest wind, drying up rivers with his bronze vessel of charcoal.

Below these figures of the winds are faint traces of sundials but none of the 47-foot tower's original mechanism remains. Indeed, it seems neglected today, filled with random stones from other sites and kept securely locked.

In the fifth century the tower was converted into a church, and during the Turkish occupation ten centuries later it became a *tekke*, a home for an order of dervishes whose shouts and exclamations brought it a reputation for being haunted. Perhaps that is why it remains almost forgotten, rarely written about, and not even depicted on contemporary postcards despite its considerable aesthetic appeal.

PLAKA: Now you might explore the Plaka, uphill from Adrianou. Along Lissiou, Mnisikleos, and Flessa are most of the tavernas and discotheques that make this the center of Athenian nightlife. During the day these streets are eerily deserted, except for the occasional tourist.

Back on Adrianou, you will pass a whole block of toy stores before coming to **Olympic Curios** at number 94, where the owner will be glad to show you his giant clam shells and other wonders of the undersea world. If you turn left on Apollonos you will soon come to the shops behind the Cathedral where ikons, church furnishings, and bishops' robes are sold.

If, instead, you continue along Adrianou to the intersection of Flessa and Nikodimou, a few steps down Nikodimou will bring you to **Mazani:** a tiny shop where the owner makes heavy metal jewelry, each piece unique, for prices beginning around $8. At this corner, Adrianou bends uphill to bring you into the center of another section of Plaka. Turn left on Kidathneion past fruit stores, a bakery and a cafe, and you will find the **Plateia Philomouson Hetairae** —literally, the square of music-loving courtesans. While the musicians are now working in the tavernas instead of strolling the square, you may be entertained by a gypsy cranking an old but beautifully carved hurdy-gurdy, as you sip your lemonade. Three restaurants also serve full meals at the tables in the square, if you're ready for lunch. A little further down Kidathneion on the left side are three antique stores that specialize in ships' fittings, cutlasses, and those vicious-looking Turkish knives called yataghans. Next comes a small church with a little square of trees, some mod clothing shops and restaurant-bars, and Nikis Street. Turn left, and you will return to Syntagma at the corner where you left it. But don't imagine that one such stroll will make you familiar with the Plaka: there are many more delightful spots to discover among those winding streets.

DOWNTOWN: As you face the fountain in Syntagma with your back to American Express, Stadiou street leaves the square to the left, beside the National Bank. Within a block, it bends sharply left again toward **Omonia Square.** Here, an arcade on the right side houses a **National Tourist Office** providing information, reservations, and tickets for the Athens Festival, the Drama Festival at Epidaurus, and other summer events throughout Greece.

On the left side of Stadiou one block further, a small triangular park features an equestrian statue of Kolokotronis, one of Greece's national heroes in the War of Independence. This marks the upper end of Kolokotroni, a narrow medium-range shopping street that runs down to the flower market on Eolou, and has several tiny fascinating streets intersecting it. If you turn left just before the Carolina Hotel, you'll find the **Kapnikarea Church** crouched right in the middle of busy Ermou street. Or a right turn off Kolokotroni on Praxitelous will bring you to another tiny church hidden among tall buildings, and back on Lada to Stadiou.

From here to Omonia, Stadiou and the parallel Venizelou provide "main street" shopping very like that of any major European city, with big shops, lots of traffic, and crowded sidewalks. At night there's one rather startling sight: a three-story shop selling hundreds of chandeliers and lamps—all burning brightly. It's awesome to contemplate their electric bill. At Korai street, you can look up toward Venizelou and see the impressive neoclassic **University** building, which is flanked by the **National Library** and the **Academy of Athens.** These are the gateway to the University district. Behind them, on Akadimias, are a major terminal point for buses, and several other institutions of learning including, at 22 Massalias street, the **Hellenic-American Union.** The Union contains an English-language library, music library, cafeteria, classrooms, galleries, and a summer schedule of concerts and plays in English sponsored by the Athens Center for the Creative Arts. Most of these, and the facilities of the Union, are free and open to the public.

Back to Stadiou street: opposite Korai, on the left, is **Plateia Klathmonos,** another small pretty square with a number of cafes and restaurants; a good place to take a break on the long walk to Omonia.

Three blocks further, at the intersection with Eolou, stands the **Lambropoulos Brothers** department store, largest in Athens. Two blocks north on Eolou is **Minion,** another large store whose basement food department offers the best bargains in Athens on imported foodstuffs and liquor, outside of the duty-free airport shops. The Omonia Square area is crowded with shopping arcades and streetfront stores which, unlike most others in Greece, stay open during the afternoon. Greeks and foreigners alike shop here, jostling and shouting in five or six languages.

Buses and cabs careen madly around the traffic circle with its tall spray, more like a geyser than a fountain; beneath it is the main subway station and an arcade containing banks and a post office as well as shops. To get away from the bustle, walk up Eolou past the square (at which point it becomes 28 Oktobriou, or Patission). In seven blocks you'll reach the **National Archaeological Museum** (discussed in Chapter VI). When your feet or your eyes give up, there is a pleasant cafe at one side of the front lawn along a curving walk, under a canopy of huge ancient vines. When you're rested, a # 12 or # 3 bus, which stops right across the street, will take you back to Syntagma.

Chapter IV

THE BUDGET HOTELS OF ATHENS

1. Between Syntagma and Plaka
2. Around Omonia Square
3. For the Backpack Crowd
4. The Hideaway Hotels

AS EVERYWHERE ELSE in the world, Greece has been suffering badly from inflation in the last few years, and even hotel prices have now zoomed astronomically, government-decreed rates often being higher than the hotel owners themselves want. A ten per cent increase is being forecast for 1978 over the last season's prices, but some proprietors have indicated they will not impose it because business has dropped correspondingly. So, although what are presumed to be 1978 prices are given throughout this book, some of them (particularly in smaller places) may not take effect until 1979—by which time there'll probably have been another increase. It's all very confusing, but please bear in mind that even with the best of intentions a travel book cannot help but be somewhat out of date even on the actual day it is published. Accept the information it contains as *a rough guide*.

Greek hotel prices are set and maintained by the government, and posted in the lobby and in each room. They are based on five categories—Deluxe, A, B, C, and D—and no hotel can charge more than the category permits, although they may, in certain instances, charge *less*. Some of the newer hotels, frankly aimed at the summer tourist trade, manage to sidestep the fixed price by requiring guests to take demi-pension (breakfast and one other meal), full-pension, or at least a continental breakfast, usually at outrageous prices.

But except for luxury hotels, these cases are the exception. Even in the very busy summer season you should be able to find a cheap room if you remember that an ancient hotel with no lobby and a narrow dark staircase may well provide rooms just as acceptable as the chrome and glass wonder around the corner . . . and it will certainly be less expensive. As is often the case in other European countries, most rooms in the older hotels are bathless, with lavatories and showers down the hall serving several rooms. Bathless rooms are much less expensive. It is common to charge 15 drs for a cold shower, 20 drs for a hot shower or bath; hotels *cannot* charge more, but they may make no charge at all . . . or they may include this charge automatically in your bill. Since the use of the shower is hardly obligatory in a bathless room, it is possible to avoid this charge by skillful planning. You should at least find out what the management's policy is before handing over your passport. If possible, you should avoid hotel meals. An example: the standard continental breakfast at a class C hotel costs 35 drs, and consists of tea or instant coffee, stale packaged melba toast or a hard roll, a pat of margarine and a dollop of jam. Two doors from your hotel there is sure to be a cafe or milk bar where you can get fresh-brewed coffee, hot chocolate with whipped cream, or tea; two eggs or an enormous warm sweet roll with fresh butter and honey, all for the same 35 drs. Case rests. If you arrive off-season, further reductions are possible for stays of over three days, groups of more than ten, and by booking well in advance. None of these reductions apply during the summer months.

Where do you want to stay? Perhaps the previous chapter has given you some idea of favorable locations, but it's a good idea to remember that such locations cost more because lots of people want them, and that Athens is an easy town to get around, before you set your heart on any one spot. Since nearly every Greek hotel room has a balcony on a street, and you'll want your window open most of the year, traffic is another factor to consider. In general, hotels on little out-of-the-way streets are both cheaper and more desirable than the ones you'll see on the major thoroughfares when you first hit town. Now we'll review some of our favorites, by geographical area.

1. Between Syntagma and Plaka

In a narrow strip between the luxury hotels near Syntagma and the tavernas of the Plaka lies a group of hotels on the tiny side streets of old Athens whose moderate prices and excellent locations have made them a prime choice for wise travelers over the past few years. Thus, their prices are rising and they are nearly always crowded during the summer, but they are certainly worth the time it takes to inquire.

Taking them in order from north to south, we come first to my favorite Athenian hostelry, my home away from home in Athens—the friendly **Hotel Carolina** (Kolokotroni 55, tel: 3220-837) named by its owner Lou, for his home state. There's nothing pretentious about the Carolina but it's renowned among readers of this book for the hospitality and friendliness of Lou and his English-speaking staff, who treat everybody with kindness and patience. There's a tiny snack bar, a place to store your luggage while visiting the islands, and a 30-drachma washing machine on the roof—a godsend to the nomadic types who are the Carolina's most frequent guests and who are encouraged to treat the place as a private club. Lou told me in 1977 that he planned to retire in a year or two, and so in readiness for the tribute I plan to write to him at that time I'd appreciate your comments and recollections of times you may have spent at this friendly hotel. (You can leave them addressed to me at the Carolina or write me c/o BCM-NOMAD, London WC1V 6XX, England). Oh yes, the Carolina's rates: about 275 drs single, 350 drs double, more for rooms with bath.

The **Achilleus Hotel** (21 Lekka, tel: 3233-197) is a six-story establishment closer to Syntagma, but also on a small quiet street. The manager John Cassimis, speaks French, Arabic, and Italian as well as English; he and his staff are courteous and helpful. Showing a bit of wear but very clean, the hotel has a bright and airy breakfast/bar room overlooking a nice-sized terrace full of flowering plants. All the rooms either have a bath or share an adjoining one, and several are actually two-room suites. Small balconies, aqua- or rose-colored walls, mirrors, and pleasant furniture make for a warm atmosphere. Singles are now unavailable, but doubles are about 520 drs including bath and breakfast. Just take Karageorgi three blocks from Syntagma, and turn right on Lekka.

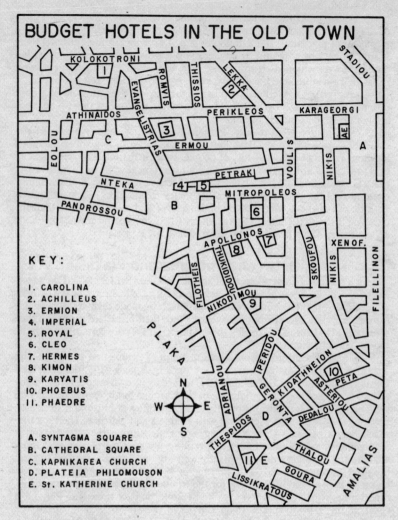

BUDGET HOTELS IN THE OLD TOWN

KEY:

1. CAROLINA
2. ACHILLEUS
3. ERMION
4. IMPERIAL
5. ROYAL
6. CLEO
7. HERMES
8. KIMON
9. KARYATIS
10. PHOEBUS
11. PHAEDRE

A. SYNTAGMA SQUARE
B. CATHEDRAL SQUARE
C. KAPNIKAREA CHURCH
D. PLATEIA PHILOMOUSON
E. St. KATHERINE CHURCH

The **Hotel Ermion** (66 Ermou, tel: 3212-753) is difficult to find and somewhat disreputable-looking as you climb the dim stairs to the tiny reservation cubicle—but it's clean enough and used to tourists of the younger, less fussy sort. An old D-class place with just 30 rooms, all bathless, it has singles for about 200 drs and doubles for 275 drs. Hot showers are 18 drs extra and there are no food facilities. To get there, take Ermou (which leaves Syntagma by the American Express entrance) down to Plateia Kapnikarias (the little square with the square with the church), and it's about two blocks below on the right.

The **Hotel Cleo** (3 Patrou, tel: 3229-053) combines a quiet side street location and handiness to Syntagma. Mrs. Cleo Nathan, a delightful Egyptian-born woman, has operated a guest house in this neighborhood for 13 years and only recently added this tiny (19 rooms) and charming hotel. She speaks at least five languages herself, and both the day and night clerks are fluent in English and helpful. The rooms (mostly doubles with bath) cost 375 drs. There are a few triples for 400 drs, a small dormitory on the ground floor at 50 drs a bed, and bathless rooms in the guest house next door. No food yet, although Cleo plans to add a cafeteria soon. A small and pleasant lounge on the ground floor carries magazines in several languages, and there is free luggage storage in the basement if you leave for short trips. Walk down Mitropoleos three blocks from Syntagma, and turn left: you'll see the sign near the end of the block. Cleo highly recommends her guest house round the corner—homelier, she says, and cheaper, too: 180 drs single, 220 drs double, 300 drs triple.

Hotel Kimon (Apollonos 27, tel: 3235-223) is just one block further down Apollonos toward the Cathedral. An old hotel recently renovated, it is simple and unpretentious but clean and inexpensive. All rooms are bathless, but have washbasins; the rates are 275 drs double, and the usual 18 drs for a hot shower. A small lobby and no food service, but very handy to the nightlife section of Plaka.

The **Phaedra Hotel** (16 Xairophontos, tel: 3238-461) has the lowest rates and, to my mind, the prettiest site of this whole group of hotels. It is just one block behind Plateia Philomouson Hetairae. Or to find it from Syntagma, simply take Amalias south from Filellinon until you're opposite Hadrian's Arch, and turn right up Lissikratous Street. The Phaedra sits at the corner of Adrianou and Xairophontos, facing the palm trees in the courtyard of St. Katherine's church. Rooms which do not face this little park have a view of the Acropolis. All rooms are bathless and toiletless, but there are at least two lavatories and shower rooms on each floor. The rooms are large, with taped music, comfortable beds, and sinks, and rent for 150 drs single, 275 drs double, hot showers 20 drs extra. You can sleep on the roof for 100 drs including breakfast. There's a bright comfortable lounge and bar on the ground floor, and the manager Stamatis Manolatos speaks English and is very helpful. The Phaedra is right across the street from two of Plaka's more famous tavernas—a little noisy in the evening, but plenty of local atmosphere.

The **Hotel Adonis** (Kodrou 3, tel: 3249-737) describes itself as "B class with C-class prices," and these are around 400 drs single, 500 drs double including breakfast. It's a pleasant little place with good views from the roof garden and very handy to everything.

READER'S SELECTION: "We reconfirmed a reservation at the Achilleus . . . but discovered they . . . lost the booking. The desk clerk found us a room at the **Nikis,** which turned out to be much nicer" (Beatrice Stein, New York City).

2. Around Omonia Square

Omonia Square and the area west of it to Karaiskaki Square is raw and lively, with plenty of open-air cafes, late-night traffic and B-girls operating out of the cocktail bars. Tourists conditioned to the genteel atmosphere of Syntagma will find it low-class and vulgar . . . and that's what it is. Nevertheless, since it's handy to the railway stations and the subway line, it has numerous hotels: some old and cheap, some new and expensive, and a few both new and cheap which are worth seeking out. Few of these have the personality of hostelries in the older part of town, but they are typically much larger, and cater to tour groups and the overflow from choicer sites. Since the National Museum is the

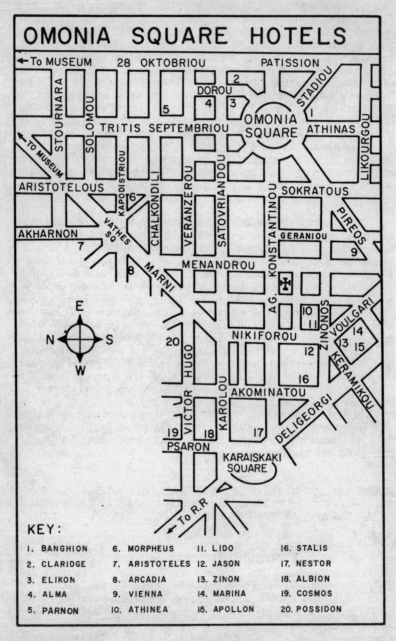

OMONIA SQUARE HOTELS

← To MUSEUM   28 OKTOBRIOU   PATISSION

OMONIA SQUARE

KEY:

1. BANGHION	6. MORPHEUS	11. LIDO	16. STALIS
2. CLARIDGE	7. ARISTOTELES	12. JASON	17. NESTOR
3. ELIKON	8. ARCADIA	13. ZINON	18. ALBION
4. ALMA	9. VIENNA	14. MARINA	19. COSMOS
5. PARNON	10. ATHINEA	15. APOLLON	20. POSSIDON

only tourist attraction in this area, Omonia may not be your first choice, but if you like open-air markets, department stores, nightclubs, and noisy crowds, give it a try.

The cheapest hotels and restaurants can all be found behind the square on the side streets which radiate out like the spokes of a wheel. Dorou is a rewarding street offering no less than three hotels in one short block.

For some reason or other, rates at the **Omonia Hotel** (tel: 5237-210) don't seem to have risen as fast as others in the area, so it's certainly the preferred place: 276 rooms, all with bath and balcony, cost 330 drs single, 475 drs double, including breakfast. The main terrace is a good spot to sip a coffee and watch the action in the square.

Across the square is the recently renovated 60-room **Banghion** (tel: 3242-259) offering singles for around 350 drs, doubles for about 450 with bath. There are some bathless rooms.

Also on the square itself is the old, unpretentious **Carlton** (tel: 5223-201) whose 33 rooms lead off wide, tall, spacious corridors which always seem cool and deserted. Quite a contrast from the bustle of the outside. Rooms here are clean and simple: 215 drs single, 300 drs double without bath.

The **Claridge** (4 Dorou, tel: 5223-013), in the first block off Omonia on Dorou, is a very old hotel, simple and clean, with bathless rooms for around 275 drs single, 330 drs double. Each nice-sized room has a phone and sink . . . but there is only one toilet per hall. Hot showers are 18 drs, breakfast 30 drs.

The **Elikon** (3 Dorou, tel: 5221-695), right across the street, is very similar. These two are not tourist hotels at all, so the clerks may not speak English—but everyone tries to be helpful. The rooms are clean and spacious, the furniture simple but comfortable. No baths, but there is a shower. Doubles cost about 365 drs.

The **Hotel Alma** (5 Dorou, tel: 5222-833), on the next corner, is a modern, eight-story, 65-room establishment with an English-speaking staff. It boasts a small mirrored lobby with an espresso machine, leather chairs, and a bright breakfast lounge and bar on the first floor. A curved marble staircase and an elevator lead to lovely rooms, each with phone. Should you be lucky enough to get one of the eight large rooms on the seventh and eighth floors you'll enjoy penthouse living, with a spacious veranda where you can breakfast and sunbathe. Singles without bath are 275 drs; doubles are about 330 drs without, 400 drs with bath. An amazing bargain. During the summer, breakfast is required at 40 drs each. Just under the Alma is a clean bright restaurant with colored tablecloths, an English-speaking manager, and lambs roasting on spits. The most expensive item on the menu is 65 drs.

The **Hotel Parnon** (tel: 5235-196) is right on the corner of Septembriou and Chalkondili, and has a street-level arcade where you can sit and watch the constant flow of activity—too noisy for some, fascinating for others. To find this modern 48-room hotel, walk down Septembriou three blocks from Omonia. All rooms have baths and cost 337 drs single, 420 drs double, with a 40-dr breakfast charge.

Just behind the Parnon is the smaller **Artemis** (corner Veranzerou and 3rd Sept.), whose 44 rooms are bathless and cost around 255 drs single, 375 drs double.

Two particular bargains are the tiny D-class hotels **Democritos** (Kapodistriou 40, tel: 5233-780), with singles for 225 drs, double for 275; and the equally old **Dido** (Victor Hugo St., opp. the Poseidon, tel: 5246-906), where singles cost 155 drs single, 275 drs double. At both, the desk clerks are friendly and speak a little English.

Another pleasant little place on Hugo St. is the 18-room **Hotel Eva** (tel: 5223-079), which costs around 245 drs single, 350 drs double without bath. Almost opposite, on the corner of Psaron, is the larger **Cosmos** (tel: 5239-201).

It sports a colorful cafe-bar just off the lobby. The 77 rooms, all with bath, are still brand-new-looking, with good beds, closets, desks, and luggage racks. The six singles rent for 350 drs with tax and breakfast, the doubles for 420. There is a large dining room, and parking for your car.

The **Poseidon** (16 Victor Hugo, tel: 5241-721) has 40 small rooms, all with bath and balcony. These rent for 375 drs single, 450 double, with breakfast at 40 drs required during the summer. There are a ground floor cafeteria and bar, elevators, and some English-speaking staff.

The staff of the **Hotel Minion** (Maizones, off Vathes Sq., tel: 5234-222) speak English well and are used to readers of this book. Rooms cost around 250 drs single, 400 drs double, but they include breakfast.

The **Vienna Hotel** (20 Pireos, tel: 525-605) is the closest to Omonia of the group of new hotels extending north to Karaiskaki Square. It is on a main road, which may discourage some, but it is very clean and light, and it does have a lobby/lounge and (minuscule) elevators. Rooms (all with bath) cost 375 drs single, 465 drs double.

The **Athinea** (9 Vilara, tel: 5234-648) is somewhat older and beautifully situated on a tiny square in front of St. Constantine's church (the cross symbol on the map). It's on a quiet street that wakes up at night when the cabarets open. Most of its 37 rooms are bathless, and cost about 200 drs single; doubles with bath rent for about 400 drs. Breakfast (35 drs) may be required in summer —the hotel has no kitchen, but there is a good cheap restaurant right next door, and a sensational pastry-confectionery-coffee shop on the corner. The cab stand in front of the church, by the way, is one of the few places near Omonia where you can be sure of getting a cab quickly.

The **Lido Hotel** (2 Nikiforou, tel: 5225-040) is just around the corner, on the same block as the Athinea, and much newer. In fact, there are three hotels on the corner of Zinonos, Nikodimou, Voulgari, and Keramikou—which is unfortunately one of the noisiest corners in Athens. The Lido's 75 rooms go for 375 drs single, 490 drs double, all with bath and including breakfast. Most of the staff speak at least some English, there is a charming breakfast room on the mezzanine overlooking the street, and the hotel has an entrance lobby with bar. Among the businesses crowded in beside the entrance is a very good, fast, cheap dry cleaning and laundry service.

The **Jason Hotel** (3-5 Nikiforou, tel: 5248-031), right across the street, has exactly the same room rates, with a few extra added attractions: air conditioning in the dining room, a roof garden, choice of two music programs in the 82 rooms, and blankets which "are the most colorful on the block," according to one of our readers. The staff speak a number of languages. Singles cost 400 drs, doubles 500, all with bath.

Hotel Marina (13 Voulgari, tel: 5229-108), just up the block and next to a pet shop, has C rates and an exceptionally helpful staff, quiet location, large lobby-lounge, dining room, and small TV room. There are also some bathless rooms at 350 drs single, 415 drs double. Breakfast is not always required.

The **Apollon** (14 Deligeorgi, tel: 5245-212) is on the back of this same block. Of its 80 rooms, all but ten have balconies on a fairly quiet street; all have phone and bath and cost 375 drs single, about 500 drs double including breakfast. There is a large dining room and an attractive inner courtyard. The friendly staff share only a little English among them.

Many of the bigger hotels in this area have raised their prices out of our range (although still offering bargains to tour groups) but there are plenty of smaller ones. Newly painted and renovated, for example, is the 30-room **Apollonion** (tel: 5224-298), on a quiet street, Leonidou, and offering rooms for 260 drs single, 375 drs double. Nearby is the newly built **Stalis** (Akominatou 10, tel: 5241-411) with plants on its balconies and all rooms with bath—340 drs single, 410 drs double.

One of the most charming hotels in this whole area is the **Solomon** (Solomou 72, tel: 5229-101), small and cool with cafe-bar and TV lounge. Not cheap—375 drs single, 475 drs double—but worth it for a hint of style.

Another of the big, modern hotels worth considering is the **Pergamon** (Acharnon 14, tel: 5231-991) whose balconies bask in the setting sun. Singles here cost 350 drs, doubles 450, all with bath.

3. For the Backpack Crowd

What are sometimes called (somewhat euphemistically) student guest houses are making an appearance all over Athens, with a particularly thick concentration in the streets off Filellinon—Apollonius, Nikis, Skoufou, Kidathineon. They change hands often and it's largely a case of hit and miss, because at busy times you'll sometimes have to wander far and wide until you find a bed at all. A very few of these are outstanding bargains; most of them are terribly overcrowded, with the only really dirty lavatories and halls I've found in Greece. Even the truly ancient hotels of the market district (like the Byron), with swaybacked beds and cracked linoleum, are neat and clean, but the student guest houses (particularly those near the intersection of Nikis and Filellinon) are a bargain in price only, with springles cots crowded into small airless rooms.

At some time or another I've looked over the following:

Acropolis House (Kodrou 6), 20 pink-painted rooms, TV lounge; about 250 drs single, 375 drs double. **Jimmy's** (Voulis 46, corner Nikidimiou, tel: 323-954); 40 bunks, doubledeckers on the top floor for 60 drs, single bunks on floor below for 75 drs; nice and airy, lots of windows. **Square Inn** (Kydatneion just above Adrianou), 11 rooms for 200 drs double. **Universal Student House** (Apollonos 22), four simple rooms, each with three beds; 100 drs per person. **Apollo House** (Apollon 8), 11 rooms; single 175, double 250, triple 300. **Manos House** (Kidathneion, just east of the square), mostly double rooms, 100 drs per bed. **Maria Carafa's** house at Imperidon and the corner of Nikis, has beds for 100 drs each in a double; add 30 drs for breakfast or a hot bath in homey but simple environs.

The couple that run **George's Guesthouse** (32 Nikis, tel: 3222-887) are a boon to young international travelers who don't speak Greek. Between them they are fluent in six or seven languages and are helpfully informative in all of them. George's has ten rooms, most with two or three beds, and additional beds on the roof with a fine Acropolis view. There's a pleasant lounge for reading, rapping or watching TV, clean showers and bathroom. Also a piano.

An English woman and her Greek husband, Manos, operate **Clare's House** (Frynichon 16A, tel: 3229-284), with comfortable, clean, and attractively furnished rooms for 175 drs per person. Hot showers are free, and Clare's a good cook who will also offer dinner several times per week.

Diogenes House (12 Xairophontos, tel: 224-560), almost next door to the Phaedra, is brand-new and has beautiful varnished wood floors. The rooms are large, and the innerspring beds are covered with sheets handwoven in traditional village patterns, pillowcases to match. Rooms which do not look onto St. Katherine's park face a quiet and lovely inner courtyard where breakfast is served under an awning. There is a comfortable lounge behind the reservation cubicle, and both Madame Ladopoulos and her reservations manager speak English and are very friendly. Prices are 100 drs per bed four in a room; doubles are about 300 drs—showers (outside the room) included. There is also a roof terrace where ten cots rent for 50 drs each, with a good view of the Acropolis, and pleasant background music of Plaka nightlife.

At the bottom of Adrianou Street where it meets Kalogrioni at what I used to call "souvlaki square" are several places to stay. A lovely peaceful area, adjoining the ancient agora and only one block from the flea market (few bargains there, by the way), it offers rooms to suit all budgets. The **Hotel Plaka** (6 Kapnikareas, tel: 3222-098) is a classy place with roof garden and upper-strata prices, with the **Adrian Hotel** (Adriamou Sq., tel: 3237-554) only slightly cheaper. But there's also the **Pericles Student Hotel** where kids bunk down for only 80 drs apiece. Rich and poor alike eat in the square under the orange canopies of the Posidon restaurant, or buy souvlaki, sandwiches and cheap snacks from the other cafes on the square.

A handful of other accommodations worth noting are **Fotis House** (6 Ag. Geronda, Filomousou Sq., just around the corner from Plaka's open-air cinema, tel: 3247-165); the **Student Inn** (16 Kidathneion, tel: 3225-165); **Ilon House** (48 Nikis); the **Outside Inn** (opposite the Phoebus Hotel on Peta St); **Lakis House** (19 Mitseon, tel: 9226-440), at the foot of the entrance to the Acropolis and **Tokyo House** (116 Solonos St.), all of which offer shared rooms, informal atmosphere and rates from about 100 drs per person.

Myrto House (Nikis 40) gets an enthusiastic nod from a reader who found it "clean, central, competent staff, fine breakfast."

A pension with a touch of class is the **Blue House** (Voukourestiou St. 19, tel: 3620-341), which is almost opposite Vassilis' restaurant: about a score of rooms for around 300 drs single, 440 drs double without bath, and about another 100 drs per person including bath and breakfast. It's a nice area to be in—relatively near both Kolonaki and Syntagma and with the cute #17 basement bar just down the block.

Of course there are many similar places in other areas of town—behind Omonia Square, just past the Archaeological Museum, in Pangrati behind the Stadium. The **International Student House** (Damareos, Pangrati, tel: 7519-530) offers "a clean, quiet and friendly atmosphere, library, TV, all types of music, abundance of flowers and fun."

A legend among the backpack set is **Diana the Huntress** (Kotsika 3, near Green Park), an efficiently run lodging house one block from the park (#2 trolley along Patissiou; alight when you see park on right). The Diana costs 80 drs per person for four or five to a room; 90 drs for three beds in a room; 100 drs each for two in a room. Kids of all nationalities pack the place for its free hot showers, free baggage storage, TV lounge, cheap cafeteria and wine shop ("We accept credit tomorrow") and the list of "Diana's Friends" (meaning similar pensions in different islands) on the open-to-all notice board. If you're really short on cash, you can sleep in your own sleeping bag on the roof for 50 drs. Across the street at Kotsika 4 (tel: 816-806) is the 20-room **Hotel Milton** (a joke?) which looks substantial enough and charges 175 drs double without bath.

The **YWCA** (XEN, as it is called in Greek) in Athens is a large, modern building that, for a single woman, is almost like a luxury hotel. It contains a good, inexpensive cafeteria, a hair-dressing salon, a library, and offers all kinds of training programs for those who want them. Membership costs 100 drs annually for girls under 16; 120 drs annually for adults; but membership is not necessary before a woman is allowed to stay. From June to October, the rates for one to three nights are 100 drs per person for two or more in a room without bath. During the summer there is room for 100 women in six- or eight-bed dormitories. Breakfast is additional. Stays are limited to 20 nights; 11 Amerikis Street, just off Stadiou (tel: 624-291).

At the **Athens Youth Hostel** (57 Kypseltis St., take trolley 2), the 80-dr charge per night includes use of hot showers. There is room for 200 sleepers.

The modern **YMCA (XAN)** at the corner of Omirou & Akadimias Streets (tel: 626-970) accepts men between 17 and 40 with a maximum stay of 10 days. Single rooms cost about 250 drs per night. Dormitory accommodation available for 100 drs a bed. There's a snack bar and travel service in the lobby but a closedown curfew of 1 a.m.

4. The Hideaway Hotels

Both the Syntagma-Plaka and Omonia areas are increasingly crowded with tourists. If you arrive at the peak of the summer season, you may want to avoid the whole hassle of searching for a room with crowds of others. If you are willing to try less popular (or less well-known) locations, there are some delightful bargains hidden away in odd corners of the city.

Three of these are in the market area between Omonia and the Monastiraki subway station, just off Athinas Street. This area is a frenzy of activity by day: fruit peddlers, butchers, sidewalk pitchmen selling miracle cleaners, all compete for the shopper's attention in shouts that pierce the rumble of trucks and the squeal of taxi wheels. By contrast, it is one of the quietest parts of the city at night. Halfway between Omonia and Monastiraki is the **Omega Hotel** (15 Aristogitonos, tel: 3212-421) just one block from Athinas: a busy, 54-room place where every room is a double with bath, for just 435 drs. Fairly modern, with sparse but comfortable furniture and tiny balconies.

One of the quietest hotels in town must surely be the comfortable **Alkistis** (tel: 3219-811) situated on secluded Platia Theatrou not far from Sokratos and Euripides Streets. Popular with most tours, it offers many of the appurtenances of a luxury hotel, including roof garden, garage, restaurant and snack bar, and yet costing only around 500 drs double including breakfast.

The **Orion Hotel** (105 Emanuel Benaki, tel: 628-441) is off all by itself on the edge of Strefi Park, to the east of the National Archaeological Museum. There are nice-sized, bright rooms with balcony and comfortable furniture for about 250 drs single, 350 drs double. Most rooms have shower and toilet right outside the door instead of down a dark hall. There are only 20 rooms, of which ten have a splendid view of Mt. Lycabettus, the Acropolis, and much of downtown Athens; the rest face the pine trees and rocky paths of Strefi Park. The roof terrace, half under awnings, is used for serving breakfast (35 drs, but not required) and for sun-bathing or lounging. Here, the view is sensational. Mr. and Mrs. Bardiambassis, the owners, speak English and prefer students. They are very helpful. Despite the strange location, the Orion is just five minutes from the National Museum, two minutes from the # 16 and # 10 buses going to Syntagma, the Acropolis, and Plaka. Still, if you're arriving with luggage, you'd better get a cab to take you up the hill from Omonia.

AROUND THISSION: An alternative area to consider making your home in Athens is over on the other side of the Acropolis in the district known as Thission (after the well-preserved Temple of Hephaistos at the edge of the Agora). There's a subway station there, plenty of buses and a different perspective on the famous Parthenon view. The three main hotels are all around 400 drs single, 500 drs double, including breakfast, the **Thession** (2 Aghias Marinas, tel: 3467-655) being the nicest. The other two are the **Phidias** (39 Apostolou Pavlou, tel: 3459-511) and the **Erecteon** (Ag. Marinas and Flammarion, tel: 3459-606). Right behind the Thession is the **Pnyka Guest House,** about 330 drs double.

READER'S SELECTION: "I was fortunate to discover the **Alex Family Guest House** (Zakharitsa and Drakou Streets, tel: 9220-761) in a quiet area not far from the Acropolis. Exceptionally warm family-style welcome, all the rooms clean and comfortable with high ceilings. Hot showers free" (Gregory D. Cokorinos, New York City).

LOW-COST MEALS IN ATHENS

DESPITE WHAT YOU MIGHT be told by well-meaning friends before you arrive, the food in Greece isn't bad. It's true that Greek chefs have a tendency to use vast quantities of olive oil with everything, especially salads, but this is much less of a problem than it might appear because you can always tip the oil off and, when you're lucky, even have the dish served without it.

As a matter of fact, compared with some countries, Greek cuisine is quite acceptable to American tastes, because it is based on many familiar staples—meat, fish, eggs, bread, pasta, etc.—cooked in many familiar ways.

Your problems in adjusting to Greek food will concern its lack of variety. Nine out of ten Greek restaurants serve lamb, veal, shishkebab, vine leaves stuffed with meat, tomatoes stuffed with rice, and moussaka (a sort of lasagna-type dish of ground meat covered with pasta or mashed potatoes). Occasionally you'll find a restaurant that also has beef, pork, and fish. Invariably, salads consist of sliced tomatoes and sliced cucumber. Lettuce is virtually unheard of and so are most vegetables.

Having said all this, I should add that this food uniformity will be barely noticed by the average tourist on a stay in Greece of two weeks or less, and is easily overcome by the long-term visitor, who can supplement restaurant meals with imported groceries.

Besides the following list of restaurants in various areas of town, the reader should also consult Chapter VII, where the different tavernas in the Plaka area are dealt with.

Here, now, is where you'll find the best budget spots:

1. Standard Tourist Restaurants

Many of the most "American-type" restaurants (by which I mean places that serve Greek food with some concession to U.S. tastes, and aren't surprised by requests for butter, etc.) are on the side streets above Stadiou or Venizelou. This isn't far from some of the more expensive tourist hotels, so the restaurants are not cheap; on the other hand, they're certainly not expensive compared with American prices. Here's a fast run down of the top four.

The word for palm tree in Greek is *gerofinikas* and in the early life of this friendly neighborhood taverna—the **Gerofinikas**—at Pindarou 10 (tel: 3622-719), one stood in the garden. Now both palm tree and taverna have disappeared to be replaced by an attractive and luxurious restaurant with surprisingly reasonable rates: entrees from about 80 drs to 180 drs, with a few little extras like caviar and smoked salmon for those with credit cards and lavish dispositions. Greek cuisine is featured, with all the old favorites prepared magnificently and accompanied by displays of fruit, mouth-watering desserts, copper placemats and flowers on every table. Try the house specialty: veal (mouskari) with vegetables cooked in a paper bag.

After a steady diet of veal and lamb *ad infinitum,* you'll be delighted to find a restaurant that actually has a variety of things to offer. Although it is frankly aimed at the tourist trade, it isn't expensive. This is the **Vassilis** (14a Voukourestiou Street, just off Panepistimiou, near Syntagma, tel: 612-801), brightly lit, cheerful, and nearly always crowded. Menu, in English, French, and Greek, includes such goodies as pork chop (115 drs), filet of fish (105 drs), goulash and rice and all the old familiar items. Peas and carrots are available, and a handful of french fries comes with most entrees. There are also soups that, unlike most Greek soups, aren't oily, and excellent apple pie (22 drs) is among the desserts. Altogether, a valuable place to know about. Open till 11:30 p.m.

Not far away the **Corfu** (6 Kriezotou, beside the King's Palace Hotel, tel: 613-011) is a good modern restaurant recommended by Greeks and not quite as touristy as the Vassilis. It's air-conditioned, has wood walls, leather seats, and upstairs tables at a balcony if you want to view fellow diners from above. The menu is extensive, with a dozen hors d'oeuvres, omelettes, spaghetti and rice dishes, more than the usual selection of fish (shrimp, squid, sole, snapper, swordfish), and plenty of different meat dishes: lamb, veal, stuffed vine leaves, tongue, grilled liver, chicken, brains, braised ham, wiener schnitzel, mostly around 80-160 drs. There are eight salads, including the rarely available lettuce or eggplant, and a random selection of cheeses, fruits, pastries, and ice cream.

A short walk down Venizelou Street will bring you to two movie houses on the right, the Ideal and the Rex. Between them is the attractive **Ideal** restaurant, at #46, which is distinguished by its sidewalk showcases (in Japanese style) displaying replicas of the available dishes. Greek dishes, stuffed tomatoes, moussaka, etc. range from 35 to 75 drs, and most other entrees—roast chicken, roast pork, etc.—are well under 100 drs.

2. Around Syntagma (Constitution) Square

Delphi Taverna (13 Nikis Street, tel: 238-205), which used to be across the street from its present location, has developed into a handsome, rustic-style establishment with all kinds of modern facilities, even a special room where you can wash your hands and have them machine dried. It's friendly, convenient, pleasant, and the food's good. The manager says he specializes in "home cooking," and from the crowds that amass here at lunchtime, it doesn't look like he'll have to eat his words. The menu's extensive with lots of specialties—

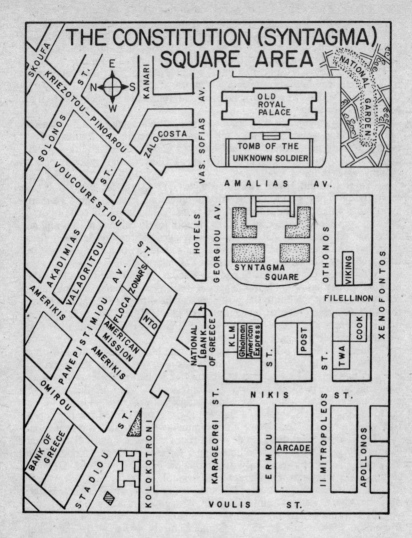

Mediterranean fish soup, stuffed vine leaves, red snapper, lamb with eggplant, omelette with sausages, rice with mince meat, veal with okra, lamb with green peas. The selection of vegetables is larger than usual.

If you continue up Nikis Street, past the Delphi, the next street you cross is Xenotontos and here, on the left at #10, is the airy **Meteora** (tel: 232-392). Nothing special about this clean bright place—except reasonable prices and good service. A few soups, including lentil, stuffed vine leaves, moussaka, omelettes, salads, grilled dishes, and fish entrees.

An open-air place not far from American Express is the **Sintrivani Tou Syntagmatos** (5 Filellinon Street, tel: 238-662), whose name means "the fountain of Syntagma." Access to the garden is via the kitchen, so if you like, you can study what's cooking before you sit down to order. Tables are in the open air, some are sheltered from the midday sun.

Menu in English includes lamb in tomato sauce or hamburger steak, veal chops, moussaka, chicken, etc. If you're lucky you'll get the friendly gray-haired waiter who can open bottles with the blunt end of a fork.

If you crave American coffee "good to the last drop" (as the menu boasts) try **The American** in the arcade on Syntagma, next to Singapore Airlines. Open till midnight, it offers cheeseburgers, meat loaf, tuna fish sandwiches as well as pancakes with syrup.

Behind Syntagma, on the corner of Nikis and Karageorghi, is the **American Coffee Shop** which does a good job of imitating second-rate Stateside food even to serving hamburgers without herbs (a normal Greek addition which improves the humble hamburger beyond belief). Okay, though, if you're homesick for tasteless filling food.

The **Restaurant Fatsio** (Efronion 5, tel: 717-421) is far enough off the tourist track to be pleasantly uncrowded at lunchtime, even though it's a mere five-minute walk from the Hilton. (A taxi from Syntagma Square costs 12 drs.) Fatsio is a spacious room, cool and bright, with lovely colorful murals and an occasional Chinese vase. All the food is displayed in shiny refrigerated glass trays, or in the open kitchen. Extensive menu with plenty of omelettes, cheeses, fruit, and hors d'oeuvres. Try a bottle of Pallini white wine.

While most people are sitting sipping sodas or coffee and watching the informal variety show beside the Zappeion (walk along Amalias out of Syntagma Square, and turn left into the park), you can be sitting at a restaurant there, the **Aigli Zappeion** (7 King Constantinos, tel: 230-939) and having a full, if late, dinner. Menu is in English and Greek, and selections include tenderloin beef steak, shishkebab and chops.

Number 18 looks exactly like a chic private house unless you know that it's a discreet little restaurant and bar. It has neat furnishings and a limited menu. Number 18 (18 Thatalou St., corner of Kondoron) is on the way to Kolonaki Square (walk straight up Voukourestiou St. from Akadimias). Half a dozen main entrees—stuffed tomatoes, cannelloni with mushrooms, chicken or shrimp curry, for example—in the 80-125 drs range. Closed Sundays, open till 2 a.m. rest of the week—except midsummer, when the staff is on vacation.

Try an occasional meal in one of the roof gardens of smaller hotels. You can usually get a decent table d'hote dinner for around 175 drs along with a view of the Acropolis and neatly dressed fellow diners. The **Hotel Arethusa** (Mitropoleos just below Syntagma) is an example.

There are two major squares in Plaka: one at the foot of Adrianou Street, near the Agora, which resembles a little Syntagma and has a nice and very popular open-air restaurant called the **Poseidon;** and the other called Plateia Philomoso Etairias just where Kydathneion meets Adrianou. In this latter square there used to be a good open-air movie theater, now converted into a theater, and there are a handful of eating places, among them the **Trattoria** restaurant, which offers pizzas (80-110 drs), hamburgers, omelettes and steaks.

It's not exactly a restaurant but it does serve such exotic English delights as fish and chips (65 drs) and sardines on toast, as well as a daily special for under 100 drs. This is the **Red Lion Pub** (Niridon St. 16, tel: 728-149), behind the Hilton Hotel. Definite pub atmosphere with bar stools, draught beer, a dartboard and English waitresses.

Busy as it is in daytime, the Flea Market area south of Monastiraki is almost dead at night, with one notable exception. This is a cheap, apparently nameless cave-like **taverna** between Ifestiou and Adrianou Streets, right opposite (and across the subway tracks) the side wall of the Stoa of Attalos. The taverna has stone walls, a rustic front, beamed ceilings, and lots of atmosphere, and is a favorite with foreign students and others who are likely to stage impromptu dances and singalongs.

Although I have recommended, elsewhere, against having dinner in the hillside area of Plaka, there are a few places that aren't quite so noisy and depressing as the rest. One of them is the unpretentious street-level garden of **T. Stamatopoulo,** at the corner of Lissiou and Tripolou, where you're shielded from the passing crowds to some extent by a tall hedge.

READER'S SELECTION: "We would like to recommend the following eating place in Athens: **Johns Place,** Patrou St. (next door to the Hotel Cleo). Tables and chairs are set up in a car park which resembles a bomb site, but in the warm evenings you don't notice the rubble and the view seems quite romantic. Moussaka or stuffed vine leaves are good value. A wandering minstrel—an old man with a guitar—serenades you as you eat" (H. Simons, London, England).

SNACK BARS: A whole rash of little snack bars have sprung up in the arcades that adjoin Syntagma Square. Most of them are very similar: a few tables in the arcade, a gleaming espresso bar offering coffee or liquor at the rear. They're very attractive and—for what they offer—comparatively cheap. The **Elysee** (Mitropoleos 1, tel: 236-924) is a good example. If you stand with your back to American Express, it's on the righthand side of the square just above Filellinon Street. Limited menu—excellent spaghetti, various omelettes, hors d'oeuvres such as sardines, salads, cheeses, and cold chicken, ham, or veal. Service is good, though, and the food is nicely prepared. It's open all night, by the way. Don't confuse it with the expensive restaurant next door.

A similar snack bar, the **Elite,** can be found in the arcade off Stadiou 7, other side of the square.

The **Seven Pans** (Souri 3, tel: 3244-739) claims to be the only place in Greece serving crêpes and Belgian waffles, and if you're into a cheap snack (crêpes with ham, cheese, spinach, or chicken cost 50 drs) it's handily close to Syntagma. Souri is the street almost opposite the Olympic Palace Hotel on Filellinon Street, and Seven Pans adjoins the 16th Century cafe.

The best coffee in Athens is served up, not surprisingly, by a series of cafes called the **Brazilian.** There are several such places, with identical menus, but the most accessible one is in the covered arcade between Ermou and Stadiou Streets, just off the bottom end of Syntagma Square. A glossy, smart place, it has upstairs tables frequented by all types, from white-cuffed businessmen to sandal-wearing backpackers. Ice cream, pastries, sodas, juices, coffees, croissants, brioches, etc. are served. A full breakfast of toast, butter, jam, coffee, ham and eggs is around 100 drs, including service. Fabulous chocolate frappes are available, but drink downstairs where they're cheaper.

If you get lonely for donuts, try the **Apolloneion** pastry shop (on Nikis, just off Mitropoleos). One huge, raised, sugared donut for 10 drs makes a whole breakfast. The menu also features "creeme pie" and "strunell," but the "donatch" are the best bargain.

3. Around Omonia Square

One of the streets behind the Hotel Omonia is called Satovriandou and on the last block of this, between Dorou and Patission Streets, are half a dozen inexpensive restaurants, any of which is satisfactory.

Right on Omonia Square itself, opposite the subway steps at September 3rd Street, is the bustling **Restaurant Hellas,** with a multilingual menu in the

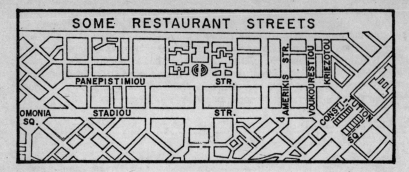

SOME RESTAURANT STREETS

window that is always surrounded by eager about-to-be customers. Extensive menu (125 items) and a spacious place, clean and informal but very efficient. Shrimp mayonnaise is about the most expensive item at 130 drs, with most entrees around 100 drs. A dish of spaghetti is a cheap snack. There are also pastries.

The arcade on Omonia Square at Dorou Street probably offers the best bet for budget eaters on the run. There are various stand-up counters, notably that of **Pikantiko Self-Service,** which offers meatballs, moussaka, shishkebab, hamburgers and chips, each for around 50 drs. Various other snackeries in the arcade proffer barbecued chicken, souvlaki, hot dogs, and sandwiches at similarly low prices.

Down Benaki, only a couple of doors off Stadiou Street (two blocks from Omonia Square), is the **Nea Olympia Restaurant** (3 Em. Benaki, tel: 3217-972), a large, white-tableclothed establishment where the waiters look very dressed up in their green jackets. It's more European-style than Greek and you can actually order chicken soup (25 drs). The menu is a bit limited, but there are such standbys as moussaka (60 drs), roast veal, and plenty of fruit for dessert.

The walk along Stadiou Street from Omonia after about six blocks takes you past the top side of a pretty square called Klafthmonos, a pleasant spot to sit and sip a soda or write postcards (which you can buy at the numerous kiosks around the square). At the bottom side of the square is the **Restaurant Sigros** (Germanou 5), which has tables on the sidewalk and also across the street under a green awning. Plenty of variety, and nothing on the menu higher than 55 drs.

Popular with students is the **Taverna Costoyanis** (Zaimi 37, behind the National Museum). So proud of their food are they that they parade you through the kitchen before seating you in the garden in the rear. Music in the evenings and low prices: chicken, fish, veal, pork chops, lamb chops, and grilled pigeons and thrushes (poor things), all for under 80 drs. Walk up Octobriou from Omonia, turn right past the Museum, and Zaimi is on your left four blocks up.

Two brothers who ran a restaurant in Canada for a couple of years have made a big success of the **Rodeo Self-Service** (17 Satobriandou, behind the Omonia Hotel). Open from 8 a.m. to 11 p.m., it offers fast service and inexpensive food. There's a remarkable selection of dishes for under 35 drs—and no waiting.

Cheap and fast (if you're in a real hurry) is **Floca Self Service** (Benaki 16), a spotless cafeteria with all dishes clearly visible and at bargain prices: baked fish (60 drs), moussaka (40 drs), veal sauté with french fries (60 drs).

4. The Fokionos Negri Area

Fokionos Negri is a winding boulevard in the north end of Athens: ask any cabby, or take the #2, 3, or 12 bus out Patission about a mile past the National Museum. Fokionos is a small street on the right side; but after you've walked a couple of blocks, it suddenly blossoms into a boulevard of trees and many fountains, lined with cafe tables. The expensive apartment buildings (no hotels) and swank shops evidence the good life. The Greeks and the international set who frequent the cafes (with such names as "Select" and "C'est Ça") like to call it "Athens' Via Veneto." While it's not that celebrity conscious an area, it is much more attractive.

The #2 trolley terminates at the top of the street and the half-dozen blocks to the bottom are filled with late-opening clothing stores and numerous counters where you can choose the ingredients for your sandwich and have it toasted. The pizza places, too, are great. Why can't America make pizzas like this?

Near the lower end of Fokionos, a fruit and vegetable market operates during the day; there's a pinball arcade with a merry-go-round for younger children, and most of the seats in the vicinty are taken by women with poodles and languid Greek playboys. A classy supermarket dominates the block which is shared by several cafes and two restaurants: the **Principos** (lots of variety) and the **Spaghetteria** (cheaper). There's also a taverna, **I Thraka,** with lots of atmosphere (beamed ceiling, barrels, straw-covered walls) and few enough tourists that the menu remains in Greek. There's tons of atmosphere in the square and plenty to watch: patrons arriving at the sex movie theater, kids patronizing the souvlaki stall and waiters challenging traffic as they cross the street with their trays.

5. "Foreign" Restaurants

The high-rent district between Kolonaki Square and Lycabettus hill is beginning to blossom with a wide choice of attractive—and mostly expensive—restaurants catering to the sophisticated tastes of wealthy Europeans and much-traveled Greeks living in the area. The charming **Je Reviens** (Xeno-cratos and Aristodimion), its tables topped with mushroom lamps under a shady arbor, has always been a favorite. Both Je Reviens and the adjoining **L'Abreuvoir,** whose terrace and trees it shares, are French in style and as popular at lunchtime as at night. But the former—with such items as stuffed tomatoes (50 drs), fried squid (80 drs), and veal with eggplant (120 drs) is cheaper; most of the entrees at L'Abreuvoir are in the 100 to 200 drs range.

Two Italian restaurants share the same street a couple of blocks further on, past the American School of Classical Studies. Our oldtime favorite **Al Convento** (Anapiron Poleman St.), with spaghetti and pizzas both under 100 drs and most entrees 140 drs to 190 drs, is pleasantly decorated but now outclassed by **La Casa** (corner of Xenocratos) further up the block. La Casa, however, seems awfully expensive.

Further up the block, just beside the steps, the pale green on burgundy tablecloths at **Jimmy's Cooking** (Loukiaou and Speysippou) are as eye-catching as the food is enticing. The cuisine is basically Greek, with heavy accent on such items as shishkebab (150 drs), pork chops (120 drs), and veal with okra (120 drs) plus cheaper entrees such as meatballs (80 drs) and chicken (95 drs).

Even the humblest Chinese restaurant in Athens, it seems, dreams of being an Imperial Palace, and **Mr. Yung's** (3 Lamahou St., off Filellinon, behind the Olympic Palace Hotel, tel: 3230-956) is no exception. Grandly decorated with paneled ceilings, Oriental prints, and elegant tableware, Mr. Yung's looks expensive and—for Chinese restaurants—is exorbitant. But everybody needs a change now and then so grit your teeth and get ready to pay for a special treat. Most fishes are in the 120 drs range but there are table d'hote specials for 200 drs for one, 380 drs for two. A foursome might try ordering the meal for two and adding a couple of extra dishes.

The food is better (but portions smaller and even more expensive) at the **Pagoda** (out by Greek Park on Alexandras Street at Bouglou)—outdoor sidewalk dining with elegant appurtenances and a wide-ranging menu. The food is good but a complete dinner for two will run to at least $14.

A classy Japanese restaurant, the **Kyoto** (5 Garibaldi St., tel: 9232-047) is also quite expensive but probably worth it for a special charge of cuisine. An attractive spot, it's situated only a block or two from where the road leads off to the Sound and Light show. Full dinners run from around 250 to 400 drs but you can get à la carte plates (tempura, tonkàtsu, sashimi, etc.) from about 140 drs. Closed Mondays. Another Japanese restaurant, **Michiko,** located in a pleasant Plaka garden (Kydathneion 27), is cheaper but not as good.

6. Snacks

Among the cheapest and tastiest snacks available in Greece are souvlaki (pita bread stuffed with meat, tomato, parsley, and chopped onion) and the hot cheese pies (pastry with melted cheese). The best souvlaki place in town, by general acclaim, is **Stefos** (Vassilissis Street, just off Aiolou Street), a semi-open stand which almost always has a line-up outside of half a dozen people. Here the souvlaki costs four drs and one can make a meal of it. The best-known cheese pie vendor is the **Ariston** pastry shop (Voulis and Karageorghi Streets), where a team of experienced women endlessly wrap fresh-out-of-the-oven pies and hand them to all comers. Get your ticket (9 drs) at the counter first and wash your pie down with icy water from the drinking fountain. Ariston sells pastries, too, but hardly anybody seems to care.

After your cheese pie, walk through the arcade which adjoins Ariston's side door (locked) and go down the steps at the end and into the street below. The police station is directly on your right as you emerge. But across the street, left, is a lovely old wine store that stays open Sundays and serves up tasty ice cream cones. The friendly man who runs it, Charles, has been sitting outside his store studying English with a dictionary on his lap for as many years as I can remember, and he finally decided that he's ready to practice on some of my readers. Drop by to say hello, he invites. Open Sundays, too.

The **Alaska Sandwich Bar** (Patission 26, first shop past the Archaeological Museum) has very tasty, large pizzas for around 20 drs.

There are dozens of little snack bars all over town which specialize in milk, ice cream, pastries, and yogurt, with or without honey. One such place, near Syntagma Square, is at the corner of Mitropoleos and Voulis Streets. Nothing costs more than about 50 drs here, and there are half a dozen tables for sitting. (More about Syntagma snack bars above.)

The most popular cafes in which to sit and watch the crowds go by are naturally the most expensive, but after you've tried the pastries you'll understand why. You won't need any help, of course, to find the cafes outside American Express or all the other, quieter ones across the street in the "sunken" part of Syntagma Square. Nor can you fail to miss **Zonar's** and **Floca's** at the Syntagma end of Venizelou Street.

But have you discovered Kolonaki Square, where all the wealthy Athenians sit around and discuss the tourists? (Walk up Vassilissis Sofias, the Parliament buildings on your right, then turn left up Koumbari.) High-spot around here is the **Byzantion,** its brick wall covered with small oval portraits of Greeks who have distinguished themselves, many of whom, as it happens, patronize the place. Late at night it is popular with actors and politicians. Like most places of this kind, it offers only pastries, coffee, and snacks and is open at least until midnight. Pastries, ice cream about 50 drs. A bit of class that's relatively inexpensive.

In the heat of midday, it's pleasant to take a taxi from Omonia to Philopapas Hill, near to where the Sound and Light takes place, and sit in a shady arbor for a beer or soft drink. There are only snacks available—cheese pies, orange juice, ice cream, pastries, etc.—but it's cool and peaceful and you can gaze up at the Acropolis while you meditate. If you don't want to splurge on a taxi, it's easy enough to catch a # 16 bus from Amalias Street, top of Syntagma Square, and get off one stop past the steps leading up to the Acropolis. Walk up the hill leading to the Son et Lumière (there's a big sign) and turn right.

Even though Greek donuts are among the world's best, some chauvinist has opened a shop to offer 61 varieties of "good American donuts" from 7 a.m. to 1 a.m. each day. This is **Jax,** at the corner of Koupa and Monis Kikkon Streets, beyond the White Tower (tel: 6910-361).

ALL-NIGHT PLACES: Each of the three major squares—Syntagma, Kolonaki, and Omonia—has at least one all-night cafe. The **Nouphara** (tel: 627-426), next door to the Byzantion in Kolonaki, is by far the most attractive. Quite elegant, it features a pond with goldfish on one of its three floors, taped music, a magazine rack, and sidewalk tables that attract some of the prettiest girls in Athens. In addition to pastries, coffee, soft drinks, liquor, and ice cream, there are also such dainties as "mini-pizza," sandwiches, and fried eggs. Nouphara means water lily, by the way. In Syntagma, the **City** snack bar (tel: 227-010) sits in an arcade over by the airline offices and offers everything from a hamburger to spaghetti or "peasant salad." In the sunken part of Syntagma Square, under the steps on the right, is a cafeteria—the **Alryoni**—which advertises "service around the clock."

The Milk Bar on Omonia Square, between Pireos and Athinas, has a limited menu but is very popular late at night and for breakfast.

7. The Big Splurge

The find of the year is undoubtedly the magnificent **Balthazar** (as in *Balthazar's Feast*) in a big old house with a lovely garden at Tsocha 27 and Vournazou Streets (tel: 6441-215). Operated by a novelist, Kay Cicellis, and her much-traveled husband Nikos Paleologos, both of whom speak English, the Balthazar's inspiring menu includes: curried eggs, parsley salad with almonds, and octopus in red wine; gazpacho or cold cucumber soup (all items so far around 50 drs); steamed trout, crab mousse, deep-fried prawns, homemade pâté or wild hare (95 drs), aubergine surprise, roast veal with pistachio stuffing, all for around 160 drs; steaks and chops, salads of lettuce, rice, carrots; cheeses and marvelous desserts. And if you give 24 hours' notice Nikos will prepare a special Indian curry evening: 1600 drs for four. The house itself, once owned by a wealthy industrialist, is delightful; Nikos' glass collection is fascinating, and the sumptuous smells with stoke your appetite to boiling point. Open till 2 a.m., closed Sundays.

Wild West saloon is the style of **The Stagecoach** (6 Loukianou, near Kolonaki, tel: 743-955), with its swinging doors, buffalo heads, and placemats recounting the inglorious saga of Captain Custer. The place has style but looks expensive and, of course, it is, although it's obvious that the food is going to be reliably satisfactory to American tastes. There's a good bar, usually patronized by local expatriates, and the place offers some relatively rare dishes for Athens, such as chile con carne (around 70 drs) and a bunch of items lumped under "range-rider brunch" which includes steak and eggs, pork chops, and stagecoach omelette (70-90 drs). Hot and cold sandwiches range from 60 to 100 drs, hamburgers to 120 drs, and salads around 60-75 drs. Bigger entrees—for example, steaks and chops—are priced at around 130 to 190 drs.

Lycabettus restaurant (top of the mountain) is a lovely spot in which to eat on a hot day—in fact on any day when you'd like a view with your meal. Menu comes in Greek, French, and English, with most entrees costing around 130-170 drs—filet mignon, pork, veal, mixed grill, all the usual items, including spaghetti or moussaka. It's not the cheapest restaurant in town, but it's certainly the highest.

No apologies for including the **Byzantine Cafe** of the Athens Hilton here. After a steady diet of cheap, nourishing, but essentially unimaginative cooking (how many times in a row can you eat veal, french fries, and tomato salad?), you'll be delighted to know that the Hilton features all those old familiar favorites that you hunger for: excellent hamburgers, frankfurters, turkey burgers, tunafish salads, cheese or ham omelettes, bacon, lettuce and tomato sandwiches, etc., etc. Naturally, there are all the more expensive dishes available, too, but this is a book for budget eaters. Still, it's a big splurge.

The **Asteria Taverna** at Glyfada puts on a big buffet dinner, with all you can eat and all the wine you can drink, at 9 p.m. Mondays. It costs around 225 drs but features fantastic selections arrayed in mouth-watering ways. The #84 or 89 bus from Amalias St. will get you there.

8. Starvation Budget

If you think that you're going to find lots of single women sitting around eating dinner in the **YWCA Cafeteria**, you're right—and you'll also find lots of men. The cafeteria (11 Amerikis Street, just off Stadiou at the Syntagma Square end) is in the basement of the XEN building. It's bright and airy and the food is pretty good—and pretty cheap. You can have lunch or dinner from an à la carte menu. Luncheon entrees include moussaka, and scrambled eggs with cheese; at dinner, the constantly changing entrees might include liver, chicken with rice, and beef with eggplant. The Y cafeteria is open Monday through Saturday from 7 a.m. to 3:30 p.m., and 5-10 p.m. Saturdays until 9 p.m. On Sundays 7 a.m. to 2 p.m., and 5 to 9 p.m.

Don't overlook the **Butcher's Cafeteria** (Kolokotroni Square, just off Stadiou). Cheap, fast, open till 11 p.m.

Some of the hotel snack bars offer good light meals for minuscule prices. Consider, for example, the snack bar of the **Hotel Diomia** (5 Diomias St.) with lusty bacon and egg breakfasts for around 50 drs, other entrees from about 70 to 100 drs.

Just past Omonia Square is the **Minion department store,** along Patission Street, and on the 11th floor is a splendid cafeteria that serves cheap meals and snacks while you sit at a narrow terrace and watch the scurrying shoppers below. Open till 8 p.m. some nights, 11 p.m. on others.

9. Further Afield

As a change from hot Athens you might want to think about going to the suburbs for dinner. Regular buses from Koningos Square run westward past the Hilton Hotel out to the suburbanite town of **Kifissia,** about a 30-minute ride. Kifissia is also the last stop on the subway line. Where the bus stops, adjoining a pleasant park, you can get a horse and buggy to take you for a ride around Kifissia, where the back streets are lined with enormous houses—almost chateaux—inhabited by wealthier Greeks who obviously don't have to run into Athens for work early each morning.

Among the nicer places to visit in Kifissia are a trio of fairly expensive restaurants, each of which has its own individual ambience: **Hatzakos** (Ag. Theodoron, old Kifissia village, tel: 8013-461) grew from a tiny taverna into two gardens across the street from each other; **Bokaris** (Acharnon and Socratous, tel: 8012-589) has a flower-filled garden in which to eat (and also a mini-zoo!); **Kirki** (Pentelis 1, tel: 8080-388) cooks Cypriot-style in clay ovens in a lovely garden.

Beyond Kifissia is **Psychiko,** a suburb with a permanent fun fair and a cafeteria/restaurant called **Peacocks** (Kifissias 228, tel: 6719-629) on the roof of a supermarket; and beyond that **Varybopi,** a tiny village which seems to consist of nothing but open-air tavernas under the trees in a circle around which the bus turns before returning. Just before entering Varibopi, however, look for a restaurant under the trees on your left. The sign is hard to read—it's **Babis** —but you'll notice a big plaster swan and other fake birds and animals set around a tiny fountain.

ATHENS: DAYTIME SIGHTSEEING

IN AN EARLIER CHAPTER, I've already noted some of the more interesting daylight walks to be made in Athens. Here I'll turn to a few specific sights and institutions, starting, of course, with the awesome Acropolis—which can provide one of the great thrills of your life.

1. The Acropolis

To all intents and purposes, the Acropolis, which towers over Athens (515 feet above sea level), dates back to the Mycenean age, about 1, 500 B.C. It was not only a palace and a fortress, but a whole city, built upon the most commanding site available that was strong enough to withstand siege. The "Cyclopean walls" owe their names to the disbelief expressed by later Greeks that human hands could have heaved such enormous marble blocks into place without the help of the mythical hero Cyclops.

The city of Athens gradually began to extend around the slopes of the hill, the citizens retreating within the shelter of the walls when trouble occurred. About the end of the sixth century B.C., by which time Athens was trading with much of the known world—its silver coin bearing an owl's head was international currency—the Acropolis was sanctified as a holy place; the homes were moved and temples built.

The rise of Athens as a city-state coincided with Persia's conquests, and eventually a clash occurred between them over possession of the Greek islands. The first battle, at Marathon, was won by Athenian troops, and Phidipides ran the 26 miles to Athens to bring the good news—falling dead after delivering the message.

Later Persian victories brought them within reach of the city. They captured the Acropolis and destroyed its temples. The Delphic oracle had previously told the Athenians that they would be saved by the wooden walls. Some thought that this meant the Acropolis, but Themistocles' interpretation that it meant the Athenian navy turned out to be correct, and the Persians were finally defeated at Salamis.

What later came to be known as the "golden age of Athens," from 450 B.C., was a time when the Athenians, under Pericles, devoted prodigious energies to making the Acropolis as beautiful a site as it was possible to create. Most of what is really universally admired about it, including the magnificent Parthenon itself, dates back to that time.

THE ROUTE: There are two approaches to the Acropolis from downtown Athens. Starting from Syntagma Square, you can walk across to Amalias Street, at the top of the square, and take a #16 bus that turns right along Dionissiou Arepagitou, and alight when you see the entrance steps leading to the Acropolis, on your right. Alternatively, and much more interestingly, you can walk down Mitropoleos Street, the hill that runs down past the side entrance of American Express. About five or six blocks down, you'll come to the Cathedral (mitropoleos), at which point watch for Mnisikleos Street (it will be written more or less like this: Mnheikleoye), two short blocks past.

Turn up Mnisikleos Street—very narrow—and walk up several blocks (passing Adrianou Street, Plaka's main drag) until you reach the broad steps. Almost deserted by day, this area really swings at night, crowded with people eating dinner around 10 p.m. or later.

Climb up the rest of the steps, then bear right at the top. You'll now find yourself on a track that winds around below the Acropolis; keep left all the way until it terminates in an open area filled with taxis, a tourist refreshment stand on wheels, souvenir stands, and tour buses.

On your way you'll pass a small open-air taverna, serving only beer, whose tables overlook the ruins of **Hadrian's Library** and the ancient ruins of the **Roman Agora** (market) below, the latter built about 25 A.D. In the market, there still stands the octagonal **Tower of the Winds,** about which more in Chapter III.

This whole area around the market is littered with ancient ruins and is interesting to walk around. It is bordered roughly by Dionissiou Areopagitou and Adrianou Streets and by Thessalonikis Street (the broad street that runs past the big building with columns—the Agora Museum—in the distance). If you want to explore it on your way back down from the Acropolis, you'll find a street leading down into the area just beside the open-air taverna you passed.

Admission to the Acropolis—and all the other ancient monuments and museums around town—is free on Thursdays and Sundays; a nominal fee (15 drs for the Acropolis) is charged at other times. Most ruins close at sunset and are also closed during the afternoon. The Acropolis is open from 9 a.m. to sunset; the Acropolis Museum from 9 a.m. to 5 p.m. on most days, and 10 a.m. to 2 p.m. on Sundays. The museum is very small and contains mostly sculptures and friezes from the seventh and sixth centuries B.C. Four works of a sculptor named Phaidimos (about 590-520 B.C.) are the high spots.

THE ACROPOLIS ITSELF: The magical, magnificent time to see it is on one of the three nights of the full moon each month, when it is open from 9 p.m. to midnight. Heavily populated though the area usually is by people of all

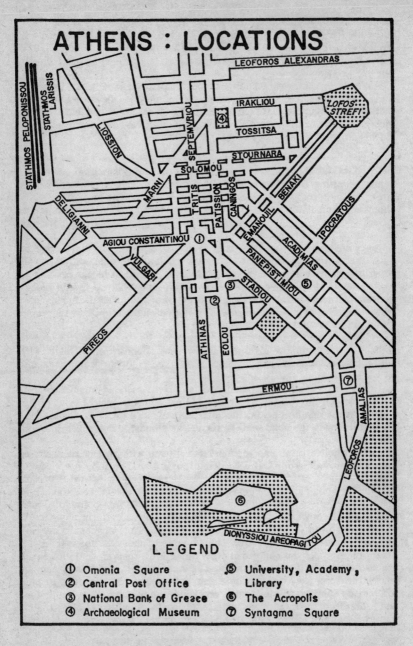

ATHENS : LOCATIONS

LEGEND

① Omonia Square
② Central Post Office
③ National Bank of Greece
④ Archaeological Museum
⑤ University, Academy, Library
⑥ The Acropolis
⑦ Syntagma Square

nationalities and all ages, it is easy, at this time, to find a tranquil spot and gaze on the massive marble columns of the Parthenon that have endured through the centuries, indeed almost from the very beginnings of what we today know as civilization.

The moon's rays, though slender, enable you to pick your way across the uneven rocky surface, but the figures that pass and repass you, discarding fragmentary phrases in a dozen different languages, are merely silhouettes with cheese-white faces. Occasionally, a forbidden flash bulb will pop or a passerby will solicit a light from your cigarette, but otherwise, in the vast area between the two main buildings, you might be alone in a world some 2,500 years long gone.

And then a stroll to the walls overlooking the city will present you with the lovely panorama of a million twinkling lights.

For 2,500 years, people have been inspecting and appraising the Acropolis and I will not presume to bore you with anything more than the barest details about how magnificent it is. If ever a place "grows on you," this is it. From almost any point in Athens, at almost any time, it can be seen, a perpetual surprise and a perpetual reassurance that mortal though human beings may be, their works survive for as long as people respect them.

As you climb up the path to the entrance, you'll see the **Theater of Herod Atticus** on your right below. Built in 160 A.D. by the Roman whose name it bears, as a memorial to his wife Regilla, it is now the site of summer events in the Athens Festival. Further over towards town is the **Theater of Dionysos,** built in the fourth century B.C.

The building at the entrance, known as the **Propylaea,** was built in 482 B.C. by the architect Mnesicles (who gave his name to the street you may have traversed on the way here). One part of it, the left wing, was used as a picture gallery. The building, five years in construction, was never finished because (it is believed) money ran out. In 1656, on the day of St. Dimitrios (October 26), while a festival was being held at the little church that bears the saint's name at the foot of the Acropolis, the Turkish governor decided to fire a gun at the church to stop the noise. According to legend, the saint asked Zeus to send a thunderbolt down from the sky as a return gesture. At any rate, something providentially struck the Propylaea where Turkish ammunition was stored, and the whole place blew up.

To the right of the Propylaea is the **Temple of Athena Nike** (generally, and inaccurately, known as "wingless victory"), which was demolished by the Turks in 1867 to make room for a cannon, but has since been re-erected. Several stone tablets, with carved figures removed from this temple, are now in the Acropolis Museum nearby (closed Tuesdays).

The **Parthenon** is one of the most skillfully conceived pieces of architecture in existence. Despite its impression of symmetry, there is not a single parallel or straight line in the whole building. It is all curves—partly because of the necessity to curve the building over the irregular surface on which it was placed and to give an impressive look to a structure that was mostly to be admired from below, and partly because the ancient Greeks believed that curves were more objectively beautiful than straight lines.

The renowned Pericles was the major driving force behind th Parthenon's construction, and the work was actually undertaken by the architects Icthinus and Callierates, and an enormous body of assistants supervised by the sculptor Phidias, who spent ten years (447-438 B.C.) on the project. It was completed only four years before Pericles' death, and because of the enormous sums of money it cost it was perhaps inevitable that charges of graft were bandied around. It is said that Pericles was undergoing investigation on some of these charges when he died. It is built in Doric style, with the usual proportion of double-plus-one pillars on one side against the other—in this case, eight columns on the east and west and 17 columns on the north and south.

In the 15th century, the occupying Turks turned the Parthenon into a mosque and in 1687, during an attack by the Venetians, it was blown up. The Turks partly restored it the following year, but it owes its appearance today to restoration work done by archaeologists who, in the early 19th century, reconstructed it, as nearly as possible, the way it was believed to have been in the fifth century B.C.

Admission to the Parthenon itself is now closed. Too many million footsteps have been wearing away the marble floor, or so the official explanation goes.

The only other building still standing on the Acropolis is the **Erechtheum,** across the open space from the Parthenon against the north wall. It is a temple that was placed on the most sacred spot in the Acropolis, where legend has it that the goddess Athena (Minerva) caused a sacred olive tree to grow. There is still an olive tree (a younger one) on the spot today. In the classical days, the olive from the tree was given as a reward to athletes who competed successfully in the quarterly games and festival, the Great Panathenaea, which took place here.

Against one wall of the Erechtheum stand six stone maidens, the **Karyatides,** one of which (second from the left in the front row) is a copy of the original which was removed, along with other statues from the Acropolis, by Lord Elgin on behalf of the British Museum. The Turks made the Erechtheum into a harem to house the 40 wives of the military governor, and during the Greek War of Independence, in 1827, a shell fell on the building and wrecked the roof.

Not the least enjoyable thing about the whole Acropolis is the excellent views it affords of the city of Piraeus and the sea, eight miles to the south. It is advisable to climb the hill as early in the day as possible, because as soon as the sun sets, the guards run around ushering everybody out of the place. It has survived 2,500 years so far, but nobody trusts present-day visitors.

THE AGORA: The ancient Agora, or Roman market place, below the Acropolis at the bottom end of Plaka near where Ermou Street meets the subway line, is dominated by an immense colonnade named after Attalos who was king of Pergamon from 159 to 138 B.C. This **Stoa of Attalos,** as it is named, contains a bronze plaque listing all the donors who contributed to its impressive rebuilding, and the museum with its ancient lead weights, sculptured heads, pottery, and an enormous bronze shield dating back to the fifth-century battle of Pilos is well worth an inspection. A caseful of Greek, Roman, and Byzantine coins includes those bearing the ancient Athens owl, which has replaced the head of the king on some of the new (1975) coins.

Also in the Stoa is another museum containing an exhibition of ancient wine flasks (sponsored by the Achaia Clauss winery whose Demestica wine is highly recommended) with a wide range of these beautiful amphora dating back to the fifth century B.C. Most of the bigger ones have a pointed base to allow greater handling when tipped up and there are examples, too, of the bases in which they were held.

At the northwest end of the Agora, nearest to the Temple of Haiphestos, is an open-air cafe, which is a popular late-evening gathering spot to sit and watch from a distance the changing moods of the Acropolis during the Sound and Light show. On the other side of the Agora, in Plaka, a winding street contains tavernas popular with Greeks for dinner. The view is great, the food less so. But usually there are a couple of wandering buskers who'll entertain during dinner.

2. The Archaeological Museum

The **National Archaeological Museum** (Patission and Tositsa Streets, tel: 8217-177, #2 or #12 bus along Patission from Amalias Street) is open 7:30 a.m.-7:30 p.m. Tuesday through Sunday, closed Monday (this, like most museums, is also closed over Easter). An enormous place, well laid out, it will take you at least one hour to peruse, even if you walk through giving everything only a cursory glance. And your time, by the way, will be well spent, for the museum contains relics, statuary, and other centuries-old objects from famous sites in all parts of Greece.

There are various printed guides to the museum, and English-speaking (human) guides can be hired on the spot. Hachette's famous *Blue Guide* gives a comprehensive, but pretty dull rundown of what is contained in each room. A better guide is *Athens and Environs* by L. Russell Muirhead (Ernest Beer, Ltd., London).

Actually, it isn't really necessary to have a guide at all, either written or spoken, because everything is clearly, if unimaginatively, labeled in Greek, French, and English, and subsidiary slabs of text dealing with various periods are appended to the walls at various places.

What follows is a thoroughly subjective, understandably incomplete, summary of some of the items that have caught my own eye as I've wandered through. Incidentally, admission to the museum is 50 drs most days, but on Sundays and Thursdays it is free.

WALKING THROUGH THE MUSEUM: Almost the first thing you'll see on turning right is an enormous pair of unattached feet, with no legs or body, on a pedestal. On the wall, in a glass case, is an enormous stone hand, also unattached. Are they related? Such fragmentation of the body has an eerie effect, almost as though different sections of the anatomy operated independently. One statue is complete except for a missing arm—nothing but air between the shoulder and the hand, which is connected to the hips at the wrist.

A row of delicately chiseled stone heads of warriors conceals a mystery. Dating back to 500 B.C., they were found buried near the temple of Aphaia on the island of Aegina, and had been replaced by another row of heads. Displaced heros? History being rewritten?

A section of the old stone wall that the Athenians built between the Acropolis and Piraeus in the fifth century B.C. appears next. Sparta, alarmed by the way Athens was beginning to fortify itself, demanded a "disarmament conference" with Athens at which Themistocles, representing the city, kept delaying serious discussion of the matter while the Athenians built furiously. As Thucydides put it: "For the circuit wall of the city was extended in every direction, and on this account they laid hands on everything alike in their haste."

All kinds of rocks and junk—second-hand used chariots, maybe—were thrown into the wall to complete it before the Spartans got too suspicious. Then, the wall finished, Themistocles broke off the negotiations—a political gambit that has served many a country since.

One of the most impressive items in the museum—throughout which there are always photographers jostling for position—is the larger-than-lifesize bronze statue of Poseidon, dating back to 460 B.C., which was dredged from the sea off the coast of Euboea (the big island to the northeast of Athens) in 1918.

The goddess of Athens, not surprisingly named Athena, is depicted on one marble jar "throwing away the double flute which she invented. She was disgusted when she saw how her face was distorted by playing on it."

Several rooms are devoted to funeral relics and the impressive steles, or gravestones, with which the burial places were surmounted. Sometimes the stone was carved depicting the bereaved family group looking wistful, at other times with a statue of the deceased. In the Greek cemeteries of today, you'll often find a grave bearing a framed photograph of the dead man or woman.

In the classic days, it was the custom to erect monuments to those killed in wars for their country, just as it is today, and there's a section here of such a monument from 394 B.C., erected by the citizens of Athens to honor the men who fell fighting at Corinth.

A large carved stone is described as an offering to Dionysos from about the same date. It shows a group of actors reclining, holding their masks and looking thoroughly languid.

In mythological sculpture, symbols say much more than labels, so a statue in which the head is bound with a band of some sort is always that of a god or an athlete-hero, just as Pan is always depicted with the legs of a goat.

The carvings on some stones have become so worn with time that one had best consult the infra-red photographs which accompany them.

Several of the galleries are devoted to different areas of Greece—Epidaurus, where the ancient theater still survives, for example—and others contain nothing but vases, with the usual subject matter: winged horses, nymphs, flute- and lyre-playing gods, dancers, archers. One vase is described as "the rape of Helen by Paris," but despite a close inspection I haven't been able to find anything indecorous enough to offend a Sunday school teacher. The principals in the "rape" aren't even touching; I guess they just mean abduction.

Ancient Greek pottery went through several stages: plain geometric forms, stylized black and white figures, incisions in the pottery to make the paint deeper and more durable, the introductions of animals, birds and other aspects of nature such as trees and flowers, the depiction of gods and myths, and finally, oriental and foreign influences.

A textual amplification in one of the galleries refers to the "imagination of the vase painters, especially those in the Athenian potters' quarter, stirred by inventive and productive genius, which succeeds in enlivening the surface of the vases with movement, with expressive gestures, with color, with smiles, with humanity."

In contrast to the sophistication of some of the vase decorations, the small clay figures—some of dolls found on the tombs of little girls—are primitive, of a style suggestive of later Mexican peasant pottery.

The most crowded galleries of the museum are the ones straight ahead as you enter—dozens of glass cases of jewelry, beaten gold bracelets and necklaces, and other small items.

Don't miss the enclosed garden between the old and new wings of the museum. It is beautifully green and cool, and sets off nicely the pieces of sculpture with which it is lined.

3. The Numismatic Museum

Adjoining the Archaeological Museum, further up Tositsa Street, is the **Numismatic Museum** (one block above Patission), the entrance to which is unmarked (the sign reads: "National Archaeological Museum offices"), and which appears to be thoroughly unappreciated by tourists. It is open from 7:30 a.m. to 1 p.m. every day except Sunday.

Thousands of people, both individually and in tour buses, pour through the adjoining show spot daily, despite the fact that it's one of the world's least imaginative museums, however many priceless treasures it might claim. Next door, laid out no more imaginatively, but with as many stories to tell if people choose to hear them, are coins preserved through thousands of years of history.

You will have learned by now that I am not one who goes into raptures over works of art. A painting, a drawing, a sculpture may very well be "beautiful" if such be the valuation that the experts place upon it; and certainly it merits attention, because some of its interest stems directly from the fact that it is old (i.e., was created by people with different standards and mores).

But a work of art, with certain exceptions, is merely that: something to give the eyes, the ear, and the heart joy. It sits there and is admired and, although life is fuller with it, life can also go on without it.

Not so the commonplace objects that are a part of every man's daily life—the clothes he wears, the tools he uses, the currency with which he has always established a trust and rapport with his neighbors. These, the items that relate to living people going about their everyday activities with no sense of posterity, are the things that make history interesting to me.

Some of the coins in the museum (climb two flights of stairs) are as small as thumbtacks holding the cords between them; others are too big for the pocket (did togas have pockets?). Silver and gold are the commonest materials, but there are also coins of other metals, even of stone. The Athenian owl, at one time a worldwide guarantee of stability, stares placidly from coins minted in the days of Pericles; other wildlife symbols include fish, bulls, and horses. But most coins bear heads, as they have always done—the sharp, hawk-like face of the Emperor Tiberius (151-171 A.D.); the fat, pompous Nero; Hadrian or Claudius.

One coin from Julius Caesar's time has a picture on it that is almost identical with the old British penny—"Little ship right out at sea, lighthouse near at hand; Britannia on a barrel wheel, a pitchfork in her hand," runs the kids' saying. The symbol of the now defunct British penny, always written as 1d, was a direct descendant of the Roman denarius—which was what the "d" stood for.

Note: It is possible to get a free pass to visit museums and archaeological sites in Greece if you are a student (accompanied by a professor) or a professor of classics, archaeology, history of art, architecture, sculpture, or painting. Personal application for such passes must be made on Monday or Friday between 11 a.m. and 1 p.m. at the Directorate of Antiquities and Restoration, 14 Aristidou St. (tel: 3234-390). Take along your passport, a photograph, a student card, and a letter of introduction and purpose from your university. Regular students can get a 50%-off pass on admission fees by presenting their ID at the above address.

4. The Benaki Museum

This one, 1 Koumbari Street, can be taken in on a visit to nearby Kolonaki Square. It's a heterogeneous collection of old locks, keys, incense burners, big bronze bells, tapestries, triptychs, jewel-encrusted crosses, religious paintings, and coins of glass and stone imprinted with whatever made currency valid in the fifth century. There are swords, guns, helmets, colored fragments of old glass and porcelain that would excite even Gaudi and, at the top of the stairs, a sedan chair. To top it off, the museum possesses two El Grecos.

Upstairs, the most interesting room is one containing paintings of Greece done by different artists at different times—Turkish soldiers stopping for a drink in a small village, shipwrecks along the rugged coastline, strong castles, views of the barren countryside around Athens in days when there was little to see but the Acropolis (as if that weren't enough!).

In the basement, plaster of paris models in glass cases are draped with the handwoven fabrics common to almost all folk cultures, but with a specially Greek accent, topped off by the red hats with tassels worn by men and women alike. Some of the women are decorated with necklaces or bracelets containing scores of gold coins, and separate cases of jewelry fill up at least two full rooms.

Look closely at exhibit #1318—it's a woven strip of colored "flowers," intricately made from fabric and looking real enough to fool a botanist.

The museum, to which admission is 40 drs, is open daily from 8:30 a.m. to 2 p.m. Closed Tuesdays.

5. The Byzantine Museum

The **Byzantine Museum** (22 Vassilissis Sofias, two blocks from the Hilton Hotel) is situated in a pleasant group of buildings with patio. The "Popular Art Room" merits your closest attention, with its brightly colored wooden and canvas pictures that look very much like the comic strips of an earlier age. In one, for example, an angel has got a tight hold of a devil by the horns and is chopping away at him with a hatchet. Presumably, religion offered our distant ancestors the outlet for violence that movies and television provide today.

There are rooms full of carved, sculptured stones, including a replica of a Byzantine church, and a couple of lecterns with carved, animal-like legs that look forbiddingly as though they'd bite anyone who stood and read in front of them. Illuminated books and scrolls, ornamental jeweled crowns, and shreds of textiles from the sixth century make up the collection. A large number of the pictures depict self-righteous angels triumphing over evil in one form or another, although one room contains a small carved stone nude about the size of a hand—so *somebody* appreciated the female form!

The museum, which offers a fine view of Lycabettus, is open from 7:30 a.m. to 7:30 p.m. Closed Monday; admission 50 drs.

NOTE ALSO: The **National Gallery of Art** (Vas. Konstantinou, opposite the Hilton, tel: 711-010), Greek painters from the 16th century plus European masters; open 9 a.m.-8 p.m. Tuesday through Saturday, 10-2 Sunday, closed Monday, 25 drs. **Museum of Greek Popular Art** (Kydathneion 17, Plaka, tel: 3213-018), folk art of all kinds from the 1700s, open 10 a.m.-2 p.m., closed Monday, free. **National Historical Museum** (Kolokotronis Square at Stadiou, tel: 3237-617), open 9 a.m.-1 p.m., closed Monday, 15 drs. **Museum of Greek Populàr Art, Ceramic Collection** (Monastiraki Square, tel: 3242-066), open 10 a.m.-2 p.m., closed Tuesday.

6. The War Museum of Greece

It all sounds so militaristic and the fighter planes, guns, and battlefield artifacts outside don't encourage the peace-loving visitor. But you're in for a surprise—it's more illustrated history book than museum, with charts, maps, slides, and dioramas of Hellenistic battles since ancient times. Models of Athenian *triremes* with three banks of oars, the mythical ship *Argo* (of Jason fame), obsidian spear tips from the Neolithic era (8,000 to 4,000 B.C.), relief maps of fifth century B.C. campaigns against Greece by the Persians, copper Corinthian helmets from a century before that. There are illustrations of ancient battles, models of hilltop forts, and cutaway sections of miniature fireships with tarred interiors. Nearer to the present day, amidst the plethora of medals, flags, shells, and busts of war heroes, are romantically elaborate uniforms, all-gold braid and epaulets with flashy skirts and rakish fezzes. There's even a piece of the tree under which national poet Fionysos Solomos wrote Greece's national anthem. Fascinating. The museum, open 9 a.m. to 2 p.m. daily (closed Monday), is situated in a cool, modern building next to the Byzantine Museum on Vas. Sophias. Admission is free.

7. The Gennadeion

One of the largest collections of literature about Greek history, especially about the Byzantine period (corresponding to medieval times in our culture), is contained in a classically built structure known as the Gennadeion (61 Sonidias Street, almost opposite the Athens Hilton on Ave. Vassilissis Sofias. Walk up the hill and you'll see the Gennadeion, with its marble pillars, deadending the top of the street).

Built in 1923 by a New York firm, from funds granted by the Carnegie Corporation, the building houses the collection of John Gennadius (1844-1932), a Greek diplomat who served in Washington, Istanbul, Vienna, and London, and honors the memory of his father, George, who was a leader in Greece's War of Independence and a renowned Greek educator.

At first glance, the library appears to be as uninspiring as any collection of old books to those not particularly absorbed in the subject they cover, but closer inspection of the contents is well worth the effort. There are copies of the first printed editions of such best-selling writers of their days as Aesop and Homer (the printed editions date back to the 15th century, when printing was invented; the writings come down from papyrus and hand-written books before that date); a 15th-century travel book about the Greek islands, hand-drawn and illustrated by an Italian predecessor of mine, Cristoforo Buondelmonte; the first edition of the Bible printed in Greece; a picture book (something like a Japanese scroll) of Turkish drawings of a marching column in bright-colored clothes, drawn in 1593; and a set of tiny books, with microscopic type and a small magnifying glass, printed only 60 or 70 years ago.

Books were much more works of art when so much individual effort went into their preparation, and several treasures illustrate this fact, including a copy of Homer's *Iliad,* printed in Florence in 1488, and profusely decorated with elaborate drawings by whatever "hack" illustrator the printer happened to have working for him at the time; Persian books with each page covered in beaten gold leaf; a 13th-century book on 175 pages of parchment, hand-written, with pictures, by a monk in the year 1226, and a whole bunch of books with gold-embossed covers, decorative spines, and ruby or precious-metal clasps holding them shut.

In the three centuries of Turkish domination over Greece nothing was actually printed in Greece, although the library has an extensive collection of books, in Greek, printed in other places: Antwerp, London, Vienna, Amsterdam, Venice. It also has copies of the first modern literary magazine, dated 1811.

Other useful libraries for reading or reference are the **American Library** on the fourth floor of the Hellenic American Union (22 Massalias St., tel: 638-114) open mornings and evenings, Monday to Friday; the **British Council Library** (Kolonaki Sq., tel: 633-211) open weekday mornings and from 6 to 8:30 p.m. on Monday and Thursday nights; and the **National Library** (Panepistimiou Ave., tel: 614-413) open mornings and evenings each weekday plus Saturday mornings.

8. Lycabettus

Almost 1,000 feet above sea level, the rocky peak of Lycabettus (the name may have referred to the wolves that used to infest its tree-covered slopes) is well worth a visit for the fantastic views it commands of the entire Athens area southwest to the sea and northwards to the mountains of which, by legend, it once was part.

There has been a church atop the mountain for at least four centuries and in recent years the terraces of an attractive restaurant have spread around the summit. A winding path is pleasant to climb but these days most visitors take the funicular (it runs till about 11 p.m.) from the top of Ploutarchou St. (taxi from Syntagma, about 30 drs). The #50 bus goes there also.

NIGHTTIME IN ATHENS

THE BIG NIGHTTIME ACTIVITY in Athens is dining or drinking in the Plaka—that sprawling old area of tavernas and outdoor cafes that covers one side of the hill leading to the Acropolis. But there are, as well, some fairly breathtaking evening spectacles available to you—the plays in the Herod Atticus Theater, the famous Sound and Light presentation, others—which we'll review before we peruse the Plaka.

1. The Athens Festival

The main theatrical event of the summer season in Athens is the nightly series of plays and concerts presented in the beautiful old **Herod Atticus Theater,** just below the Acropolis. It usually begins early in July. In addition to the numerous classical performances by the National Theater of Greece (works by Aristophanes, Euripides, and Sophocles), and the concerts by the Athens State Orchestra, there's a wide range of presentations by orchestras, opera companies, and choruses from other European countries. A full program of the scheduled events is available some time in June from the National Tourist Office and also from the ticket office in the arcade at 4 Stadiou Street (tel: 3221-459), near Syntagma Square. Tickets range from as low as 100 drs (depending on the production), and if you want "good" seats, it is advisable to get them well in advance. My personal view is that the cheapest seats, high up at the back, are the best, and these can usually be obtained just before the performance (which begins 8:30 p.m.) at the theater itself.

The theater, which sits just below the Acropolis, on Dionyssiou Areopagitou Avenue, was built in the second century A.D. by the Roman whose name it bears. It can seat up 5,000 people on its marble benches (a limited number of thin cushions are available free on each row), and the view and acoustics from the very topmost rows are exceptional.

At one time there was a roof, but no traces of it remain. There are wide niches in the front wall of the theater which once held statues, and from the upper rows you can see the twinkling lights of the city. Behind you, atop the hill, the Acropolis is floodlit and competes strongly with the stage in front for your attention.

2. Sound and Light

Every night at 9 p.m. except Tuesday and Friday, you can (and you should—at least once) gather on a small hillside, the Pnyx, at the south side of the Acropolis, and watch what skillful use of 1,500 lights can do for the already impressive Parthenon. There are nightly performances of the French-invented Sound and Light show, in which the entire hillside is illuminated in such a way that you'll suddenly realize what it is that makes for a truly great piece of architecture.

The answer, for me at any rate, is that it can be seen or lighted from any angle, with any section spotlighted out of context, and somehow everything belongs. There is a period when, as if an abstract painting were to glow one section after the other, lights flash on and off, each time revealing a new overlapping aspect of this amazing building.

All the time the lights are going on and off, there's a flowery commentary over loudspeakers, of which one sentence will give you the idea:

" . . . The deep mauve of night hath seeped away, the soft dawn of day doth creep its way to the Cephissus banks—The first flowing rays of sun fondle the sacred trireme as it urges on towards the Propylae, undulating its way up the hill, as over the crest of the waves. . . . "

In fact, if you go at 8 p.m. for the German presentation, or at 10 p.m. for the French one, you might not miss much. The text is rather pretentious, and one reader, Richard Grant of Stoneham, Mass., makes a valid point. "Where," he asks, "are the words of Plato, Socrates, Aristotle?"

On a sandy path that leads around to the entrance of the Acropolis is the small control room from which the Sound and Light performance is beamed each night. Packed with green steel lighting equipment and tape recorders, it looks like a mixture of a Con Edison power plant, a radio station studio, and a dentist's office.

The machines are French-made, and the operators who work them speak French and English, so as to coordinate their actions with the French and English commentaries which drone from a tape recorder at one side of the room. But "you don't need to be a technician," jokes the man who pulls the switches, and as if to prove it, he keeps up a running conversation with visitors, the waiter who brings his coffee, and such friends as happen to be around.

The Acropolis cannot be seen from inside the room, because the window which overlooks the hill is blocked off with a corrugated iron ventilator. But operating the switches and levers apparently comes as a matter of habit, and the operator's hands never falter as he chats, a fascinating counterpoint to what is going on outside.

To get to the Sound and Light presentation, take the #16 bus that goes along Dionyssiou Areopagitou, past the Acropolis, and get off one stop past the Herod Atticus Theater, on your right. You'll see the neon sign reading "Son et Lumière." A path leads down to the Pnyx from the crossroads here.

When the presentations were begun in 1964, it was possible to pay 20 drs for a cushion and sprawl comfortably on the ground. But formality came—as it apparently always must—and now there are row upon row of seats, all of 50 drs each. (Half price on presentation of a student card.) There are no performances on full-moon nights.

There's an extremely smart snack bar and restaurant just back to your left at the crossroads. Downstairs is a bar proffering a wide range of drinks, sandwiches, coffee, pastries, and ice creams. Upstairs is a very chic restaurant, the **Dionysos,** with some inexpensive entrees such as spaghetti, but most items (veal, chicken, shrimp) are expensive. Lovely view of the Acropolis, though.

If you go one stop past the Sound and Light crossroads on the bus, you'll come to a row of cheap sidewalk restaurants and a cafe, which has a group of tables across the street on a little plateau that itself possesses an uninterrupted view of the Acropolis, illuminated à la Sound and Light, across the valley. It's a delightful spot.

3. The Dora Stratou Folk Dancers

The nicest thing about summer entertainment in Greece is that so much of it takes place in the open air. It would be pleasant enough to spend an evening sitting under the stars watching a heterogeneous audience file through the wispy trees and take their places to the accompaniment of casual chatter and the chirping of wandering soft drinks sellers, whose repetitive "Pago menes, pago menes, pago menes. . . . " sounds like birds in the woods.

It's an enthusiastic, talkative European crowd, constantly in flux, and always ready to exchange a few good-natured sallies with the little boys who circulate with baskets of nougat (marvelous nougat) candies, cookies, and chocolate bars.

Fifteen minutes after the scheduled starting time, the audience begins to get restless, and sets up a rhythmic clapping to indicate its impatience. It is rewarded instantly by somebody turning on the stage lights, and the appearance of the **Zygia** (small orchestra consisting of clarinet, violin, lute, santouri, drum) in white stockings, blouses, and skirts with black waistcoats.

The dances and songs have been preserved from the days of ancient Greece, and the young men follow the steps of the old. There's one instrument that looks like a bagpipe, but it's made from the almost uncut skin of what was once a sheep.

The dances take place on the Hill of Philopappou, directly across from the Acropolis. The theater itself is called the **Dora Stratou Theater** (tel: 3224-681) and can easily be reached from Syntagma Square by bus #16.

Dances are presented nightly at 10:15 p.m.—timed to take in the crowd as it emerges from the Sound and Light—May to October, with admission ranging from about 60 drs (little advantage in paying the higher prices). Take a sweater in case it gets chilly that late at night. Give the usherette who shows you to your seat a tip of a couple of drachmas. On Wednesdays and Sundays there are additional performances at 8:15 p.m.

4. Piraeus' Veakio Theater

All during the summer there are nightly (except Monday) performances by visiting operas and ballet companies at the hilltop Veakio Theater in Piraeus. In Athens you can buy tickets for these productions at the Palace Theater (Voukourestiou 1, tel: 3222-434) in the mornings. A nightly bus is supposed to run to Veakio from outside the Hotel Amalias, just off Syntagma Square, at 8:45 p.m., but I found it unreliable.

5. Movies

In summertime, all Athens' movie theaters, and most of its drama and variety theaters, move outdoors. There are plenty of them, so it isn't really necessary to single out one or another—all you need do is walk down any of the main streets until you reach one and then study the stills outside. Many movie theaters show foreign movies with Greek subtitles, but even the foreign and Greek movies where you don't understand the language, are a gas—and so are the advertisements before the program.

There are several outdoor theaters and movies in the Greek Park area of Patission Street; indeed, most of these are actually on Patission Street.

There used to be an open-air movie theatre at the foot of Kydathneion Street in Plaka but it's been closed in recent years. Now your best bet is the little one beside the Zappeion in the National Park. To find this walk along Amalias Street (top right off Syntagma Square), enter the park and follow the red signs reading "Zappeion." Eventually you'll come to an open space filled with cafe tables, where afternoon and evenings an orchestra plays tea-time classics and at night there's a free variety show. The movie there opens late evening. Look at page 8 of the *Athens News* for listings of other movies.

Some of these others are: the **Ideal** (Panepistimiou St., tel: 614-596); the **Astor** (Stadiou St., tel: 231-297); the **Aigli,** in the Zappeion; the **Rex** (Panepistimiou St., tel: 614-591); the **Kotopouli** (Omonia Sq., tel: 529-761); the **Palals** (Voukourestiou St., tel: 224-435).

Free concerts and movies are often available at the **Hellenic American Union** (22 Massalias St.) in the evenings, and the building also houses reading room, art gallery, and cafeteria. On the same block are a couple of student-type cafes: the **Latin Quarter** and the **Rue de Marseille.**

6. Theaters

There are 12 open-air variety theaters in Athens and three in Piraeus which offer a tremendous array of live talent for a little as 50 or 60 drs. Top movie and recording stars appear in comedies and revues; the bill may include everything from operatic arias through juggling, acrobatics, and skits to modified striptease. The pace is fast and funny.

Most of the theaters are concentrated along the strip of Patission between the museum and Fokionos Negri, with three on Leoforos Alexandras, and the most highly respected (Carolus Koun's **Art Theater**) at the intersection of Iouliannou and Septembriou. Koun's company may be doing Shakespeare, but the rest are doing things called *I Want Love. Not War* and *Aunt Olga Knows.*

Settings, costumes, and sketches have the nostalgic quality of American musicals of the '30s and '40s. A dreamy fairytale castle may incorporate a real tree into the setting. A chorus line of brightly dressed young men and women, the girls in frothy petticoats and the boys heavily made up dance into view singing. A lovely girl is lowered from the trees in a basket of flowers, singing all the way down. A schoolroom sketch has four hefty adults dressed as kids in shorts and smocks; a singing star croons before a cutout moon; Jackie and Ari are shown aboard their yacht, making bored conversation while a harassed steward attends their every need with the agility of Buster Keaton. For a grand finale, all the lovely chorus girls don floppy hats and wander among the audience singing and smiling.

All the shows are clean enough for little kids, mostly incomprehensible to anyone who doesn't speak Greek, yet still, somehow, vastly entertaining. Partly it's because Greek acting (like the real-life arguments you'll sometimes see in the streets) is valued for speed, volume, and emotional intensity rather than for nuance or sincerity. This can make a simple conversation sound like the critical moment of a lifetime. Once you learn to relax and enjoy it (they won't really assault each other) the theater stops being a museum of culture and takes on the youthful zest of a ZAP! BIFF! YEOW! living comic book.

Besides those in the theater district, there are two (**Perroquet** and

Vembo) on Karaiskaki Square which are popular with Greek young people. But the best in town is the **Alsos** in Pangrati Park (take the #12 bus on Stadiou, and stay on until the third stop past the Stadium). Here, the Free Theater group, ten immensely talented and inventive young people, present a satiric revue so pungent that language is no barrier.

Most theater programs do not begin until 10 or 10:30 p.m.

The **Minoa** (91 Patission, tel: 810-048) often stages elaborately costumed comedy revues for which knowledge of Greek is minimal.

Somewhat different from the others is **Green Park** (take the bus or trolley out Patission from Omonia to the first stop after the museum and look for the sign up a side street to your right). Here, pop singers, acrobats, jugglers, and dance teams entertain you for the price of the coffee or soda you sip as you sit at an open-air cafe table. (The nearby **Hotel Park,** by the way, has a rooftop swimming pool where you can get lunch.)

There is still one of the traditional **Karaghiosis** shadow puppet theaters in the Plaka, right behind the Lysikratos monument at the top of Lysikratos Street. Here, a single puppeteer manipulates as many as five puppets at a time, providing voices for all of them, and putting them through violent slapstick plots for two hours, beginning at about 8:30 p.m. Admission is 15 drs, and the audience is at least half adults so there's no need to be embarrassed to go even if you don't have a kid to drag along. "Shadow" puppets really gives the wrong idea: they're made of buffalo hide, which is transluscent, and painted in bright colors—the effect is like Cinerama color TV with an endless series of violent Saturday morning cartoons. A splendid way to get into the spirit for an evening in Plaka if you arrive before the tavernas get started.

READERS' SELECTION: "In winter the **Aliki Theatre** (4 Amerikis St., tel: 3244-146) presents folk dancing in native costume at 6:30 p.m. on Thursday nights. Tickets cost 50 drs and reservations are necessary. Excellent and a must!" (Captain and Mrs. Richard Johns, New York, N.Y.).

7. The Plaka

Sprawling across the hillside directly below the Acropolis is the city's oldest quarter, Plaka. By day it's almost a ghost town: a bus boy sleeps, his arms and head sprawled across a table; the faded green shutters of the old houses remain closed while their inhabitants lie abed; ice melts untended on a marble doorstep.

Only tourists wander abroad in Plaka during most of the day. Even at the busiest times, the streets are too narrow for most traffic, and nothing much disturbs the tranquility beyond the regular services—three-wheeled garbage truck, ice wagon, an occasional delivery of bread or wine to one of the tavernas.

Three French women in shift dresses and sandals plod wearily up the steep hills, past the closed shops, pausing for shelter from the sun under an awning. Two cats regard them sleepily from a window ledge. So scarce are the residents, it is hard for the women to find anyone to give them directions about how to get to the Acropolis.

Late in the afternoon, Plaka starts to awaken. The early employees of the tavernas turn on the hoses and cool down the sidewalks, small boys sit at tables and hand-chop sacks of potatoes into raw french fries, a score of barbecue grills begin to smoke. By six or seven o'clock, the tables are laid and the city is beginning to light up below. The view from Plaka roofs—always glorious—is taking on its most unforgettable characteristics.

The dinner hour begins about 9 p.m., and from then until 2 a.m. or so there's hardly a street without music. It should certainly be visited for dinner,

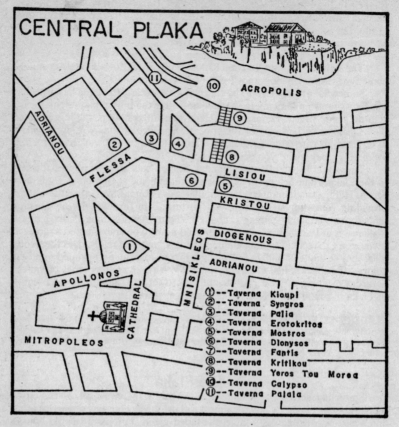

CENTRAL PLAKA

ACROPOLIS

ADRIANOU

FLESSA

LISIOU

KRISTOU

DIOGENOUS

MNISIKLEOS

ADRIANOU

APOLLONOS

CATHEDRAL

MITROPOLEOS

①--Taverna   Kioupi
②--Taverna   Syngros
③--Taverna   Palia
④--Taverna   Erotokritos
⑤--Taverna   Mostros
⑥--Taverna   Dionysos
⑦--Taverna   Fantis
⑧--Taverna   Kritikou
⑨--Taverna   Yeros Tou Morea
⑩--Taverna   Calypso
⑪--Taverna   Palaia

but your knowledge of it is incomplete until you have also seen it by day.

And now I shall admit that the preceding few paragraphs are pure nostalgia. The images are of a decade ago, for the Plaka has, alas, changed drastically. At nights now, in these late '70s, the streets are bedlam, the area's denizens catering to the tourist traffic. The food is no longer "authentic" and the service has declined correspondingly. It's impossible to hear the music at the restaurant at which you might be eating because it's usually drowned out by the noise from the restaurant next door—and the noise is enough to stun an ox.

The best advice I can proffer is go elsewhere to eat—the little square at the bottom of Adrianou is nice, or the restaurants beside the Agora on Eolou—and then take a stroll up Mnisikleos to what must be one of the world's most interesting crossroads, on the steps where Mnisikleos crosses Thrassyboulou. (That tiny, two-story house that's now a cafe/bar was a private residence in the early '60s and I lived there when I was first compiling this book—hence my nostalgia.) All the cafes here charge outrageous prices, but it's fascinating to hang around and watch the crowds go up and down the steps. And every evening the man at the **O Yeros Tou Morea** (Kolokotronis, leader of the Greek revolution) dances with a table in his teeth!

PLAKA GEOGRAPHICALLY: Plaka is bordered roughly by a line drawn up Nikis Street straight to the Acropolis at one end, from Monastirion Square up to the Acropolis at the other end, and with Mitropoleos Street between them.

Plaka's main street, Adrianou, is singularly lacking in anything of interest to a tourist. There are a couple of indifferent souvenir shops, but mostly the stores sell items for the local community: plastic bowls, ironing boards, children's toys, fruit, bread and pastries, canned goods, meat.

Several streets run off Adrianou at right angles up the hillside; the busiest one is Mnisikleos, lined with tavernas, all of which swing at night. Turn right at the top of Mnisikleos and you're on the circular path that leads to the Acropolis. At the bottom (righthand side) end of Adrianou is a small square adjoining the Roman agora or market; at the top end (lefthand side) is the statue of Lysikratos.

Chapter VIII

ATHENS LISTINGS

1. The ABC's of Life in the Capital
2. Out-of-Town Buses from Athens

WHENEVER I HAVE FOUND myself in some foreign country, there have always been dozens of questions in my mind that guidebooks have neglected to answer. Often these questions have concerned very minor things—how to operate a telephone or where to find a good mechanic for the car—except that no question is minor when you don't have the answer to it.

In this section, I have tried to anticipate some of the questions about Athens—and about life in Greece—that you may find yourself asking. You will probably think of many such items yourself; if so, I would appreciate hearing about them. Such listings will be included in the Readers' Selections near the end of this chapter. At the very end of the chapter are lists of buses from Athens to various out-of-town destinations, near and far—prepared in anticipation of your transportation frustration. Here now, some vital statistics, from A to Z (Y, actually).

1. The ABC's of Life in the Capital

AIRPORT BUS: Olympic Airways buses run frequently to town but you can save money by walking outside the airport to the main road and taking a local bus to Piraeus. From there it's a quick and cheap subway ride to Omonia Square in Athens.

Olympic's airport bus runs to its office at Syngrou 92, a longish walk or 20-dr taxi ride to Syntagma Square. To the East airport (all lines except Olympic), the airport bus runs every 20 minutes from Amalias 4 between 6:20 a.m. and midnight—30 drs.

AIRPORT INFO: Call 92-921 for Olympic Airways schedules or 144 for its recorded timetable. For international flight information call 90-091.

AMERICAN EXPRESS: An invaluable service but if you don't want to wait on line for hours, arrange for your mail to be sent elsewhere and change your checks at a bank (same rate).

AMERICAN LIBRARY: 22 Massalias Street (corner of Didotou St.), tel: 637-740. Open 8:30 a.m.-1:30 p.m., 5:30-8:30 p.m. every day except Saturday and Sunday.

ANTIQUES: The most frequented shopping area for antiques is Pandrossou Street near Monastirion Square.

ART GALLERIES: In the **Hilton Hotel** (46 Vass. Sofias Ave.); **Naees Morfes** (9a Valaritou Street); **Zygos** (8 Omirou Street), and **Sarla** (9 Kolokotroni Street). All show works by comtemporary Greek artists.

ART SCHOOL: Athens Center for the Creative Arts operates a comprehensive summer school at the **Hellenic American Union** (22 Massalias Street, tel: 629-886) with classes in yoga, art, dance, theater, Greek drama and folklore, etc. There's a cheap cafeteria at the Union and also a notice board with rides, things for sale, etc.

ATHENS FESTIVAL: Most events are held in the marvelous **Herod Atticus Theater** on the slopes of the Acropolis. Get the cheapest seats and sit at the back (high up—binoculars will be a help). Programs are available at the tourist office on Syntagma Square or at the Athens Festival office in the arcade at Stadiou 4 (tel: 3221-459). You can purchase tickets at the Festival office or at the theater itself on the night (by which time they've often sold out). Events are also presented at the **Lycabettus Theater**—and if you have a chance to hear Mikis Theodorakis, don't miss it.

BANKS: Open on weekdays from 8 a.m. to 1 p.m. The **National Bank** (8 Venizelou Street) is open from 5:30 to 7:30 in the evenings and on Sunday mornings from 9:30 to 12:30.

BARBER SHOP: The Greek word for it looks like Koypeion, and the charge is about 50 drs for a haircut or shave in an A-class shop. Add 5 drs for the tip to the barber and 3 drs for the person who brushes your clothes. Most barber shops are closed on Wednesday afternoons.

BEAUTY PARLORS: The Greek word looks like Komothirion, and although they vary greatly in price, most will charge about 35-60 drs for a hair set. Like barber shops, salons are usually closed on Wednesday afternoons.

BLOOD DONORS: Outside American Express you'll see cards offering "average $11." Don't be conned—it's usually more like $3.

BOOKSTORES: The well-stocked **American Bookstore** is at 23 Amerikis Street, another good bookstore **(Panetelidis),** located on the same block, is at 11 Amerikis Street. Also try the store at 4 Nikis St.

BUS FARES: Within the city, fares range from 6.50 to 9 drs, doubling after midnight. Most lines are serviced by both the blue buses and the yellow "trolleys" (really electric buses), each with its own stops marked by signs corresponding in color and indicating the numbers of the vehicles that stop there. The "Athine" map given to tourists at the National Tourist Office indicates the major bus and trolley lines. Get on the back and give the money to the conductor as you walk past his cash desk. If you're unsure of your stop, he will usually be glad to tell you when to get off.

BUSES THROUGH EUROPE: The famous **Magic Bus,** once known only to a dedicated few, has grown into a largish organization with offices in Amsterdam, Frankfurt, Paris, London, and other cities on the route. The Athens office is upstairs at the foot of Kydathneion St. in Plaka— #24 (tel: 3224-407)—just below the little square. Fare to London is now around $47. This is by no means the cheapest offered, because other tours go as low as $28. Check the student travel agencies on Filellinon Street. **Economy Travel** (18 Panepistimiou St., tel: 3634-045) quotes a price 100 drs less than Magic Bus; **Consolas Travel** (102 Eolou St., tel: 3219-228) quotes a price 100 drs more but sounds a bit more luxurious.

BUYING CARS: Lots of hippy types offer their vehicles for sale via notices in the arcade off Fillelinon Street that leads to Viking's Tours. It's also possible to buy a "transit" car from a dealer, obtaining all the necessary papers in the transaction. The car bears foreign plates and can usually be sold again before leaving.

CAMPING: Greece is a wonderful country for camping, and almost everybody welcomes lovers of the outdoor life. If you're planning to bring camping equipment (it can be bought in Athens and many other places), you might like to apply to the **Automobile and Touring Club of Greece (ELPA)** 2 Messogiou St., Athens Tower (tel: 7791-615), for a list of official sites, although you can pretty much camp anywhere.

CAR RENTALS: Most of the firms are out on Syngrou Avenue, about ten minutes' walk from Syntagma Square toward Piraeus. **Batek** (Syngrou 43, tel: 9215-795) has Fiats and VWs from about 300 drs daily or 1900 drs weekly plus mileage. With unlimited mileage, it comes to around 6000 drs weekly. **Tourent** (Syngrou 6, tel: 238-821) has Fiats from 240 drs daily or 1600 drs weekly plus mileage. **Ilios** (Solonos 138, tel: 3624-059) has small Fiats from 210 drs daily or 1400 drs weekly plus mileage. **Hellascars** (Stadiou 7, tel: 3233-487) and **Avis** (Amalias 48, tel: 3224-951) are expensive but allow you to drop off cars outside Greece (for a high fee).

CERAMICS: Just off Syntagma Square at 26 Voulis Street (tel: 3223-366) is **Tanagrea,** an attractive store with high-quality colored bowls, vases, plates, etc. The store's card is almost as attractive as its contents, and the young women who work there wear dresses that are reminiscent of riotously colored vases.

CIGARETTES: Because of import duties, American cigarettes are very expensive when you can find them—usually 36 drs. The better quality Greek cigarettes cost between 15 and 20 drs.

CLIMATE: Greece is very hot (but not as humid as New York) in summer, slightly cooler in the islands than in Athens, but still too hot for a jacket every day and almost every night.

CLOTHING: Light clothing required, informal and easy to carry. A sweater, maybe, for nights aboard ship and on the islands, but virtually no need for a topcoat or raincoat in summer. Most Greek women wear heels, most tourists wear sandals. You can get away with wearing virtually anything except topless bathing suits. However, you will not be admitted to churches in shorts or halter tops.

DRINKS: If you wish to buy ouzo, cognac, or any of the wonderful fruit brandies cheaply, never buy them bottled. Take a bottle or container to a grocery store and have it filled. If one grocery doesn't carry what you want, another one nearby will. The saving is at least half, often more, though the quality may be slightly less.

DRIVING: You'll need any valid driving license or an international driving license, the latter available from the **Greek Automobile and Touring Club (ELPA),** and costing 150 drs (you'll need a current photograph, obtainable at one of those coin-in-the-slot machines). ELPA's office in Athens is at 2 Messogiou St. (Athens Tower, about one km past the Hilton, tel: 7791-615); in Salonika at 45 Franklin Roosevelt St.; in Patras at 30 King George Square. Offices also in Xania, Corfu, Rhodes, etc. Main offices of the National Bank will sell you reduced-price gasoline coupons, good for 15 liters each, on production of passport and car registration. These can be purchased in five- or ten-day batches for up to a total of 60 days altogether. For emergency road service call 104 in Athens or Thessalonika.

DRUGSTORES: For name and address of a late-night one, dial 180 and ask.

EMBASSIES: The **British Embassy** is at Ploutarchou Street (off Vassilissis Sofias Ave.), tel: 736-211; the **Canadian Embassy** at 4 I. Gennadiou Street (tel: 739-511); the **U.S. Embassy** at 91 Vassilissis Sofias Avenue, near the Hilton Hotel, tel: 712-951. Open until 3 p.m.

ENGLISH-SPEAKING DENTISTS: Dr. Dem. Papadopoulos, 43 Stadiou Street, tel: 226-478; Dr. Mary N. Sarantopoulou, 11 Likavitou Street (Amerikis Street becomes Likavitou when it crosses Akadimias), tel: 613-176; Dr. Nikitas Demetriou, 3 Pindarou St., tel: 639-056.

ENGLISH-SPEAKING DOCTORS: Dr. S. E. Dimitrouleas, Skoufa 75, tel: 3636-466, or Dr. A. Mandekos, Akadimias St. 15, tel: 3615-216, each of whom advertise in tourist publications. For others check with the **Athens Medical Association** (Iatrikos Syllogos) at Themistokleos 34.

EXTENDED STAYS: After three months, you'll need a special permit, available from the **Athens Alien's Department,** 9 Chalkokondili Street, tel: 622-595, or from the police station in small towns (bring three photos).

FESTIVALS: Around May 21, there is a fire-walking ceremony (called Anastenaria) at Langadas, near Salonika; sometime during July is Naval Week, with ceremonies in Piraeus and other naval harbors; the open-air drama festival at Epidaurus takes place during July and August; the Athens Festival (see above) during July, August, and September; from late July to mid-August, there's a drama festival at Philippi in Macedonia; Epirus stages its drama festival in the middle of August in Dodoni's ancient theater; the island of Corfu celebrates the day of Saint Spyridon on August 11; there's a literature and art festival on the island of Lefkas in the latter half of August; August 15 is the day of the Feast of the Holy Virgin in several places in the Cyclades islands, notably on the island of Tinos, the Greek Lourdes; the Wine Festival at Daphni, near Athens, lasts from July 12 to September 14; an international world's fair of industrial products takes place at Salonika in September.

GOLF: There are two golf courses near Athens: an 18-hole, par-72 course at Glyfada (tel: 8946-820), a seaside resort about nine miles south on the Sounion Peninsula, and a nine-hole course 20 miles to the north at Varibopi (tel: 8019-488). There are also 18-hole courses on Corfu and Rhodes.

GREEK: The simplest Greek language book available is *A Phrase Book of Modern Greek,* by Julien T. Pring (David McKay Co., New York), a slim, hardy volume with simple words, phrases, and pronunciation in both Greek and English lettering.

HISTORICAL PERIODS: Until about 10,000 B.C. was the Paleolithic Age, evidence of which—tools and fossilized bones—can be found in Thessalia, Beotia, Attica, the Peloponnese, and Ionian islands. Next came the Neolithic Period (until about 2650 B.C.). Remains of Neolithic settlements can be found in Crete and some other parts of Greece. The Bronze Age lasted until about 1100 B.C., and what remains is best seen at Mycenae, Crete, and in parts of the Peloponnese. (The first Olympiad was held in 776 B.C.) Next came the Archaic Period (seventh century B.C. to 480 B.C.), which produced Pythagoras, Sappho, the temple of Delphi, the Acropolis at Athens; closely following was the Classical Period (450 B.C. onwards was "the golden age of Athens" under Pericles), in which Zeno, Democritus, Socrates (470-399 B.C.), Plato (427-347 B.C.), Aristotle (384-222 B.C.), Aeschylus (525-456 B.C.), Sophocles (496-406 B.C.), Euripides (480-406 B.C.), and Aristophanes (453-385 B.C.) lived and worked. At this time most of the temples (Parthenon, Olympia, Sounion) were built. The Hellenistic Period (196 B.C. onwards for half a century) ushered in the Roman Period (146 B.C. onwards), when Hadrian and Herodus Atticus went on a building kick and changed the face of Greece.

HORSEBACK-RIDING: Non-members can ride for about 250 drs hourly at the **Riding Club of Athens** (Geraka, tel: 6593-830) or for 300 drs per hour at the **Hellenic Riding Club** (Paradisos, tel: 6812-506).

LAUNDROMAT: The **Self Service Laundry** (although you can actually leave the stuff and pick it up later) is at Didotou 46, corner of Zood, Pigis, not far from Omonia Square (tel: 610-661). Open Monday through Saturday, 8 a.m.

to 9 p.m. Not expensive. And the **Carolina Hotel** has a coin-operated washing machine on its roof.

LEFT LUGGAGE: Only a couple of blocks from Syntagma Square, at **Pacific Ltd.,** a travel agency, you can leave bags or pieces of luggage for 10 drs a piece per 24 hours, 50 drs per week. This is at 26 Nikis Street (tel: 3223-213). Open 7 a.m. to 9 p.m. (8 a.m. to 2 p.m. Sundays and holidays).

LONG DISTANCE TELEPHONE CALLS: From your hotel or at 15 Stadiou Street, open from 8 a.m. to midnight. Dial 161 for overseas service from a regular phone.

LOST PROPERTY OFFICE: Dial 817-606. It's at the corner of Bouboulinas and Totsitsa.

LOTTERY: Held every Monday; winning numbers announced in Tuesday papers. Tickets cost 20 drs, a quarter section selling for 5 drs.

MONEY: There are now so many different shapes and sizes for the same denominations of coins that it's advisable to take a few moments to study them all before conducting any transactions.

PARKING: There are special areas for tourists. They include the following: Kolokotroni Square, Klafthmonos Square, Totsitsa Street, Konstantinou Avenue, Deligianni Street, Gregory V Street, Ippokratous Street, Satovrindou Street, and Halkokondyli Street. Check these streets for signs denoting specific permitted locations.

PERIODICAL GUIDES: Hellenews Publishing Co. Ltd. (6 Karytsi Square, tel: 3236-313) publishes an attractive, glossy annual called *Tourism in Greece,* which is more interesting than most guides. Illustrated. Hellenews also publishes a Greek financial newspaper, a weekly newsletter in English, and other periodicals. Like most large cities, Athens has a *This Week in Athens,* which can be bought at kiosks or perused in the better class hotels. It includes lists of theaters, cinemas, tourist attractions, etc., with prices and times in three languages. The *Athenian Magazine* (20 Alopekis, Kolonaki, tel: 724-204) is invaluable, as well as interesting, for news and views about contemporary Greek life in the capital as well as current listings.

POSTAGE RATES: Surface mail from Greece to European countries takes as long as a week, to the United States two or four weeks. Airmail to the U.S. takes about five days. By airmail to the U.S., postcards are 9 drs, letters 11 drs.

POST OFFICE: The main one is in Plateia Kotzia, the square near Omonia that also houses the Town Hall and lots of tree-shaded tables. Near here, at 29 Koumoundourou, is the building at which most parcels will arrive if taxable, and you'll have to show up between 7:30 a.m. and 8 p.m. to collect them. (The tax is usually waived for tourists on production of passport.) The post offices most patronized by tourists are those near American Express in Syntagma

Square (open 7 a.m. to 10 p.m.), and the one at 100 Aiolon St. near Omonia (open 7 a.m. to midnight). Many newsstands and all hotels sell stamps, although most hotel desks merely accept the money and letters and mail them later.

Readers report that the most efficient post office from which to mail parcels is just opposite the Ethnic Theater and St Constantine's church, three blocks west of Omonia Square on Ag. Constantine St.

RAILROADS: Timetables for all of Greece (in English) are available from the **State Railways** office, 31 Panepistimiou St., Athens. There are two major stations in Athens, **Larissa (S.E.K.)** for all trains north and **Peloponesse (S.P.A.P.),** both reached by subway from Omonia, the first and second stops in the direction of Kifisia; or by walking five blocks up Deligianni from Karaiskaki Square.

RAILROAD TICKETS: Kosmos, next to TWA in Syntagma Square, specializes in international rail tickets. The **Hellenic Railways** office is at 1 Kavotu St. If you want a sleeper, go to **Wagons-Lits,** 2 Karageorghi Servias St.

REAL ESTATE AGENTS: The National Tourist Office, inside the bank on Syntagma Square, has a mimeographed list with phone numbers, addresses.

SAILING: Rent a yacht? It's possible. Sailboats, motor yachts and caiques accommodating four to as many as 20 passengers can be hired. Contact the **Yacht Brokers' Association,** 25 Loukianou St., Athens. (See "Yachts" below.) You can take sailing lessons and rent boats at the **Glyfada Sailing School** (Glyfada Marina, tel: 8942-115) or the **Piraeus Sailing Club** (Tourkalimano, tel: 4177-636) for nominal fees.

SALES: There's a whole street of shops that have sales at the same time, which is frequently: mostly cheap-quality clothing, shoes, and fabrics. The street is Agiou Marcou, three or four blocks below Stadiou and parallel to it, between the Cathedral and Euripidos Street.

SECOND-HAND BOOKSTORE: A basement place near Monastiraki is **Vassiotti's,** at 24 Ifestou Street. Thousands of tattered volumes in many languages plus American, English, French, and German paperbacks. Also old movie stills and cheap postcards.

SHOE REPAIR: They do good work at the corner of Karageorghi and Voulis Streets (two blocks up the righthand street of American Express as you face it).

SHOPPING HOURS: Almost all except tourist shops and cafes close between about 1 p.m. and 5 p.m.—and now shops in Athens close at 2:30 p.m. Wednesdays and Mondays and do not reopen until next day.

STUDENT FLIGHTS: You're eligible if you have a student card. Student charter flights are usually about one-third the cost of regular tourist fares.

SWIMMING: There are no public pools but the public is admitted to the **Hilton** pool for the cost of lunch (around 250 drs). The **Park Hotel** also has a (rooftop) pool.

TAILOR: On the third floor (room 315) of Kolokotroni 6; turn left as you leave the elevator. No English spoken—but the desk person at the Hotel Carolina will be glad to write a note.

TAXIS: When the flag drops, you'll automatically be at 12 drs (an extra 5 drs if you're going to the airport). The fare increases 3 drs for every km in the city center, 6.40 drs for every km outside. At night, an extra 10 drs is added to the fare. Tipping is not essential, but a few drachmas is customary. For every suitcase add 5 drs. From Syntagma Square to the airport costs about 100 drs.

TAXI STATIONS: You can usually pick up a cruising taxi, but if there isn't one available, try one of the stands. These are located at Mitropoleos and Nikis, Amerikis Square, Thission Square, Kaningos Square, Klafthmonos Square, Kolonaki Square, and Omonia Square.

TELEGRAMS: Overseas telegrams can be sent from the **OTE** office at 85 Patission Street, any hour of the day or night. There is a branch office at 15 Stadiou Street which is open from 8 a.m. to midnight.

TELEPHONE: Most newsstand kiosks have telephones. It costs one drachma to make a call from there. Pick up phone, dial the number, and pay only if you get an answer. Pay phones are available at various other spots and these also take one drachma. To make a call outside Athens or Greece, go to the OTE office nearest you (there's one in the subway concourse at Omonia, and the main one is on Stadiou between Omirou and Lada Khristou).

TENNIS: Tourists can play at the **Athens Tennis Club** (1 Olgas Avenue, tel: 910-071). Guest membership is available.

TIPPING: It seems to be impossible to eradicate it. Even here in Greece, where 15% is added to most bills automatically, people still tend to tip in addition. You're perfectly correct to square it off to the nearest drachma and leave only that, but the more touristy places (you'll have to play it by ear) have come to expect more. Disappoint them.

TOURIST INFORMATION: For any kind of aid or information, dial 3222-545.

TOURIST OFFICE: Headquarters is at 2 Amerikis Street (tel: 3223-111) but the only one most visitors need to have dealings with is the one inside the National Bank on Syntagma Square where you can get maps, boat schedules (new every week), and various other helpful folders.

TOURIST POLICE: Are extremely helpful both in emergencies and with solving problems. Call 171 day or night.

TOURS: The most exciting tour company of Athens (primarily for trips outside the city) is **Viking's Travel Bureau** (3 Filellinon St., just off Syntagma, tel: 3229-383), run by the extremely friendly and helpful Cocconi brothers, who are among the most knowledgeable experts on all aspects of Greek tourism. Viking's will get your tickets, change your money, act as a meeting place (lovely garden at rear) and answer all your questions.

Among their most popular tours are: (1) a five-day tour of the northern Peloponnese and Delphi, via bus departing Thursday year round, every Tuesday, Thursday, and Saturday from April through October; and costing $100. This includes accommodations, transport and guide. (2) A four-day visit to Mykonos, including accommodation in a restful beach hotel out of town, plus side trip to the island of Delos, leaving daily except Sunday from April through October; $75. (3) A five-day visit to Crete, departing every Monday and Thursday, $108. Viking's also runs some fascinating cruises aboard its two private yachts (see Chapter II).

Particularly to be appreciated about Viking's tours—and they have many others—is that they're aimed primarily at young people of all nations; hence, the guides are knowledgeable and interesting. Also, participants are given a great deal of freedom to improvise and roam within the confines of the tour—and students and teachers are granted reduced prices.

The Cocconi brothers have been extraordinarily helpful to this book and it's strongly recommended that if you want assistance in seeing Greece you call their office and talk over your plans. Or you can contact their newly opened office in New York: Viking's Tours, 500 Fifth Ave., Suite 923, New York, N.Y. 10036 (tel: 212//221-6788 or 6789).

The other main agencies in Athens are **ABC** (57 Stadiou St., tel: 3249-704); **Bell** (3 Stadiou St., tel: 3224-138); **Key** (2 Ermou St., tel: 3232-520); and **CHAT** (4 Stadiou St., tel: 3222-886)—all of which operate dozens of tours of Athens and Greece at roughly comparable rates. All can be booked through any travel agency; tours start from central points often with bus pick-ups at the major hotels. Most of these tours are relatively expensive and favored by older, more sedate people.

TRADITIONAL DRESS: Now seen only occasionally in country districts or less urbanized islands, such as Crete. Male costume consisted of the *fustanella* (full, pleated kilt) or *yraka* (baggy britches) and *kapa* (hooded cloak). It is still worn in some places on feast days or weddings—and at funerals.

TRAIN SCHEDULES: To Northern Greece and Europe in general call 813-882; for Peloponnese trains call 5131-601. *Key Travel Guide* has some train schedules but more comprehensive is *Odigos Dromologion* or *Indicateur des Horaires,* the blue-covered annual bilingual train schedule available for 25 drs from 1 Karolou St., Athens.

TURKEY: Rika Tours (among others), at 60 Khalkokondyli St., tel: 523-5905, runs daily bus tours from Athens to Istanbul, leaving 6:30 a.m. The trip takes about 30 hours, costs 750 drs.

VOLKSWAGEN REPAIRS: Numerous dealers and mechanics around town but one we have dealt with who is fast, and efficient and apparently honest is **Kag. Karabella** at Antisthenous and Fotomara Streets (behind Fix Brewery on Syngrou Ave). Tel: 3220-869.

YACHTS: Can be rented in almost any size by hour, day or week. Open sloop costs around $100 daily, can accommodate six persons. There are also larger sloops, catamarans, and motor yachts.

YACHT CHARTERS: Valef Yachts Ltd. (Themistetelious 22, Piraeus, tel: 4529-571.

YOUTH HOSTELS: Most Greek ones charge 30 drs per night or less. Complete list with addresses and prices is available from **GYH,** 4 Dragatsaniou Street, Klafthmonos Square, Athens, tel: 3234-107.

READER'S SELECTIONS: "Please warn everybody that the **Flea Market** is one big rip-off and the 'considerable reductions' you get by haggling are not bargains because invariably you'll see the same goods priced less in other shops" (Hilary Simons, London). . . . "As you know there are thousands of craft and souvenir shops but all their best stuff can be seen at the **Greek Cooperative of Craftsmen** (56 Amalias Ave.) and their prices are cheaper" (M. MacDonald, Montreal).

2. Buses from Athens

Local

To **Piraeus:** #165 from Filellinon St., off Syntagma Square, every few minutes till 1 a.m., then hourly, 7 drs.

To **Glyfada:** #85 from Olgas Av., Zappeion corner, until 1 a.m., 13 drs.

To **Daphni:** #100 from Koumoundourou Sq., every half hour until 11:45 p.m., 7 drs.

To **Elefsis:** #68 from Koumoundourou Sq., every ten minutes to midnight, 13 drs.

To **Kifissia:** #49 from Kaningos Sq, till 1 a.m., 13 drs.

To **Rafina:** from Mavromateon and Alexandras Aves., from 7 a.m. every hour (or more) until 11:30 p.m., 25 drs.

To **Varkiza:** #90 from Olgas Ave and Zappeion, every couple of hours till 11 p.m., 13 drs.

To **Varybopi:** #138 from Kaningos Sq., till 10 p.m., 13 drs.

To **Vouliagmeni:** #89 from Olgas Ave. and Zappeion, till midnight, 13 drs.

Long Distance

To **Delphi:** at 7:30 and 10:30 a.m., 1:30 and 5:30 p.m., from 260 Liossion St. (tel: 8616-489), three to four hours, about 270 drs.

To **Halkis:** every 30 minutes, from 5:30 a.m. to 9 p.m., from 260 Liossion St. (tel: 874-915), 90 minutes, about 80 drs.

To **Kalamata:** 8, 9:30, 10:30 a.m. and 12:15, 3:45, 8:45, and 9 p.m., from Kavalas and Kifissiou (tel: 5134-293), five to six hours, about 250 drs.

To **Kamena Vourla:** every hour from 6:15 a.m. to 8:15 p.m., from 260 Lissiou St. (tel: 874-809), two to three hours, about 40 drs.

To **Kavala:** 7 a.m. and 7 p.m., from Kifissiou and Kratilou Sts. (tel: 5129-407), 12 hours, about 500 drs.

To Corinth: 5:50 a.m. and every hour from 7 a.m. to 9 p.m., from Kavalas and Kifissiou Sts. (tel: 5129-232), 90 minutes, about 90 drs.

To Lamia: every hour from 6:15 a.m. to 8:15 p.m., from 260 Liossion St. (tel: 874-809), three hours, about 150 drs.

To Larissa: 8, 10, 11:30 a.m. and 1:30, 3:30, 5, and 10 p.m., from 260 Liossion St. (tel: 842-694), five to six hours, about 300 drs.

To Lefkas: 7 a.m., 1 and 9 p.m., from Kifissiou and Kratilou Sts. (tel: 5133-583), seven hrs, about 325 drs.

To Levadia: 6, 7, 8:30 a.m. and every hour thereafter to 8:30 p.m., from 260 Liossion St (tel: 8617-954), two to three hours, about 130 drs.

To Marathon: hourly from 9 a.m. to 10 p.m., from Mavromateon and Alexandras (tel: 8210-872), one hour, about 35 drs.

To Megalopolis: 8:05, 11 a.m., 1:45 and 11:30 p.m., from Kavalas and Kifissiou (tel: 5134-575), six hours, about 250 drs.

To Nafplion: 6, 7, 8:15, 9:30, 10:30 a.m. and every hour thereafter to 8:30 p.m., from Kavalas and Kifissiou (tel: 5134-575), three hours, about 150 drs.

To Patras: 6:30, 8, 9 and every hour thereafter to 6 p.m., 7:30 and 9 p.m., from Kavalas and Kifissiou (tel: 5124-914), three to four hours, about 250 drs.

To Pyrgos: 6:45, 7:30, 9, 10:30 a.m., 12:30, 2, 5, and 9:30 p.m., from Kavalas and Kifissiou (tel: 5134-110), five to six hours, about 290 drs.

To Sounion: 6:30, 7:30, 8:20 a.m. and every hour thereafter to 5:20 p.m., from 14 Mavromateon (tel: 8213-203), one to two hours, about 60 drs.

To Sparta: 7:15, 8, 10 a.m., 1, 3, 5, and 6 p.m., from Kifissiou and Kavalas Sts. (tel: 5124-913), five to six hours, about 250 drs.

To Trikala: 7:30, 9, 10:30 a.m., noon, 1:30, 3:30, 5, and 8:30 p.m., from 260 Liossion St. (tel: 852-333), five to six hours, about 300 drs.

To Tripolis: 6:15, 7:15, 8, 8:45, 11 a.m., 1:30, 3:45, 5:30, 8:30, 9:30 p.m., from Kavalas and Kifissiou Sts. (tel: 5134-575), four hours, about 210 drs.

To Volos: 7, 9, 10:30 a.m., noon, 12:30, 1:30, 3, 4, 5, 9:30, and 10 p.m., from 260 Liossion St. (tel: 874-151), five to six hours, about 300 drs.

Note: It is important to check these schedules, which change frequently. Have a Greek friend make enquiries from the telephone numbers listed.

Chapter IX

PIRAEUS

1. The Town
2. Boats from Piraeus
3. Beaches West of Athens

PIRAEUS, ONCE KNOWN ONLY for its attraction to sailors (vide the movie *Never on Sunday*), and as an embarkation to the isles of Greece has become one of the world's cleanest and most attractive ports. Flowers bloom everywhere, and its citizens spend most of their leisure time strolling or eating in the numerous outdoor parks and sidewalk cafes.

New areas are constantly being reclaimed from the sea, new beaches have been created, and even the street cleaners fitted out with spotless white uniforms. Whereas you might once have nipped down to Piraeus just in time to catch your boat it's now well worth spending a day or an evening there, particularly in the open-air Municipal Theater which sits on a hill with a fine view of the coastline and its twinkling lights.

It's long been a favorite excursion to visit the seafood restaurants in famous Mikrolimano, as the old "Turkish" harbor is now called, but actually the whole coastline around Piraeus (which is much too long and curving to follow on foot) is dotted with charming little restaurants and cafes, many of them overlooking bays or beaches. (The sea, however, still isn't clean enough to bathe in.)

Little squares are still being created in odd spots around town; flowers in pots are still being hung from lampposts; 8,000 flowering trees from Italy have already been planted along busy streets (Americans always ask why they don't get stolen—they never are); hammock seats, simple sculptures, and stretches of durable plastic "grass" are still being installed.

The harborside square, Plateia Kanaris, where most of the boats leave for the islands, has been changed and rebuilt. An attractive park and fountain now adjoin St. Nicholas Church, the oldest church in the city.

To make things easier for non-Greek visitors, the city's street signs are being replaced with ones in both Greek and English lettering.

1. The Town

ORIENTATION: Piraeus is located on a fat peninsula—shaped like Spain—which is narrowed at one end by harbors at each (north and south) side.

The central port where boats to the islands dock is on the north side of the peninsula; the town's main square, **Passalimani,** is situated on the smaller,

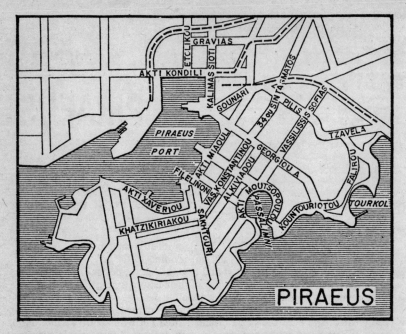

more attractive harbor to the south. Slightly back towards Athens along the coast is tiny **Mikrolimano,** a beautiful yacht harbor renowned for its view and its seafood restaurants. Overlooking it is Piraeus' open-air theater, **Veakio,** described in Chapter VII.

Running from the main harbor to Passalimani is **Sotiros Street,** which runs through one of the city's main squares, **Karaiskon,** where City Hall is located (as is the old theater, at whose box office you can also get tickets for the Veakio Theater). Well, Sotiros doesn't *exactly* connect with Passalimani— it's one block short—but it's easier to remember that way.

One block north of Sotiros is one of the city's main streets, **Georgiou A Avenue,** which also runs through Karaiskon Square and whose northern end is the central port, beside a beautiful park and fountain. The buses to Athens depart from near here; the subway station is further north, up the coast a few blocks. In this general area, along the port, are shipping offices for the various lines.

WHAT TO DO: By day the central port is fascinating, what with the constant hustle of people setting off for the islands. In the evening the action shifts to Passalimani, where free performances of the Dancing Waters (illuminated programmed fountains) and visiting dance troupes can be seen while sitting at cafe tables.

Piraeus is only a few kilometers from the **Planetarium** (Syngrou Ave., opposite racetrack, tel: 933-331), which is a part of the **Eugenides Foundation,** featuring scientific exhibits of the physical universe. In Piraeus itself, there is an interesting **Maritime Museum** (Freattis Bay, just past Passalimani, tel: 456-264), which is open 9 a.m. to 1 p.m. daily, and 5 to 8 p.m. on Wednesday and Saturday (Sunday 10 a.m. to 1 p.m. and 5 to 9 p.m.), admission 5 drs; also an as yet unopened **Archaeological Museum** (Charilaou Trikoupi Street, runs off Passalimani to the west; the road past the Taverna Kalyba leads down to it). Admission 5 drs, free on Thursdays and Sundays.

WHERE TO EAT: Piraeus doesn't exactly abound in good restaurants. There are two passable ones right opposite the subway terminal on Plateia Roosevelt, and the six-story department store (air-conditioned, by the way) **Dragonas Junior** at Sotiros and Vas. Konstantinou, has a cafeteria and snack bar. There's a tiny ice cream place at Kolokotroni 74 which is always (deservedly) crowded. And the cafes beside Passalimani have expensive snacks. Most of the nightlife is also centered around here, with an open-air theater (Sotiros and Sophias) and two movie theaters. Beside the park at Gladstonos and Kolokotroni is an open-air cafe, **Le Jardin,** which stays open all night serving pizzas and spaghetti. Incidentally, the expensive **Park Hotel** (550 drs double, tel: 4524-611) on this park has a disco and a rooftop garden (with a great view), which is expected to reopen shortly.

WHERE TO STAY: Most of the best hotels are at the far end of the port nearest to the customs house and where the ocean liners and cruise ships dock. Where the harbor (Akti Miaouli) meets Trikoupi Street, on Trikoupi itself, are four, big modern hotels—the **Serifos, Capitol, Glaros,** and **Santorini**—with only a few drachmas difference in price: around 350 drs single, 420 drs double, all with bath. The Capitol has a rooftop garden bar. On the side street, Notara, behind the Serifos, is the bargain-priced **Faros,** with singles for 270 drs, doubles for 335 drs. It's slightly smaller than the others but otherwise very similar.

Filonos, the next street down, is the center of a somewhat lowlife nighttime area with Arab cafes, "Egyptian" nightclubs, seamen's bars and the Ilysian movie theater, which specializes in spaghetti Westerns, Italian vampire epics and German porn. If you want to be in the center of this sleazy atmosphere (some people do), the **Hotel Lux** (Filonos 115) is a bargain at 240 drs (singles negotiable). Actually, your best bet at this end of the harbor is the old but freshly painted (hideous hues of green) **Hotel Mykine,** right on the Akti Miaouli, with simple, balconied, bathless rooms overlooking the busy harbor: 125 drs single, 250 drs double.

The other side of the harbor, near the subway station, where most of the island boats embark, offers the **Hotel Ionian** on Kapidistrou Street, one block from the subway. It's a passable bargain at 220 drs single, 375 drs double without bath. On the next block is the somewhat plusher **Delfini** (Leoharos 7, tel: 4123-512), whose 51 rooms, all with bath, cost 385 drs single, 460 drs double.

Just up Tsamada, off the big waterfront square, is the pleasant **Triton** (Tsamadou 8, tel: 4173-457) with singles for 340 drs, doubles for 443 drs. Finally there's the youth hostel (65 drs a bunk) at Bouboulinas and Notara, with a colorful cafe next door.

Between Passalimani and Mikrolimano harbor is Piraeus' public beach, and above this, on the main road, is the attractive **Hotel Cava Doro** (Castella, tel: 4113-742), which is certainly not cheap but is a suitable hideaway if you must stay in Piraeus: singles around 500 drs, doubles 730 drs; doubles with demi-pension are around 1200 drs.

WHAT TO DO: In **Zea Marina,** from which the Flying Dolphins (hydrofoils) speed to Hydra and Spetsai, is a public swimming pool (adm. 50 drs) which is open daily all year around. It has regularly changed sea water and adjoins a nice cafe. The **Diogenes Hotel** has a rooftop pool.

And if you want to rent a yacht, Zea Marina is again the place to be. Just outside the marina itself is **Valef Yachts Ltd.** (tel: 4529-571), whose customers include some of the world's best-known celebrities. But you, too, can rent your own yacht (complete with fuel and crew) from about $300 per day. These are big enough for eight passengers, but obviously there are smaller types available.

Mikrolimano

Once called Tourkolimano (meaning "the Turkish harbor"—there used to be a Turkish prison here) is an easy walk up the coast from Passalimani (the road past the Taverna Kalyba leads down to it). The tree-covered hill at the side of the harbor is dominated by the ritzy Greek Yacht Club.

By day or night, Mikrolimano is always charming. At night, the tables outside all the cafes around the bay are crowded with noisy eaters and drinkers. My personal opinion is that the sleepy daytime air is the most pleasant: fishermen are drying and coiling their yellow nets (most of the fishing is done at night from boats equipped with lights), small boys row boats that are twenty times their size, the ubiquitous kittens snooze on piles of cork floats under the midday sun. Tourists? There aren't any.

By and large, the restaurants charge pretty much the same rates and are approximately equal in quality. Which is to say, very good. Fish, of course, is a specialty, and it is common to sell some fish—especially lobster—by weight in bulk. A kilo of cooked lobster, for example, is sometimes enough for three or four diners.

There are plenty of restaurants in Mikrolimano, so take your time in making a choice and don't be rushed into eating too early by the overly ambitious hucksters who try to sweep you through their doorways.

The hill next to the Trata restaurant will lead you back up to the main highway, from which you can get a yellow trolley bus to the subway station.

Although Mikrolimano is delightful at any time, try to visit it when the yacht races are taking place in summer. These are usually held on Wednesday, Saturday, and Sunday afternoons from 3 to 5 p.m. Also from 10 a.m. to 1 p.m. on Sundays.

If you think you can handle a score of different dishes at the same meal try out the **Taverna Vassilena** (Etolikou 72) on the #74 bus route from the subway station. Set meal (everybody is served the same menu for about 150 drs) includes shrimp, octopus, other kinds of fish, taramosalata, soup, rabbit, salad, pastries, and melon. A big bargain for hearty eaters.

The Bouzouki Area

Hop the subway and travel just one stop—to **Phaleron**, a formerly "good" suburb that has seen better days. The beaches here are polluted, but at night it's fresh and cool, and a stroll along the seafront, as you leave the station, will take you past about half a mile of open cafes. A Mobil station on the left marks the beginning of a string of three or four bouzouki joints—enclosed gardens with tables, a bandstand, and mostly idle waiters, because bouzouki, after a brief spell of popularity, has now returned to the half-neglected state it was in before all the publicity of several years back. Most places open for the night at about 10 p.m.

By general consensus, the best bouzouki player in Greece is Vassilis Tsitsanis, who plays (in summer) in the **Hayama Club** (18 km mark on the

National Road to Thessaloniki). You'll have to wait until at least 1 a.m. to hear the master himself.

HOW TO GET TO PIRAEUS: Bus #165 from Filellinon St., opposite the Viking's office in Athens, takes about half an hour, costs 6 drs. Subway from Omorias or Monastiriki stations takes about 20 minutes, costs 7 drs. Taxis are faster, cost around 100 drs. Bus #70 from Piraeus will also get you back to Athens.

READERS' SELECTIONS: "Anyone ending up in Piraeus in the early hours of the morning will be glad to know of the **Astoria,** an all-night cafe near the Peloponnese station" (Chris Austin, Chatham, Kent, England). . . . If one happens to be traveling by one's own boat and something goes wrong with it, it might mean several days of headaches trying to find parts and someone to repair the vessel. This is especially true if one spoke little Greek or was on a tight budget. The cure for this is one **Roger Stafford,** 319 Ave. El. Venizelou, Athens, tel: 9517-665. He has been in Greece for ten years, calls it home, and is the only person who can efficiently get American boat problems together with Greek cures" (Carl Semezak, Detroit, Mich.). . . . "The **Hotel Santorini** (Trikoupi 6, tel: 4522-147) is spotless and has helpful staff" (Wm. Sherrill, Mesa, Ariz.).

2. Boats from Piraeus

SOME NOTES ABOUT RIDING BOATS: Sooner or later, you're going to find yourself in Piraeus at the first stage of a boat ride to the Greek Islands. You may be making a comparatively short trip to say, Mykonos (six or seven hours), or you may be en route to Samos, Crete, Rhodes, or some relatively distant place that will take you at least a day, and probably a night, to get there.

In any event, there are several things you need to know. The first concerns the different classes. Whether the boat is old or new, plush or shabby, there'll be a choice of various categories—first or second class, with a bewildering range of sleeping subdivisions (private cabin, shared cabin, bunk), plus sometimes "tourist" class, and always "deck" class (which is sometimes called tourist).

First or second class, without the specification of a bunk or cabin, merely means that you'll have a lounge to sit or recline in, or maybe a deck chair or a private piece of deck.

Plain old "deck class," always very cheap (as little as four or five dollars for journeys lasting several hours), gives you a choice of bunking down in the open on a barren piece of upper deck, or joining the older people stretched out on the deck or on the handful of benches down below near the heat and noise of the engines.

Younger people of all nationalities, Greeks included, tend to prefer the upper deck, and as soon as the boat opens its gate for boarding, there's a mad scramble for favorable positions. Sometimes the lifeboats are left uncovered, in which case they provide relatively comfortable shelter; other favored positions are atop or behind the lifebelt boxes, stretched out on the seats or in corners protected by piles of luggage, ropes, or other obstacles. Advisable to get there early.

The very best thing to have with you for these excursions is a light-weight, padded sleeping bag that rolls into a small bundle for easy carrying. The other possibilities are an inflatable air mattress (in Athens this will cost about 300 drs) and a blanket, or just the blanket alone. It is not advisable to travel without any covering because: (1) the deck isn't soft enough or smooth enough to sleep on bare, and (2) it gets cold during the night.

There is, usually, a kind of snack bar where food is limited to cheese, dry bread, tomatoes, baklava, and soft drinks. Mercifully, there is usually a tap of that magnificently cold, fresh Greek water on deck—even for the peasants like ourselves.

So it's advisable to take food. Good staples, I have found, are jars or cans or tubes of fish or meat paste or jam or even caviar, which is readily available in tubes fairly cheaply. You can almost always buy bread on board, but it doesn't hurt to spend a few drachmas for a loaf to take along with you, just in case. (German pumpernickel bread, wrapped in tinfoil for durability, is available in many Athens stores.) Other good staples are fruit, boxes of foil-wrapped cheese, cookies, and canned beans.

Imported (American) canned foods are relatively expensive in Athens, but considering that you're not eating regular meals for what amounts to a whole day, you're not being that extravagant.

A good area for familiar foods is the one between Athinas, Sofokleos, and Ermou Streets. This is the market area. Lots of little stores there specialize in imported foods, mostly for the wholesale trade. Sofokleos itself is a particularly good street.

As the miles and miles of sea go by with only occasional stops or views of islands, and rare encounters with other boats, to break the pleasantly lulling monotony—it will occur to you that there could hardly be a better time to read that lengthy paperback you've always intended to get around to. Take it with you. One infallible rule about island-hopping in Greece is that you've never got too much to read. But take paperbacks that you can dispose of when you've finished with them, thereby always keeping a little extra room in your luggage. Other useful, virtually indispensable items for cheap travel: bottle opener, can opener, knife, folding cup, spoon, packaged towelettes (or damp rag in plastic bag), soap, towel, toilet paper or Kleenex, and salt and pepper (in the same shaker).

BOAT SCHEDULES: Boat companies in Greece, I'm sad to report, are notorious for their lack of information regarding schedules, the irregularity of passages between the islands, tardiness, and the lack of sufficient inter-island transportation. I'm only saying this so that you *don't base your plans too strictly on boat schedules,* which vary from week to week. Actually, this isn't too serious when you consider that island life (and boat transportation) simply isn't as regimented as city life. There are many different boat companies and no agent of one can give you help regarding another line. They seem to be trained to give information only on boats to and from the island on which they live. Here, though, are some helpful ideas: (1) In Athens, right before you leave, buy the latest copy of *What's On In Athens,* at any kiosk. This lists the most up-to-date inter-island schedules. (2) Get a copy of the Tourist Map of Greece from the Tourist Office on Syntagma Square (free). The dotted lines between the islands denote boat routes. This will show you some general, though by no means all, routes. (3) Remember that Syros, once a major world port, is today still a key as far as inter-island transportation is concerned. The paths of many ships cross here and it is often possible to make a connection—on the same day, if you're lucky. (4) Purchase the latest steamship schedules either from the NTOG's Information Desk at 2 Karageorghi Servias Street (Syntagma Square) or from a travel agency.

The following table shows some sample boat fares (in drachmas). Although valid at the time of this writing, they may not be tomorrow. Duration of the trip depends on the number of stops.

	1st Class	2nd Class	Tourist	Deck Class
Crete	660	517	301	283
Rhodes	963	605	—	350
Mykonos	500	303	233	193
Samos	900	478	357	270
Ios	750	378	300	248
Naxos	500	388	239	201
Patmos	779	444	—	260
Monemvassia	450	291	233	193
Santorini	750	378	300	248
Mytilini	705	479	—	283

From Piraeus, embarkation tax is a few drs for all classes.

Note: Any information you might pick up about boat schedules from one island to another will be very useful to readers of this book, so if you get a chance, slip it in an envelope and mail it to me (c/o BCM-NOMAD, London WC1V6XX).

3. Beaches West of Athens

The National Road from Athens to Corinth crosses and recrosses a local road which runs along the shore, allowing access to the sea only occasionally because of the steep cliffs. (Transfer to the local road at Eleusis.) Having few hotels, the island of **Salamis** offers little for the tourist and even the beaches aren't that great.

The stretch west of **Kinetta** is best, most of it staked out by expensive hotels, of which the most accessible is the **Siagas Beach Hotel** (tel: 0741-67454) at Ag. Theodori. Here bed and breakfast (the minimum you can arrange) is around 475 drs single, 700 drs double. But of course you could drop by for lunch and a swim.

A more satisfying trip is to head north on the main road at Eleusis and make the turnoff west through Vilia, heading for the charming little fishing port of **Porto Germeni**. Avoid weekends, when this tiny beach is too crowded for comfort. There are primitive rooms for rent here, but the best bet is to book a room in advance at the only hotel, the 80-room **Egosthenion** (tel: 0263-41226), which is about 400 yards up the hill behind the beach. It's comfortable, charming, and cheap (350 drs single, 400 drs double with bath) and can only get more and more popular as Porto Germeni—90 minutes' drive from Athens —undergoes its predictable boom.

Chapter X

ONE-DAY TRIPS FROM THE CAPITAL

1. Aegina
2. Epidaurus
3. The Beaches and Sounion
4. Delphi
5. Around Attica
6. Eleusis

NOW WE TURN to a cluster of interesting sites that can be visited (there and back) on a one-day excursion from Athens.

1. Aegina

The nearest of the innumerable Greek islands to Athens is Aegina, a strangely peaceful place—before the midsummer tourist rush begins. It is famous for pistachio nuts and its many small, cream-colored churches with round blue domes and belltowers.

Aegina can be reached from Piraeus in about one hour's sailing time and, if schedules are checked carefully with a travel agent, it is sometimes possible to arrive on the island at one side, cross by bus, and leave for Piraeus from the port of **Aghia Marina** on the other side of the island. In any case, it's an easy trip there and back the same day.

Another alternative is to take one of the "Three-isle cruises" which allows you to pay brief visits to Aegina, Hydra, and Poros all in the same day, leaving Piraeus (Zea harbor) at 8:30 a.m. and arriving back at 7 p.m. Several different companies operate these pleasant one-day outings (cost about $25) including lunch) and my advice is to make a booking through Viking's Travel Bureau.

Boats for Aegina leave Piraeus from opposite the Melissa Restaurant several times daily. Fare is about 70 drs each way (third class), and the journey is uneventful, except for a man selling one-drachma raffle tickets for boxes of candy (the drawing is made before the boat docks). Most boats contain a small snack bar. It's best to buy a one-way rather than round-trip ticket. Different boat companies leave Aegina at different times, and since tickets are not exchangeable, you may discover another company has a boat leaving at a more convenient hour.

WHAT TO SEE AND DO: In the **Archaeological Museum** in Aegina town is a small fragment of inscribed stone that convinced the 19th-century archaeologists A. Furtwaengler and V. Stais that the **sanctuary** they had uncovered near Ag. Marina, 12 kms north of Aegina town was dedicated to the goddess Aphaia, who provoked the passion of King Minos while dallying in Crete. She supposedly fell into the sea and was rescued by fishermen who brought her here. At any rate, it's worth climbing up to see, just for the marvelous view—and if you've been to the Parthenon and the Temple of Poseidon at Sounion you've completed an equilateral triangle.

Also worth the climb (50 minutes from Aegina via the Perdika road) is **Oros** mountain, which in ancient times was known as Mt. Hellanion. A sanctuary to Zeus once stood on Mount Hellanion (1,700 feet) and a cloud above the peak, even today, is popularly supposed to indicate impending rain, just as Theophrastos wrote in the fourth century B.C.

Aegina has had some famous sons dating right back to Aristophanes (said by Thucydides and Theogenes to have owned land on the island around 450 B.C.). The 20th-century writers George Finlay *(History of the Greek Revolution)* and Nikos Kazantzakis *(Zorba the Greek)* both wrote their classic works here; and—sadly—Ioannis Capodistriou, first president of post-Turkish occupation Greece, was assassinated here in 1831.

Aegina was also the first place in Greece to mint its own coins: silver, with the image of a turtle, back in the seventh century B.C.; and bearing a phoenix when the new independent republic minted its first coins in 1829.

The island has not been so lucky with its natural resources, and even today has to import water by tanker. Until recently, writes Anne Yannoulis in her informative guide *Aegina* (Lycabettus Press), each household had water only every other day, and some houses kept drinking water in huge pottery jars similar to those used over 3,000 years ago.

Peter Edmund Laurent, visiting in 1818, wrote that the island used to abound in partridges to such an extent that the islanders had to destroy the birds' eggs in order to save the grain crop.

Buses run regularly across the island to **Aghia Marina,** the trip taking about half an hour from the narrow streets of Aegina (where the bus driver sometimes has to get out and close somebody's shutters before he can negotiate a corner) to the beautiful port.

The bus is soon out into the countryside, climbing past terraced hillsides and farms so tiny that the solitary ploughed field would fit easily into the swimming pool of the average-sized Texas ranch. The startling whiteness of the houses is relieved by the red, green, or yellow trim and red or blue doors. Soon, the **Monastery of St. Nektarious,** protector of the poor, appears on the left, and it is a common thing to alight here, look around the monastery and hop onto the next bus.

The bus goes past hillsides barren of all but an occasional fig tree. The sea pops back into view from time to time and eventually, after a long, twisting climb, the columned ruins of the **Temple of Aphaia** (fourth century B.C.) appear atop the hill to the right. The bus stops here and so can you, for a short guided tour, catching the next bus on to Aghia Marina. But don't bother to get off in the early afternoon: the temple gates are locked and the refreshment stand operator sleeping between 1:30 and 3:30 p.m.

Aphaia, a god of the sea like Poseidon, was held in high esteem in the fourth century B.C. when the temple was built, and, indeed, Aegina was the rival to Athens and Corinth. Declining interest has served the temple well, however, for it remains one of the least visited and best preserved in all of Greece. And its setting is lovely: on one side a terraced hillside looking like a green and brown striped awning, on the other a valley to the sea dotted with white houses and what look like miniature people tending their tiny fields.

From the temple it's only a mile to Aghia Marina, and you can walk down if you prefer. Both the road and a small path going straight down through the woods give a lovely series of vistas of the bay. There are often 40 people waiting for the 20-seat bus (which departs about every half hour after 3 p.m.), so better get in line early if you're not planning to take the boat back.

You may just decide to stay over, since the beach here is far nicer than those on the west side of the island. People are camping under the bushes at the edge of the beach and in the olive grove behind it. A tethered donkey stares in amazement at the bikini'd bodies spread out around him. On a hill at the far end, a tiny chapel is almost hidden beneath awnings that create a picnic pavilion. Greek families eat lunch here, while their candles burn inside; over the door, an ikon shows the Virgin solemnly holding a little devil by one horn.

There are crowded beaches near town and a smaller, private beach (with entrance fee) past Kolona. Take a boat across to **Moni** (fee for entrance), with its beaches, woods, wild goats, and pungent herbs.

STAYING OVER: In Aegina itself the 26-room **Hotel Brown** (tel: 22271), with its seahorse murals and seashell-decked lounge, is the most attractive. There's a small garden terrace at the rear and friendly service. Rooms without bath cost around 300 drs single, 450 drs double; doubles with bath, about 500 drs. Slightly cheaper and more or less sharing a small beach just east of the harbor is the eight-room **Hotel Aktaeon** (tel: 22241), with spacious lobby and rooms for 300 drs single, 400 drs double. Going past the Aktaeon and the movie theater and walking for ten minutes or so will bring you to the charming **Hotel Pharos** (tel: 22218) with its tiny beach and outdoor restaurant. Here the 26 bathless rooms cost 250 drs single, 400 drs double.

The town of Aegina has three movie theaters, two of which usually show features in English. That's about it for entertainment if you're staying overnight, for there is a conspicuous lack of tavernas with live music, or discotheques: Aegina caters primarily to day-trippers.

In Aghia Marina, the **Hotel Ammoudia** (tel: 32313) and the **Hotel Oassis** (tel: 32312) sit side by side on the beach, both offering simple, pleasant rooms with bath for around 400 drs single, 475 drs double. The classier **Hotel Argo** (tel: 32266) has some rooms at the same price, but the **Hotel Marina** (tel: 32307) is slightly cheaper.

There are numerous private homes offering rooms and a few pensions, of which the most prominent is that of **Evangelos Pavlou** (tel: 22795) whose rooms have balconies and comfortable beds.

ANGHISTRI: Fifteen minutes west of Aegina—boats every two hours—is the smaller island of Anghistri, suitably remote to offer peace and tranquility from the day-tripper crowd. Here, not far from a sandy beach, is the **Anghistri Club** (tel: 23894), whose 45 rooms cost upwards of 400 drs per person. There are also small apartments available. The hotel has a restaurant, bar and TV room; boating, fishing, and water skiing are among the activities available, as are Sunday visits to the Epidaurus Festival in season.

TO EPIDAURUS: There are boats to Epidaurus from Aegina, but one nice way to go is to book with **Saron Tours** in Aegina town for an excursion departing at midday and allowing for time on the beach.

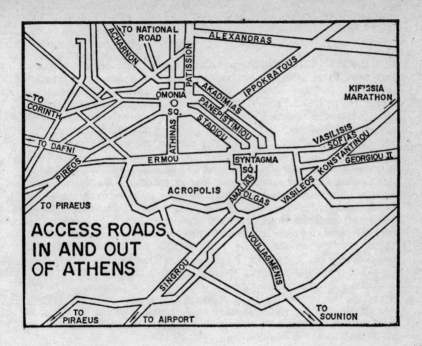

ACCESS ROADS
IN AND OUT
OF ATHENS

2. Epidaurus

During July and August, there are performances of ancient Greek dramas every weekend in the centuries-old theater at Epidaurus, about 110 miles from Athens by road.

THE JOURNEY: The bus takes the superhighway out of Athens, skirts Piraeus to the north, and then forks right on the road to Corinth. And off to the left is that blue sea, with, here and there, a small shore town.

Suddenly, surprise! The sea appears to the right, too, a white ship making its way slowly to one of the small ports nearby on the isthmus. The bus crosses the Corinth canal. A ten-minute stop in Corinth—a small sleepy town despite its age and reputation; afterwards the countryside is softer, with cultivated fields of corn and lush green plants and faded advertisements for Melisa or Stella macaroni emblazoned on the walls of the red-tiled barns.

Several high peaks dot the horizon on the left, and for a while the road parallels the railway track. Through another village, a friendly wave from the bus driver to the uniformed cop, and a last, lush stretch of greenery with lemon trees before the pretty town of Nafplion, with its flower-filled squares and attractive bay.

The public bus to Epidaurus goes from Syntagma Square in Nafplion, three or four blocks from where the bus from Athens stops. A hurried dash, and you're on another bus for the 12- or 15-minute ride through the barren, rocky peninsula to Epidaurus. There are even a few cactus plants now and again, but there is cultivated tobacco hanging to dry, too, and even a village or two for the last mile or so.

AROUND THE TOWN: Epidaurus is a lovely place, something like an overgrown Tanglewood. The bus takes its place along with scores of others, so be sure to remember its number and location if that's the way you plan to return. The path to the right leads to snack stands, a small post and telegraph office, a tourist information office (they can answer questions in a dozen languages), and the theater and museum. Also in this direction is the terrace cafe of the **Hotel Xenia,** (tel: 21003) in a lush green setting with flowers and bushes growing all around in what appears to be carefully cultivated abandon. Rooms here on the demi-pension plan: around 800 drs single, 1100 drs double.

Coming from the village, about four kms from the theater, the barren landscape suddenly blossoms with bright red signs advertising the **Scarlet Beach Hotel** further down the coast (bungalows, snack bar, taverna, nightclub) and the **Hydra Beach Hotel,** at least 60 kms away. Closer is the **Hotel Alkyon,** only a few yards from the sign, and a nearby pension with a cafe bar. Continue up the road towards the theater, past old ladies on donkeys so laden with branches they look like trees with tails, and you'll find an open-air restaurant.

Visiting the theater during the day is an interesting experience, for the workmen will be busy preparing stage sets, working on papier-mâché "rocks" so realistic that unwary visitors have sat upon them before realizing they were fake. Inside the theater you can stand on the center stone and drop different-sized coins on the stone floor, noting how the different tone of each can be heard all the way up to the rearmost seats.

The best advice is to take along a bag or basket filled with food, drinks, and other appurtenances of country living, and have a picnic on the grass. An inflatable cushion or blanket, binoculars or opera glasses, some mosquito repellent and sunglasses are about the only other things you need. It doesn't get cold enough for other than a very light jacket.

Before the performance begins, you can wander around the grounds looking at everybody, and if you walk to the cabana-type colony, which is the hillside portion of the Hotel Xenia, you'll see the actors and actresses, handsome devils all, idling around in their costumes. There's a museum just below the theater entrance, but rather strangely it closes at 6 p.m., just before about 90 per cent of the visitors arrive.

Epidaurus once sheltered a sanctuary for Asklepios, son of Apollo to whom the sick flocked to be healed in the days preceding the fourth century B.C. Many left their thanks inscribed on stone slabs (on display in the museum along with intricately carved cornices, columns and friezes) but not all were so grateful. One tale tells of the blind man whose sight was restored, but being too miserly to offer a thanksgiving gift had it taken away from him again. Responding to his further pleas, the god then restored sight to one of his eyes.

THE PERFORMANCE: From the stone benches in the theater you can look down a green valley bare of all but scrub and an occasional fig tree. A slight haze drifts in front of the rugged peaks at each side of the valley, and a row of trees forms a backdrop to the simple lines of the stone stage.

High up here on the topmost row of stone seats, the view of the stage and the sandy, circular arena in front of it is impressive, and the acoustics are as perfect as when the theater was first devised by the architect Polyclitus, four centuries before the coming of Christianity.

There are 55 rows of seats, tiered as in a bullring. They are set into a gently curving hillside to comprise three-quarters of a natural bowl, the remaining section taken up by the stage, its broad central steps leading down into the arena and two sets of side steps leading to an upper terrace of the set.

At 8 p.m. exactly, as the sun disappears behind the hill, the olive-uniformed policemen who have been guarding the aisles sit down, and the audience applauds a file of performers who can be seen marching across the open space towards the back of the stage. They appear to be majestic lords and ladies in togas and diaphanous dresses, a legion of soldiers with blouses and pleated kilts, and a score of lovely dark-haired maidens. But all disappear behind the stage and the audience quiets down to wait apprehensively.

Two cymbals crash, a random snatch of music rises to the mountains, and the performance begins.

Well, I'm not going to go into the details of what goes on. Unless you know Greek or dig the exclamatory style in which these ancient plays are presented, you may be bored—unless, of course, you get a copy of the play in advance and read it in the afternoon or on the way from Athens. That way you can follow the action and really enjoy the performance. In fact, bring the play along with you to the performance. You'll be amazed at how well you can follow the action, and if you get lost, there's usually someone nearby doing the same thing. The trilingual programs aren't quite as helpful, although they do give brief story outlines. You shouldn't have any trouble finding a copy of any ancient play. Kiosks and bookstores in the Syntagma area of Athens are always stocked with them.

Once the performance ends—it lasts just over two hours—there's a frantic scramble to get out of the theater and back onto the buses. If you are returning by bus, grab the same one you arrived on.

GETTING THERE: You can make your way to Epidaurus from Athens either via Nafplion (buses from Kavalas and Kifissiou Streets, tel: 5134-575); or you can go direct by private bus at 4 p.m. on Saturdays and Sundays from Polytechnion St. 12 (tel: 5248-000); or at 8 a.m. on Sundays by coach, which stops to allow a swim before proceeding to Epidaurus at 6 p.m. The cost is around 225 drs. There are also evening hydrofoils to Epidaurus from Zea Marina in Piraeus.

3. The Beaches and Sounion

The beaches of Athens are dotted more or less continuously down the coast to the south of the city. There are, of course, beaches at Piraeus and in its environs but, other than those mentioned in Chapter IX, these are usually polluted and aren't much in use by fastidious swimmers. Athenians and visitors usually head further down the coast, where there are several fine beaches.

Most of the hotels down the coast are new and very attractive: marble staircases, gardens or lawns bordered with flowers, open balconies and spacious lobbies. Unfortunately, most of them are not very cheap, owing to their insistence that visitors take full pension. Because the whole trip to Sounion is only a matter of a two-hour drive or bus ride, it is probably wiser to plan on spending the night back at Athens, unless you happen to like camping.

In general, campers are welcome throughout Greece, and may pitch their tents in almost any open country, except near archaeological monuments.

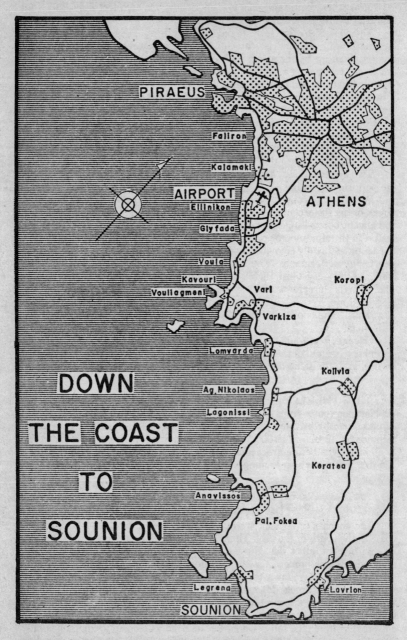

PIRAEUS

Faliron

Kalamaki

AIRPORT

Ellinikon

ATHENS

Glyfada

Voula

Kavouri

Koropi

Vouliagmeni

Vari

Varkiza

DOWN

Lomvarda

Kalivia

THE COAST

Ag. Nikolaos

Lagonissi

TO

Keratea

SOUNION

Anavissos

Pal. Fokea

Legrena

Lavrion

SOUNION

Sleeping on beaches in sleeping bags is not uncommon.

    Buses leave Athens regularly to run down the coast, all the way to Sounion, an attractive headland at the southernmost tip of the peninsula. As the trip is a mere 45 miles, it can be made comfortably in a day, with time out for beaches at many points en route.

Bus schedule from Athens to Sounion: every hour or so from the corner of Mavromataion and Alexandras Avenues, which is two blocks beyond the National Archaeological Museum on Patission Street. Telephone 813-203 for more information.

It is easier, however, if more costly, to take one of the tours to Sounion. Almost all the tour companies—Elite, CHAT, Key, ABC, Bell—operate afternoon tours. They offer comfortable buses with English-speaking guides who point out such easily missed phenomena as lamb-roasting villages and salt-drying beds.

And now, let's get going . . .

THE ROAD TO GLYFADA: Actually, it isn't necessary to go all the way down to Glyfada, or beyond to the official swanky beaches. If you merely want a place to sit or be by the sea, you can take a bus down the coast and alight at almost any point beyond Phaleron—wherever the coastline takes your fancy.

Many buses travel this route—the #84 bus to Ano Voula from Amalias Street (just off Syntagma Square); the #1 bus to Edem; the #85 bus to Glyfada; or the #125 or #159 buses from Piraeus to Voula or Varkiza, respectively.

The area you'll first come to is that just below the airport, and it's easy to see that it is rapidly changing its character with the army camps, buggy racing tracks and waste land gradually being transformed into marinas, beaches and restaurant developments. But there's still years of work ahead and meanwhile there are occasional little spots—often beside a cafe or taverna—where you can sit beside the sea on the rocks. **Kalamaki** is about the first place where the sea is clean enough to bathe safely—but hang on! There's plenty of nicer coastline to come.

GLYFADA, VOULA AND VICINITY: Next we reach the best of the beaches close to Athens—Glyfada, often thronged with wealthy tourists because of its smart ambience. Admission here costs 50 drs, so money-conscious sunbathers head further along to Voula (which marks the end of the residential area), Vouliagmeni (admission 15 drs, including locker facilities), or to the free beach of **Varkiza,** the latter as jammed as Coney Island on hot weekends.

The tiny seaside town of Glyfada is worth a stop if you're driving. Most of it is set just back from the main road and its half-dozen streets are easy to walk around. There are several restaurants, an "English pub" and cutesy bars with names like Pussy Cat, San Tropez, etc. The hamburger stand is thronged with American teenagers who live with their families nearby, and English is heard as much as Greek. There are two or three big hotels—the 61-room **Niki** (tel: 894-6231) is typical with doubles from about 500 drs—but none is really cheap. You'd be better off down by the sea, at one of the modern hotels lining the main road such as the **Themis** (tel: 894-0824) or the **Rial** (tel: 894-4209) both of which theoretically have doubles with bath for around 400 drs, although in summer it's doubtful if you'd get a room without advance reservation, and even then you'd probably have to add another 300 drs or so per person for full board.

One place you might find useful to know about is the 31-room **Villa Katerina** (6 Vass. Sophias, Glyfada, tel: 894-7281), a charming hideaway with flowers, trees, singing birds, and a terrace on which to eat overlooking the pine garden. It's one of the nearest hotels to the airport and therefore somewhat noisy, but it is a useful place near the sea for an overnight stop en route to somewhere else. Simple bright rooms cost about 400 drs single, 500 drs double including breakfast: for half board (probably obligatory in season) add 100 drs per person.

Go back to the main highway where the 19-mile stretch of coastline is speckled with numerous resort hotels, most of them pretty expensive. At **Asteria** beach just south of Glyfada, there are a couple of modern apartment houses that rent to transients, a typical one being **Kyknos,** on the main road, in which small apartments containing two beds, a living room with two sofas, kitchen with refrigerator, bathroom and hall, rent for around 700 drs per day, with a reduction over two-month periods. Fine for two compatible couples. Most of the glossy hotels around here, incidentally, are booked up months in advance. (The big-splurge **Asteria Taverna** is recommended in Chapter V.)

Next comes **Alimos** beach, its snack bar offering American-style pizza and hamburgers, also southern fried chicken. Among diversions here is a miniature golf course.

Just before **Voula** beach (15 drs admission) is the privately owned, very fancy and equally expensive **Astir** beach (admission 50 drs) where young, rich social types hang out. The Astir boasts private dressing rooms, paved walks lined with flowers, brightly colored umbrellas, and grass to stretch out on as well as sand.

Buses to Glyfada and Voula leave Athens at the Royal Garden entrance along Amalias (just off Syntagma Square); they run almost continuously from 5:30 a.m. until 1 a.m. Buses to Vouliagmeni go from lower down Amalias, at the Zappeion corner of Olgas Avenue, regularly, from 6 a.m. to midnight.

At Voula there's a state beach (admission 10 drs) which is open all year round from 8 a.m. to 8 p.m., and a camping site charging 50 drs per person plus 35 drs for a tent or 50 drs for caravan or bus. There are also a batch of medium-priced hotels such as the **Rondel** (tel: 895-8605) or the **Noufara** (tel: 895-3450), the latter separated from the road by a tranquil lake filled with water lilies. Both these C-class hotels have rooms with bath for about 500 drs double although both will probably require that at least half-board be taken (at least another 175 drs per person).

After Voula there's a lengthy stretch of undeveloped coastline where you can get off the bus and walk to the sea almost anywhere that takes your fancy. **Pamela's,** an enormous restaurant, rises like a white concrete castle out of this wilderness and makes an excellent stopping place. In addition to the elegant dining room with its pale pink tablecloths and caged canaries, there's a self-service cafeteria with good food, low prices, and a terrace overlooking the sea. Adjoining is a state beach (15 drs) and a concrete "island" in the bay that you can swim out to and dive from. Half a mile further south is the **Apollon Palace Hotel** (expensive) with a 24-hour coffee shop, and a mile or two beyond that is the beautiful beach of **Kavouri,** on a promontory off the main road, with extensive camping grounds and picnic areas.

The two hotels at Kavouri couldn't provide a greater contrast. On one side of the road is the sleek, expensive modern **Kavouri Hotel** (tel: 895-8461) with swimming pool and package-tourists sunbathing on the lawn; on the other, overlooking a quiet sandy beach is the old **Kastello Beach Hotel,** enclosed in a charming garden with an olde-worlde air and view of the sea.

VOULIAGMENI: There's a junction of the road here with the main highway continuing south past more and more beaches, sidewalk cafes, and lots of restaurants and action. Off to the right is a mile-long peninsula, jutting out to sea, with a curving road servicing some expensive hotels, a large marina, a classy private beach, **Astir** (50 drs) and—at its extreme point—a fabulous stretch of rocks from which you can swim or just lie upon in the sun listening to the transistor radios of neighboring Greek sunbathers. There's a mobile snack bar offering drinks, sandwiches, and other snacks, and it's a fine place to park your VW bus for a day or two and just enjoy the sun and the sea. Crowded by day, it's virtually deserted at night.

Back to the highway. Just beyond the Greek Coast Hotel watch for signs indicating the fresh-water lake to your left. It's an unusual place (20 drs admission) with snack bar, changing rooms, rowing boats for rent and an opportunity to swim in and out of several grottos carved into the cliff face.

VARKIZA: After Vouliagmeni, the coastline curves and the road passes through a stretch of barren, rocky hillside before descending into the vast bay of Varkiza, its beaches crowded on weekends; dozens of buses bring bathers in from many surrounding areas. It's a free beach and is dotted with all the usual appurtenances of such a place: snack stands, restaurants, and strolling vendors.

Entering Varkiza, there's a fish restaurant so strategically placed on a bend in the road that the enticing smell of frying fish grabs the attention of all who pass. There are more beaches here—one private and one state, beside which is another Pamela's restaurant. No cheap hotels although below Varkiza there is so much construction going on that it looks as though every little cove will soon have its own hotel and/or taverna.

A few miles beyond Varkiza, past a large sheltered harbor and occasional large private homes with swimming pools, there's a turnoff to the swanky self-contained bungalow colony of **Lagonissi,** complete with flower-filled gardens, swimming pools, shops, golf course, tennis courts, and even a movie theater. Expensive, of course.

SOUNION AND VICINITY: Next comes the whistle-stop village of **Nea Folkea,** at the 53-km mark from Athens, with its fishing boats and a few roadside restaurants, and from here on the view gets prettier and prettier: a flock of sheep gathered under a hillside shack; shallow pools of water where salt is being prepared, the piles of salt nearby; a boat en route to Piraeus visible in the shimmering sea, and finally, in the distance, the pillars of the **Temple of Poseidon** (built in the fourth century B.C.) on a promontory jutting out to sea.

There is very little cheap accommodation at Sounion, most hotels costing at least $12 per person and being booked up well in advance by German tour groups. There are numerous bungalow colonies set back from the road and one of them, **Cape Sounion Beach,** boasts a pedestrian walkway underneath the road to the beach. Just about the only cheap hotel is the 17-room **Saron** (tel: 39144) which has bathless rooms for about 250 drs single, 350 drs double.

Centuries ago, the island across from Sounion was fortified, partly to protect the narrow water passage and partly because the area was loaded with silver and lead mines. Today only shepherds live on the island, their water supplied by the rain. Sounion was an early "meteorological station" which transmitted weather reports to Athens via an elaborate system of hilltop bonfires. The temple of Poseidon is only five years younger than the Parthenon in Athens.

A brief excursion up to the temple is well worth the climb, for the archaeology or the view. The temple was built to the glory of the Greek equivalent of Neptune and built so well, of marble brought from Penteli north of Athens, that most of the pillars still stand. Carved and written all over them are inscriptions made by 24 centuries worth of visitors (including Lord Byron) and some of these have been carved with exquisite care. For about 15 drs, a man will take your photograph, with the temple as a backdrop, and develop it on the spot.

Just below the temple is a restaurant for tourists (it is called **Tourist Pavilion**), with a menu in English. Cheaper prices, but fewer choices, are offered at the small restaurants on the beach.

Admission to the ruins is free on Sundays, 10 drs at other times.

Most of the day-trippers to Sounion spend an hour or two on the sandy beach outside the big hotel, but if you glance over the cliffs at the other side you'll see a tiny, pebbly cove that's a perfect spot to get away from it all. My Australian friend Barbara, accustomed to long, sandy stretches back home, was amazed to discover how pleasant it can be on a beach only large enough for half a dozen people.

From Sounion you might like to go back by an alternative route, more or less up the eastern side of the peninsula although the road heads inland almost immediately and offers a panoramic mix of industry, unspoiled countryside, and small towns where tourists are rarely seen. This trip, of course, is much easier if you have your own transport and this is certainly to be recommended. If there is only one day during your stay in Athens when you rent a car, the round trip down the coast and back should be the occasion for it.

The bus fare from Athens to Sounion and back is 100 drs.

4. Delphi

The history of Delphi was for centuries the history of Mediterranean politics. For much of the time, there was hardly an action taken without consulting the gods at the **Apollon Temple.** The entrails of birds and animals and the drugged or drunken ravings of an old woman decided the fate of nations—and all in the name of religion.

From the depths of the mountain, misty vapors poured, so potent, it is said, that the first sheep which grazed there "had spasms," and shepherds who breathed the fumes were able to prophesy the future. There has been much speculation about what those mysterious fumes were and certainly some version of kif (hemp) is not unlikely. Whatever, they certainly played their part in history.

Many Greek legends surround the famous site, but the most persistent one is how it got its name. Apollo, it seems, jumped into the sea one day, disguised himself as a dolphin (for which the Greek word is *delphini*), and kidnapped a shipload of Cretans, hauling them to the place that is now called Delphi. From that mythical day onward it was a holy place, and whoever initially thought of dispensing advice, and charging a fee for it, instigated the world's first unbeatable con game.

On a summer day the sun seems to spotlight different sections of the surrounding valley quite arbitrarily, as if Apollo the master designer was playing with the lighting effects.

It is easy to see how, given the right circumstances, the place could be chosen as a holy one. The site of Delphi, in an impressive ravine, looks over a valley that drops sheerly almost two thousand feet. There is nothing to distract from nature at its most awesome. It is a sight that the visitor will probably never forget.

The journey to Delphi takes almost four hours, with a brief rest stop about halfway, and when you arrive in Delphi you'll be on the main street, with the ruins about half a mile back.

The last few miles have been through majestically awesome granite hills and canyons, and you're perched on the edge of a cliff that falls steeply, at one point, to the valley 1,700 feet below.

LODGINGS: The main street of Delphi (pop: 800) is lined with about a dozen hotels, most of them brand-new, small, and extremely light and airy. The ones on the lefthand side of the street are preferable, because at least some of their rooms overlook the valley.

The **Iniohos** (tel: 82316) claims to have the best food, and while that isn't really true, it does have the friendliest owner who has always looked after readers of this book. Pleasant rooms and restaurant terrace with good view of the valley below. Fifteen rooms, all with bath, cost 375 drs single, 475 drs double.

The **Hermes** (tel: 82318) is comfortable enough, with 24 rooms for 400 drs single, 520 drs double. Keep in mind: you don't have to buy souvenirs from the owner's store.

Next to the post office, and still on the valley side, is the **Baronos** (tel: 82345), a relatively new hotel which is a bargain at 300 drs single, 415 drs double with bath.

Across the street, the 20-room **Parnassos** (tel: 82321) is probably the nicest on the street but a bit expensive: about 425 drs single, 500 drs double.

The **Pythia** (tel: 82328), the **Greca** (tel: 82248), the **Lefas** (tel: 82324), and the **Sybylla** (tel: 82335) are all pretty much the same, which is to say perfectly acceptable, and roughly the same price: about 250 drs single, 350 drs double with bath, although at the Greca these prices are for rooms without bath. The Pythia (tel: 82328) is more expensive.

Cheapest hotels—the **Athena** (tel: 82239), **Dionyssos** (tel: 82257), and **Phoebos** (tel: 82319)—are hotels with either no rooms with bath or very few, and rates at these are around 250 drs single, 300 drs double.

All these hotels are on the main street, and maybe you would prefer to be on one of the upper streets which run parallel. (It's somewhat quieter up there.) In which case, consider the **Lito** (tel: 82303) with singles for 400, doubles 475; and the **Stadion** (450 double) or the inexpensive **Kotopouli**.

The **youth hostel** (tel: 82268) is also on this upper street. It has 70 beds and charges 70 drs. Sign says the doors are closed at 11 p.m. and won't be opened, but since there's nothing to do in Delphi at night, it scarcely matters. Cheap restaurant at this hostel, open to all.

On occasions when all Delphi's hotels and private rooms are already booked (not uncommon in midsummer), you might have to seek refuge at **Arahora** or **Amphissa**, about 20 kms east and west of Delphi respectively.

THE MUSEUM: This should be your first stop. The highspot of the Delphi museum (open 8 a.m. to 1 p.m., 3-8 p.m. Tuesday through Saturday; 10 a.m. to 1 p.m., 3-6 p.m. Sundays; 11 a.m. to 1 p.m. and 3-6 p.m. Mondays, admission 30 drs) is a lifesize bronze figure of a charioteer, dating back to 478 B.C. It is hypnotic in its effect on visitors, who pause, momentarily stunned by the repose of the figure whose hands clutch a tangle of reins and whose eyes stare icily into space. The figure is barefoot, and every fold of the gown enhances the naturalness of its pose. The statue, excavated in 1896, is often reproduced in literature about Delphi and is described as the "masterpiece of an unknown artist." The racetrack, incidentally, was circled 23 times in what were nine-mile races, and the tense look on the charioteer's face may be due to the fact that as many as 40 chariots had been known to overturn during the course of it.

The museum was built by private donation back at the turn of the century, when Greece was hard pressed to find the money to finance the continuing excavations. It was reconstructed in the late thirties and is today a cheerful airy place, with glass ceilings in some rooms and an inventory of more than 10,000 items found in the ruins nearby.

These include carved stone friezes, numerous statues of toga-clad men, a pedestal containing a group of three dancers on different sides, a 12-foot-high sphinx donated to the Delphic oracle by the island of Naxos early in the sixth century B.C., and many carved stones, fragments of pottery, and other artifacts. Some of the items in the museum represent the Mycenean period—1600 to 1100 B.C. An interesting curiosity is a pink statue: the head and the body do not match. They were stuck together when found, and it was years before anybody realized that the head belongs to a child and the body to an adult.

In one of the rooms, stone slabs are said to be inscribed with centuries-old musical notes, but it would be more interesting if such notes could be rendered in some way for visitors to hear.

The History It Reflects

Much of the information about Delphi's early days is speculation, but from the writings of various Greeks and Romans, and from what has been found at the site, a fairly clear picture has at last emerged.

In the center of the temple, beside the altar, a copper and gold tripod was set up above the fissure in the ground from which "intoxicating vapors" sprang. The woman known as Pythia was led to this area and the fumes apparently caused some kind of trance or fit, during which she uttered the incoherent sounds which were "interpreted" to the questioners by the priest by her side. To be chosen as Pythia—at first a young woman, until one of the early pilgrims made a pass at her—one had to fulfill certain conditions: she had to be handsome, more than 50 years of age, from a poor farmer's family, and not too bright. (The priests didn't want a thinking man's Pythia.)

Before making her pronouncements, Pythia had to fast for three days. On the day in question, she bathed in the nearby Castalian Spring, burned some laurel leaves at the altar, put some more on her head, and drank a little water. Then taking her place by the tripod, she would work herself into a hysterical frenzy and start muttering—something like the mediums of today.

At first the pronouncements were delivered in hexameter, on the grounds that verse was easier to remember, but eventually they began to be given out in simple prose. In the early days, too, the oracle was in action only during February (believed to be the month that Apollo was born), but eventually—presumably as the magistrates of Delphi became greedier—other pronouncement days were scheduled throughout the year.

There were many oracular sites throughout Greece at this time, but Delphi was the only one with a human voice and eventually it became the most influential one to which only the most important problems of state were presented.

The decline of Delphi began at about the time of the Christian era, and despite efforts to revive it by Plutarch, who served as one of the priests early in the second century A.D., it gradually became merely a tourist attraction. The Christian Emperor Constantine took away many of its treasures, and in 381

A.D. the Emperor Theodosius outlawed "paganism," and the shrine was soon forgotten. Earthquakes and landfalls covered the site, and a village, Kastri, was built on top. Excavations did not begin until the last century.

The Persians figured in a great many of the oracle's replies, because they were always threatening Greece with invasion. In the year 490 B.C., for example, all the signs were that they were going to overrun Greece, and Delphi really didn't want to be on the losing side. So its vague pronouncement was to the effect that the Greeks must either leave the country or surrender.

Actually, what happened, according to historians, was that when the Persians came over the top of Mount Parnassus and seemed to be on their way to sweeping Delphi in their path, a tremendous thunderstorm sprang up, which both sides interpreted as Apollo defending his shrine—and the Persians fled.

Ten years later they were back again, and this time the oracle's injunction to the Greeks to "Trust the wooden walls" resulted in the Greeks' wooden fleet, although surrounded at Salamis, breaking out and putting the Persian ships to rout.

Every time one of the oracle's predictions appeared to come true, the prestige of Delphi was enhanced and riches and praise poured in from the pleased petitioners. (Some were not so pleased: the Roman emperor Nero had been warned, "Beware 73," and chose to interpret it as meaning that he would die at the age of 73. Instead, he was overthrown, aged 36, by Galvus—who was 73.)

Eventually the place was rich in gold, statues, monuments, and other material goods, not to mention the influence held by the priests who ran it. To strengthen their power and to eliminate the sceptics, Delphi originated the tradition of holding trials for doubters who, when inevitably found guilty of sacrilege, were thrown bodily from a high rock adjoining the temple. Aesop, the author of the fables, is said to have died in this way. If so, he must have been one of the earliest of a long line of writers who were killed by religious fanatics for daring to suggest that a creed might have alternatives.

It seems amazing now, in retrospect, that for almost one thousand years (from the seventh century B.C. onwards), the lives and fortunes of commoners, kings, and even countries hung on the words of an uneducated peasant girl—the Delphic Oracle. Can't really blame her, though: her words were "interpreted" by priests, a shrewd and knowledgeable bunch who had mastered the art of ambiguity. "Know Thyself" and "Nothing in Excess" were supposedly the basic principles behind all the advice rendered.

In the end, it was the money rather than the ambiguous advice that finished them off. They couldn't resist placing a little more emphasis on the things people wanted to hear than what they objectively believed might be the more likely, and their influence waned as the value of their advice lessened.

In its heyday, though, Delphi was renowned throughout the civilized world. In 548 B.C., after much of the temple had been destroyed by fire, contributions for rebuilding flowed in from all over the Mediterranean, including Italy and Egypt, and a similar fund was raised from international sources after the earthquake of 373 B.C.

On balance, the Oracle was decidedly a positive thing, if only because the general effect of its pronouncements was to encourage the expansion of the Greek state and the extension of Greek philosophy and civilization to other parts of the world. Without this expansion it is highly probable that the Greeks would have killed each other off in a series of civil wars.

THE RUINS: Outside the museum, a lovely mosaic has been spread along the ground, its colored tiles bearing pictures of ducks, peacocks, fish, rams, and bears. It's in surprisingly good condition and very beautiful. It dates back to the fifth century A.D., and was probably part of a Roman villa. It was found some ten years ago, and contemporary houses had been built on top of it.

Stone pavements (which, like red brick, denote Roman rather than Greek builders) lead up into the temple area. The impressive building with the pillars was the **Treasure House** of the Athenians, a stronghold for the riches offered to the gods of Delphi to celebrate the victory at the battle of Marathon (the word "Marathon" can still be read on one of its base stones). The treasury's walls are covered with carved inscriptions relating to everything from the release of slaves (liberated after victories or after having paid a ransom), recipes, oracular pronouncements, etc. Some of these inscribed stones are in the museum.

Just behind **Sybil's Rock,** which follows the treasury on your upward climb along the **Sacred Way,** is a flat pedestal which once held the **Sphinx,** which now sits in the museum. Another pedestal, this one circular, is on your right, just after you turn the corner past the outer walls of the central temple. This base once held the sacred tripod, three intertwined snakes as "legs," inscribed with the names of 23 Greek towns. Another stone, with holes and a channel carved into it, is believed to be the one that held the tripod during the ceremonies when the oracle delivered her messages. This stone is now in the center of the ruined temple. A ramp, rather than steps, leads into the temple, because it was believed that such an approach was more dignified.

Looking over to the right from the temple, you can see the pedestals on which stood the statues which are now in the museum. The cliff beyond that is the one from which disbelievers were thrown. Up to the left are the remains of the ancient theater (fourth century B.C. and restored by the Romans).

High up on the hill, to the left, is the ancient Stadium which seated 7,000 spectators. The procession of athletes, which preceded every event there, began from a **Triumphal Arch,** four pillars of which are still standing.

From below the temple a grassy footpath leads off to the right to the **Castalian Spring,** where Pythia used to bathe, and from there down across the road to a lower group of ruins known as the Marmaria. These include the ancient gymnasium and—the most often reproduced feature of Delphi on picture postcards—the remains of the Temple of Pronaia Athena. The climb up to the Stadium, above the amphitheater, is worth it.

There don't seem to be any especially good books written about Delphi. The best I have been able to discover, and which has assisted me in my own research, is *Delphi: Legends and History* by Panagiotes Loukatos. The publisher is George Papademetriou, 50 Stadiou Street, Athens.

DELPHI RESTAURANTS: Most of the food around here is pretty uninteresting. Even the 200 dr dinner at the **Hotel Vouzas** (which, by the way, has a good selection of English paperbacks in the lobby) in no gourmet treat. The two cafes past the Hotel Hermes have good pastries.

BUSES TO DELPHI: Buses leave from 260 Liossion Street (tel: 8616-489) in Athens at 7:30 a.m., 1:30 and 5:30 p.m. The trip takes about four hours and costs around 270 drs. Buses from Athens pass thru Delphi twice daily en route to Nafpaktos where you change buses for Antirion with its 15-minute (automobile) ferry across the gulf. It's a lovely drive along the coast from Itea (where the ferry used to go from) to Nafpaktos, past groves of olive trees.

5. Around Attica

Aegina, Sounion, and Delphi are considerably further from Athens than the many mountain villages and ports of the Attic peninsula—and several of these are well worth a trip. Most of them can be reached by public bus from one of the two suburban bus terminals on either side of Leoforos Alexandras, just off Patission, for about 40 or 50 drs.

Porto Rafti is a beautiful fishing village on the east coast; just north of it is **Vraona** (the ancient Brauron), a site of recent archaeological discoveries. To get to either of these, you'll go through Markopoulon (I wonder if Marco Polo stopped there?) which is famous for its wine. North of Vraona is **Loutsa,** one of the longest and finest beaches near Athens. Still further north is historic **Marathon,** where the grave mound of the Athenians who died in the great victory against the Persians can still be seen. At **Dionissos,** on the way there, you can drink wine in tavernas on the very spot where the wine god showed the Greeks how to make it. Here are three of my favorite local spots:

MONT PARNES: On the hottest day of the summer leave Athens for the cool, verdant beauty of Mont Parnes (3,600 feet), 15 miles northeast. There's a spectacular view—one of the widest-ranging in Greece, with the Bay of Piraeus dimly visible through the industrial haze—and a magnificent swimming pool to plunge into when the breezes drop and the afternoon sun reaches its peak.

The **Mont Parnes** (tel: 246-9111) is a luxury 160-room hotel with a casino to which the fantastic cable railway (teleferique) runs 24 hours a day (30 drs, runs every half hour during the day; 50 drs, runs every ten minutes in the evening). The restaurant is open all the time, with breakfast served until 1 p.m. and reasonably priced snacks—eggs, sandwiches, spaghetti, etc.—always available.

The hotel's minibus from Syntagma takes staff only; you'll have to take a regular bus from Sourmeli St. Last bus back is 8 p.m., so you won't get to see the casino in action unless you thumb a ride or pay for a taxi home. Skip Parnes unless the weather is almost perfect or you'll find yourself in clammy clouds.

KESARIANI MONASTERY: This hardly counts as a day trip from Athens, because it will take only about one hour on the bus, but it's a lovely spot to which to take a picnic lunch—so you could stretch it into a day's outing if you choose. What I'm referring to is the old Kesariani Monastery, on the hillside to the south of Athens. Take the #39 bus from behind the university on Akadimias Street and get off at the little village of Kesariani. From there it's about a 1½-mile walk up to the old monastery, built in the 12th century but unused since 1830. A beautifully tranquil spot with only the smell of flowers (and incense from the chapel) and the sound of birds to disturb your thoughts. There are no facilities for eating or drinking so take a little food along with your sketch pad.

DAPHNI AND THE WINE FESTIVAL: Every summer, from mid-July to mid-September, the numerous wineries of Greece show off their wares at a ten-week festival at Daphni, five miles southwest of Athens on the road to Corinth. The festival is held from 7 p.m. to 1 a.m. each night in picturesque hilly grounds, with lights hanging from the trees and numerous (temporary) open-air tavernas where you can sit and dance and drink.

Buses (#100) to Daphni run every half hour from 6 a.m. to 11:30 p.m. from Koumoundouro Square.

Admission to the festival grounds is 50 drs, but you can wander around at will drinking as much as you want of the 50 or 60 different varieties of wine, dispensed from various barrels by smiling girls in Greek costume. You'll need a glass or decanter, both of which are available on the spot for 20 drs. Food is served cafeteria style and on paper plates. There's also a first-class restaurant where 200 drs brings you a four-course meal and cabaret. There's also dancing to a live band.

There's dancing outside most of the tavernas, and tables are ringed around the dance floor, so that it's almost as much fun to watch as it is to dance. Keep your admission ticket stub: there's a midnight drawing for a barrel of wine.

Greek families tend to bring their own picnic baskets stuffed with food, collect a decanter of wine, and sit there all evening watching the fun. There's a donut stand, several places to buy roast corn, souvenirs and other items, but no salt available. If you want to enjoy the corn, bring some.

Daphni is also the site of a sixth-century **monastery** that contains some of the finest mosaics in the world, according to the experts. One guide says that "Daphni is to Byzantine what the Acropolis is to classical art," so you might plan to take a look. Come to think of it, you'd better go there on your way to the festival rather than afterwards—you won't be able to see the mosaics for the wine.

6. Eleusis

Fifteen miles northwest of Athens, along a noisy, shabby road that once was The Sacred Way, lies the small town of Eleusis, known today for the production of oil, aluminum and soap. But once Eleusis (pronounced "Elefsis") was a site renowned throughout the world for its annual rites, known as the Eleusinian Mysteries, which brought as many as 30,000 pilgrims at a time along The Sacred Way for nine-day ceremonies culminating in a dramatic performance that initiates were forbidden (under threat of death) ever to talk about.

For almost 1,300 years, until the seventh century, the Eleusinian Mysteries were the world's pre-eminent secret society. The Roman writer Aeneas Gazaeus wrote that those who presided over the Mysteries "boast that by their magical songs they are able to evoke superior intelligences and the spirits of the dead." Notwithstanding all the secrecy, later writers seem to have concluded that the Mysteries were largely devoted to freeing the initiate from his or her fear of death.

What remains of ancient Eleusis is surprisingly impressive, despite the distinctly unmystical surroundings (oil refineries, cement factories, ship-building yards) and in some ways is more interesting than the Acropolis in Athens. For anybody who likes to potter among old ruins, dreaming and speculating, Eleusis is a delight. Very few tours ever go there and visitors are few and far between. Perfect!

The site is open 8 a.m. to 7:30 p.m. (Sundays: 10 a.m. to 2 p.m.); the museum on the grounds is closed between 1 and 3 p.m. Take the #68 bus from Eleftherias Square; trip takes about half an hour. Next to the ruins is a delightful open-air cafe, **Cava Doro,** where you can eat and drink under the vine trees very cheaply.

THE PELOPONNESE

THE PELOPONNESE is the vast slab of variegated terrain in the southwest corner of Greece. It is rich in legendary names—Corinth, Sparta, Tripolis—and in historic sites, but because much of it is both rural and relatively inaccessible, it has changed less than many other sections of the country.

Epidaurus, where a festival of ancient Greek drama is held in the centuries-old theater (see Chapter X) is a mere three-hour boat ride from Piraeus, and Corinth, where a 70-year-old canal technically turned the Peloponnese into an island, is only a couple of hours by bus, but the rest of the Peloponnese requires more specific planning.

Parts of the east coast are accessible via twice-weekly boat; thrice-weekly flights go to Kalamata in the southwest; trains visit most of the big cities, and buses, both local and long-distance, cover the rest.

But the best way of all to visit is by car, and in the pages that follow, I have outlined a trip taking about three days, covering almost 600 miles. Be sure to get gasoline coupons (by producing your car registration papers at the National Bank) before you set off.

The trip covers Corinth and its ancient ruins a few miles away, the ancient tombs at Mycenae, the lovely port of Nafplion, Tripolis, the ruins of Megalopolis, the seaside town of Kalamata, up the west coast from Pilos to Pyrgos, to Olympia where the Olympic Games began in 776 B.C., and back to Athens via Tripolis and Corinth.

But first a word about—

TOURS OF THE PELOPONNESE: You might consider letting **Viking's Tours** do all the work for you on a tour of this interesting peninsula. Five-day tours start from the Viking's office in Athens (3 Filellinon Street, tel: 3229-383) every Thursday all year round (also on Tuesday and Saturday April through October). Tours cost $90 for students, teachers, military and airline staff, and senior citizens over 60 ($100 for others) and include transportation, accommodations, and the services of a knowledgeable English-speaking guide.

Viking's also conducts a one-day tour to Delphi ($18), and a one-day tour of Corinth, Mycenae and Epidaurus ($25 with lunch, $21 without).

1. Corinth

A comparatively narrow stretch of land—less than two miles—sits between the waters of the Gulf of Corinth and the Gulf of Saronikos. But ships too big to cross this stretch of land (for several hundred years, smaller ships were actually hauled across on rollers!) had to go all the way around the Peloponnesian coast, an extra 200 miles, before continuing their journey east or west.

Not surprisingly, the idea of cutting a canal across the narrow isthmus occurred to many people, Caligula, Hadrian, Caesar, and Nero among them. Nero actually got the work started (in 62 A.D.) after discovering earlier plans from the seventh century B.C. and, with the aid of several thousand slaves, dug wide trenches. But the work was interrupted and, for some reason, never resumed, although piled-up earth was discovered along with other traces of digging.

It was not until the late 19th century that the canal was finally dug.

Just after crossing the canal, you'll arrive at Corinth. The town itself hasn't much to offer except a beach—pebbly but popular—and some nearby cafes at which you can sit and listen to rock-and-roll-filled jukeboxes.

In the early days, Corinth took advantage of its situation to concentrate upon commerce. It exacted heavy customs duties on traffic between the Peloponnese and the Greek mainland, and did a lot of export trade. St. Paul came here to address the Corinthians, because he regarded them as lascivious and pleasure-loving.

At the end of the second century A.D., it was considerably improved by Hadrian and Herodus Atticus, and its beauty was renowned throughout Greece.

The city of Corinth today is a new one, situated on the Gulf, more than three miles from the ancient city, which was devastated by earthquakes.

Buses to Corinth leave from Kavalas and Kifissiou Streets in Athens—this is the new Peloponnese station from which all buses to this region leave (tel: 5129-232). A taxi to the station from Omonia will cost you 240 drs.

EATING AND SLEEPING IN CORINTH: Right by the railroad station, at the beginning of town, is the **Hotel Apollon** (18 Prinis, tel: 22587) with singles for around 350 drs, doubles 400 drs all with bath, plus a handful of cheaper, bathless rooms; this hotel has seen better days. Slightly cheerier is the **Acropolis** (25 Vas. Georgiou, tel: 22430) with bathless rooms at a slightly cheaper price. Two blocks further down, on the square overlooking the harbor, are the tiny **Hotel Acti** (1 Vas. Constantinou, tel: 23337) with singles for 200 drs, doubles 320 drs, all without bath; and the attractive **Belle Vue** (41 Damaskinon, tel: 22088) which charges 220 drs single, 300 drs double without bath, 360 drs double with.

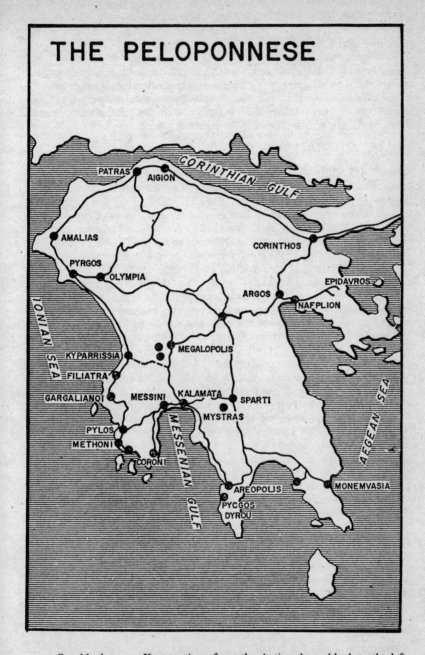

THE PELOPONNESE

CORINTHIAN GULF

PATRAS AIGION

AMALIAS

CORINTHOS

PYRGOS

OLYMPIA

EPIDAVROS

ARGOS

NAFPLION

IONIAN SEA

KYPARRISSIA

MEGALOPOLIS

FILIATRA

GARGALIANOI

MESSINI

KALAMATA

SPARTI

MYSTRAS

PYLOS

METHONI

CORONI

MESSENIAN GULF

AEGEAN SEA

AREOPOLIS

PYCGOS
DYROU

MONEMVASIA

One block up on Konstantinou from the Acti and one block to the left,
at Theokoti 41, is the **Hotel Kypselos** (tel: 22451) whose 18 rooms, all with
private bath, cost 385 drs double; with breakfast, an additional 40 drs. It's a

modern, clean place, with black leather chairs, wood beams in the lobby, and attractive, well-lit rooms with larger-than-usual double beds, desks, large mirrors, and tiled bathrooms.

In midsummer, it is often hard to find a vacant room in Corinth.

Also on the square here is the town's best restaurant, the spacious **Pantheon** which has a wide selection of dishes and a well-stocked bar. If you're around at night be sure to walk down Vas. Sophias to the water where you can sit outside the Taverna Nichtereda on an otherwise remote piece of seashore and listen to the crashing waves—and the jukebox.

WHAT TO SEE: The old town is really a small village built around the extensive ruins, in the center of which seven of the impressive columns of the **Temple of Apollo** and the skeletons of several buildings are still standing.

Towering above the whole area are the impressive ruins of the **Acrocorinth,** the amazing fortified castle atop the hill. A rough road winds up the hill, which is a long, long climb, and no buses make the trip (90 drs by taxi); it's well worth every step of the climb for what's to be found at the top.

If ever an historical site can stimulate the imagination, it is this one. The fortifications, almost as forbidding as when they were built—in medieval days—occupy a vast stretch of land around the top of the rugged mountain, and they are a child's dream, what with their towering battlements, secret underground stairs coming out below the walls, and narrow enclosed gateways with the holes still in the walls where the barricading beams slipped into place when the enemy attacked.

Although the fortress appears to be virtually invulnerable, it was captured over and over again—once in the 12th century, twice in the 13th, once in the 14th, twice in the 15th, by the Knights of Malta in the 17th, by the Venetians 75 years later, by the Turks in 1715.

Where the road ends, still several hundred feet from the summit, a path winds around through a gate in the lower walls. Between the first and second gates, and between the second and third, are two big, open areas—perfect for an ambush of invaders by defenders mounted guard on the walls ahead and above. Every inch of the upward climb must be fought on the defensive, with attacks coming from three sides. Because the high walls are virtually insurmountable, it is difficult to see how the castle could ever be taken except by a long siege. A half-concealed hole in the ground houses steps leading through underground tunnels to unobtrusive openings below the walls—exits presumably used by people in the castle who didn't want to leave by the front gate (patrols, maybe, sent out at night during attacks?).

The view from the summit of the mountain is magnificent and proves conclusively that whoever held the castle controlled the gateway between the Peloponnese and the Greek mainland. The gulfs at both sides of the canal can be seen, and the panoramic view covers miles of countryside in every direction.

Not the least of the attractions of the old fort was its female population: 1,000 sacred prostitutes whose function, or at any rate details of it, is rather squeamishly overlooked by all the guide books. The temple in which they operated was said to be "luxurious" due to the rich tribute they were paid, but the historians display their usual reticence about a subject as potentially interesting as this.

2. Mycenae

About 40 miles from Corinth, halfway along the road to Argos are the ancient ruins of Mycenae, mentioned by Homer in the *Iliad* and the *Odyssey*. A thriving civilization existed at Mycenae at least 1,500 years before the Romans began to dominate the world, and it became a rival empire to that of King Minos of Crete.

Golden Mycenae flourished mainly between 1600 and 1100 B.C., its decline beginning with the death of its king, Agamemnon, who was murdered by his wife Clytemnestra and her lover Aegisthus, when his triumphant return from a victory over Troy proved inopportune. Many later writers—among them Aeschylus, Sophocles and Euripides—dealt with this tragedy, the subsequent avenging of Agamemnon's fate by his children and their own tragic deaths. Mycenae, clearly, was steeped in bad news and only too vulnerable to attack by the Dorians when they invaded the Peloponnese later in the century.

It was the German archaeologist Heinrich Schliemann who first decided to investigate Mycenae, and from 1876 onwards he and his successors uncovered remains of palaces, aqueducts and tombs proving to Schliemann's satisfaction that Homer's writings about the place were based on fact. Excavations still proceeding have recently uncovered the remains of a perfume and cosmetic factory, in front of the citadel (nearest to the road), and it is thought that the Mycenaeans built up a thriving export trade in these commodities.

The citadel's walls are so massive they became known as "Cyclopean," after the one-eyed monster from Asia Minor whose strength, it was felt, must have been called upon to erect them.

The vaulted tombs, including one said to be that of Agamemnon (found empty), are probably the most interesting to visitors. Skeletons were found in some, along with at least 30 pounds of gold brooches and precious objects.

The remains of the ancient city are on, around, and underneath a cone-shaped hill about half a mile up the main road from the village. It was a commanding position dominating the roads from Corinth across the isthmus, and a lookout on the adjoining mountain, Prophet Elias, gave it a view to the sea. It was from here that a sentry warned Clytemnestra of Agamemnon's return from Troy.

The renowned **Lion Gate,** one of the few features to be situated above ground before excavation, depicts two lions resting their paws on a central column which sits on an altar—interpreted by historians as a symbol of the power granted by the gods to the king.

Mycenae is open from 7:30 a.m. to sunset weekdays, 10 a.m. to 1 p.m. and 3 to 6 p.m. on Sundays. Nearby is the charming 13-room hotel **Le Petit Planette** (tel: 66240), with friendly English-speaking owners and rooms for 500 drs double including breakfast. Dinner (usually excellent) costs 165 drs. Another choice, a little further away at the entrance to the town of Mycenae, is the **Hotel Agamemnon** (tel: 66222) with similar rates. There is also a youth hostel nearby with bunks for 50 drs.

Buses run to Mycenae from Argos and Corinth, with the last bus back to each at 8 a.m. and 11 p.m. respectively.

The road from Mycenae to Argos is through fertile country, with melons for sale piled up beneath the trees that line the road. An ancient castle upon the hill (**Kastro**), to the right, identifies Argos.

3. Nafplion

Said to have been founded by Poseidon's son Nauplios, this pleasant waterfront town became the seat of the revolutionary government in 1822 during the long fight against the Turks. It was proclaimed first capital of the Greek state.

Buses to Nafplion leave from Kavalas and Kifissiou Streets in Athens—see the schedule at the end of chapter VIII.

WHAT TO SEE AND DO: The cafe-filled stretch along the harbor makes for a pleasant stroll at night, and when you reach the end of the waterfront you can continue, along a more romantic path, leftwards under the carved rock tunnels at the foot of the cliffs and around the bay to bring you back into town. This whole walk takes about 25 minutes. Towering 600 feet above you, towards the end of this stroll, is the proud **fortress of Palamidi,** which guarded the approach to the city and was later used as a prison. A paved road to the top has made the 899 steps somewhat obsolete but some hardy adventurers still make the climb.

Other interesting buildings around town are the Venetian-built **Archaeological Museum** housing finds from Mycenae and Tiryns; the graceful structure, with pillars and palm trees, on Sediras Merarx Street which houses the tourist police, but would not be out of place on a Georgian plantation; and the picturesque fortress on the islet of Bourtzi in the harbor. Once the home of the Palamidi executioner, it was, for a while, a luxury hotel but is now deserted. Boat rides out to the island and back can be made from the harbor.

At night take in a movie at **Trianon** (shows at 8:30, 10:30, and 12:30) just down a side street off Sediras Merarx, or visit one of the discotheques. By day head for the beach at **Tolos,** a 15-dr ride on buses that leave Nafplion every hour and return on the half hour. A much more secluded beach is that of **Candia,** seven kms beyond where the main road forks right to Tolos. It is accessible by car or motor cycle. Two kms past the last horseshoe bend where the road enters a ravine, continue to the end of the gorge and take the dirt road past the house on the right and drive about one mile to the sea. Watch out for tar on the beach.

WHERE TO EAT AND STAY: Most of the hotels are near to the harbor or around Syntagma Square not far away.

The **Hotel King Othon** is your best bet, just off the harbor at 3 Farmakapoulou Street (tel: 275-85), charging 300 drs single, 400 drs double for rooms without bath. It's old and comfortable, the interior dominated by a metal spiral staircase winding to the upstairs rooms. The friendly manager speaks English.

On Syntagma, the **Hotel Athena** (tel: 276-95) has rooms without shower for 275 drs single, 350 drs double. Breakfast costs 40 drs showers are 20 drs. A simple, clean place.

The attractive **Hotel Dioskouri** (Zigomala and Vyronos, tel: 286-44) is on a hill overlooking the town; its 51 rooms offer a charming view over the sea. Rates are 400 drs single, 500 drs double, all with bath.

The **Hotel Rex** (Navarinou and Bouboulinas, tel: 280-94) is a happy choice: around 360 drs single, 475 drs double. All rooms with bath. Much cheaper is the D-class **Argolis** (26, 21st of April St., tel: 272-71), whose 13 rooms cost 250 drs single, 350 drs double including bath.

Nafplion's **youth hostel** (Oreston Harmonta St., tel: 277-54) has 150 beds for 60 drs per night plus 15 drs for a sheet. Meals available.

A charming place to eat is under the trees in the center of Syntagma Square itself. Neat rows of tables, covered in spotless white cloths, with sparkling wine and water glasses, await the late diners in the evening. They are serviced from the **Ellas** restaurant (its blue neon sign merely reads "Restaurant") and prices are low.

More picturesque, is the outdoor **Grill Room** of the Hotel Bretagne, around the corner from the King Othon Hotel and facing the water and the Hotel Bourdzi.

The lovely **Restaurant Fikos** is set in a pretty, leafy garden with a 187-year-old tree. It's a cool spot with menu in Greek only, but feel free to look into the kitchen across the street to choose your dinner.

On the edge of town, within walking distance (and a bus stop right opposite) is the attractive, modern 18-room **Hotel Alkion** (Argons 40, tel: 28114) with balconies to every room, bathtubs (instead of the more common shower), and lounges overlooking the sea. Rooms are around 350 drs single, 450 drs double.

As befits a town founded by the sea god's son, Nafplion excels in seafood. **Elatos,** on the harbor, is one of the best places to eat and if you can't find it rest assured that the woman who runs it will find you, dragging you back to her tables to feast on red snapper or shrimp. Finish up with a coffee at the swinging cafe—that is to say the cafe with real swings further down the waterfront.

From July onwards the best view with your lunch or dinner is from the rooftop of the Hotel Agamemnon. Try one of the breath-taking pastries from the cafe with the Kodak sign just down the side street from the harbor.

READERS' SELECTIONS: "Just outside of Nafplion we came across a real find, the **Plaka Hotel** (tel: 594-20). It's new, very attractively decorated, with balconies with two views in all rooms, an airy dining room overlooking a flowery terrace, and its own small beach across the road. The cost was about 500 drs a night for two including breakfast. The best way to find it is to ask directions of the police in Nafplion and then follow the signs" (Beatrice F. Stein, New York, N.Y.). . . . "I found **Tolos** to be a very pleasant place. A few good hotels, an excellent little restaurant called the **Argiris,** and a lovely view from the rooms to rent beside the beach" (John Hekkenberg, Bussum, Holland).

4. Tripolis

The road westward to Tripolis is lined with lush tobacco fields and racks of the drying leaves; then the road begins to climb, looping backwards and forwards around the contours of the hill. The view at night is probably the most spectacular, the lights gradually receding into the distance behind.

Tripolis (pop: 18,400) is not much of a town. Primarily an industrial center specializing in carpets, tin plate, and leather, it is also a market town for the products of the fertile countryside round about, and among the crops (says Hachette's *Blue Guide*) is hashish.

It makes a suitable resting place, however, before heading south to Sparta or west to the coast, and there are two good hotels on Kolokotroni Square (named after the Greek revolutionary hero who captured the town from the Turks in 1821): the 20-room **Hotel Semiramis** (tel: 22244; 375 drs double without bath, 450 drs with) and the 32-room **Hotel Alex** (275 and 450 drs, 35 drs for breakfast). All rooms have balconies.

Same rates at the pleasant little **Hotel Anactoricon** (Konstantinou 66, tel: 22545, just off the main square). Breakfast 35 drs. Rock-bottom rates at the **Krystal** (K. Palaiologos 3, off JFK Street) and the **Hotel Byron** (Filellinon 20, tel: 22783) with bathless rooms for around 200 drs single, 330 drs double.

The expensive **Hotel Menalon** has balconies overlooking a wide square where cafe-sitters listen to the band and others stroll. It's a pleasant part of town, adjoining a small park with shady cafe.

John F. Kennedy Street, parallel to Konstantinou Street, is also the home of the town's two best eating places—the **Kepossosoli Lounge** and the nearby **Sosolis** restaurant. Both pleasant, offering little gardens filled with tables and a warm welcome to customers who check out what's available in the kitchen.

There are nine daily buses to Athens in summer, the first at 5:30 a.m.; the last at 10 p.m., and others to Olympia, Pyros, Patras and Astros. All these leave from the large modern bus station. Buses to Sparta (four daily) leave from a subsidiary bus station around the corner.

The buses to Tripolis leave from Kavalas and Kifissiou Streets in Athens. Call 5134-575 for schedules.

READER'S SELECTION: "I spent a week on a beach near the town of **Diakofto.** Every guest gets a small hut on the beach and pays for items with a string of beads in the style of the Club Med. Meals and drinks are excellent and the interesting man who runs the place is friendly and speaks four languages. The beach is called **Engali-Z-Plage** and maintains an office in Athens at 6 Ag. Konstantinou Street" (Geoffrey Wilson, Long Beach, Calif.).

5. Megalopolis

You may have gathered by now that in my opinion a small dose of ruins goes a long, long way. And I'm not the kind of traveler who goes out of his way to check off as many ancient sites as he can find.

But **Megalopolis**, about 20 miles west of Tripolis, is definitely my type of ruin. It is so undeveloped and untouristy that in the peasant village nearby, there isn't even a sign to direct you to the old site.

Coming from Tripolis, turn right at the main square, head up the road for about a mile, and then you'll see the signpost directing you to the ruins of the old theater.

A bumpy trip across the sandy path through the fields, and you'll find yourself by a cemetery. Park the car just to the right of this, and over the brow of the hill on the left is the semi-circular old theater. Only the stage area and a few of the first rows of some seats have been excavated, but a series of ridges denote where the rest are.

If it were allowed, you could probably take a spade and dig among the rows yourself and heaven knows what you might find—programs from the year 300 B.C., old opera glasses, lipsticks, maybe even chewing gum under the seats?

The setting of this theater—once the largest in Greece—is really delightful: the tranquil shade of trees, a dried up (in summer) river just across the meadow, the faint tinkle of distant goat bells, and all the sticky sleepiness of a rural pasture.

Megalopolis, of which only a few random rock piles remain (apart from the theater), was a planned town that turned out to be a failure. Originally, in 370 B.C., it was planned to be one of a chain of towns in the state of Arcadia, which would act as a buffer between warlike Sparta to the southeast and the rest of the Peloponnese.

But the manner of its founding—with citizens taken from nearby villages to populate it, like stocking a pond with fish—was unsuccessful. There was no unity, a dissatisfaction among the villagers who liked their old homes better, and no chance of saving the town when it was besieged. By the end of the first century B.C., it had almost disappeared.

The road from Megalopolis to Pyrgos, a beautiful trip, passes through the mountain village of **Andritsena,** where you can stay at the inexpensive **Hotel Bassai** (185 drs single, 275 drs double), which has a friendly owner and rooms overlooking the village fountain.

6. Sparta

Sparta, a name that once terrified the rest of the Greek world, is today a quiet town with a few traces of its ancient grandeur. It has fulfilled, with astonishing accuracy, the words of Thucydides that if someday it were to be laid waste, with only its foundations remaining, "posterity will find it difficult to believe that its power corresponded to its fame."

The Spartans of pre-Christian days were always terrifying their neighbors. War was a virtue to them and not an inconvenience, and they were trained to be tough and as ready to fight as possible. Hardly a schoolboy has not heard how the weaker babies of Sparta were left exposed to the elements on barren hillsides, on the principle that only those who could endure would make good Spartans.

Sparta, sometimes with allies and sometimes alone, was always fighting its neighbors, but until the Peloponnesian war (440-430 B.C.) against Athens and its allies, it retained a certain amount of communion with the rest of Greece.

Although it won the war, Sparta went into a gradual decline afterwards, and further wars and battles finally subdued it.

Today, it is known for its olives, oranges, and lemons, and very few of the ancient ruins remain. There is much more to be learned from the ruins of the medieval city of **Mystra,** on a hillside about five miles to the east. It is well worth the trip, a picturesque cool spot with villagers dressed much as they must have years ago, lots of donkeys, and two restaurants near the ruins. Mystra was built by the Franks in 1249, but soon captured by Byzantine Emperor Michael Palaeologus, and today is a fairly well-preserved Byzantine town with winding alleys, churches, palaces, and monasteries. It has been called "the Byzantine Pompeii." (Buses run regularly from Sparta to Mystra.)

Buses to Sparta leave from the station at Kavalas and Kifissiou Streets in Athens (tel: 5124-913).

An enormous bronze statue of a Spartan warrior wielding sword and shield is about the only tangible reminder of Sparta's ancient glories. It looms over Stadiou Street, on a pedestal outside the Stadium, facing away from the dirt road which winds around to what remains of the ancient city (not much). Stadiou Street, which boasts a row of fine palm trees, houses most of the town's hotels.

HOTELS AND RESTAURANTS: The 35-room **Dioskuri** (Lykourgou 96, tel: 28484), all rooms with bath, 400 drs single, 475 drs double; the 13-room **Cecil** (Stadiou, tel: 26371), 200 drs single, 300 drs double without bath; the **Panhellinion** (C. Paleolougou 43, tel: 280-31), 14 rooms, single or double, 250 drs without bath; and the nearby **Laconia** (C. Paleolougou, tel: 289-51), some bathless rooms averaging 240 drs single, 300 drs double. All other hotels in town are expensive.

Best restaurant in Sparta is undoubtedly the **Diethnes** on the main square. Rock-bottom prices are charged (say readers) at the **Semiramis.**

7. The Southeast Peloponnese

On Tuesdays at 8 p.m. the *Cyclades,* and on Thursdays at 9 a.m. the *Kalymnos,* leave Piraeus for the southeastern coast of the Peloponnese; calling at **Monemvassia** and **Kythera.** There's also the *Kanaris,* leaving Piraeus at 8 a.m. on Saturdays. The trip takes about seven hours.

The southeastern section of the peninsula, centered on Monemvassia (62 miles from Sparta, all except ten miles over paved roads), is interesting because of the character and history of its inhabitants.

Many of its towns and villages were fortified against the Turks, and during the centuries of Turkish rule it was the one part of Greece that was never really subjugated. Indeed, other Greeks came from all over the country to avoid persecution, and in some places this caused dissension and feuds between the newcomers and the original inhabitants.

One place where these disagreements were carried to ridiculous lengths was the village of **Pyrgos,** down on the other leg of the peninsula. A few of the houses there survive in the shape of the turret-like forts that their inhabitants built to protect them from their neighbors. (It's not worth a special trip just to see them.)

There were even occasions when they fired upon each other with miniature cannons.

Although the feuds are a thing of the past, a couple of the houses still stand.

Monemvassia itself means "only access," and the town is renowned for its Venetian and Byzantine fortress atop an enormous rock, accessible only by a stone bridge, which connects it to the mainland.

8. Kalamata

The nicest thing about Kalamata (or "Kalamai," as it is shown on some maps) is the **car camping** area about three miles east of town.

Here are two or three camping grounds amidst the orange trees right on the beach and you can either rent a tent or bring your own. There's a small restaurant, showers, cooking facilities, and a beach, and it's a cheap and painless way to try the outdoor life right beside the sea. The last time I was there, campers and trailer-travelers from numerous different nations were sunning themselves.

Two items are helpful: a sleeping bag to put on the mat floor of the tent, and rubber-soled shoes for the pebbly bottom of the sea at the point where it laps the beach.

If you don't have a car, the camp is accessible by bus from the town of Kalamata.

In the town itself, the best cheap hotel is a delightful one along the waterfront, the **Hotel Amerika** (Marzina and Navarinou, tel: 22719), which has 22 bright, spotless rooms for which it charges about 200 drs single, 300 drs double, without bath.

Two other budget choices are the **Achillion** (Kapetan Krompa 12, tel: 223-48) and the **Acropolis** (Aristomenous, tel: 220-42), both small and both with bathless rooms for about 250 drs single, 350 drs double.

Best all-around hotel in town is the **Rex** (Aristomeros Street, just off King George Square, tel: 22334). This is surprisingly luxurious, has 54 rooms, and a restaurant, bar, and roof garden—half-pension only, and expensive. From here, the #1 bus goes down to the beach.

A good restaurant for seafood is the **Acroyali,** along the waterfront a few blocks to the left of the Hotel Amerika as you face the water.

A weekly excursion tour to **Pyrgos Diron** (where the fortified homes are) departs from Kalamata every Sunday. There, a separate trip is made into subterranean grottos by a smaller boat. No regular bus runs to Pyrgos Diron, but a party of 20 or 30 can hire a bus to make the trip at the bus station at Messiris and Antemidas Streets.

Buses to Kalamata from Athens take about seven hours and leave from Kavalas and Kifissiou Streets. Call 5134-293 for schedules. Take local bus from Ag. Konstantinou Square to the bus station.

There are also daily trains (call OSE ticket office, Ag. Konstantinou St., tel: 5131-636), as well as daily Olympic flights (tel: 9292-444)

9. Pilos

The small attractive port of Pilos, on the west coast, has the remains of a 16th-century Turkish fort atop the promontory, but the most prominent event in its history is one that left no traces. This was the 1827 Battle of Navarino, which was the decisive final battle of the Greek-Turkish War.

Britain, France, and Russia agreed to impose an armistice on the two countries. Greece accepted the mediation, but Turkey did not. An Allied fleet, entering the harbor with the intent of forcing the Turkish fleet to withdraw, was fired upon, precipitating a day-long sea battle in which 84 Turkish ships were lost and 6,000 men killed. The Allies were somewhat embarrassed by this surprising victory, but Greece was finally freed as a result.

The town itself doesn't have much to detain the traveler, although it's good to take a swim off the dock in front of the **Nestor Hotel** (just around from the harbor). The Nestor's rates are around 700 drs double.

Almost next door is the inexpensive **Hotel Navarinon** (tel: 22291), whose 13 rooms without bath cost 225 drs single, 300 drs double. There's a good restaurant across the street from the Navarinon, overlooking the water. There are also two restaurants on the square, charging similar prices. Best bet is to walk around and take a look at what people are eating.

On high ground above the sea, about half a mile from the Nestor, is the modern **Castle Hotel** (tel: 21264) with roof garden and restaurant/bar. Rooms are large, with balconies overlooking the sea, and cost around 500 drs double.

Other cheap hotels are the **Galini** (tel: 21208) and the **Astir** (tel: 21204), both with bathless doubles for around 250 drs.

10. The Coastal Trip from Pilos to Pyrgos

There's a stretch of 82 miles between Pilos and Pyrgos, much of it along the coast and all of it beautiful. Two stretches of road—and a total of seven miles in all—are rocky and unpaved, but to anybody who has traveled on bad roads in Mexico or Central America, these are quite good in comparison, and any car should be able to negotiate them without trouble.

It is very fertile country, rich with sugarcane, palms, grapes, lemons, and watermelons, and gardens filled with bright orange chrysanthemums and other flowers. Thick bunches of purple grapes line the highway for the first few miles north of Pilos.

THE PALACE OF NESTOR: After several patches of cactus and groves of olive trees, a signpost indicates the Palace of Nestor (open 9 a.m. to 1 p.m. and 4-6 p.m.; Sunday 10:30 a.m. to 2 p.m.) to the left.

(One of the best guide books seen in Greece is the one prepared by the archaeologists from the University of Cincinnati. It costs 15 drs and is worth it for the clear orientation it gives to this site.)

Excavations began in 1939 after the discovery of apparently royal tombs in the region indicated that there might be a palace. Sure enough, on the most dominant hill, digging revealed pottery and other artifacts. Resumed after the war, the digging uncovered the ruins of a royal residence that, apparently, was destroyed by fire about 1200 B.C. Inscribed clay tablets, identified as economic and administrative records, were found in what appeared to have been the tax collector's office.

Despite the passage of time, much of the decorative art work on walls and tiles remained, and the booklet mentioned above includes reproductions of Piet de Jong's drawings of what the palace must have looked like. Thousands of drinking vessels and vases were discovered, and tablets bearing the word "Ela-won" (olive oil—the word still used in Greece today) identified the several storage rooms found with the remains of larger pitchers. A bathtub, with a step to assist getting into it, is undamaged and apparently had a sort of shower—a servant who poured water over the bather from a pitcher found standing nearby.

A museum at nearby **Hora** (same opening hours at the palace, closed Tuesday) has more objects from the collection.

ON TO PYRGOS: After the Palace of Nestor, you'll negotiate five miles of unpaved, rocky road punctuated with potholes, which in some ways is the most beautiful portion of the trip, with its isolated villages and fertile countryside. Then the paved road reappears just before the village of **Gargaliani.** Back onto the coast, with **Proti** island offshore, two more miles of unpaved road, and then a procession of farm wagons, kids on donkeys bearing baskets of melons and tomatoes, and wandering goats, pigs, sheep, horses.

At **Filatra,** notice the lovely bronze fountain of a nymph holding aloft a bunch of grapes and, at the far side of the village, a wire unisphere with the countries of the world shaped upon it in colored metal.

More groves of olive trees, rich red soil, and an irregular chain of cypresses on the skyline. Then a small church with a cafe attached! **Kyparissia** is a somewhat dull, oversized village, despite its prominence on the map. But the road straightens out immediately afterwards, and the next stretch is fast and easy, the road following the coast.

From Kalamata to Kyparissia, including a stop at the Palace of Nestor, takes about four hours.

Just after Kyparissia, a sign denotes the village of **Kalonero** ("good water") off to the left. Off the road about ten kms, between Kyparissia and Pyrgos, is **Bassai,** site of the fifth century B.C. **Temple of Apollo,** one of the best-preserved ruins in Greece, in a quiet picturesque setting among the trees. Just before Pyrgos, a road to the right leads to thermal baths, with a few nondescript hotels of little interest to tourists.

Pyrgos, too, is disappointing, and if you're planning to visit Olympia, it's better to head straight through; it has better hotels.

THE SHADOW THEATER: Pyrgos offers one attraction, though, that's hard to find anywhere else: a theater, the **Orpheus,** that sometimes presents shadow plays—a dying art in Greece since the arrival of movies, and presumably one that will disappear forever when television comes into its own.

The Orpheus, a little backstreet open-air theater that charges four drs admission, is filled with people of all ages, because shadow plays are truly theater of the common people, replete with topical references and scatological humor. Even if you don't understand Greek, you'll be infected by the excitement and enthusiasm.

An illuminated screen is the "stage," and one-dimensional puppet-like figures are manipulated behind it. All the different voices are delivered by the same man, who also jiggles the puppets. The characters are widely varied: women in flowing dresses, a clown with an exceptionally long nose that other characters are always reaching out to touch, a double-jointed contortionist type whose legs keep collapsing, village stereotypes who swear and spit, one who continuously puts his hand up his back to tip his hat, a couple who dance. The humor is earthy (at one point, a character greets an apparently pregnant woman as "Mrs." and stares wordlessly at her belly when she says she's not married) and provincial, with occasional scathing references to landmarks in Athens (the big city). Slapstick is another major element, with characters knocking each other down, and humorous treatment of handicaps (a man who stutters just about breaks the audience up).

Despite the language difficulties, you'll learn a great deal about Greek provincial life from shadow plays, and the reaction of the audience to each character, as he or she appears, will give you a clue as to their roles.

11. Olympia

According to the weight of historical evidence, the first Olympic Games were held in the year 776 B.C. They took place at four-year intervals after that, until they were abolished in 394 A.D. by the Roman emperor Theodosius, largely on the grounds of their being a "pagan festival."

While they lasted, they acted as a sort of latter-day United Nations, with all rivalries suspended during the seven-day duration every four years. Athletes and spectators from all parts of the Greek and Mediterranean world attended, and social intercourse was as much a part of the festivities as was the competition. There were stringent rules against passing through the area armed, and on at least one occasion Sparta was fined for an infringement of this rule.

In the years between the races, Olympia was merely a religious sanctuary. It was not a town, and only people connected with the temple lived there. But for the time of the games—during a period of full moon in midsummer—a sacred truce was proclaimed, and otherwise hostile foreigners accepted the invitations of the festively dressed heralds who had come to their countries to announce the games.

The games themselves were barred to women, presumably because the athletes mostly competed in the nude, and any woman found within the grounds was tossed from the nearby mountain top. Earliest event was a foot race of 192.27 meters, which is the length of the Olympia stadium. Later contests were combined into the pentathlon (jumping, javelin-tossing, foot race, throwing the discus, and wrestling), and after the fifth century B.C. there were even such cultural events as oratory contests, painting exhibitions, and writers reading their own works. The poet Pindar is known to have entertained in this way.

At first, the religious content of the games was stressed, and wreaths of laurel leaves or branches of wild olives were regarded as being satisfactory prizes, because of the considerable honor that was attached to winning. (Short of conquering an empire or writing an epic poem, the games were about the only route to stardom in those days.) But as the religious significance began to fade, the games became more secular and more commercial. Professionals were allowed to compete for valuable prizes, and once the Romans entered the picture, even the administration gradually became corrupt. The emperor Nero inaugurated a few new events—guitar-playing was one—in which, coincidentally, he always seemed to be the winner.

Less than half a century after the emperor Theodosius suspended the holding of the games, his son, Theodosius II, ordered the Temple of Zeus destroyed, and earthquakes and the natural ravages of time completed the destruction of the site. The ruins, at once majestic and forlorn, sit quietly at the edge of the modern town today. A couple of local guide books (the preferred one is *A Concise Guide to Olympia* by Maria Tompropoulos, published by C. Cacoulides, 39 Venizelou Avenue, Athens; available at the Olympia Museum for 30 drs), describe them adequately.

Excavations to restore the site were begun in 1829 by the French and were continued by the Germans. Another Frenchman, Baron Pierre de Coubertin, was responsible for the idea of reviving the games; in 1894, he called together the International Congress of Paris to lay the plans. The first modern games were held two years later, in 1896, at Athens, subsequent ones in Paris and St. Louis. They were suspended during World War I, and resumed afterwards. The last ones held before World War II were staged in Berlin, where the Nazis used them mainly for propaganda purposes.

Since 1936, it has been the custom to have a symbolic lighting of the Olympic torch (ignited by rays from the sun through a magnifying glass) in the sacred site at Olympia, and for this torch to be carried by relays of runners to the site of that year's Olympics.

While walking through the sanctuary be sure to look for the remains of the oldest hotel in Greece: it had 80 rooms and housed visiting dignitaries back in ancient times. Also note the gray, square pedestals which dot the site and which once held bronze statues (there were said to be over 200) called Zanes, paid for by fines imposed on the athletes for misbehavior. Zanes is the plural of Zeus, whose sanctuary this was, and despite his association with thunderbolts and sudden anger he was also known for his compassion and harmony—traits this tranquil, sun-dappled site was specifically chosen to reflect.

MUSEUM OF THE OLYMPIC GAMES: A rich collection of Olympic memorabilia, including stamps issued on the occasion of the First Olympic Games of 1896; a large number of rare photographs from Olympic Games held in Greece in 1896 and 1906; all the torches used for the transfer of the Olympic flame since the first torch relay in 1936; about 150 engravings printed in Berlin in 1892, with representations of all the objects found by the German archaeologists Curtius and Adler during the 1875-1890 excavations in Olympia; many ancient coins and tokens, and a rich library with books dating back to 1700. Also featured is the box into which was transferred the embalmed heart of Baron Pierre de Coubertin (founder of the modern Olympic Games), later deposited in a specially erected stele of marble by Prince Paul, then heir to the Greek throne (1938).

There is no question that this museum is unique in the world. Founded in 1961 by Mr. G. Papastefanou-Provatakis, it was donated to the Hellenic Olympic Committee in 1964, which now runs it.

THE OLYMPIA MUSEUM: The old museum, sitting on a hill overlooking the ruins, and the new museum, situated some 200 meters north of the ruins, contain magnificent stone statues, bronze statuettes, richly decorated weapons, and pottery, among other things.

The museum is open 8 a.m. to 1 p.m.; and 3 to 6 p.m.; 10 a.m. to 1 p.m. and 3 to 6 p.m. Sundays and Mondays. Admission (all-in ticket) 50 drs plus another 30-dr camera ticket, which comes complete with pin, if you want to take pictures in the museum. Guards strictly enforce this. Take note that certain items (such as the Olympic flame holder) are constantly being switched from one museum to the other.

In the lobby is a scale model of what the site was once like. Two rivers—one running into the Ionian Sea—crossed at Olympia, and early visitors to the games could come by boat, tying up right beside the sanctuary. Subsequent earthquakes and floods destroyed most of the site but preserved a large number of the ancient statues in 20 feet of mud.

One of the things that the statuary proves is the total realism of the sculptors of those days—the exactness of feet that couldn't even be seen (as in the case of the charioteer at Delphi) because a horse was in front, or the hole in the chest of a warrior who was being stabbed. The basic thought was that "the eye of God" was always watching so you did the job right.

The most dramatic statue in the museum is that of the Nike of the Paionios, dedicated after the victory of the Messenians over Sparta, 421 B.C. It was originally in the Temple of Zeus on a column tapering upwards for 30 feet. "The Nike seems to be flying down from Olympus in order to proclaim the victory," says the label. And the fact is that to get the impression of flying, the statue was tilted so much that it had to be weighted in the back or it would have fallen off the pedestal.

In another room, a statue of Hermes carrying Dionysos (Praxiteles was the sculptor, 340 B.C.) rests on a pedestal in sand, because Olympia has had numerous earthquakes and it is hoped that a fall onto sand will preserve it.

Some very enlightening work has been done with fragments of objects found: sketches of what the whole item would look like, incorporating the piece, invariably accompany the segment on display. There is a heavy stone, weighing 316 pounds, with a sixth century B.C. Greek inscription that, when translated, reads: "Bybon, son of Phola, has lifted me over his head with one hand."

In the lobby, in addition to a statue of the Emperor Hadrian (117-138 A.D.), is a wooden reproduction of the way Olympia possibly looked at this period or before.

But the highspots of the museum are the group of statues found on the east and west side of the Temple of Zeus. The eastern group (left side of the hall) illustrates the legend of Hippodameia and Pelops. According to the legend, a king named Oinomaos was told by an oracle that he would be killed by the man who married his daughter—but before the marriage. In an attempt to defy the prophecy, he would challenge suitors to a chariot race, with the condition that the loser of the race would forfeit his life. At least a dozen times, the king ran the race and, according to some versions, stabbed the suitor in the back before the finishing line.

Finally came the turn of Pelops who, asking for help from Poseidon (the Greek Neptune), was offered four winged horses that would never tire and could beat any that the king chose. Another version of the story has it that Pelops and the king's daughter conspired to remove the lynch pin from the king's chariot—with the aid of Myrtilos, the king's charioteer.

On the righthand side of the hall, a group of figures depicts the mythical wedding of king Peirithos and Deidameia—a wedding feast which turned into a drunken brawl, with battles between the half-horse-half-man centaurs and other wedding guests.

Note: Don't wander too far off the beaten track when you're nosing around the ruins at Olympia. There are snakes.

The **Socrates restaurant** on the main street has open-air dining and reasonable (if not inspiring) food. The charcoal grill, in an enclosed cubicle right by the sidewalk, plays a large part in enticing in the customers. Good list of wines and liquors.

By day you can take a gaily decorated buggy, drawn by a spry horse, from the old museum to the antique stadium. By night visit one of the two discotheques, **Zorba's** on top of the hill beside the Hotel S.P.A.P. and the other downtown.

HOTELS IN OLYMPIA: The cheapest hotels in Olympia are the **Hereon** (tel: 21539) on the main street, with bathless rooms for about 150 drs single, 200 drs double, and the similar **Hermes** (tel: 22577). Another bargain in Olympia is the **Hotel Pelops** (tel: 215-43), a 25-room structure on a side street just by the church, at the beginning of town as you come in from the west. It is new, without any frills, but clean and attractive and facing a nice, quiet grassy town square. Single rooms about 275 drs, double rooms 400 drs, all rooms with shower.

On the major side street are the **Hotel Olympia** and the **Hotel Apollon.** There is not much to choose between them, both being fairly plushy. The Apollon (all rooms with bath) charges 260 drs single, 320 drs double. The Olympia has 31 rooms, is slightly larger, and charges about the same.

The two major luxury hotels include the 36-room **Xenia,** which offers only demi-pension for around 1400 drs double. There's a fancy restaurant upstairs. Usually good food and a wider selection than the run-of-the-mill main street restaurants can offer. The preferred hotel in this class, though, is the older, 51-room **Hotel S.P.A.P.,** set on a hillside behind the museum, with neatly manicured lawns, a lovely flower-filled garden, the chirping of birds, mucho romance. Expensive though: all rooms with bath cost at least 700 drs double.

Even if you don't stay here, you might like to drop into the Hotel S.P.A.P.'s cute little cocktail bar and try a liqueur made by the monks at Mount Athos; the flavor will linger with you all night.

Olympia also has a **youth hostel.**

For buses (from Athens) go to station at Kavalas and Kifissiou Streets (tel: 5134-575). The trip takes six hours, costs 300 drs one way.

12. Monemvassia

Monemvassia means "only access" and the little town itself clings to the far side of an immense rock connected to the mainland by a narrow causeway. Neither the old town itself nor the ruins of the abandoned ancient city atop the rock itself can be seen from the mainland village, a sleepily charming harbor that welcomes two or three boats per week.

There are places everywhere that travel writers are instructed not to talk about by well-meaning people who wish to protect them from "the crowds" and occasionally writers go along (there's this taverna with an English-style garden and swans on the lake somewhere near Khania, for example . . .). But it is difficult to imagine crowds coming to Monemvassia—to which access can be made only by the rare boat or via an eight-hour bus ride from the more populous regions of the Peloponnese. So in a sense only those who are willing to undertake the gruelling journey to Monemvassia deserve the spoils.

For those who make the trip to this town, seemingly at the edge of the world, it's well worth the journey. There are no movie theaters, no television, and few tourists beyond the handful of nomadic types en route to Crete or an occasional pair of academics who have deliberately sought out its solitude.

WHERE TO STAY: There are three small hotels by the harbor: the preferred-choice **Akrogiani,** right above the Shell station; the **Likineion** and the tiny **Aktaion** (the only one looking over the water). All are around 150 drs single, 225 drs double.

Rooms are available at private homes for 100 or 150 drs per person. The best hotel, the six-room **Monemvassia Hotel** (tel: 61381) overlooks what passes for the town beach, a pebbly cove with gentle waves that all-too-often collects the oily tar discharged from boats so far away they are never seen. Pleasantly luxurious (simple as it is) by comparison with the rest of town the Monemvassia's rooms—all with balconies overlooking the sea—cost around 500 drs double and are an ideal place to rest up and, say, do some long-neglected typing or thinking. There are few distractions.

WHAT TO DO: Don't fail to visit the fruit shop in the alley next to the laundry, where you can buy a *karpouzi* (watermelon) and sit and eat it right at the greengrocer's own table.

To really get away from it all you must cross the causeway and visit the **old town** whose precipitous narrow streets cling precariously to the hillside on the far side of the gigantic rock. There are a couple of tavernas here and innumerable houses where you can stay for a pittance. And when you summon the energy a climb up the hillside to visit the **ruins** of what must have once been a magnificent hilltop city is absolutely mandatory.

The island was formed by an earthquake in the fourth century and by the end of the following century was already fortified because inhabitants from the region of Lakonia took refuge there when chased by the Slavs. Over the years the castle was made more and more impregnable and withstood a siege by the Normans in 1147 and another by the Franks in 1246. This last siege lasted for three years during which the inhabitants were reduced to eating rats.

Monemvassia's heyday was during the reign of the Emperor Paleologos (1283-1341), a period of cultural and economic development when a considerable navy was developed and the number of homes reached 800. There were also 40 churches of which many ruins remain today.

Because of the close proximity within which Turks and Greeks lived there was considerable harmony during the centuries of Turkish occupation, and the Byzantine churches were neither damaged nor converted into mosques. The 13th-century **church of Agia Sofia,** built by the Emperor Androuikos, still stands at the north side of the castle today and is the only complete building.

Allow plenty of time to wander among the castle ruins; they are quite extensive and usually deserted. Be careful as you walk about, however; there are no clear paths and at dusk there is a danger of falling into the unguarded cisterns sunk deep into the hill in which the inhabitants collected and stored water.

Until about a century ago a wooden bridge, built by the Venetians, connected the island with the mainland. It was destroyed when the main road to

Sparta was constructed but traces of the 14 arches that supported it can still be seen at both sides of the causeway.

GETTING THERE: The trip to Monemvassia by boat takes about six hours from Piraeus via the *Kalymnos,* which leaves at 9 a.m. on Thursdays. On Saturdays, the *Kanaris* sails from Piraeus for Monemvassia at 8 a.m., arriving around 3 p.m. On Tuesdays the *Cyclades* sails at 8 p.m.

Chapter XII

THE GREEK ISLES

1. The Cyclades
2. The Argo-Saronic
3. The Sporades
4. The Northeastern Aegean

DON'T LET THE TITLE of this chapter mislead you: I'm not going to ship you off to all the Greek islands in one chapter. Even the three chapters devoted to the islands are woefully incomplete. Greece is bordered by three seas—the Aegean, the Mediterranean, the Ionian—and in those waters lie : . . how many islands? Some, like Crete, are almost small countries unto themselves. Some seem like mere villages placed incongruously in the middle of an ocean. Some belong to just one family. Some aren't populated at all. Perhaps you'll discover your very own island. Perhaps you'll buy it. But first let me introduce you, here and in the next two chapters, to the island style of life.

1. The Cyclades

The biggest and best-known group of Greek Islands, the Cyclades, are so named because they circle **Delos,** in ancient times the holiest place in Greece. Each of the islands in the group is different in character—easier to experience than to explain—and each has its own special fans.

ANDROS: Andros is one of the greener islands, with woods and fresh mineral springs. The main town, **Hora,** on the east coast, has a pleasant cheap hotel: the 15-room **Aegli.** It is quite a prosperous island, with several small resort towns, including the beaches at **Batsi** in the west and **Korthion** to the south.

READER'S SELECTION: "The island of Andros is the closest thing to paradise I have seen. Our stay at the **Xenia Hotel** (tel: 222-70) was memorable due to the kindness of manager Diana Pendeli, who speaks English, French, German. Hotel is on the water, half the rooms overlooking the sea, and the beach is nearby." (Faith Webb, Trinidad).

TINOS: This is an island known mainly for an ikon (who made the famous remark that the trouble about iconoclasts is that they become ikons?)—one that reputedly restored the sight of a man who prayed to it. The ikon, the **Madonna of Tinos,** prompts an annual parade through the streets in late March and mid-August each year, the rest of the time sitting in the lovely church atop the hill in **Agios Nikolaos,** the main port where the m/s *Richmond* docks.

It's an easy 15-minute walk up the hill to the church, now greatly enlarged. Its semi-enclosed patio is as white as whitewash, marble, and painted trees can make it. (Do you remember in *Alice in Wonderland* when the courtiers painted the roses red because the queen also wanted to improve on nature?) A mosaic of colored pebbles leads to the steps, and inside, the church is thickly hung with gold and silver lamps, boats, and other offerings.

The hill leading up to the church is actually the town's main street and, at its foot, a green and orange relief map of the island sits in the center of a stagnant pool, its sickly colors giving the appearance of a bloated animal. The island has 60 small villages, most of them nestling into the hillside, like nuts in the nougat sold by all the harbor cafes.

In the Middle Ages, the Venetians occupied the island (13 miles by 7 miles), and traces of their capital, **Exoburgo,** now a ghost town, still remain. Another small village, **Pirgos,** has a school of fine arts, and is likely to produce many more fine sculptors to add to the considerable number who have come from Tinos in the past.

The streets leading up from the harbor have a special charm. One is chiefly a tourist market, lined with stalls selling four-foot candles, bags, ikons, baskets, but the others are quiet, narrow, and full of uncommercial life. "Steps and steep alleyways slip between cubic houses," is the way the tourist bureau's folder poetically puts it.

Restaurants and Hotels

With the exception of the clean, modern **Hotel Theoxenia** (tel: 22274), on the hill leading up to the church, most of the town's hotels and restaurants stretch around the harbor. The Theoxenia has 31 rooms, for which it charges 350 drs single, 400 drs double, without bath; with bath, around 550 drs.

The hotels along the harbor are nearer to the center of activity and there's not much to distinguish one from another. The tasteful, 42-room **Poseidonian,** with creamy white walls and duck-egg-blue shutters, charges 200 drs single, 300 drs double without bath (400 drs single, 500 drs double with); the older-looking **Flisbos,** 200 drs single, 300 double, with some rooms with bath for 400 drs double; the 17-room **Avra,** a low-slung building compared to the others, same rates as Flisbos. Completing the group, on the left side of the harbor, is the 25-room **Tinion,** around 500 drs double.

READER'S SELECTIONS: "The pension of **Mrs. Alexandra Psaltis** (on your left when facing the big church on the hill, behind the main street) is very pleasant. Sign says 'Chambres à Louer.' Nearby is good local restaurant of **Satirias Phisas,** whom everyone seems to know, and whose prices are about half those of tourist places" (John Hekkenberg, the Netherlands).

Boats to Tinos

Elli at 8 a.m. Monday, noon on Tuesday, 2 p.m. on Saturday; *Aegeon* at 9 a.m. Friday; *Samena* at 8:30 a.m. Saturday.

SYROS: The only reminders that Syros was once Greece's major port are the remains of some impressive buildings, what's left of the shipbuilding industry, and the fact that it's still a stopping-off place to catch boats to some other islands without having to go all the way back to Piraeus.

A smaller harbor than the main one curves around behind the Hotel Hermes, opposite the boat dock, and this is punctuated with tiny strands of pebble beach. One imagines the water here is not too pure but townspeople use

the beaches extensively. At its far end, a small taverna charges 5 drs for use of the showers and changing cubicles.

The main action in **Hermoupolis,** as Syros' port is called, centers around **Miaouli Square,** dominated at one side by the twin-towered government building with its enclosed patio and (padlocked) well. The post office, telegraph office, and two movie theaters are located on this square, which is a pleasant place to sit at a cafe table under the trees.

Thirty-nine wide steps lead up to the government building, behind which you can keep climbing indefinitely. The **museum** is up this way but if you keep heading right you'll eventually come to the blue-domed **church** from which steps lead down into the secondary harbor and the little beaches.

The best beaches, however, are in the other direction, right out of town. Buses run to **Azolimnos, Vari, Megas Yalos,** and **Poseidonia** to the west and to **Finikas, Galissas,** and the fishing port of **Kimi** to the north. You can also catch a bus to **Ano Syros,** the original capital with its picturesque streets and **Capuchin monastery.** This is situated on one of the conical hills that you can readily see as you approach Hermoupolis by sea.

Perhaps the most colorful sections of the port are the narrow, cobbled streets down by the shipyards (opposite side of the harbor from where you disembark). Here are crumbling houses with balconies and shops selling ancient paintings and ships' supplies. The water carrier, his mural-painted tank pulled by a decrepit horse, still patrols these streets filling up tanks and jars at shops and homes that lack plumbing.

Where to Stay

Almost opposite from where the boat docks is a **tourist office** whose staff willingly find rooms (from 100 drs single) for all comers and also have news of houses for rent at the various beaches.

The nicest hotel is the nearest: the 28-room **Hermes** (tel: 28510), with cool, comfortable lobby, good restaurant, and a pleasant garden in the rear. Rooms here cost around 235 drs single, 375 drs double without bath; 425 drs single, 550 drs double with.

The aging **Aigaion** nearby is a bit tattered but clean enough, and its spacious airy rooms overlooking the harbor seem reasonable at 200 drs single,

300 drs double (without bath). On Miaouli Square the venerable, sturdy-looking **Kykladikon** (tel: 22280) has bathless rooms for 200 drs single, 275 double. A quieter hideaway is the pleasant **Hotel Europe** (Odos Proion, a street parallel to the harbor towards the shipyards). Thirty-eight rooms here, ranged around a garden patio, cost 300 drs single, 360 drs double.

Boats from Syros

Monday: *Lemnos,* 2 p.m., to Piraeus; *Cyclades* at 1:30 p.m. to Paros, Naxos, Ios, and Santorini. Tuesday: 9:30 a.m., *Chrisi Ammos* to Tinos, Andros, and Raphina (about 30 kms north of Athens); *Cyclades* at 11 a.m. to Piraeus. Wednesday: *Chrisi Ammos,* same as Tuesday. Thursday: 2 p.m. *Lemnos* to Piraeus; 11:30 p.m., *Cyclades* to Paros, Naxos, Ios, and Santorini; *Chrisi Ammos,* 9:30 a.m., to Tinos, etc. Friday: *Cyclades* at 9:30 a.m. to Piraeus. Saturday: *Cyclades* at 1:30 p.m. to Paros, Naxos, and Amorgos; *Lemnos* at 2 p.m. to Piraeus. Also daily sailings at 5 p.m. of the *Apollon* and the *Naias* to Piraeus.

Boats to Syros

From Piraeus at around 7:45-8 a.m. daily, with extra boats on Thursday and Saturday.

MYKONOS: Mykonos, almost everybody's favorite island, has become host to the widest range of tourists. Campers there are a-plenty—Paradise and Super Paradise beaches have become glorious nomadic towns for youthful wayfarers on their way to and from Israel and India. But even for those who sojourn with more sophistication, such as the older first-class adventurers at the Xenia and Lito, Mykonos is reminiscent of our own lost moments, when the most innocent childhood discovery could transmute an ordinary day into a golden one. Mykonos is for those who can rediscover the luxury of a life that needs nothing beyond bare necessities to supplement the pure diet of sun, sea, and sky.

The winding alleys, they say, were built to confuse pirates but resident and visitor alike savor their secrets. Perhaps you'll drag yourself away from the crowded harbor cafes to take a walk up the hills into the barren countryside where infrequent farms are surely outnumbered by tiny chapels topped with shiny domes, and where, on a steep path, the pastoral solitude will be interrupted by the sudden bleating of a herd of goats and the jingle jangle of their bells.

The lesson of Mykonos is the richness of simplicity.

Most of one's time in Mykonos is spent sitting aimlessly at the port cafes watching the crowds go by: the harbor life always seems to be a confrontation between those on the way somewhere and the others who like to watch them getting there.

New arrivals take photos of the famous hammy pelicans (which have been proliferating so fast they now seem to be in almost every alley) and the birds have become so closely associated with the island that they have now been immortalized on T-shirts.

Where To Stay

Dozens of householders meet every boat as it docks and anybody offering a room can be trusted implicitly. Rooms in private homes now cost 100-150 drs, doubles 250 drs. Single rooms are hard to come by and in midsummer it's almost impossible to get a room for only one night.

The solitary cheap hotel, the 19-room **Apollon** right on the harbor, is fine (if you can get a room) and costs around 230 drs double; 330 drs double with bath.

Just to the right of the **youth hostel** (go up steps to your right as you leave boat dock) is the **Pension Maroulena,** which, although it caters to package tour groups from England, usually has a room available (about 150 drs per person). If not there are three or four places within a hundred yards of it to choose from. This entire street is now almost all rooming houses, in fact.

Nicest hotel in town is the **Kouneni** (tel: 22301), off the main shopping street behind the harbor, next to Fouskis' restaurant. It has spacious elegance in an otherwise crowded town—but it's expensive: around 420 drs single, 750 drs double including breakfast. More pleasant are the **Theoxenia** (tel: 22230), near the windmills, and the lovely **Leto** (tel 22207), at both of which you'll be required to pay for at least half-board. This costs around 700 drs single, 1200 double at the Theoxenia, slightly less at the Leto.

Biggest bargains may be the 15-room **Monto** (tel 22330) just off taxi square, or the nearby 15-room **Delfini;** each of them charge about 400 drs double. No breakfast is served, but the tastiest donuts in Greece are available hot and fresh at the bakery a few doors away. Of the two, readers prefer the Delfini.

You can live expensively at **San Stefanos** beach, about three miles north of town, at the **Alkistis** (about 1000 drs demi-pension); or somewhat more economically in the lovely **Hotel Rhenia** bungalows (tel: 22300), whose owner always meets the boat in a station wagon—ask him if he has a room. If you want to stay at the Rhenia, it makes good sense to book through Viking's in Athens, as their tour groups occasionally stay there. Rooms around 700 drs double including breakfast. The Rhenia's comfortable bungalows are about 15 minutes' walk from town—two thirds of the way toward San Stefanos beach— and just up the hill from the sea. Buses run every hour until 11 p.m.

Just outside town in the other direction (south) is the charming **Hotel Mykonos,** whose 16 rooms cost around 400 drs single, 500 drs double including breakfast. Nearby is the new and similarly priced **Hotel Rochari,** whose 40 rooms overloook the town. Both, within easy walking distance of the harbor, are on the road that encircles the back of town, a main road from which side roads run off to **Ano Mera** (a dusty hilltop village in the island's center) and **Plati Yalos,** the most popular beach.

If you don't turn off this road, you'll head past the somewhat shabby **Megali Ammos** beach (location of the otherwise attractive **Mykonos Beach Hotel**) eventually to **Hornos** beach, site of both the **Paralos Beach House** and **Ornos Bay Hotel.** Each costs around 400 drs single, 500 drs double.

Best idea of all is to book your room before arriving (phone from Athens or book through Viking's), because otherwise you might end up sleeping, as hundreds do, on the beach. Of course, if you have a sleeping bag or blanket (or better still, a tent) it makes a lot of sense to head right for **Paradise Beach** and do just that. Taverna there and daily boats back to town.

If worse comes to worst, leave your bags in the custody of some friendly cafe, after eating there, and watch for "Rooms for Rent" signs in windows. The **tourist police** will always act as a last resort and find you a room if there's one left in town.

Where to Eat

You'll find several restaurants among the bars, shops, cafes, and whatnot on the town's "Main Street," the one that starts just before Taxi Square, leads behind the harbor, and winds around for about a mile back to the bottom end of the harbor. A walk along this street is a good way to get your bearings; stroll the length of it, then return to one of the restaurants you found attractive. If it's sheer setting you're looking for, head for the area along the waterfront below the windmills—picture postcard perfect.

There are several restaurants right along the harbor, and plenty of souvlaki stands in Taxi Square and in the area just behind the harbor at its bottom end (good french fries here, too).

Right in Taxi Square is **Antonini's,** a perennially popular place, especially with Mykonos residents, who move in later in the evening after the tourist throngs have moved on. All Antonini's food is neatly laid out for inspection. After dinner, the nearby **Manto Cafe** is a choice stop for pastries and cappucino as well as the most favorable spot to watch the late-night drinkers cavorting at the adjoining **Pierro's.** Check out the two **bakeries** behind Manto.

New restaurants keep popping up in lesser-traveled side streets. Among the nicest are the stylish **Katrin** and the **Edem,** set in a pleasant garden.

What to See and Do

The pier, where all boats dock, forms one side of what is an almost perfectly horseshoe-shaped bay. If you bear right, and keep going right when you leave the pier, you'll follow the coastline around a series of bays, above one of which, on a slight incline, is a trio of windmills. One of them is always operating, and a sign in three languages invites visitors to enter.

Upstairs, the flour-covered miller, cramped into a space about as big as a Volkswagen, explains with gestures the working of the mill. As the big canvas-fitted sails revolve in the wind, their fluttering blends with the uneven wobble of the meshing wooden gears inside—and so the corn is ground. Atop the sacks of unground corn sits a wire rack of colored postcards and souvenir picture books of Mykonos.

Behind the windmill are the grounds of the plush Hotel Xenia, and in front of the mill is the town's most famous photographic landmark—a row of old houses whose walls are lashed daily by the sea, as they have been for centuries. Stumbling upon this little bay at night, lured from a casual stroll through nearby streets by the sound of waves lapping on cobblestones, brings memories of Venice.

The twisting turning alleys, spotlessly scrubbed and clean enough for bare feet (their rough cobblestones are outlined in whitewash, as is the Greek custom), form a maze impossible for the uninitiated to fathom quickly. The only rule it is helpful to remember is where the sea lies, always keeping its location clearly in mind, even when it can't be seen or heard.

Nighttime invests these same alleys with a very special mood and a silence (for they are too narrow for traffic) that is impelling. The leaves of a tree rustle, a youth sings to his girl (they pass, arm in arm, moments after his voice was first heard from blocks away); every sound is an incident. A woman sits making lace on her doorstep, the blouses and dresses for sale spread out on the bed inside the narrow room.

A stop at a museum would not be at all inappropriate: the pleasant **Mykonos Folk Museum** illustrates with objects the impression you probably have already formed about the island. In the tiny rooms are the likes of regional cooking implements, embroidered samplers, ikons, nautical instruments, portraits of modern Greek greats, and, for some reason, a self-portrait and letter from the late Werner von Braun. The museum has some old things too: pieces of marble and pottery from Delos, and a marble relief picturing a young man lying on the ground, under a Latin inscription meaning, "I sleep and my heart keeps watch."

To find the museum, follow the steps to the right of the Tourist Police and bear right. No admission is charged, but it is customary to give a few drachmas to the woman who takes you on a tour of the place.

Beaches Around the Island

Boats leave the harbor until 11:30 a.m. for the distant **Paradise, Super Paradise,** and **Ilia** beaches. All are nude beaches by common consent, although technically this is still illegal and every now and then there's a bust. Super seems to have become almost entirely gay. Paradise and Super are a longish walk across rocky hillsides past **Plati Yialos,** which is reached via crowded buses from the harbor. (No buses during siesta.) Little boats ply fairly regularly between Plati Yialos and the trio of beaches already mentioned. All beaches mentioned have tavernas, and Plati Yialos also has a hotel (300 drs without bath, 400 drs with bath, doubles only) and rooms for rent.

Just before Plati Yialos you can hop off the bus and walk down the hillside to **Psarrou,** a lovely beach but unsuitable on windy days.

San Stefanos, three miles north of town (bus or taxi), is popular but fairly dull. There are two tavernas here, and the expensive Hotel Alkistis is nearby. On the way are the small beaches of **Tourlos** and **St. George's,** each with a taverna.

Across the island is the beautiful beach at **Kalafatis,** a long bus ride (**Ano Mera,** the only other town on Mykonos, is two-thirds of the way) but worth it for a change. The expensive Aphrodite Bungalows adjoin the beach, but the snack bar operated by the hotel is good and fair-priced.

Other beaches, known only to the cognoscenti, and with no facilities and no direct bus service, are **Ftelia** and **Kapari.** Avoid the grubby town beach.

Briefly Noted

Mykonos has an excellent **free clinic** (8 a.m. to 12:30 p.m.) just off the circular main street to the left past Kalogera. . . . If you need medical care at other hours, consult Dr. Yiorgos Giovannis, on the main shopping street near the Artemis cinema (hours: 5-8 p.m.); Dr. Ioniss Kapsipis, on the street beside the Apollon Hotel (hours 5-8 p.m.—he runs free clinic in mornings), or Dr. Athenassius Poussalogiu, above Antonini's restaurant (8-1 and 5-8). Each charge a couple of hundred drachmas for a visit, prescriptions, etc., extra. . . . The **Commercial Bank** (harbor) and the **National Bank** (behind the Tourist Police) are open 8-1 Monday through Saturday, 5-8 most weekday evenings. . . . The **Post Office,** past Taxi Square beside the town beach, is open daily from 8 a.m. to noon and 4 to 7 p.m.; lines for poste restante mail are long unless you go just after opening time. . . . The **telephone** and **telegraph** office, open until midnight in summer, is behind the Tourist Police. . . . The *Apollon,* one of the better ships on the Mykonos run, shows TV videotapes (usually Westerns) when out of range of regular Greek television transmissions.

Shops stay open late (often till 11 p.m.), since they close from 1 to 4:30 in the afternoon, so shopping is a good way to spend the evening. Be sure not to miss the store of **Yannis Galatis,** just off Taxi Square, if you're looking for designer dresses. Not cheap, but Yannis has style. (He's designed a score of stylish houses around the island.)

Nightlife

Every year there seem to be more and more bars and discotheques in Mykonos. The **Remezzo,** past the Hotel Lito, is probably the most popular, but the **Nine Muses,** just past Taxi Square, is always crowded. At the bottom end of the harbor, the **Thalamis** is small and friendly; nearby, the **Windmill** gets the one-day trippers. Most of these places operate on a basis of a one-drink minimum, as does the **Mykonos** dancing bar near the "Venice" area. Friendliest bar is the **Minotaur,** whose bearded owner, Nunyos, is a longtime Buddhist. Give him my best wishes. Other recommended bars include the **Montparnasse** (folk music and art shows), **Pierrot's** ("the beautiful people"), and Paulo's (dancing), up the alleyway off the harbor near the Apollon.

Billy's Club has eye appeal but **Fouskis' Anchor Pub** with its early Mae West and Chaplin pix has the most style. Also check out the interesting crowd at **Vengera,** on the back street where it makes a right-angle turn.

Both movie theaters are off the semi-circular main shopping street: the **Artemis,** on the square opposite the police station (turn off at fruit store on corner), and the outdoor **Lito,** behind the wine store opposite Kalogera Street. Greek movies on weekends, movies in English during the week, usually at 8 and 10 p.m. Watch the notice boards in the harbor for program details.

One unique spot that might be of interest is **Cafe Christo,** which is a combination cafe-bar and *lesky* (Greek word for card-playing casino). Owners Christos and Pamela Vasilas say it's the only place on Mykonos where gambling is legal. (Unfortunately, they didn't send me the address, but say it's "centrally located with an upstairs view of the harbor.")

Getting to Mykonos

Boats run from Piraeus at least three times daily in the busiest part of summer: usually the *Apollo* at 7:30 a.m., the *Naias* at 8 a.m., and either the *Aegeon,* the *Mimika,* or the *Elli* in the afternoons. Deck-class fare is about 200 drs, duration about seven hours.

Olympic Airways flies to Mykonos three times daily (45 minutes) for about 600 drs each way.

Boats from Mykonos

To Paros: daily excursion, except Sunday, aboard the *Megolohari,* 9 a.m. to 7 p.m.; also the *Margarita,* at 4 p.m. Monday and Tuesday, and 9 a.m. Thursday and Saturday; *Actaeon* at 8:30 a.m. Monday, Wednesday, Friday; *Naoussa* at 9 a.m. Thursday and 4 p.m. Monday, Tuesday, Wednesday, Saturday; *Elli* at 8:30 a.m. Tuesday.

To Naxos: daily excursion, except Sunday, on the *Megolohari;* also the *Margarita* (onwards from Paros) and the *Elli* (ditto).

To Ios: *Margarita* at 9 a.m. Thursday and Saturday; *Actaeon* at 8:30 a.m. Monday, Wednesday, Friday (and onwards to Santorini); *Elli* at 8:30 a.m. Tuesday (and onwards to Santorini and Crete).

To Tinos: *Naias* at 2:30 p.m. daily (and onwards to Syros and Piraeus); *Chrissi Ammos* car ferry Saturday and Monday (and onwards to Andros and Rafina).

To Piraeus: *Naias* and *Apollon* every afternoon and *Elli* at 11 a.m. Sunday, Wednesday, and Friday.

DELOS: The famous marble lions of Delos are well worth the morning excursion from Mykonos. The island of Delos was for centuries a sacred place, its history so intertwined with legend that there's no clear-cut version of what really went on. Even the island's origin is disputed.

Some versions have it that Delos just floated around, an island without fixed abode, until Apollo was born, and then was covered with gold and flowers and proudly took up its central position as the focal point of the Cyclades group of islands. Another story is that it miraculously appeared out of the sea, a gift from Zeus or Poseidon to offer hospitality to Leto, Apollo's mother, at his birth. Leto, incidentally, was supposed to have conceived Apollo illegitimately after sleeping with Zeus. Reputedly, Zeus' real wife, Hera, was chasing her vengefully—hence the sudden need for a home. All authorities are agreed about one mythical fact: that Apollo was born on Delos.

With this kind of background, it's no surprise to learn that Delos was treated with varying degrees of reverence by one ruler after another. Even the Romans seemed to have adopted its gods, and they encouraged its growth as a busy commercial center. It lay at the crossroads of important sea routes.

Long before the Romans, in the sixth century B.C., one of Athens' rulers, Pisistratus, had interpreted something said by the Delphic oracle to mean that the island should be purified by removing the graves from it. After that time, nobody was allowed to be born or to die there, seriously ill people and pregnant mothers being carefully removed to neighboring islands.

Apart from sheep, lizards, and the handful of people who operate the **tourist pavilion** (where you can stay overnight for 75 drs, but there's absolutely no necessity), waterless Delos is uninhabited today. In the summer, French archaeologists live on the island. They have been excavating for more than 100 years now, and will presumably still be at it when our current civilization also lies buried.

A guidebook to the ruins is on sale but unless one follows it dutifully step by step it is almost useless. Perhaps it's better to wander freely among the ruins allowing the island's mysteries and the many unexpected delights to manifest themselves: inside one of the temples the sound of crickets echoes their pagan song to Apollo . . . a magical mandrake plant is draped theatrically over a fluted column . . . Cleopatra (minus her head) stands against a natural backdrop of blue sky and mountain peaks. There are some fine mosaics to inspect mostly in the ancient agora but most of the treasures found during excavations— bronze statues, jugs, etc.—are on display in the museum (open 8 a.m. to 1 p.m., 3 to 5 p.m.) adjoining the tourist pavilion.

Boats leave Mykonos every morning at 8:30 a.m., allowing four hours to inspect the island (admission, 30 drs) before returning. Souvenir sellers display expensive trinkets and snacks and drinks are available at the tourist pavilion.

To the left, as you walk up from the boat, is the **Terrace of the Lions,** a fine row of carved lions (one of which is propped up with an uncarved stone "leg") which is all that remains of Naxos' gift, in the fifth century B.C., to the Sanctuary of Apollo. Who knows what secrets might be uncovered if one would but condescend to scratch the earth with his paw. Nearby is the ancient agora with attractive mosaics.

It's hot during the day, and you may not have the energy to walk all the way to the edge of the island to see what remains of the wall paintings in the **House of the Actors.** A more likely trip is over to the right, past what remains of the ancient theater, and up to the summit of the hill. Here the view is bracing, and so is the wind. The tiny island nearby is **Renia,** now also uninhabited, where Delians were taken to give birth and to die.

IOS: From the rock music beating softly down from the hills at 3 a.m. to the cafe signs offering cut-price flights to Colorado, Ios is obviously the island for young people. They come swarming off the boats to dance in the numerous discos or lounge on the gorgeous beaches, and if you are under 30, Ios is the place you're likely to run into your old college roommate or cousin's ex-boyfriend eating cheaply in one of the cafes or fishing off the pier.

Even more than Santorini, which it faintly resembles, Ios is two different communities: an exceptionally bustling one in the port, where all cafe tables in the main square are jammed the day long with travelers awaiting boats or just having disembarked; and the village on the hill—which is immensely larger than might seem at first sight. A bus from the port's eastern end connects the two every hour.

This bus stops beside a post office (where the village "begins") and continues onwards to **Mylopotos** beach. A schedule outside the post office lists buses which run late into the evening. The bus takes a circuitous route, looping back and forth across the hillside, but the pedestrian path (and steps) follows a shorter (and more laborious) route.

Where to Stay

There are rooms for rent everywhere: behind the harbor, on the path up to the village, in the village itself, or on the town beach just west of the port. Rooms cost as little as 100 drs per person, and before you commit yourself take time to sit in the harbor and have a coffee while you debate whether you want to be at sea level (so you won't have to tote bags up and down) or in the more colorful village up on the hill.

As you alight from the boat, the building to your left is **Fragipani's pension,** where doubles cost around 300 drs and the balconies offer a lovely view westward across the bay.

The hotels are all at sea level, most of them further to your left than Fragipani's and beside the town beach. First comes the pleasant **Hotel Corali** (400 drs double with bath and hot water), then, across a cow-filled field, the **Elena,** a definite bargain at 150 drs single, 225 drs double in bathless rooms. Finally, at the far end of the beach, is a **restaurant** with a big terrace sporting a dartboard and a bar, which offers rooms for 255 drs double with cold water, 350 drs double with hot water.

At the other side of the port is the **Hotel Sea Breeze** (about 425 drs double, 340 drs single, including bath and hot water), beside the bus terminal, and the **Hotel Armadoros** (with similar rates), a couple of hundred yards up the hill beside the path to the village.

Life on the Hill

Streets in the village are an intricate maze which meander up, down, and around, dead-ending just when you think you're getting somewhere. They are laid out seemingly so that wherever you are it's impossible to *see* where you are, and until you get used to it (once you stray from the main street) the only solution is to keep an eye on the sun and keep heading west. White-outlined steps will guide you to one hilltop where there's a taverna, a reconverted windmill and a discotheque. Sometimes the wind blows for days on end, ebbing and falling, propelling everything (including you) before it through the narrow streets like a bowling ball down a polished chute.

Much of Ios' water supply comes from wells at which householders fill their buckets, sometimes with the aid of a donkey hitched to the drawing mechanism and persuaded to walk round and round hauling up the water, which it is then obliged to carry on its back in cans. A double injustice.

Nightlife

In addition to the hilltop **disco,** there's another one on the road to the beach (about half a mile past the post office) and a third on the town beach near the Caroli Hotel.

The major event each evening is to sit on the balcony of the **Ios Club** (just off to the right before the bus arrives at the post office) and watch the sunset. There's a two-hour "classical" period at 7 p.m. (program listed on a board in the harbor) and disco dancing after that. Drinks around $1 apiece.

Briefly Noted

Homer's tomb, at Placotos, is a 2½-hour trip by mule and on foot. . . . Best cooking is at the **Pithari** restaurant, first one you come to in the village, although most people prefer to cluster with the crowds further along the main street. You can sit on the wall here and watch. . . . Nude beaching is officially against the law, with warning signs and the occasional bust. But nudists still gather on the rock at **Mylopotos beach.**

Boats from Ios

The comfortable *Lemnos* is the main one. On Mondays it leaves Ios at 9:30 a.m. for Naxos, Paros, Syros, and Piraeus. On Tuesdays at 3:45 p.m. for Thira, Paros, and Piraeus. On Wednesdays at 4:30 p.m. for Oia, Thira, and Iraklion. On Thursdays at 9:20, same as Monday. On Fridays at 3:45 p.m. for Thira and then back at 7 p.m. for Paros and Piraeus. On Saturdays at 3:45 p.m. same stops as Friday. On Sundays at 4:30 p.m. same stops as Wednesday.

Additionally, the *Aktaion* leaves at 3 p.m. on Monday, Wednesday, and Friday to Santorini. On Sunday, Tuesday, and Thursday at 8:30 a.m. to Santorini, and then at 1:30 p.m. to Paros and Mykonos.

The *Cyclades* leaves at 7 a.m. Monday to Thira; and at 4 p.m. Tuesday to Naxos, Paros, Syros, and Piraeus.

The *Elli* goes to Santorini at 3:30 p.m. on Tuesday, and then at 7 p.m. to Paros, Mykonos, and Tinos. At 2 p.m. on Tuesday to Santorini and Iraklion. At 8:15 p.m. on Wednesday to Mykonos, Tinos, and Piraeus.

The *Margarita* leaves at 8:30 a.m. on Friday to Paros, Naxos, and Mykonos. There's also a daily departure to Santorini (return 8 p.m.) of the *Kritikaki.*

Boats to Ios

The *Elli,* the *Cyclades,* and the *Leto* —all at 8 a.m. Monday; the *Lemnos* 8 a.m. Tuesday, Wednesday, Friday, and Sunday; the *Kanaris* at 1 p.m. Thursday.

SANTORINI: In recent years the talk has been going around that the volcanic explosion on Santorini caused the destruction of the ancient site of the legendary Atlantis, but this romantic fancy only enhances an island already unique. From the first sight of the towering red cliffs, rising steeply out of the water, you'll appreciate that this is an island like no other. You are, in fact, sailing directly over the "mouth" of an extinct volcano, which erupted more than 3,500 years ago, forming a deep bay that is seven miles long and almost five miles wide. (If you arrive on the car ferry you will dock on the far side of the island, making your way to Thera, the capital, by bus.)

One's first view of the island, and one that lingers for a lifetime, is of layer upon layer of red volcanic rock interspersed with white buildings and specks of greenery, all floating on a deep blue magnetic-looking sea.

Thera, sometimes spelled Fira, is a terraced town perched seemingly precariously on the edge of the cliffs in a picturesque manner. It's easy to walk around and strangely peaceful, considering how many tourists it attracts.

The only way up the extremely steep cliffside is via the 587 steps arranged in a zigzag path followed by the donkeys, and if you can afford it this is by far the most colorful way to go. Prices are negotiable beginning at about 30 drs and one solution is to split the price with somebody else and pile all your luggage and theirs atop one beast, walking behind in the best tradition of the downtrodden Eastern wife.

Be sure to visit the little **museum** (8 a.m. to 1 p.m. and 3 to 6 p.m., admission 5 drs, except Thursdays and Sundays when free) displaying some of the finds from ancient Thera and **Akrotiri** (in the southeast and southwest parts of the island respectively).

An exhibition of rug-making techniques is open daily (behind the museum, near the convent), as is the building known as **E.P.S.,** which stands prosaically for "Exhibition of the Products of Santorini" (these include wines, embroideries, textiles, pumice stone, beans, and nuts. The wine comes in three grades—dry, medium, and sweet and is sold for about 30 drs per bottle by many stores).

Major tourist activity is to go to the black sand beach at **Kamari** (seven buses daily between 7:15 a.m. and 6 p.m.), to the picturesque village of **Oea** (three buses daily, first one at 11 a.m.), or to the excavations at Akrotiri (three buses in the morning, first at 8 a.m.). The island's tourist office was inexplicably closed down a few years ago, so organized tours are now suspended.

The ancient town of Thera atop the mountain Messa Vouno is accessible only by taxi, and as the trip costs more than 400 drs it is advisable to find somebody with which to share the cost. Thera's outstanding feature lies in the fact that traces of seven distinct civilizations have so far been uncovered.

All bus schedules are listed on a blackboard across from the bus station and boat schedules can be found displayed in most cafes, hotels and the OTE building.

Archaeology, Atlantis, and More Things to Do

The path to the harbor, Spyr. Marinatos, is named after the archaeology professor at Athens University who was in charge of the diggings on Santorini for many years and who is among those who believed that Santorini (once called Stronghili) was the site of the fabled Atlantis. The island, 128 miles from Piraeus and 150 miles from Rhodes, has had a long history of volcanic eruptions, the most recent of which was in 1956.

It is the massive eruption of almost 3,500 years ago, however, that appears to fit the Atlantis legend. On that terrible day in or around the year 1520 B.C., the entire center of the island—an area of 35 square miles—sank into the ocean, causing tidal waves that virtually wiped out the flourishing civilization on Crete, 70 miles to the south. Santorini was covered with volcanic ash to a depth of more than 100 feet and traces of the old civilization are being uncovered as this is dug away.

Professor Marinatos wrote: "This is not a usual excavation. One has the feeling of living among men who were suddenly driven away, terrified by the fury of the elements."

The excavations at **Akrotiri** (open 8 a.m. to 1 p.m. and 3 to 6 p.m.; Sundays 10 a.m. to 1 p.m., 3 to 6 p.m.) are impressive for their scope and size but contain very few relics; most have been removed to Athens. There is a 20-dr entrance fee but this includes the services of a guide (nobody is allowed to wander alone so there are often delays). When digging was suspended for a year after the death of Professor Marinatos in a fall (he is buried on the site) it was still uncertain whether the site was a complete settlement or one large palace. At any rate, it has been estimated that the population was once as much as 30,000. Many rooms have been excavated and in one case a complete building.

Some of the buses to Akrotiri also pass **Perissa beach,** so it is possible to combine a visit to both in one journey.

Where to Stay

The best hotel is the **Atlantis** (tel: 21232), whose 25 rooms are an expensive 1200 drs double, demi-pension. Only a few doors away, and with the same view, is the simpler **Hotel Panorama** (tel: 21481) with rooms for 400 drs double, and both this and the even cheaper **Hotel Loucas** (about 300 drs double) have pleasant terraces for dining. Breakfast costs 30 drs. Note, however, that staying in your room past 4 p.m., even if you arrive at midnight and leave the following night, will entail a charge for two nights.

All boats and buses are met by eager men and women who will offer you rooms for about 150 drs per person. No need to be hesitant.

Adjoining the Loucas and about the same price is a complex of rooms for rent including cafeteria and shady hillside courtyards.

READERS' SELECTIONS: "Our apartment in the pension of **George Kavalari** had several cave-like grottos for sleeping and living. Private bath and balcony with clothes line and the cost was still only that of a D-class hotel, and all rooms have a magnificent view" (Micki & Don Schallock, Boulder, Colo.). . . . **"Taverna Babis,** just across from the Hotel Loucas, is family run and has good food, good vibes, good prices" (Greg Dyer, Mill Valley, Calif.).

Restaurants

The two best are the **Taverna Aris** and the snack bar **Canava** "the cafe with soft and classical music." Both the hotels **Panorama** and **Atlantis** open their dining rooms to non-residents. The first street left past the bus station (or, coming through town, past the Handy jewelry store) is a very Greek cafe, the **Apostolis,** serving cheap and oily food. Its major attraction is the eccentric customer who, fired with enthusiasm by the music, jumps to his feet, dons a handkerchief and a glass of wine and jigs around the tables without spilling a drop. It may be preferable to watch this floorshow from the street, however, opting for one of the nearby restaurants in which to eat.

Getting to Santorini

The *Cyclades* sails at 8 a.m., the *Leto* at 8:15 a.m, and the *Kanaris* at 11 a.m., all on Monday; the *Lemnos* at 8 a.m. Tuesday, Wednesday, Friday, and Sunday; and the *Kanaris* at 1 a.m. Thursday.

Olympic Airways has a daily flight to Santorini (and back). The trip takes about 55 minutes and costs 700 drs each way.

Briefly Noted

Thera boasts three discos—the **Yellow Donkey** below the Hotel Atlantis; the **Neptune** and the **Volcan,** en route to the museum. . . . Handmade sandals are cheaper here than in Athens or Mykonos. . . . A store called **Wheels** rents bicycles (from 30 drs hourly, 150 drs daily) and mopeds. . . . A daily boat leaves the harbor at 3 p.m. for **Nea Kameni,** largest of the uninhabited volcanic islands in the bay. Fare around 50 drs. . . . **Kamari beach** boasts six tavernas and a tame pelican who swims in the sea, takes showers with bathers and steals food to share with the local dogs. . . . Last bus back from this beach: 6:30 p.m.

PAROS: The way Paros is now is presumably the way Mykonos was once—before the crowds came pouring in. There are the same charming, narrow, cobbled alleyways and confusing streets; the same sudden views of sea and sky, or an occasional lazily turning windmill; the same midget, whitewashed churches with bell-towers. One of the churches, **Ekatontapyliani,** dates back to the tenth century, some parts of it to a couple of centuries before that.

"Beautiful, smiling and simple" is how the government travel folder describes **Parikia,** the capital, and I have no arguments. In addition to the town itself and the pleasant sandy beach across the harbor (ten drs by boat, no boats between 1 and 4 p.m.), there are many interesting places to see around the island. It is well worth at least a couple of days' stay.

Don't miss a walk around the narrow streets of the town (you can begin by entering the main shopping street between the two cafes to the right of the harbor). It dates back to the 17th century and, from the quality of some of the houses, must have been lived in by wealthy merchants who made their living from sea traffic. As you walk along the main street, if you look to your right, you'll soon see a wall composed of what appears to be a strange arrangement of various archaeological finds—doric columns lying on their sides fit between flat pieces of rock, a tower from an old castle, all together suggesting a piece of abstract art. The place actually turns out to be what once was used as a hostel for pilgrims about 300 years ago.

Nighttime activities are the same as everywhere else: sitting outside the cafes along the waterfront, walking through the streets with their numerous souvenir shops, and going to the open-air movie, the **Cine Rex,** and three discos.

Paros sweeps around in a horseshoe shape at the point where the boat docks. As you disembark, there are low-lying hills behind you and at the left. The harbor area is small, consisting only of the pier, two hotels and a cafe. Up to the right is the town, with a choice of an inland path leading into a maze of narrow streets with stores and whitewashed houses, and another road along the water's edge which follows a route to outdoor cafes, a restaurant or two, and, on the slight hill at the extreme right, maybe half a mile or so from the dock, two more expensive hotels.

Where to Stay

As there are very few rooms available in the town itself, the best bet is a "room-to-let" place along the waterfront road to the right of the harbor area. These usually cost around 250 drs double and include a view of the sea. In town beside the dock the 16-room **Hotel Oasis** (tel: 21227) is invariably filled because of its convenient location. If you can get a room there it will cost around 450 drs double. The owners also run the **Hotel Galini** on the edge of town. The **Kontes** (tel: 21246) with 36 rooms is just around the corner and worth trying:

singles about 230 drs with bath, doubles around 350 drs. It also has some rooms without baths. Further out along this road are the delightful **Pandrossos** (tel: 21229) on a hillside with a terrace restaurant and rocks for bathing below, and the luxurious **Xenia.** The former has doubles for 300 drs, the latter is demi-pension obligatory.

Take the road to the left of the harbor and you'll come to three hotels directly on a small beach. Preferred choice is the **Alkion** with doubles for 400 drs with bath, 275 drs without, but the **Stella** and the **Paros,** with similar rates, are also fine.

READER'S SELECTION: "I have nothing but the highest recommendation for the pension of **Dina Patellis** in Parikia (across from Niko's art gallery), where we stayed in a lovely immaculate room in this plant-filled Greek home." (R. Geismar, London, England).

What To Do

Unless you speak Greek the Tourist Police (in the harbor windmill) are not terribly helpful although bus schedules are posted outside their office. Just up the road is the **Paros Travel Agency,** which offers half-day bus and donkey excursions to the **Monastery of Langovaradias** (whose monks are renowned for their ikon paintings), to the **marble quarries,** or **Psihopiana,** known as "the valley of butterflies." All these places can be visited on your own of course—the Monastery via a 15-minute climb after leaving the Naousa-bound bus about halfway, and the valley of butterflies via taxi or donkey, the latter trip taking about two hours. The Paros Travel Agency also dispenses info, sells bus tickets and helps to find accommodation. Skip their gruelling excursion to the caves on the nearby island of **Antiparos;** the caves—filled with stalactites and stalagmites—are more interestingly visited via bus to **Pouda** and then a caique ride across to Antiparos.

Backpackers and those looking for a good beach that offers almost no other distractions head for the far side of Paros—the tiny fishing village of **Pisa Livadi** on the southeast coast from which caiques occasionally sail to Naxos. Buses leave from the harbor for Pisa Livadi in the morning only (usually 9 a.m. and noon), the trip taking one hour. You can camp on the beach, rent a cheap room or return to the capital by bus about 3 p.m.

The port of **Naousa,** in an inlet to the north, also boasts fine beaches but seems to have been blighted by the tourist boom. You'll have no difficulty in finding a room in any of the numerous hotels. Buses go there about every two hours with the last one returning about 9 p.m. Incidentally, nude sunbathing has spread from Mykonos to Naxos where it has been treated with much less tolerance. Some nudists have recently been jailed without warning.

About halfway along the waterfront, the attractive **Corfo Leon** cafe and bar in the little square has recently been joined by **Nick's Hamburgers**—for homesick Americans. There are two movie theaters, the **Rex** and the **Paros,** but most of the community's nightlife centers on the cafes and restaurants which line the waterfront road. The sunsets are superb, the discos (**The Limon Tree, Psarades**) sleepy. Restaurants are all pretty much the same though locals give the edge to **Vassili's.** The **Xenia Hotel** has a pleasant restaurant with a diversified, cosmopolitan menu.

There's a well-known year-round art center, the **Aegean School of Fine Arts** on Paros. Applications and information can be obtained by writing to the director, Brett Taylor, Paros, Cyclades, Greece. Courses offered include studio subjects, photography, and creative writing, all at university level. The Paros Chamber Ensemble resides here in the summer, when not on professional tours.

Paros marble is no longer mined, but ample supply of water helps the island grow plentiful amounts of lemons, oranges, apricots, pears, plums, melons, figs, and all kinds of vegetables as well as olives. So thoroughly is the Parian soul "rooted in the earth," say Jeffrey Carson and James Clark in their charming book *Paros* (Lycabettus Press), that there's hardly a shopkeeper, bureaucrat or taxi driver "who doesn't have his own orchard, garden or vineyard somewhere in the nearby countryside." This guide to Paros is one of a series of attractive books produced by Lycabettus Press (owned by American John Chapple) and which include guides to Spetsai, Aegina, Plaka and Delphi with many more in the works. Recommended.

Boats from Paros

Paros is quite well served by boats running to other islands. The *Megalohari,* for example, sails at 2 p.m. daily, except Sunday, for Naxos, Mykonos and Tinos. The *Aigaion* sails at 2 p.m. on Saturday, Monday, and Wednesday for Naxos, Kalimnos, Kos, and Rhodes. The *Elli* sails at 10:30 a.m. on Tuesdays for Naxos, Ios, Santorini, and Iraklion. The *Miaoulis* sails at 7 p.m. Thursdays for Naxos, Amorgos, and Iraklion. The *Cyclades* sails 3:30 p.m. Monday and 1 a.m. Friday for Naxos, Ios, Thira, Anafi, Folegrandos, Sikinos; and Sunday at 3:30 a.m. to Naxos and Amorgos. In addition to all these boats to Naxos, there are also daily round trips to Naxos and Ios, leaving 8 a.m., returning 8 p.m., allowing three hours on each island and costing around 300 drs.

To Mykonos there's the daily *Megalohari* (except Sunday); the *Elli* at 9:45 a.m. on Monday; the *Actaeon* at 5 p.m. on Sunday, Tuesday, and Thursday; and daily round-trip excursions at 8 a.m. returning 7 p.m.

To Piraeus, there's the *Aigaion* at 9 p.m. on Tuesday and Thursday and 10 p.m. on Sunday; the *Kanaris* at 8:30 p.m. Friday; the *Miaoulis* at 10 a.m. Friday (via Syros) and the *Cyclades* at 7 p.m. Friday, 9:30 a.m. Thursday, and 5 p.m. Sunday (all via Syros).

There are round-trip excursions to Sifnos at 8 a.m. on Tuesday, Thursday, and Sunday.

To Santorini, the *Elli* sails at 10:30 a.m. Tuesday and the *Actaeon* at 11 a.m. on Monday, Wednesday, and Friday (via Ios).

To Iraklion, there's the *Kanaris* at 8 p.m. on Thursday (via Ios and Santorini); the *Elli* at 10:30 a.m. on Tuesday (via Ios and Santorini); the *Actaeon* at 11 a.m. Monday, Wednesday, and Friday (via Ios and Santorini); the *Cyclades* at 3:30 p.m. Monday and 1 a.m. Friday (via Naxos). There are also daily round trips to Ios, allowing three hours on the island.

NAXOS: The very first time I went to Naxos, the *meltemi,* or violent summer wind, was blowing. A good third of the journey from Piraeus was as rough as anything I have ever experienced, and there wasn't a happy face or a pink cheek aboard. The trip was worth it, though, for Naxos proved to be charmingly unspoiled, with virtually no concessions to the tourist trade, most of which is Greek anyway. There's a sprinkling of the more adventurous young European crowd that favors a place of this kind: no attractions beyond that of walking, swimming, and climbing the narrow, whitewashed alleys of the old Venetian town behind the harbor. It's exactly the kind of island that artists and writers eventually choose to settle on, buying cheap homes and working quietly in near-isolation until the pseudo-artists and writers come looking for them.

During its history Naxos has seen many occupiers and most have left their traces on the island. The diligent seeker after remains can track the Mycenaean (1600 to 1200 B.C.), pre-Classical and Classical (up to 338 B.C.), Hellenistic and Roman (up to 326 A.D.), and Byzantine (to 1207 A.D.) eras as well as the Venetian (to 1564) and Turkish (to 1821) occupations of the island. Some of these relics are scattered around the countryside, a few others are preserved in the museum atop the ancient citadel. In mythology Naxos is the island where Theseus abandoned Ariadne—an event memorialized by Ariadne's Gate on an islet called Palatia in the harbor. This marble gate, dating to the sixth century B.C., was part of a projected Temple to Apollo which was never completed.

The **museum** (25 drs, open daily except Monday from 11 a.m. to 1:30 p.m., free on Sunday and Thursday) is situated in what remains of the 13th-century Venetian castle on the hill above town. Apart from a fragmented mosaic, it's not very interesting and its extensive view northwards overlooks a tranquil but pretty arid terrain.

Famous for fruit (pomegranates, figs, lemons, and oranges) Naxos makes a special liqueur from lemon tree leaves and this can be sampled free at the wine shop on the harbor.

The early-afternoon scene on the wharf is particularly absorbing, with long-eared burros and dusty trucks unloading sacks of potatoes piled chaotically around the luggage of departing passengers, all bound for the same destination: Paros. The winch aboard one caique unloads sacks of flour onto a horse-drawn wagon, while another small boat stockpiles sacks of potatoes; the sacks occasionally split open high in the air, raining spuds on dockers and visitors alike.

Beyond all the luggage, massive numbered blocks of white marble, quarried in the northeastern section of the island, sit precariously one on top of the other, while in the background giant white waves leap and tumble across the breakwater and matching white clouds spill over the craggy brown hills behind the town.

On Naxos the **Aegean School** now offers a summer course (July, August) in cultural anthropology. For details write to Dr. Russell Barnard, Naxos, Cyclades.

Where to Stay

The largest selection of rooms is to be found behind the harbor's southern end (furthest from where the boats dock), in what is practically a brand-new community around the area of the town beach. Behind the **Hotel Ariadne** (450 drs double without bath) is a whole bunch of pensions: **Kymmata, Nissaki,** and **Domatia,** among others. All will ask for around 350 drs double but this is negotiable unless Naxos is unusually crowded. The jolly lady at the **Galini,** who speaks some English, says she'll "make a good price" for singles, which is fairly unusual as it's common to insist on the double rate even for singles.

There are numerous other rooms along the harbor and in the streets ascending to the old castle behind it. These are usually cheaper than the ones near the beach.

Nearest hotel to the boat dock is **Protos,** whose balconies overlook the harbor: about 150 drs single (hard to get) or 250 drs double. The refrigerator is always filled with icy water. Nearby is the **Okeanis** (250 drs double without bath, 350 drs double with).

At the other end of the harbor (nearer the beach) are the **Hotel Hermes** (235 drs single, 350 double without bath; about 400 drs double with) and the **Aigaion** (about 500 drs double including breakfast), both pleasant and cool.

Climb the colorful, winding alleys behind the harbor and you'll find a batch of cheap hotels near the castle: the 16-room **Panorama** (tel: 22330), charming, with bathless doubles for around 400 drs and doubles with bath for 450 drs; Also the cheaper **Anoisis** and **Dionysos,** beneath which is a multi-bunked room which serves as the local **youth hostel** (60 drs per person).

What To Do

The town beach, on a gently curving, enclosed bay behind the Hotel Ariadne, is a bit tatty. It's better at night, when the **Naxos Club** disco is operating (there's another disco at the far side of town, right below the marble gate on the hill). There are daily boats at 10 a.m., noon, and 1:30 p.m. to **Ag. Anni beach,** returning 4 or 6 p.m. **Apollon,** a charming fishing village about 30 miles across the island, is a popular trip; an excursion (stopping for three hours at a beach en route) leaves daily at 8 a.m. You might like to make the trip to Apollon on your own by catching the bus at 8 a.m. Last bus of the day is at 2 p.m., and it turns right around and comes back. The trip, through majestic hills dotted with tiny villages, somewhat resembles a stagecoach ride, with sack-carrying policemen, cargo drops here and there and the occasional tempestuous (and inexplicable) arguments between driver and passengers that seem such an inevitable part of any bus ride in Greece. Goats, sheep and the occasional backpacker are the only living things to be seen for most of the way and the scenery is impressive. Once past Profitis Elias, the magnificent olive groves of **Tragea** come into view and soon there's a stop at **Filotis,** overshad-owed by **Mount Zas** (or Zeus), at 3,200 feet the highest mountain in the Cyclades and one that offers a panoramic view from Greece on the west over to Turkey. It takes about an hour to make this climb (from Filotis out on the Danakos Road), at the end of which is an enormous cave, said to have been one of the innumerable homes of the infant Zeus. Past **Koronos,** with its nearby emery quarries, is a series of spectacular spirals round and round the moun-tains, swooping down into sleepy communities for denizens of which the bus stop is a major daily event. At **Apollon** (where there are rooms for rent), the bus stops only a few moments before returning. Be sure to get on the bus early or you'll have to stand all the way—for two hours.

Briefly Noted

Best book on Naxos is John Freely's *Naxos* (Lycabettus Press), which, as well as describing all the local sights and excursions, is peopled with such fascinating characters as the octogenarian who tells jokes by the numbers and the Greek prime minister (Protopadakis, 1860-1920) who was arrested, tried, and executed for treason within one week as the War of Independence ended. His statue stands on the *paralia,* or waterfront promenade. . . . **Bicycles** can be rented for around 150 drs daily, **motorcycles** from about 350 drs daily. . . . Occasional trips are arranged to visit the marble quarries at **Melanes** (ask at the tourist office along the harbor). . . . During your evening stroll along the harbor, be sure to drop into the little cafe with the long name—**Zacharoplaste-ion**—and sample some of the platesful of little donuts soaked in honey. You'll see everybody eating them. . . . There are daily trips to the beach at **Mohtsouna** at 10:30 a.m., returning at 5 p.m.

Boats from Naxos

Monday: 9 a.m., *Margarita* to Delos, Mykonos, and back; 3 p.m., *Naxos* to Paros and Piraeus; 3:30 p.m., *Aigaion* to Kalymnos, Kos, and Rhodes; 5 p.m., *Cyclades* to Ios, Santorini, Anafi, Folegrandos, and Sikinos.

Tuesday: 8 a.m., *Cyclades* to Paros, Syros, and Piraeus; 9 a.m., *Margarita* to Delos, Mykonos and back; 11:30 a.m., *Elli* to Ios, Santorini and Iraklion; 3 p.m., *Naxos* to Ios and Santorini; 7:30 p.m., *Aigaion* to Paros and Piraeus; 10:30 p.m., *Naxos* to Paros and Piraeus.

Wednesday: 1 p.m., *Margarita* to Mykonos; 3 p.m., *Naxos* to Paros and Piraeus.

Thursday: noon, *Margarita* to Ios; 3 p.m., *Naxos* to Paros and Piraeus; 7:30 p.m., *Aigaion* to Paros and Piraeus.

Friday: 8:30 a.m., *Miaoulis* to Paros, Syros, Piraeus; 1 p.m., *Margarita* to Mykonos; 3 p.m., *Naxos* to Paros and Piraeus; 6:30 p.m., *Cyclades* to Paros, Syros, Piraeus.

Saturday: noon, *Margarita* to Ios; 3 p.m., *Naxos* to Ios and Santorini; 3:30 p.m., *Aigaion* to Kalymnos, Kos, and Rhodes; 10:30 p.m., *Naxos* to Paros and Piraeus.

Sunday: 5 a.m., *Cyclades* to Amorgos, Kouonisi, Iraklion; 3 p.m., *Naxos* to Paros and Piraeus; 3 p.m., *Cyclades* to Paros, Syros, Piraeus; 7:30 p.m., *Aigaion* to Paros and Piraeus.

Boats to Naxos

At 7:45 or 8 a.m. (sometimes both and/or 9 a.m.) every day. Also 6 p.m. Thursday.

2. The Argo-Saronic

The three islands on the Argo-Saronic boat circuit—Poros, Hydra, and Spetsai—form part of an area known as the Argo-Saronikos (the Saronic Gulf), and even the travel folders wax more poetic than usual:

"One's first impression of the Saronic," says one, "with its austere surrounding mountains rising bare and abrupt, is of its Doric character, but then the transparent light, the myriad colors of the atmosphere, the play of the silver sea washing the islands and its shores, come as a wave of relief and delight to the traveler, inspiring painter and photographer alike."

SPETSAI: Someday, it seems certain, the horse will be just a memory—something that survives in wooden reproductions, on midway roundabouts, or outside those Paris shops that sell the meat as a cheap alternative to beef.

To visit the island of Spetsai is to remind oneself of the days when the noble horse played a fuller role in life. There are few cars on Spetsai—only motorscooters, bicycles, tiny trucks, and horse-drawn surreys. To jog along the meandering coastline in one of the latter, the sun overhead and the gentle waves lapping a few yards away, is a treat worth traveling far to experience. Roads cover only parts of Spetsai, and cars are allowed on the island only with a special permit. The wooded island's major assets are its innumerable fragrant harbors and bays, as well as the splendid mansions built by earlier residents, many of whom were sea captains who fought long and recklessly in Greece's War of Independence. A renowned Spetsai heroine was Lascarina Bouboulina (1771-1825), who built her own fleet of warships with a fortune inherited from her sea captain husband.

Although Spetsai, with its key position at the entrance to the Argolikos Gulf, probably always played an important role in naval history, the island was not substantially developed until the 16th century, when a fortified community was established at **Kastelli,** on the hill above the present capital. It was sacked by the Albanians and not rebuilt. Instead, when the islanders who had fled returned, they built on the slopes below the hill—and also laid the groundwork for Spetsai's eventual navy by building fishing boats from local pine.

Although tourism is the main activity today, there is still a tradition of shipbuilding and, says Andrew Thomas in his delightful book *Spetsai* (Lycabettus Press), "many young Spetsiots continue the island tradition and join the merchant navy."

If you arrive at the best of times and have the best of luck (i.e. getting a room), it's easy to fall in love with the island and end up wearing one of the popular local T-shirts, emblazoned: "I'm a Spetsai-maniac."

You can rent a bicycle through the tourist office. (Completely around the island is a 21-km ride.) Or you can take a horse-drawn "taxi" to get around town, for anything from 50 drs upwards, depending on the journey.

One pleasant activity is to rent a horse and buggy for a one-hour tour, from the little square in front of the port 50 yards from the pier: past the beach, towards the lighthouse, through the narrow streets by the church with the white heads all around the top, to the museum.

The **museum** is an old two-story house (open daily, 10 a.m. to 2 p.m., closed Tuesday) with an enormous anchor in the yard, and inside are ancient weapons, faded figureheads framed with 19th-century newspapers, and the original Spetsai flag (cross and upturned anchor), which inspired the island to fight so courageously in the Revolution of 1821. The mansion in which the museum is housed was built by one of Spetsai's richest 18th-century shipowners, Hadziyannis Mexis, and it combines Moorish and Venetian styles of architecture.

Where to Stay

In midsummer it's not easy to find a room in Spetsai, even in a private house, and the hotels, of course, are filled up first. These are: the **Saronikos,** the cheapest and first one you encounter after disembarking, which costs around 250 drs single, 375 drs double; the **Faros** in the square behind it (to your left), whose 58 rooms cost around 330 drs single, 400 drs double; the quite ritzy **Soleil,** about 100 yards further east, whose 26 rooms, all with shower, cost around 540 double, 440 drs single, including breakfast; and two hotels back in the main harbor (called Dapia) where you docked—the 32-room **Roumeni** (tel: 72244), with doubles for 475 drs, and the 38-room **Star,** about 250 drs single, 400 drs double. The Star's sidewalk cafe (only snacks, no meals) is the best place to sit around and relax.

At the foot of the harbor, below the Olympic sign, is the tiny and perpetually full **Hotel Acropol,** and beyond, going west, are first the luxurious **Posidonion Palace** (tel: 72206), the island's first hotel (built in 1914), whose 55 rooms cost 750 drs single, 1200 drs double demi-pension; and then—a kilometer or so out of town—the equally expensive **Spetses** and **Xenia** hotels.

There are various ways of finding a private room. One is to wander around checking out places that advertise rooms for rent. Except in spring and fall, this is usually fruitless. Alternatively, check with the **Mania Express** office (main tourist office in the harbor), with **Takis'** tourist office (eastwards towards the old harbor), or, as a last resort, at the office of the **Tourist Police,** which is 200 yards up the narrow street behind the Saronikos hotel. A single room is hard to come by; you'll probably have to pay for a double, which costs around 250 drs.

On the way around to the old harbor, just past the seashore pools where fishermen can be seen cleaning their octopus catch at sunset, is **Yolanda's House,** an attractive place with blue shutters and patio, where a self-contained apartment which sleeps four costs 800 drs daily.

READERS' SELECTION: Check out the **Pension Kamelia** (tel: 72415), smothered in flowers and nestled among the white-washed houses in the village. About 400 drs double with breakfast, served on a lovely balcony" (Tom and Linda Monahan, Albany, N.Y.).

Beaches

Within walking distance along the coast you can find rocky little coves with not very good beaches, most of them to the west of the harbor. The seaside road passes the majestic Posidonion hotel, several 19th-century houses, a derelict cotton mill, and the Town Hall (on the street behind which, not far away, is the house where Lascarina Bouboulina, Spetsai's famous lady admiral, was shot to death in 1825). After this comes the coastal district called **Kounoupitsa,** the name of a lilac-type shrub which once grew here in abundance. From here onwards are small beaches, the most popular being those near the famous **Anargyrious and Korgialenios school** (where novelist John Fowles used to teach) and the Xenia hotel.

In the other direction from Dapia (Turkish word for "a fortified place"), heading east, it's about two or three kilometers to the **old harbor,** the route passing through a series of other harbors, all filled either with moored yachts or the bare-ribbed skeletons of boats still being built.

Most beach-freaks board one of the 10:30 a.m. boats from the harbor to go to a beach elsewhere on the island. First choice: **Aghi Anargyri**—a gently curving bay with sandy seashore and a taverna, and jagged rocks at one end between which you can find relative privacy. The adjoining bay, **Paraskevi,** is also popular, and between them is **Bekiri's Cave,** once accessible only by sea, where islanders hid during pirate raids in ancient times. Boats also run to **Zogheria,** a vast bay on the island's northwest corner where a Roman watchtower once stood guard.

Another alternative is to take a boat across to mainland **Kosta,** or to nearby **Hinitsa Beach** (where there's a big hotel and a rocky headland on which you can find a niche of your own).

Nightlife

Two open-air movie theaters, the **Marina,** and **Titania,** change programs daily and usually have two or three shows each evening. There are three discotheques, the remotest being the **Karnaya** in the old harbor, and there's live bouzouki music at **George's** in Aghia Marina, on the coast east of town. Check with Taki's tourist office for evening barbecues. **Lazaros' taverna,** up the hill beyond the police station, is usually lively.

Transportation and Excursions

There are at least two daily boats to Piraeus—four on days when the speedy but sometimes unpredictable *Mania Express* operates. Monday through Saturday, the *Mykinai* sails at 6 a.m. and the *Maria* at 2:30 p.m. (both calling at Poros); and the *Mania Express* runs (theoretically) at 11 a.m. and 5:45 p.m. Two boats sail to Piraeus on Sunday afternoons. In addition are the twice-daily *Flying Dolphin* hydrofoils to Piraeus on which it's often hard to get a seat. Hydrofoils also operate to Nafplion, at the head of the gulf (from which you can readily get a bus to Athens), and to Porto Heli, an attractive resort at the southwestern tip of the Peloponnese mainland. Every hour caiques run across to the mainland at Kosta. It's a short trip, costing 10 drs.

There are excursions to Epidaurus on Saturdays and Sundays, and a one-day tour comprising Epidaurus, Mycenae, and Nafplion on Wednesdays. The *Daphne II* operates one-day cruises to Leonidon (on the southeast Peloponnese coast) at 10 a.m. on Mondays, to Hydra at 10 a.m. on Wednesdays, and to lovely Monemvassia (southeast Peloponnese) on Thursdays at 9 a.m. The *Daphne II* also departs at 9 p.m. on Saturdays for a bonfire and barbecue at Anaghiri beach, returning at midnight (250 drs). There's another outdoor feasting and dancing party, departure by boat, at 8:45 p.m. on Thursdays.

The easiest way to look around the whole island is to take any of the morning boats to Anaghiri beach, for the boats usually come back round the island the other way.

Across on the Peloponnese mainland, at Kosta, is a small airport from which you can fly to Athens. Ask at the tourist office for schedules.

A side trip from Spetsai to the coastal resort of **Leonidi** is worth considering. Boats go weekly. At the tiny port community of **Plaka** nearby you can relax and usually find a simply furnished room for about 100 drs per person.

HYDRA: Hydra was a rich island in the 19th century—a pirate's hideout—and many of the big mansions built in those days are still standing. Rich people live there, or maintain seldom-visited homes, and the island has earned a reputation as an artists' and writers' colony (which means that every second building along the harbor is either a "gallery" or an artsy-craftsy souvenir shop).

Less than five miles from the Peloponnese coast, Hydra has sometimes been called "the St. Tropez of Greece" and it does have something of the same glittering elegance. But Hydra has a proud history, too, something of which is reflected in the wonderful old mansions built by ships' captains in the island's 19th century heyday. One of these—the former Tsamados family home at the entrance to the harbor—is now a Merchant Marine school while another, the Emmanuel Tombazi house (above the harbor's southwest corner) now accommodates a fine arts school.

The stone water cisterns that can still be seen below some of the houses were once, it is said, used as hiding places for the gold, silver and treasures amassed by their wealthy owners. Hydra's water supply then as now is still largely imported from neighboring Poros, although a minuscule supply is still extracted from two wells at the far end of Miaouli Street and this is supplemented by what can be collected in the rainwater tanks.

Boat building began on Hydra in the 17th century and the following century saw the island's fleet grow to almost 200 ships which traded all over the Mediterranean and piled up large fortunes for its captains. During the war for Greek independence in the 1820's, Hydra's fleet—and the fortunes of its owners—provided the main naval power.

One of the particular talents of the sailors from Hydra was the dangerous task of manning the brullots (fire ships) which—soaked in tar and stuffed with explosives—were rammed into enemy fleets, abandoned by their brave crews only when set afire.

In the decades that followed the successful war against Turkey, Hydra's ships found a profitable new occupation with the development of sponge fishing off the North African coast, but when the age of steam-driven ships arrived the value of the old wooden ships declined and gradually Hydra lost its importance. But not its beauty.

It's a pretty town and many of the buildings are painted in bright colors and have lovely old doors with quaint knockers. The harbor is hidden away in an inlet and can't be seen from the sea until the very last few minutes before arrival.

The population, once more than 20,000 is now less than one quarter of that figure.

Where to Stay

On the harbor the tiny **Hotel Sophia** (tel: 52313) is somewhat shabby, quite pleasant—but usually full. Bathless rooms, if you can get one, cost 200 drs single, 300 drs double. The even tinier (seven rooms) **Argo**, right where the boat docks, is simple and pleasant—and invariably full—350 drs double without bath, no singles. There are rooms for rent next door to Antonio's Snackbar. The attractive **Leto** (tel: 52280), which has a bar and roof garden, has a lot more rooms (240 drs single, 350 drs double without bath; 330 drs single and 400 drs double with bath). The 16-room **Miranda** (tel: 52230, Athens 521-004), with its antique telephone in the lobby, is easily the most stylish but also fairly expensive: a few bathless rooms at 450 drs single, 600 drs double; doubles with bath almost 800 drs. To this add compulsory breakfast at 75 drs per person.

The **Xenia**, in a spacious old house behind the harbor, is Hydra's biggest and most expensive hotel, its 40 rooms costing around 750 drs single, almost 1,000 drs double (including breakfast).

The **Hotel Hydra** (tel: 52597) is the marvelous old mansion atop the hill that's been converted into a hotel. Quite a climb, but quite a view when you get there. All rooms without bath, clean and spacious, costing 300 drs single, 425 drs double. On the way up the hill you'll find several homes with signs offering rooms (these cost about 150 drs per person), but you may be accosted by their owners as you disembark, which will save you the trouble of looking.

Another way to find a cheap room is to turn left at the narrow alleyway beside the bakery in the harbor and then right at the first street watching for a blue sign offering "Rooms for Rent." Further up this street is the **Pension Amarilis**, whose ten rooms cost 368 drs single, 443 drs double. All these prices, by the way, represent rates in the off season: in July, August, and early September, expect to pay 15 per cent more on prices listed.

It is increasingly hard to find a room in a private house because many of the owners, disgusted with the red tape and paperwork involved, have gone out of the rooming business. As for a single room—forget it, it's a rare commodity.

What to Do

Up on the hill, about two hours' walk from town, is the **monastery of Prophitis Ilias,** which can be visited only on foot. The start is made early in the day to avoid returning in the heat of the afternoon.

Not far from the monastery, at a slightly lower level, is the **convent of Aghia Eypraxia,** where the nuns are happy to demonstrate the ancient looms on which they weave a variety of fabrics which they offer for sale. There's also a wide choice of crafted goods and clothes available at the shops and boutiques down in the harbor.

Donkeys can be rented for trips up into the mountains—to the monastery and convent or to the little villages of **Palamidas** and **Episcopi,** about one hour and two hours' ride respectively.

Beaches at the villages of **Kamina** and **Molos,** both to the west, are also likely stops, as is **Mandraki,** where the old shipyards used to be. Small boats run back and forth all day to these beaches.

Eating and Drinking

Hydra wakes up with a vengeance at nights when there's dancing until 3 a.m. at the **Lavouclera** (to the right of the harbor as you dock), at the nearby **Kavos** on the other side of the harbor, and at the appropriately named **Cannons** on a promontory further around the cliffs past the yachting club. Here the view is spectacular—and familiar if you saw Sophia Loren in *Boy on a Dolphin.* All these places charge around 30 drs for sodas, 60 drs for spirits, but otherwise there's no admission charge. In the daytime you can also go swimming off the rocks beside the Lavoudera. The discos, incidentally, have a sneaky habit of increasing drink prices at the busiest time of the evening, lowering them again later. No warning is given, so take this as one. Liveliest bars: **Bill's** and the **Pirate.**

Not too much difference between the restaurants on the harbor, but you might like to check out **Jimmy's Taverna,** just behind the harbor at the left-hand side, and the pleasantly remote (relatively speaking) **Kaminia** taverna, beyond the Cannons disco on the cliffs.

At Kamina

The tiny harbor of Kamina, with its one taverna and the hilltop **Hotel Dimitra** (tel: 52335) is worth the 15-minute walk. The Dimitra is charming but owner Pete Turton plans to turn it into a private club this year, so rooms may not be available. Just off Kamina is a rocky island which used to be popular with nudists, but Hydra's police are not fond of this habit (recent fines have been stiff), so caiques have been prohibited from taking visitors there.

Briefly Noted

The solitary movie theater, the **Gardenia,** has nightly shows at 9:15 and 11:15. . . . The **post office** is open 8 a.m. to 1 p.m. and 5 to 7 p.m. weekdays, till noon on Sundays. . . . The **clinic** is open 8:30 a.m. to 12:30 p.m. and 5:30 to 7 p.m. weekdays, 10 a.m. to noon on Sundays. . . . The **Commercial Bank** is open from 8 a.m. to 2 p.m. weekdays, one hour later than the **National Bank,** which, however, is open Friday evenings as well as the Monday evenings of its competitor. . . . There's a daily boat to Piraeus at 2 p.m. and extra boats on some days. . . . Fast hydrofoils (the *Flying Dolphins*) leave Zea Marina in Piraeus (8 a.m. and 2 p.m.) daily calling at Poros, Hydra, Spetsai, and Porto Heli. Another hydrofoil goes to Aegina. Tariff is high: almost 300 drs for the one-way trip to Hydra.

POROS: A channel of water so narrow that you can almost throw an olive across separates the island of Poros from the mainland. Supposedly it was an ancient volcanic eruption that separated the two portions of land, and although the channel between them is now quite deep it is so narrow that one gets the impression of sailing down a watery street. Little motor-powered boats run to and fro all day and most of the night. The fare is a couple of drachmas.

But Poros *is* an island and, because of all this activity, a particularly interesting one. It is not nearly as commercialized as Hydra, and most of the tourists here are Greek tourists.

Along the waterfront, where all the cafes and hotels are, there is always something happening. It might be big ships coming and going, or ferries to the mainland, or people promenading, or shopkeepers selling fruit and vegetables from floating markets rigged up with a seat for the proprietor and canvas for shade.

Sometimes, especially in mid-afternoon and late at night, the harbor is quite still, except for the putt-putt of the inevitable little ferries, but there are always things to watch—a circular bread loaf with a hole in the center hooked over a boy's bicycle handlebars, or a cafe waiter holding a chair on his head, on which his friends have playfully hung six other chairs.

Around the bay to the west (your boat came up the narrow channel from the east), is a tremendous harbor in which part of the Greek fleet is sometimes quartered, and from this side of the town you can climb broad steps leading to the hillside. There's a tall clock tower atop the rocks, and the view (even when the tower is closed) is panoramic and quite overwhelming, especially at sunset.

There are other routes up the hillside—almost any path behind the water-front will lead you there—and your expedition is likely to be rewarded with the smell of gardenias, the tinkling bell of a captive goat, and dozens of cats of all shades and sizes. The clock is illuminated at night and is a famous landmark as is the mountain range in the distance (best viewed at sunset) known as the Sleeping Woman because of its resemblance to the torso of a woman lying horizontally.

For the Afternoon

A pleasant, brief excursion from Poros is across the island to the lovely old **monastery.** The trip could be made by bus from the harbor, but by far the more pleasant route is by boat. Ask one of the old men in the harbor how much he will charge to *monastiri.* You should expect to pay about 10 or 15 drs per person each way, with a couple going roundtrip for 50 drs.

With the boat's motor sputtering away at full tilt, the journey will take about 30 minutes, docking near a tiny restaurant overlooking the sea, called **Sandy Beach.** (The beach, however, is not sandy.) A path leads up the hillside to the large monastery, about ten minutes' walk, but don't expect to find anything much there except whitewashed walls, the glimpse of an occasional monk, and a small chapel (light a candle for me). A marble plaque inset in the floor reads: "Beneath this marble are deposited in Christ the mortal remains of Brudnell Bruce late ensign in the British Foot Guards who having accompanied His Majesty's Ambassador from England unhappily died of a fever at Poros on the 8th day of Oct., 1828."

If you want to make an afternoon of it, take the boat one way, pack a picnic, or eat at the restaurant and swim off the rocky beach, returning to Poros by bus in the late afternoon.

Not far from the monastery are the sparse remains (one pillar standing) of the ancient **Temple of Poseidon,** notable now only for its tranquility and magnificent view.

A more ambitious excursion might be the trip to the vast lemon groves at **Lemonodassos,** which is reached by first taking a boat from Poros across to the mainland beach of **Aliki** and then hiring donkeys (around 150 drs per person) to ride through the grove whose 30,000 trees will stupefy you with their acidic, distinctive perfume. Top off this trip with a fresh lemon drink at the taverna in the grove.

Bicycles can be rented for around 120 drs per day, and water-skiing is available at **Askelli beach.**

Eating and Sleeping

There are three hotels right on the harbor; all their rooms which face the sea provide, therefore, a beautiful view. As with most Greek hotels, rates drop a few drachmas if you stay more than one night.

The most tasteful is the impeccably clean **Hotel Saron** (tel: 22279), complete with marble steps and marble furnishings. It has 30 rooms: a few doubles without bath for 400 drs; the rest double with bath for 580 drs. Most beds come with bright red blankets, adding a spot of color. There are two toilets plus a shower for women on each floor and the same for men. The manager speaks very little English but she does speak French and is intelligent and helpful.

Most prominent of the hotels is the **Hotel Aktaion** (tel: 22281), right in the center of the sidewalk cafe block. Not as modern as the Saron, but spotless nonetheless, its rooms have that wonderful smell of clean linen. It also has brighter room lights than most hotels in Greece, along with the usual necessities: sink (all rooms are without bath), closet, chairs, and luggage rack. As at the Saron, there are separate facilities for men and women. Rates: 250 drs single, 380 drs double, all without bath.

Not as bright as the above is the 27-room **Hotel Manessi** (a bit further along the harbor to the left when facing the cafes), where doubles cost 250 drs without bath and 375 drs with. There are worn but adequate facilities in each room, along with a sink.

Around the bay to the right (while facing the sea), and out of sight of the main harbor, is the 39-room **Hotel Latsi** (tel: 22392)—clean and new but relatively isolated: it takes ten or 15 minutes to walk from the boat dock—but it's that much closer to the beach, about halfway. It has a pleasant restaurant and charges 470 drs single, 700 drs double, including breakfast, for rooms with bath.

The **Villa Maria** has ten rooms for rent without bath, two or three beds to a room. These cost 150 drs per person the first night and 120 drs for subsequent nights. The hotel is clean and sunny and situated opposite a Fina gasoline sign, around the right of the harbor past where the navy ships tie up (i.e., on the way to the Hotel Latsi). Ask at the **tourist office,** up the steps beside the Hotel Saron entrance, for other private rooms available. About 250 drs double.

The owner of the Perfect Elektra Art Shop (beside the Hotel Aktaion) has a modern **apartment** that can be rented by the month. Sleeps four or five.

A trio of hotels outside the town is accessible by bus, taxi, or boat, the last mentioned being the most pleasant way to get to them. Each place is self-sufficient, so it is hardly necessary to come into town at all. All are expensive.

Best tavernas are the **Seven Brothers,** entrees in the 80-110 drs range, and the **Kerras,** but you might want to combine a trip to the monastery with dinner at the nearby **Platanas** taverna (by taxi from the harbor, around 80 drs).

Another good taverna in town is the **Lukas,** whose manager, George, has traveled the world giving exhibitions of Greek dancing. Naturally you can dance at his taverna. Poros also has a disco named the **Dirlanda.**

READERS' SELECTION: "We highly recommend the **Hotel Angyra** (tel: 22368), located in **Norion** village on the outskirts of Poros. Quiet atmosphere, very clean, good restaurant, near nice beaches" (Linda and Tom Monahan, Albany, N.Y.).

Crossing the Water

Across the narrow channel, on the Peloponnesian mainland, is the small town of **Galata** (pop: 3,000), which doesn't have much to offer except a good view of Poros. In Galata, where trees and flowering shrubs shield the waterfront cafes, there are two hotels, both modern, with balconies overlooking the water, and not more than 100 yards apart.

Better of the two, the three-story **Hotel Galatia** charges 240 drs single, 370 drs double without bath; 13 of the 30 rooms have bath and these cost 340 drs single, 420 drs double.

The other hotel, the **Saronis,** has 14 rooms and the same rates. Best eating place in town is the **Hotel Galatia's** restaurant. The owner of the Galatia has orange trees and he gives their produce to his guests. A third hotel nearby, the **Papasotirion,** has rooms for about 400 drs double.

There isn't much in town. In a walk through the streets back of the waterfront, you'll see lots of houses half-smothered with grape-bearing vines, and a blue-topped church next to which the buses are parked overnight. The tavernas here are real tavernas, that is to say they're pretty bare except for massive barrels of resinated wine and a few tables and chairs.

Crossing to Galata at night, I once forced myself to keep my back to Poros until I had reached the other side and could gaze at it from the peaceful sanctuary of the other bank. What a marvelous sight! The lights of the little town are spread up the hillside in twinkles and sprinkles, like the lights of a discreet Christmas tree. And somehow, the black velvet cubes of darkness between each light were exactly the right size (how do they do that?).

Getting to Poros

There are at least half a dozen boats every day from Piraeus (call 451-1311 for info), including twice-daily hydrofoils from the Zea Marina in Piraeus. For current schedules from Poros to Piraeus inspect the blackboards beside the harbor cafes. The voyage takes about 2½ hours. In addition to the regular boats from Piraeus to Poros there are several one-day cruises which also take in Hydra and Aegina, offer a swimming pool and a bar on deck and return to Piraeus about 7 or 8 p.m. Cost is usually about $25 including lunch, and Viking's Travel Bureau can give you full details and make reservations.

The drive to Athens from Galata takes around four hours via Nafplion and buses are frequent. Epidaurus is a mere 20 miles from Galata and could be visited en route.

3. The Sporades

The Sporades, not yet so famous as the Cyclades, have the advantage of not being overrun by tourists in the month of August.

They are still more popular with Greeks than with tourists which sometimes has the effect of making the English-speaking visitor actually feel as though he is in a foreign land.

SKIATHOS: The easiest to get to (at the mention of its name, any Greek will say "Ah, Skiathos!"), Skiathos is truly beautiful: magnificent beaches and woods of pine, plane, and oak trees. Wild strawberry bushes and thousands of olive trees combine to give Skiathos one of the most fragrant atmospheres anywhere.

The island's favorite son, the novelist Alexandros Papadiamantis (1851 to 1911) second only to Kazantzakis in world renown, lived in a charming house behind the harbor, now preserved as a museum. A deeply religious man with some of the prophetic strains of Dostoevski, Papadiamantis was a tireless celebrant in the long vigils the Greek Orthodox Church stages on the eve of major festivals, and his house (just to the right off the street named after him) with its simple furnishings and writing artifacts reflects his pious simplicity. It has been written of him: "Papadiamantis made one of Mount Athos and Athens."

It was in the northern part of Skiathos, at the Evanghelistria Monastery, that Greece's current flag—a white cross on a pale blue background—was raised for the first time in 1807 at a meeting to plot revolution against the Turks.

The best months for a stay on this island are April, May, June, September, and the first half of October. There is a new harbor; the old one is used for the mooring of yachts only.

Where to Stay and Eat

When the boat docks from Ag. Konstantinou the major part of the harbor is around to your left along with two cheap hotels, the **Avra** (tel: 42044) and the **Sporades** (tel: 42065), both of them so tiny that they are usually full. Doubles cost about 250 drs if you can get one.

Three other hotels are all very near to each other, about 300 yards around the street Filokleos Georgiadou which slopes slightly upwards, following the line of the coast to the right of the harbor. These are the **Akti** (tel: 42024), with 11 double rooms without bath for 300 drs; the 15-room **San Remo** (435 drs double with bath), and the marble-fronted **Koukounaries** (tel: 42048) whose 17 rooms all have bath and cost 300 drs single, 430 drs double. The **Hotel Agnodema** (a converted house, and slightly cheaper than the hotels thus far mentioned) is but one of the many places with rooms in the area.

Skiathos sometimes gets so crowded that there are no rooms left in town, but you can almost always find a bed by setting off on the road at the back of town that heads for **Koukounaries.** Opposite the post office, for example, is a narrow alley sheltering **Mary's Guest House,** a modern building with 25 rooms costing 300 drs double with bath, but only 200 drs double before June. Buses run about every 40 minutes to Koukounaries (one of the most beautiful and famous beaches in Greece—see below). There's a taverna here, as well as discreet semi-nude bathing on the rocks at one end.

On the way to the beach you'll pass several inexpensive pensions (mostly within walking distance of town) and then—a few miles from town—a few expensive hotels: the **Nostos** (tel: 42520), a hotel-bungalow setup with water-skiing, a private beach, and other delights (from about $40 double daily); and the equally expensive **Xenia** (tel: 42041) and Skiathos Palace (tel: 42242) at Koukounaries beach itself. The Skiathos Palace has good food but is usually fully booked.

The first bus from Koukounaries to Skiathos town is at 7:30 a.m., the last bus at 10 p.m. The last bus from town is at 9:30 p.m. Fare is 13 drs. A taxi would cost 110 drs.

READER'S SELECTION: "The pension of **Ilias Tsaprounis** at Ikonistrias 36, situated on a bluff near a small beach, has a lovely view and kind and friendly owners. They speak no English but do their best to make you feel comfortable" (Terry Tagney, Quebec, Canada).

Skiathos Nightlife

Before dinner, at about 9:30 p.m., walk up the steps to your right as you face the water and you'll come to an area much like Plaka in Athens, except on a small scale. The first place to stop is at **Stamatis Bar,** where you will be served octopus, charcoal broiled, and an ouzo for five drachmas. You'll recognize Stamatis by the smoke pouring out the front window. Further up the steps, at Auriou 24, is a taverna where you can see some excellent *sirtaiki* dancing (remember *Zorba the Greek?*). The people on this island are especially nice, and you feel a very personal thing as you watch the men dance to the bouzouki. Further up is an outdoor place, with a bamboo ceiling and no walls; from here you'll see an unforgettable view of the harbor at night, cafes, lights reflecting on water.

Later, you can go to the **Bourtzi Nightclub.** It usually has the best live band playing everything from watusi to tango and rhumba. There's usually some new dance—hard to say from where—that you've never seen before. I saw one that looked like a cross between a Russian kazatzga and an Irish jig, and they were all doing it. Another popular place, **Scuna Club,** is down the dirt road to the left as you face the harbor. There are signs to follow and it's pretty hard to miss the string of green lights as you approach it. Drinks are around 45 drs here so check the menu before ordering. There's a free spaghetti-eating contest at midnight if you're hungry; winners get a bottle of champagne. Back in town, the **Talagria,** at Papiamondi 12, has a singer and bouzouki music in an open garden. But you can join the entertainment, as many of the Greek men do, and break into dance. It's a splurge for dinner, but then again there's the entertainment.

There's a big demand for *loutraki* (bottled spring water) in Skiathos because the local water supply is brackish and—possibly—unhealthy.

Beaches

Boats leave about 8:30 every morning for the various beaches. (If you get up an hour earlier, you can watch the fishermen bring in the nets.) The boats return about 1 p.m. for lunch; take an afternoon siesta so you can stay up late at night.

Koukounaries is noted for its beautiful golden sand and water, set off against a backdrop of fragrant pine trees. Buses go here as well as boats, and you'll find them leaving from the statue across from the self-service restaurant around the corner. The bus ride is beautiful, crossing over hills and through the countryside. Fare is 13 drs for the 20-minute trip. Contender for the most-beautiful-beach-in-the-world award is **Lalaria,** half hour by boat. It's been described as the "pink seaside with the silver pebbles," and the water here is an extraordinary shade of blue (there is, however, little sand). Nearby are two incredible grottos—**Skotinia Spilia** (dark grotto) and **Galezia Spilia** (blue grotto). You can swim in the dark grotto, which looks more like something from the science fiction world than reality. It takes your eyes a few minutes to get accustomed, but once they do you will see rock formations in the most incredible colors of blue, red, purple, pink, and green. You'll need a lantern to see the stalactites, and the rocks are slippery so be careful. Nearby, the Blue Grotto, which has no visible available light source, has *air* of the most incredible shade of blue, the same as the water, and you won't believe what you are seeing. Ask Jimmy Delianni at the seafront to take you in the canoe, which he keeps on his excursion boat *Richmond* that goes to Lalaria.

Another sandy beach, **Tsoungria,** is noted for its rare seashells, but if you simply want to go for a quick swim, you can dive off the rocks at the Bourtzi Club.

Boats from Skiathos

Daily boats to Volos at 8:15 a.m. and 5 p.m. Mondays; 9 a.m. and 8:15 p.m. Tuesdays; 10:30 a.m. and 7:30 p.m. Wednesdays; 5 p.m. Thursdays; 10:30 a.m. and 5 p.m. Fridays; 8:15 a.m. and 7:30 p.m. Saturdays; and 5 p.m. and 11:30 p.m. Sundays. There are also daily boats to Skopelos (and an excursion daily, from 8 a.m. to 8 p.m., visiting Skopelos and Alonnisos) and a daily boat sailing right around the island.

Getting to Skiathos

The best source for information and bookings is **Alkyon** (98 Akadimias Street at Kaningos Square in Athens, tel: 3622-093). Tickets can be purchased from them for the 5½-hour combination bus and boat trip. The bus leaves every morning at 8 a.m. (except Friday, when it leaves at noon) from the corner of Psaron 45 and Aghiou Pavlou; but it's not a bad idea to get there a half hour early to present your ticket and then pick up some fruit and cheese at the store across the street. The buses go to **Aghios Constantinos** (on the Evian Gulf), where the boat meets them around noon. If you happen to be driving, you can simply buy the boat ticket at the port.

It's good to remember, by the way, that the bus ride from Athens to Ag. Constantinos takes almost four hours and as most Greeks hate fresh air, keeping all windows closed and most blinds tightly drawn you'll probably need an oxygen mask—or at least some place where you can open a window without other Greeks being able to close it. There are also daily ferries to Skiathos from Volos, from Kimi on the east coast of Evia (8 a.m. Monday, Wednesday, and Saturday), and from Thessaloniki, if you happen to be working your way south instead of north. This last is a seven-hour cruise.

Olympic Airways operates two daily flights to Skiathos from Athens. These take 50 minutes and cost around $17 each way. The airport on Skiathos is around to the right of the harbor in a spot that's still marked on tourist maps of the island as a freshwater lake.

SKOPELOS: Though its name means "rock," Skopelos is another fertile green island, famous for its plums, which are dried in the sun and slowly baked in an oven before emerging in their final state as prunes. The island grows an abundance of fruit and nuts—pears and plums, walnuts and almonds—which it exports in large quantities, and a trip across into the countryside astonishes visitors who are used to more barren islands. As your boat pulls in (two hours from Skiathos), you'll see the white houses set amphitheatrically into the hillside, with blue, green, and golden shutters accenting the picture. To the right, an ancient church juts out from the rocks and looks out to sea.

As soon as you alight from the boat you'll spot a "Rooms for Rent" sign above a taverna slightly to your right. These are pleasant simple rooms with balconies overlooking the bay and cost around 150 drs single, 250 drs double. Many other houses around the harbor offer rooms (there are said to be 1,200 beds available at any one time) and usually you'll be offered one as you step off the boat. If not, head for the **Lemonis** (no sign), a building with balconied rooms next to the Alkyon office. More or less the same rates apply everywhere, including the spotlessly white **Hotel Amerikis** with brown shutters which overlooks the harbor at the eastern end (entrance from the street behind).

The nine restaurants lining the harbor are shaded by plane trees with their big palm-like leaves. At any of them—**Octi, Klimataria, Regas, Kimatia**—you can be served the usual Greek fare for about 70 drs. Have a look at the diners' plates and in the kitchen to see what's good. There are some island specialties worth trying: stifado (meat cooked in tomato sauce with baby onions), and glyko mygdalato (a sweet cake made with almonds—very good and very rich).

Some time during your stay, take the five-minute walk up to that church on the rocks, **Aghios Michael**, which has super ikons. There's an amazing fresco of the Panocrator (Christ the Almighty) in the dome, highlighted with pounded silver—one of those things an art historian would be tempted to have put in a museum.

Nightlife here is less sophisticated than on Skiathos—just a few jukebox clubs with names like **Sirtaiki, Monica, Lina.** An ouzo at any of them is about 5 drs.

There are 7 a.m. departures most days for a **boat tour** of the island; this takes 4½ hours and includes a stopover at one of the beaches and lunch at Loutraki or Glossa. Another popular tour (either by foot or rented mule) is to the group of **monasteries** in the center of the island. Two tourist offices in the harbor will give advice on these and other activities.

A **bus ride** across the island is a pleasant trip and has the additional advantage of passing several beaches along the way, each with its own taverna. In order of appearance these are **Stafylos, Agnontas** and **Linarakia,** each exceptionally beautiful and virtually deserted. If you have the time and patience, however, stay on the bus to its terminus at the port of **Loutraki,** about one hour's ride. Be careful not to get off at the hilltop town of Glossa which, despite its magnificent view, has little else to offer.

The bus is apt to be crowded but most passengers get off before the final stop, the pretty little port of Loutraki from which you can either get an occasional boat back to the mainland at Volos or to Skiathos itself. Last bus returns to town late afternoon, but meanwhile you can have lunch at the solitary taverna or at the pleasant hotel **Avra** (rooms with bath for around 260 drs double). If you really want to get away from it all this hotel, or the equally unpretentious **Flisbos,** is a good place to stop.

ALONISSOS:

ALONISSOS: Alonissos is one of the world's simpler places, popular with an international set who have houses about the island, and a number of French people who live near **Marrounta,** a beach 20 minutes from the main port. The port town itself is a mere babe, built in 1965 after an earthquake destroyed the old village. You can stay at the newly built **Artemis Bungalows** (tel: 5210) for about 400 drs double including private bath, or you can easily find a room in town for about 150 drs. Mr. Kalogrides at the Artemis speaks excellent English and can help find a room and answer questions. His 20-room hotel has a club attached which seems to be the meeting place at night for music and dancing.

It's a friendly island for those looking for a quiet place. The main attraction is **Krissamilia beach,** part sand, part stones, with beautiful golden water and gray and white striped fish that swim around with you. Find a speedboat to take you around for an hour, and ask to see the 3,000-year-old cemetery on the hillside, the ruins of the old castle, and the nearby place where the ancient city has been buried under water for the millennia. It's an eerie feeling to look down at this point, even though you probably won't see anything besides the fish looking around too. Maybe Dorotheos, a familiar resident who dresses in flowing monk's robes, will be standing at the mast of a large sailboat, his long hair blowing in the wind. If you're lucky, he'll come onto your boat for a chat.

SKIROS: This island, with its associations with Achilles and with the English poet Rupert Brooke (who is buried here), is the most inaccessible and least visited of the Sporades. It's a beautiful place, its port crowned with a medieval castle and the countryside dotted with fig trees. There are numerous private homes offering rooms and also a classy **Xenia Hotel** (tel: 91209), offering demi-pension only, for around 1100 drs double. Skiros is reached via bus from Athens, across to the Evia peninsula by ferry, and then a boat from Kimi to Linaria on the island's west coast.

The map guides to the Sporades (printed in 1967) offer some rather charming advice to both residents and visitors alike: "The local inhabitant . . . should know that every visitor is not the millionaire who will give him the opportunity of becoming rich in one day. . . . A warm and hearty behavior enslaves the most exacting visitor . . . (and) the visitor should know that he will meet with a population of good faith and character, natural gentleness, simplicity . . . he should not have any extravagant pretensions. . . ."

4. The Northeastern Aegean

LESBOS: The third-largest island in Greece, **Lesbos,** offers a variety of scenery and a happy mingling of the mood of Greece to which it belongs and Asia Minor which it adjoins. First settled more than 30 centuries ago, it has changed ownership frequently over the years and traces of its former masters linger on, as do proud memories of some of its ancient citizens—the statesman Pittakos, one of the Seven Sages of antiquity, and the lyrical poets Alkaeus and Sappho, all three of whom lived on the island around the seventh century B.C.

Sappho, in particular, whose group of young maidens worshipped Aphrodite (the Greek goddess of love, beauty, and fertility) is still much admired today for the candid and direct way she expressed her feelings ("Love shook my heart like a mountain wind that falls upon the oak trees . . . .") and for what the *Oxford Classical Dictionary* terms her "excellent eye and ear for natural things." Sappho was sometimes described as "the tenth Muse," an allusion to the traditional Nine Muses, Greek deities of poetry, literature, and music.

With a population of around 150,000, Lesbos boasts 11 million olive trees and enormous herds of sheep and goats. It has thermal spas, beautiful scenery, castles, a petrified forest, and interesting harbors, of which the biggest is the capital, **Mytilini** (pop: 16,000) on the southeast coast.

Where to Stay

The four hotels in Mytilini itself are usually filled. They are the 38-room **Lesbos** (tel: 28177), which costs about 400 drs double without bath, 500 drs with; the 31-room **Sappho** (tel: 28415), about 225 drs single, 330 drs double; the 16-room **Rex** (tel: 28523), about the same as Sappho; and the classier 39-room **Blue Sea** (tel: 28383), which is the most expensive at 400 drs single, about 550 drs double.

The Lesbos and the Sappho are in the middle of the harbor, the other two at the end where the boats dock. This is also where the **Tourist Police** can be found, and it's there you'll probably have to go in search of a room, which will cost around 175 drs single, 300 drs double. **Maria Marigli** at Logu Street 3 (tel: 28547), runs a pleasant place but you may need help in finding it: head along the main street away from the harbor and ask for St. Sophia and St. George, two churches with streets named after them.

About two miles south of town is the 74-room **Xenia** (tel: 22713), on the coast not far from the airport. Here the tariff is around 1200 drs double for demi-pension.

What to Do

There isn't much to do in Mytilini. You might wander past the **docks** on your way to the beach, pausing to commiserate with a boatload of fettered cows, waiting to be shipped to some nearby island while standing mute and uncomplaining, apart from restless feet and flicking tails. But even the dock isn't too active most of the time.

The **museum** (open 9 a.m. to 1 p.m., and 4 to 6 p.m.) is at this end of town, but you're probably more intent on finding a beach, in which case head on past the docks, past the unfinished rotunda, past the minuscule **town beach** with its showers (if you sit by the **war memorial** here at sunset you can hear musicians practicing at the nearby disco), and right around the big bay to the **castle.** Here, beyond the building on the headland, you'll find a small deserted beach which doesn't fill up until late afternoon when Greek families bring their children.

As you come back around the harbor you'll pass the various shipping offices near the Blue Sea Hotel, then notice a bus station from which buses run to nearby **Thermi** and eastern parts of the island. Most of the buses go from another square, at the far side of the harbor beside a little park. This is where the busy shopping street behind the harbor terminates and also where the Olympic Airways office is located. En route you'll pass the magnificent marble **theater** (with sidewalk cafe), the impressively oversized **Town Hall,** and the open-air **movie theater** on a rooftop opposite.

Buses from Mytilini: to Mythimna at 9 and 11 a.m. and 1:30 p.m.; to Mandamados at 1:30 p.m. (returns 6 p.m.); to Sygri (petrified forest) only on Wednesdays and Saturdays; and to Plomarion at 7:15 and 11 a.m., 12:30, 3, and 6:30 p.m.

You might like to rent a car and explore the island leisurely, in which case avoid the harbor places with their high prices—around 700 drs for one day, with 100 free kms and 5 drs per km thereafter. Many of the island's roads are unsurfaced.

The nicest places to visit are **Plomarion** in the south and **Mythimna** (see below) in the north. Both are readily available by bus, as is nearby **Thermi**, once a famous thermal bath but now a sleepy seaside village (about 5 kms north).

The road beyond Thermi follows the coast towards **Mandamados,** offering a wide choice of narrow little beaches. Then it turns upwards and inland, heading over the hills beyond which, across the straits, is Turkey.

Beyond Mandamados, which has little of interest, the road is unpaved for several miles and it is not uncommon to find an unmarked junction with no sign of life save a blue-robed scarecrow with a fur collar. But rest assured— most roads lead to Mythimna, and your first glimpse of it, guarded by its lovely castle, is worth the wait. (The buses from Mytilini follow another route, through the dense olive groves around **Kalloni**—famous for its sardines—and up the coast to the fishing port of **Petra,** with its church on a projecting rock, where most of the fine sand is mined. Soldiers are to be seen everywhere, because this close to Turkey tensions are high.)

Apart from soldiers and the occasional man on horseback, the countryside is largely deserted. Sun dapples the road, shining through the millions of olive trees which line both sides of the highway, and frequently a little brown bird scuds across the path as though it were on wheels.

Mythimna

Mythimna has no hotels but it does offer about 500 available beds in private homes, one of which the friendly young lady in the **tourist office** (where the bus stops) will find for you on request. Singles from 150 to 200 drs, doubles from 250 drs to 400.

The cobbled street behind the office passes the cafes and shops before doubling back and forth across the hillside. This is woman's terrain—the men are all at the cafes—and every corner brings an encounter: a Medea-like figure in long black gown seems startled as a stranger passes . . . a housewife with two eggs in her hand nods *kalispera* . . . three generations of a family sit on the steps beside their home cutting up vegetables for dinner.

The walk along Dionysos Street leads to Logos, ("the word") and thence, still climbing, to the magnificent Byzantine and Genoese **castle.** A small stage has been built into one end of the castle forecourt and "backstage" steps lead up to the castle's ramparts, from which there's a glorious panorama of both sides of the cape and the red-tiled houses of the village.

After dinner at one of the tavernas, be sure to drop in for loukamades (fresh-cooked donuts with honey and cinnamon) at the cafe opposite Aristides the silversmith. The cafe next door to Aristides is the liveliest late-night one, with jukebox, impromptu Greek dancing, and lots of heavy drinkers (and offkey singers). There's a dimly lit disco down on the beach.

An alternative place for dinner is the little, near-perfect fishing harbor of **Molivos** (old name for Mythimna) where, if you can get a room, you can stay at the charming **Sea Horse,** with its geranium-decked balconies, for around 450 drs double. This one's a suitable place for honeymooners.

The cobbled street leading to the harbor—so quiet at noon that the only sound is waves lapping against the fishing boats—is Odos Poseidonos. An ancient legend relates that King Macareus, the mythological founder of Lesbos, drove Poseidon's son from the island and named its first two cities after his daughters, Mytilini and Methymna. Another charming tale is of one of the island's native sons, Arion the Methymnean, a contemporary of Sappho, who made such beautiful music that a song he sang, to delay being robbed and murdered by sailors on a ship in which he was traveling, was so sweet that it attracted the attention of a dolphin who sailed by the ship and carried Arion on his back safely to shore.

Mythimna's **town beach** is small, rocky, and not too attractive. (In fact, the town's summer residents urge me to emphasize this in the hope it will discourage more tourists from coming in and "spoiling" the place.) It's best to keep walking south, past the abandoned olive-oil factory on the shore, and around the bay towards the **Hotel Delfini** (1100 drs double, demi-pension), where not only is the beach minimally better but there's also a swimming pool and reasonably priced hotel restaurant.

More beaches can be found on the other side of the cape—about one hour's walk from town or 60 drs by taxi. But there are no facilities or tavernas, so take everything you might need for the day.

Plomarion

It's a pleasant 40-kilometer trip to the sheltered harbor of Plomarion along roads with lots of black and white sheep and goats, donkeys, and, at **Papados**, a disused factory chimney housing a family of storks, just like you see in old picture books. At the turnoff for **Aghiassos** (famous for its pottery and its annual religious festival, on August 15) there are rooms to rent; to stay here and visit this pleasant inland town, surrounded by walnut and chestnut trees, is to experience Greek rural life at its most unspoiled.

Plomarion's major industry is making ouzo, and the 118-year-old **Barbayani** factory, beside the Esso station at the edge of town, will allow you a glimpse of its manufacture. It's a simple process: sacks of the brownish-yellow herb fennel (anise) are boiled in copper vats set into concrete ovens, the distillate being led off by pipes and purified by four more successive distillations. The clear liquid that results is ouzo, turning the familiar milky color when mixed with water, and packing a hefty kick.

Not too many tourists are seen in Plomarion and when you walk around at night you'll feel almost an intruder. There's only one hotel, the **Oceanis** (tel: 498), which is usually filled. Rooms cost 330 drs single, 400 drs double. The night manager's brother, Jimmy, runs the adjoining **movie theater,** and his wife rents rooms (250 drs single, 350 drs double) about 200 yards up the main street (road to Aghiassos) on the other side of the square.

Heading West

The drive westward to tranquil **Sigri,** with its little harbor and 18th-century **Turkish fortress,** passes some interesting sights. Past **Antissa,** in a region of wild, mountainous ravines, is the restored **Monastery of Saint John Theologos Ipsilos,** whose foundations date back to the ninth century. A turnoff south leads to **Eressos** (probable birthplace of Sappho) and Roman **ruins,** and beyond that to a fine beach at **Skala Eressou.** The **petrified forest,** between Antissa and Sigri, is one of the most impressive in Europe: hundreds of tree trunks fossilized and preserved by violent upheavals as much as one million years ago. There are some samples of the fossils in the Mytilini museum. A small hotel at Sigri, the **Nisiopi** (tel: 6) is fairly expensive, but there are rooms for rent in private homes.

Getting to and from Lesbos

Olympic Airways has three daily flights to Mytilini. The trip takes about 50 minutes and costs $37.

The *Sappho* sails from Piraeus to Xios and Lesbos at 6 p.m. on Monday and Wednesday and at 4 p.m. on Friday, when it continues on to Thessaloniki. The *Arion* sails to Xios and Lesbos at 7 p.m. on Tuesday.

From Lesbos there are daily sailings (except Friday and Saturday) to Xios and Piraeus at 3 p.m. A boat sails to Limnos and Kavala on Wednesdays and Fridays. There is a Saturday boat to Rhodes and Cyprus, a Sunday boat to Thessaloniki, and on Tuesdays a boat to Samos, Ikaria, Patmos, Leros, Kalimnos, Kos, and Rhodes.

LIMNOS: The mythological home of Hephaestus, the god of iron-working after whom one of its towns is named, this peaceful, relatively unvisited island is rich in ruins, some of which date back to the Neolithic era. **Myrina,** also known as Kastro, is where the boats dock, and it has good beaches and historic sites. The **Limnos** (tel: 22153) and **Sevdalis** (tel: 22691) hotels are both around

350 drs single, 400 drs double. The view from the cliffs at **Kotsino,** north of Moundros, is famous.

IKARIA: Rich in the remains of Roman baths, this is another tranquil, unspoiled island. You can eat barbecued goatmeat here—thousands of goats roam wild—and sample the local liqueur, raki, which is made from berries of the koumaro bush. Ikaria also grows pears, apricots, grapes, walnuts, and almonds. There are trails, not roads, but boats can be hired to reach various coastal spots. In the capital, **Aghios Kirikos,** are rooms for rent as at **Therma,** a mile away, where there are two C-class hotels: the **Apollo** (tel: 4) and the **Icarion** (tel: 3). Needless to say, the island is named after Icarus, who is reputed to have made the first flight—until the sun melted the wax on his wings and plunged him into the ocean.

XIOS: Homer is supposed to have been born here, and a rock platform cut from the slope of **Mount Epos** is said to have been where he addressed his pupils. The island's main port, also called Xios, is dominated by an ancient **fort** which offers splendid views: Turkey is only four or five miles to the west. Mountains as high as 4,000 feet cover the northern end of the island, where the famous **Nea Moni monastery** (founded in the 11th century) was a completely self-contained community for centuries. Today it is mostly deserted. The fertile southern section of the island produces citrus fruit, figs, wine, and the famous sticky white gum known as mastic. The 28-room **Actaeion** (tel: 23287) and the 39-room **Kyma** (tel: 22309) are C-class hotels in the main port.

SAMOS: Even closer to the Turkish coast than Kos in the Dodecanese, Samos is one of the most beautiful of all the Greek islands. The lush greenery includes date palms, pines, poplars, and, of course, the vineyards that produce its famous wines. There are miles of sandy beaches, awe-inspiring cliffs and mountains, and dozens of small and large towns full of hospitable people.

At one time, before Athens rose to power, Samos was the undisputed master of the Aegean, and under the enlightened despot Polycrates, its capital city was a complex considered immense even by today's standards (it surrounds modern Pythagorion for miles). The philosopher and mathematician Pythagoras, the astronomer Aristarchus, and the first sculptors to cast bronze monuments came from Samos. Its Temple of Hera was the largest in Greece until the Parthenon was completed, and a four-mile-long Sacred Way paved with white marble and lined with statues led to it.

Today, Samos is perhaps best known to tourists as the jumping-off point for a visit to the ruins of Ephesus in Turkey. A few yachts visit **Pythagorion;** the Piraeus boat stops briefly at **Karlovassi,** and the rest of the island remains largely unvisited. This isn't surprising: the western end is inaccessible by bus, and the buses to much of the rest of the island are infrequent enough to discourage all but the most curious. But it also means that prices are low, that the beautiful beaches are free and nearly empty, and that the people are wonderfully friendly.

Samos Town

You will probably get off the boat in Samos town. (The steamship schedules say "Vathi," but that's the old town up on the hill.) Coming from Piraeus, the boats stop at Karlovassi first . . . but it's not an easy town to get out of (the bus schedule is murderous) and since there are few hotels you may have trouble finding a room there in summer. So, Samos town.

Right at the end of the wharf is a **tourist office.** The English-speaking director, Stergos Horiatopoulos, sells maps, tickets for tours, trips to Turkey, Patmos, and Fourni, and gives advice on bus travel.

To the left (toward the open sea), the road leads to Gangou beach and several hotels; to the right, five long blocks will bring you to the small and charming town square with its palm trees and statue. If you leave the square at the left rear corner, you'll find the little church square from which the buses leave. How they maneuver there is a mystery . . . and even stranger is how they get into the square through that narrow alley. Just don't be going through it when one comes along, because they fill it wall-to-wall.

The ticket office is on the harbor road two blocks away (you passed it a block before reaching the main square).

Where to Stay and Eat

The choice of hotels ranges from the **Xenia** (23 Themistokli Sofouli, tel: 27-463), a little further along the harbor, with air conditioning, a lovely (and expensive) restaurant, and demi-pension terms only (about 1100 drs double); to the **Hera** (five minutes' walk toward Gangou), where singles with bath cost 250 drs drs, doubles 400 drs.

In between is the **Samos** (6 Themistokli Sofouli, tel: 28-377) a very pleasant C-class hotel with a roof-garden restaurant and 83 rooms (all with bath) which rent for about 400 drs single, 500 drs double.

Other than the Xenia restaurant, there are no outstanding eating places in Samos town—it seems to be mainly a place to pass through from and to the boats. Nor is there any hotel or restaurant in **Vathi** (1 km uphill), which is smaller and older—but it's certainly worth a walk through the narrow cobbled streets just to admire the strange old houses leaning together overhead, their carved wooden balconies filled with flowers. Around the main square of Samos there are several pleasant and inexpensive cafes, good for snacks.

READER'S SELECTIONS: The **Pythagora** pension has doubles with showers. You must ask for the hot water to be sent to the room but there is no extra charge for it. The word for hot water is *zestoon nero.* Breakfast is not included, so don't eat it there. Go down to the cafes in the square. A restaurant in Samos town named **O Baghalis,** before the square if coming from the pier, next to a car rental place, is a super Greek restaurant and cheap" (Thomas Pellechia, Tehran, Iran).

What to Do

On the way to Vathi (just behind the Xenia Hotel) is a **public garden** with a tiny **zoo.** Behind that are, from right to left, the O.T.E. (telephone center), cathedral, post office, and **Archaeological Museum.** Downstairs, the museum has the usual small collection of broken statues found locally, but it's worth the five-dr admission charge (free Thursdays and Sundays) to watch the archaeologists in action on the second floor. The digs on Samos are recent, and at the top of the stairs is a huge table covered with boxes of broken pottery that keep coming in daily. Here, with ruler, notebook, photographs, and presumably glue, the local experts labor at ancient jigsaw puzzles, oblivious to the tourists.

There are also some beautiful bronze griffin heads—so many, in fact, that they must have been the symbol of ancient Samos. But I didn't dare disturb the archaeologists to ask, so don't quote me.

A little further up the hill toward Vathi, an old tree stands in the middle of the road. Just opposite is a simple inexpensive restaurant, where you can have a pleasant lunch on the terrace while watching the local boys race their cycles up and down the hill.

On the other side of the bay to the town of Samos is the town's major industry—the **wine factory**—set at the edge of a small forest on the shore. Hundreds of barrels sit on the beach awaiting shipment, for Samos wines were renowned far and wide long before the day they were included on Lord Byron's lyric list. Swedes, especially, have an appreciative palate for the wines of Samos.

To visit the factory is a joyous experience. There is very little to see of the manufacturing process, but you'll be invited to sit in the manager's office while a woman brings you glass after glass of the different kinds of wine. Some are dry, some sweet, some old, and one particularly attractive (says the manager) to American tastes. The bouquet from the wine is as memorable as the taste.

Buses run around the bay but turn off before the wine factory (all buses, for example, to Malagari, Kokari, or St. Constantin). The walk from town will take about 40 minutes.

Bicycles can be rented just off the main square, and taxis are available at reasonable rates. Taxi rates to all points are posted on a board in the tourist office.

At Night

Samos closes down early—before midnight—although there is usually one cafe still in business long after the others. The main evening activity is to stroll along the seafront and back, between bouts of sitting in the square and watching others do the strolling. The two **movie theaters** are open to the sky in summer, and it is advisable to take along a jacket or a sweater when visiting them. The films, some in English with Greek subtitles, tend to be of a rather low standard and I found myself disagreeing more with their basic assumptions (a sort of feudal deference to the kind, sweet people who live in the old house on the hill, etc.) than bothering about technical flaws. Take my advice and skip the movies here.

Visiting the Old Capital

Many names, famous throughout Greece, are associated with Samos: the astronomers and scientists Aristides and Aristyllos; Conon, a geometrician who was Archimedes' teacher; Dionysios, the historian; Homer's friend, the poet Creopyllos; Callistratus, who first devised the 24-letter Greek alphabet; Glaucos, who invented the process of soldering iron; and, in 1821, Lycurgus Logothetis, leader of the 1821 revolution against the Turks, whose statue can be seen in the town.

Other Samians became renowned even further afield, as, for example, Aesop, author of the fables, the philosopher Epicurus, and the mathematician Pythagoras, whose own philosophy was expressed in his statement: "Numbers take man by the hand and conduct him unerringly along the path of reason."

About Pythagoras, a name that at one time or another confounds every schoolboy, MIT professor Giorgio de Santillana wrote that he was the first to discover the connection between mathematics and music, and that he regarded numbers "as a heavenly host of perfect entities which rule the world of men."

The professor added (writing in *Life* magazine in 1963): "The Greeks realized that beauty depends upon right proportion, but it was Pythagoras who showed them that that same proportion that forms the structural principle of the universe also rules man and his works. Hence music, sculpture, architecture and science all obey the same law."

The birthplace of Pythagoras was the town now called **Pythagorion,** on the southeast side of the island. At one time it was called Samos, the capital. It is a pleasant ride of about half an hour (9 drs) to the sleepy town, with the sea at one side disappearing just as the sea at the other side of the island comes into view. Buses leave from the little square at rare intervals in daylight and not at all at night. Tickets must be bought before boarding the bus. The ticket office is along the narrow street connecting the two squares.

Alighting at Pythagòrion, you'll find yourself on a tree-lined hill leading down to the sleepy port. A caique is usually in the building stages but, if you arrive in the early afternoon, nobody is even standing up, much less working.

The harbor is a popular stopping point for owners of private yachts who rarely stay more than one night.

On the waterfront are a couple of pensions, the **Delphini** and the **Iraion,** each of which costs about 140 drs double. It's possible to spend a cheaper night—about 50-65 drs per person—by staying at homes in any of the side streets that carry signs advertising rooms.

Pythagorion has four restaurants, none of them very interesting, and an elegant new cafe, the **Dolphin,** with limited menu (steak, bacon and eggs, toasted ham or cheese sandwiches) and slightly higher prices than its neighbors.

The best beach, **Portokali,** is about half a mile from town.

Just up the hill from the harbor are the ruins of the fortress of **Lycurgus,** built by the revolutionary leader in 1823. From these grass-infiltrated ruins and the adjoining whitewashed church, you can gaze at Turkey across the narrow straits of Mycale.

From the "center of town," where the bus stopped, it's a half-hour walk up the hillside to the monastery of **Spiliani.** Tiny cultivated fields, rocks, and the occasional cypress tree are the backdrop to one's walk, and it really doesn't matter too much if one decides merely to sit in the shade of a more opulent tree and contemplate the peaceful landscape. There is, however, an interesting landmark on the way: the **Efpalinion Tunnel,** 1,000 miles long and eight to ten meters deep, which was built with the labor of thousands of slaves in the days of the ruler Polycrates (560 B.C.). Although he is usually known as "the tyrant Polycrates," he undoubtedly got a lot accomplished, and the tunnel (which was chopped through the mountain to bring a spring water supply to the then-capital) has endured mostly undamaged. You can go into the tunnel, but not right through it, because sections of the roof have collapsed.

A gigantic wall around the city was also built during the time of Polycrates, but little of this remains.

Don't forget, the last bus back from Pythagorion is before evening.

Further Afield

The excursion around the island, starting early on Sunday mornings, takes the whole day, costs about 200 drs, and visits virtually every landmark. But most of the places, of course, you can visit on your own.

The great **Temple of Hera,** built in Polycrates' time, has been undergoing archaeological excavation for the past 50 years, and what has been uncovered so far is of great interest to history buffs. Ireon is a few miles further west of the airport, itself a few miles west of Pythagorion.

Other places of interest: **Platanos,** a mountain town in the west, famous for its magnificent water and views, and **Mount Kerkis** (1494 meters), west of Platanos.

The **Monastery of Panaghia,** near Vourliotes, is an adventuresome excursion to make, because there is only one bus each day (at 1:30 p.m. from the little square, 25 drs), and there is therefore no guarantee that you'll be able to get back until the bus returns at 6:30 the next morning. Even if you take the bus, there's still a long walk ahead when you dismount. The round trip by taxi costs about 350 drs. If you walk down the hillside from Vourliotes to the main road while it is still light, you can probably thumb a ride back to Samos, because almost any driver will stop. And if not, you can invariably find a home in the village of Vourliotes where they'll give you a bed for the night. Oddly enough, the monastery won't.

What comes as something of a surprise is the monastery itself. Built in 1566, it is today inhabited by only one monk (surrounded by two or three women, said to be relatives, who do the housework) and not by a majestic choir of saintly men. Secondly, the residents seem by no means eager to shelter the weary traveler, although I'd always believed this was one of the main functions of remote monasteries. They will serve you a meal, though—olives, cheese, tomatoes, cucumber—and watch with amusement while you eat it.

The Beaches and Villages

In general, the beaches on the north side of the island are rocky, with breathtaking cliffs behind, crashing breakers in front, and (surprisingly) slightly warmer water than those of the south side, which are calm and sandy.

Three beaches—**Gangou, Psili Ammos,** and **Posseidonion**—can be reached only from Samos town. The first has a 3-dr entrance fee and is an easy walk from town. The others are free, but about a 20-minute drive away; 20 drs by bus, twice daily. Both are set in deep cozy bays and boast sandy shores and pebbles like jewels—there are no seashells on Samos, but the red, green, yellow, purple, and translucent white rocks turned me into a pebble-picker. Posseidonion is also famous for its fishing, and has a good seafood restaurant (not particularly cheap). The view from both Posseidonion and Psili Ammos across the narrow strait to the mountains of Turkey is worth the ride, even if you don't feel like swimming in the rather chilly water (the brochure describes it as "bracing").

Despite what the National Tourist Office brochure says, **Tsamadou,** the most photogenic beach, is *not* on the south coast, but two kms past Kokari.

Kokari is my nomination for the perfect seaside village. Twenty minutes from Samos, on the north corner of Vathi bay, it lies between two great rocks in a small bay. Beyond the righthand rock is another small bay with a sandy curve of beach; beyond the lefthand rock, the north coast begins with a mile-long stretch of pebbly beach and thundering breakers. Take your pick. In the middle, a tiny square faces moonrise. There is no traffic (the streets are too narrow), and so the whole square is scattered full of tables and cafe chairs. At a few, old gentlemen are playing backgammon and drinking coffee or ouzo; at the rest an international array of bearded youth are drinking wine and playing chess.

There are two restaurants and two cafes on the square (all good, and cheap), but the favorite restaurant is hidden away down an alley and around a corner—just follow everyone else about 9 p.m.

Kokari has no hotels, but several excellent **pensions.** All provide simple cooking facilities as well as private rooms with comfortable beds. On the lane from the bus stop to the square, the tiny (eight rooms) pension over the bakery shop offers doubles for 200 drs, provided you stay three nights. The baker's wife is the woman to see. The **Lito** is more expensive, larger, and right on the main road just before the bus stop (above the cafe). Here doubles are 250 drs. Right on the north beach is the brand-new **Dina,** charging the same prices.

Kokari has absolutely no classic ruins, museums, or flashy nightlife. The young people that frequent it are there for the beaches: first the mile of breakers north of town, then two small bays, and finally (about a mile and a half away, and a pleasant walk), **Tsamadou,** reached from the road by a small path that winds down a sheer cliff.

If you want a break from the sea, try climbing the hills behind town to the **Louloudas Castle.** It's a nice spot, and the view of mountains behind and coast in front is beautiful.

East of Pythagorion there is a small beach beyond the quay; but west of town the beach stretches four miles to **Ireon.** The best part of it—sandy, clear, and warm—is closest to town, just beyond the castle. When you've explored the town, you can take a taxi to Ireon to see the **Temple of Hera,** and swim at that end of the beach; or you can take the bus to one of the small mountain towns like **Pirgos,** for a leisurely lunch on the pine-shaded terrace of a restaurant that is a favorite with the local folks.

When you're ready to move on, take the bus west to **Marathocambo.** This is a two-hour ride through pine forests, mountain towns, and breathtaking scenery to the village of Aghios Nikolaos, where you have a 1½-hour wait before intercepting the bus from Karlovassi. (You have to climb back to the highway intersection where you were dropped, because the road into Aghios Nikolaos is not paved.) Marathocambo is a pretty but activity-less town on a hillside, with a view embracing Agathonissi near Turkey and the Fourni islands to the west. The D-class **Kerkis** is the only hotel, charging 150 drs for a bathless single, 250 for a double. There is just one restaurant.

You must take a taxi down the mountain to reach **Ormos Marathocambos** on the beach: one good restaurant, two cafes, and three miles of warm sandy coast, usually completely deserted. There are a few rooms to rent (for example, over the restaurant) but no hotel.

At 5 p.m., a bus leaves for **Karlovassi,** which is actually four towns, connected by mile-long stretches of road: a town seemingly designed for the benefit of taxi drivers. **Neon Karlovassi** on the hillside, where the bus stops, is clean and attractive, with plenty of shops, two theaters, and several good cafes and restaurants, particularly around the lower square where the taxis park.

There are two good cheap hotels: the **Morpheus** (21 Apriliou, tel: 32262), with bathless rooms for around 200 drs double, and a few singles with bath for about the same price; and the **Samion Palace** (on Vliamou, tel: 323-09), old, pleasant, and spotlessly clean, with singles for 200 drs, doubles for 245 drs, all bathless.

There are no hotels or even pensions in **Meson Karlovassi** or **Paleo Karlovassi**—although the latter is a quaint spot, with its two tiny chapels perched on high rocks like stork nests with blue egg domes.

The **Port of Karlovassi** offers the ancient **Aktaeon Hotel,** with bathless rooms for around 200 drs; and three primitive pensions where prices are negotiable and beds sag. By contrast, nearby **Pefkakia** boasts the beautiful B-class **Merope,** air-conditioned, with a flashy restaurant, and rooms—all with bath—for 350 drs single, 500 drs double. The taxi ride out there will cost around 80 drs (depending upon which Karlovassi you leave from), but the beach and the setting beneath a cliff are splendid. Unless you want to make the long trek to town at mealtimes, however, you'll pay 175 drs for lunch or dinner, as well as the required 40 drs for breakfast. All the hotels on the island offer 20% discounts off-season.

For information, tours, tickets, and Samos wine to take back, see Mr. Andreas in the tourist office on the harbor, unfailingly friendly, and busy extolling the virtues of his island in four languages. Right next door is the best restaurant in town, with excellent roast pork.

The beach in front of Meson Karlovassi is marshy and reedy, but half a mile to either side are good beaches, and just around the headland west of the port is the most spectacular scenery on the island: a series of fjord-like ravines that end in small beaches between majestic cliffs. A good spot for a final swim before catching the boat back to Piraeus.

You should somehow also try to see **Mytilene, Aghios Constantinou,** and all the other delightful and individual towns of Samos. As the brochure says, "At every bend of the road, every beach, fishing village, or inland hamlet, the visitor to Samos is confronted with the unfamiliar, and altogether these contrasts form the smiling face of Samos."

Getting to Samos

The *Samena* leaves Piraeus for Samos at 8:30 a.m. Monday and Wednesday, the *Aegeon* at 9 a.m. Friday. But you can also get there from Patmos and Rhodes. Cheapest (deck class) one-way fare is about 180 drs, and the trip takes 10-17 hours depending on which island it stops at. There are two daily flights by Olympic from Athens, this taking one hour and costing about $25 (office in Hotel Xenia, tel: 27-237).

Samos can also be reached from Kavala in the north (see Chapter XV), with stops at Lemnos, Lesbos, and Xios. This is a 24-hour trip.

CRETE

CRETE, THE LARGEST of the Greek islands and the nearest to the African coast, has been an archaeologist's paradise for the last century. The discovery of elaborately decorated palaces at **Knossos** in the north and **Phaestos** in the south confirmed what historians always suspected: that a highly sophisticated civilization existed in Crete at least 1,500 years before Christ, when the rest of Europe was little more than warring groups of barbaric tribes.

King Minos ruled Crete in those days, and of all the legends associated with his name, none seems to have lingered more persistently than that of the half bull/half man who took his name, the Minotaur (said to be the result of the union of the last king's wife and a white bull).

The Minotaur was imprisoned in a labyrinth or maze, and every year seven youths and seven maidens were supposedly sacrificed to his lust or greed or whatever Minotaurs suffered from. The miserable beast was finally slain, but civilization in Crete degenerated from that time, and the history of the next centuries is of invasions and occupations.

Of more contemporary interest was the fierce fight waged by Cretans in May 1941, when British and Commonwealth forces retreated to the island from mainland Greece and, despite what appears to have been thoroughly inept direction from armchair generals who were not even on the island, put up a tremendous battle until overpowered by German paratroopers, tanks, aerial strafing, and bombardment from the sea.

For the next two or three years, the German occupation was resisted with amazing courage by the people of Crete, many of whom risked their lives to hide soldiers who had escaped capture by the Germans, or who had broken out of resistance camps on the island. Guerilla warfare was waged from the Crete mountains (riddled with limestone caves in which it was easy to hide), and once the German commander of the island was kidnapped and smuggled off the island into British custody—presumably by the same means by which so many soldiers escaped, via British submarines surfacing near the deserted coastline.

There is record of at least one of the British soldiers returning to Crete after the war to marry the daughter of the family who had hidden him away.

Most of Crete's tourists, of course, come to immerse themselves in the ruins—the distant past, apparently being of more interest to them than the present—and their first stop is the island's major town, **Iraklion,** from which Knossos is but a 20-minute bus ride.

Knossos was excavated and partly reconstructed, complete with brightly painted columns and murals, by a team led by British archaeologist Sir Arthur Evans, and there has been considerable controversy about his work. My own view is that, considering that he spent partly his own money, and that he probably possessed more knowledge than anybody then living about what the ancient Knossos looked like, he was perfectly entitled to re-create the place in any way he wished. The pure culture vultures, however, prefer Phaestos, which was merely dug up and then left with its crumbling walls simply ouflining the shape of the way things were.

The Cretans are proud, vigorous, and independent people—many of them mountain men with traditional black costume and high boots (to guard against thistles, thorns, etc.)—and something of their spirit is reflected in the works of Greece's famous novelist, the late Nikos Kazantzakis, whose most famous book, *Zorba,* is set on that island (where Kazantzakis himself was born). (Two other famous Cretans were the painter, El Greco, and Venizelou, prime minister of Greece in the 1930s.)

A beautiful island, with plenty of good but untamed beaches, impressively high mountain ranges, and millions of brilliantly colored and gloriously aromatic flowers, it now has a high priority on the list of places for tourist development. "Crete, because of climate, abundance of natural beauties, length and variety of coast, its picturesqueness, its interest from a folklore point of view and the proverbial hospitality of its inhabitants fulfills all the necessary conditions for its development," says one published report.

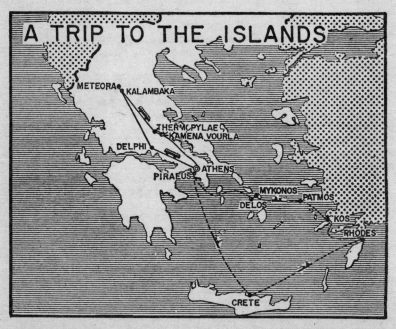

BOOKS OF INTEREST: Lawrence Durrell's book set in Crete is a novel, *The Dark Labyrinth* (Faber paperback), and like most of Durrell's works has.

more mood than plot. Good reading, though, and based at least partly on existing circumstances. . . . Nikos Kazantzakis, of course, was born in Crete, and his most famous work, *Zorba,* is set there. It's a story of an individualist whose way of life changed the lives of people he met. "Zorba had got so far beyond contemporary events that they had ceased to be anything but out-of-date rubbish." . . . Alan Clark's *The Fall of Crete* (Four Square paperback, London, is an historian's account of the five-day struggle, in May 1941, for the possession of the airfield at Malesse near Heraklion—a battle won by the Germans with appalling losses, and which decided subsequent control of the island. The appendix at the back contains a series of accounts of survivors who courageously fought as guerillas after the battle, some of whom were captured, some killed, some of whom escaped. . . . *Minotaur and Crete* (Spiros Alexiou Sons, Heraklion), by Robert Grantham, is an often delightful study of Crete and its customs by a Kansas-born schoolteacher who lived there for many years. Part history and part guidebook, it also contains many anecdotes and stories about such customs as arranged marriages, harvest time, and dances. . . . John Bowman's guidebook *Crete* (Secher & Warburg, London) is well written, interesting, and comprehensive. It has photographs, maps, history, geography, and also a section on driving around specific portions of the island by a man who spent several months doing just that. . . . Mary Renault's *The King Must Die* (Four Square Books, London,) is a fascinating novel spun around the legendary king of Athens, Theseus, taking place largely in the Palace of Knossos and packed with all the legends surrounding Minoan culture (Ariadne's ball of thread, the youths who danced the bulldance for the Minotaur). . . . Robin Bryans' *Crete* (Faber & Faber, London) is a charming personal account. . . . Check also *The Wooden Swallow* (World Publishing) by Dana Faralla, whose novels also include one about Corfu: *Children of Lucifer* (J. P. Lippincott Co.).

1. Chania

Boats rarely dock in the harbor of Chania itself, preferring the more spacious facilities of **Souda Bay** naval base. Buses meet the boats for the run of three or four miles into town. The ride by taxi costs about 80 drs. There is no advantage in staying in Souda, a dull naval town with few good facilities (the six-room **Hotel Knossos,** on the harbor, charges about 140 drs double).

Chania, the former capital of Crete, is an aged, peaceful city with crumbling sandstone walls and the characteristically narrow, winding streets of Greek island towns, except that here the medieval influence of the Venetians can be detected. Much of it was bombed during the last war, when British and Germans were fighting on the island.

For a drachma or two, the sexton at any of two or three churches with minaret-like towers will let you climb, and from the top the city comes into perspective. The most attractive part of town is around the harbor, but Konstantinou and Sfakianaki Streets are both lined with pleasantly set, large houses, many of them homes of the wealthier Greek-Americans or British sea captains. Bright flowers abound.

Following Venizelou Street westwards takes you to the most attractive part of the shoreline, where calm clear waters encourage most of the town's bathers. A coral bank acts as a natural breakwater against heavy tides.

The house where Venizelou lived (to repeat, Venizelou was the Crete-born prime minister of Greece in the 1930s) stands opposite a statue of him at the point where Avenue Venizelou meets Konstantinou Street.

You might look through the town's two **museums**—one containing historical archives of Crete, at 20 Sfakianaki Street, and the other at 30 Chalidou Street, between the harbor and Plateia 1866. Both are open from 9 a.m. to 1 p.m. and 4 to 6 p.m. daily, closed Sundays and Monday afternoons. Admission is 25 drs.

The most central part of Chania is Venizelou Square, where the covered market is, and where the buses leave for Rethymnon and Heraklion.

The highest point from which to obtain a good view of the city is from the **Akrotiri** (promontory), about three miles east of town. There's a statue of Eleuteria, goddess of liberty, here, marking the spot where Cretan insurgents raised the flag against the Turks in 1897. Venizelou's grave is nearby.

During the war for liberation, the blue and white flag of Greece was raised atop the peak and, though bombarded fiercely by the enemy, was kept flying. "This grave manifestation of the deep desire for freedom and the contempt for death was the result of many years of uninterrupted sacrifices which convinced the world that the Cretans deserved to live free. Crete was liberated," says the official brochure. And it closes with the translation of a verse written by a Greek poet to commemorate the occasion:

"Our blue flag which raised up there
And was torn down by bombs coming from the edge of the mountain
It is raised again and gloriously reaches heaven
Until it becomes part of the blue sky."

Today, the point is marked by a modern representation of Athena, goddess of wisdom and war (strange combination), carved by the sculptor Thomas Thomopoulos in 1937.

There's now a new luxury restaurant up on the Akrotiri called the **Asteria**, very popular at night for its views of both Chania and Souda. Meals are expensive, but drinks are reasonable. No bus service; taxi from Chania charges about 100 drs.

ORIENTATION AND HOTELS: Many of Chania's foreign resident writers have pleasant apartments overlooking the harbor and rarely leave the vicinity. You may also find this the most pleasant part of town and if so there are various rooms for rent plus several hotels to choose from. The modern **Lucia**, unobtrusively right on the harbor (tel: 21821) is comfortable with lovely views and an attractive, cool dining room. All rooms with bath: around 320 drs single, 425 drs double. Somewhat simpler and older is the unpretentious **Hotel Plaza** with the same rates.

Attractively located right around at the eastern end of the harbor is the pleasant **Porto Venezia** (tel: 29311), one of the nicest hotels in Crete, though hardly cheap (about 700 drs double including breakfast). In the opposite direction, past the harbor to the east, is the plush **Xenia** (tel: 24561), with its own private beach and swimming pool. Demi-pension only: about 1200 drs double.

There are two cheap rooming houses towards the eastern end of the harbor. **Yani's** is the nicest and its friendly, English-speaking proprietor points out that there's always plenty of hot water. Forty beds available for 100 drs each or 250 drs for a double room.

If all the harbor places are filled you'll have to walk up the short hill back into town.

Where the buses come in and leave is **Plateia Venizelou** (Venizelou Square), and here is the big covered market, a not-yet-complete luxury hotel, and a good drugstore. The hilly street climbing out of the square is called **Tsanakakis**, and a couple of hundred yards up it, on the left, are the post office (open 8 a.m. to noon, 3 to 5 p.m.), the hotels **Cyprus** and **Minoa,** and a lovely little park with fenced-in aviary, lake for swans and ducks, children's playground, and open-air theater.

Opening off the square at the same side are **Konstantinou Street** (a short way up this street is one of our recommended restaurants, the Pik-Nik), which leads past several schools, the army barracks, and three separate movie theaters, two of them open-air ones; and also **Venizelou Street,** which leads ultimately (about two miles) to Venizelou's statue and the beaches.

At the other side of the square is the main street, **Hatsimikili Jannaris,** which leads into **Plateia 1866,** full of taxi stands and the bright, modern **Hotel Canea** (tel: 24673). Its 50 compact rooms with balconies cost 350 drs single and 450 drs double with bath; the few rooms without bath are cheaper. Breakfast can be taken in a small first-floor lounge for 40 drs. The **Hotel Kydon** (tel: 26191), which dominates Venizelou Square, is too expensive for budget readers (single 500 drs, double 800 drs), but there's a pleasant alternative only a couple of blocks away, the relatively new **Hotel Diktynna** (beside the cathedral, tel: 21101) whose 35 rooms all have bath and balcony. Singles 340 drs, doubles 420 drs. Another recent (and expensive) addition to Plateia 1866 is the **Hotel Samaria** (tel: 51551), with cafeteria and roof garden.

The biggest hotel bargain is the 20-room **Hotel Cyprus** (singles 200 drs, doubles 330 drs, bathless) on Tsanakakis Street, just above the post office. It is a very cheerful, bright, airy place with vines and plants in all kinds of odd corners and a sort of enclosed garden in the rear. Rooms are small, but clean and bright, and bathrooms are spotless.

Chania's **youth hostel,** very civilized, with helpful manager and plenty of hot water, is at Drakonianou 33 (tel: 53565), which runs off Dexameni Square. It's the fifth stop on the Ag. Ioannis bus from Kotzabassi Square.

EATING PLACES: A 328-year-old soap factory, later used for the manufacture of cheese and candy, is Chania's newest taverna. Called the **Aposperida** (Kondylaki 37, tel: 51423), it's attractively done up with timbered ceilings and benches, but few of the items on its varied menu were available on a recent visit. Kondylaki is the street that runs back from the harbor beside the Hotel Lucia. It crosses Zambelliou (which is parallel with the harbor) just about where the tiny cellar called **The Experimental Cafe** is located. Here, mornings and evenings until 10 p.m., you can "play chess, read a good book, listen to music or find oneself in a quiet place full of creation."

The preferred place to eat—by foreigners living in Chania—is the **Kavouria** on the harbor. At first glance it looks dark and dingy, but the food is good. It's easy to recognize because of all the big barrels in the back of the restaurant and a sort of wooden minstrels' gallery running around the interior. Another friendly spot is called **Pik-Nik,** a narrow bar with picture-lined walls, on Konstantinou Street, about 200 yards on the right out of Venizelou Square. The Pik-Nik has lamb chops, chicken, and a host of snack-type items such as meatballs, spaghetti, souvlaki, cheese pies, etc. It's intimate, lively, and friendly. One of the best of the outdoor restaurants is the **Padogiannis,** just up Kossourakie Street, where it turns off Venizelou, about a mile from the square. Take a taxi or a horse-drawn surrey. There's a movie theater right opposite the restaurant, too. Also recommended, the **Zepos** and the **Selini.**

Best cafe in the harbor is the enormous, classy **Pharos,** its sundeck bar overlooking the sea and adjoining the enclosed dining room.

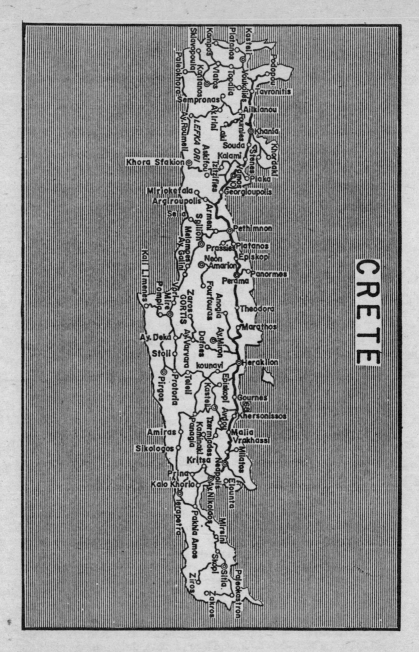

OUT OF TOWN: Best excursion from Chania is to the magnificent **Samaria Gorge,** which begins at Xiloskalon, about 25 miles south of the city, and runs almost 12 miles to the sea at Aghia Roumeli. You can take a tour or, better still, get one of the half-dozen daily buses to the tourist pavilion at **Xiloskalon** and hike for four or five hours to Aghia Roumeli. Here boats run to **Chora-Sfakion,** a charming little fishing port where you can get the bus back to Chania. Or you can hang around for a while, rent a cheap room in the village or stay at the new **Xenia Hotel** and pay a visit to an ancient Venetian castle with the sweet-sounding name of **Frangocastello.**

The drive to Xiloskalon where the gorge begins is absolutely magnificent but, of course, it makes no sense to drive if you plan to hike through the gorge because then you'll eventually end up in Chania and have to come all the way back to retrieve your car. So take the bus. (If you do drive make sure your gas tank is full; the only gas station en route is at Fournes.)

It might also be more to your liking to stay overnight at the tourist pavilion (about 150 drs single) before setting off on your hike early next morning. The trip must be made between sunrise and sunset and it is advisable to carry a light lunch and some fruit. Fresh water available courtesy Mother Nature's streams. The flora and fauna will enchant you and you won't lack for company on the way.

Even if you don't make the gorge trip try to fit in a ride at least to **Omalos** and back. The road gets increasingly beautiful with spectacular views constantly changing as the highway loops around one hillside after another, and valley vistas unfold panoramically below. The highway comes to a dramatic end at Xiloskalon where the gorge swoops dramatically downwards. There's a bus (around 65 drs) to Omalos at 6 a.m.; but you may find it more congenial to catch the one at 9:10 a.m., which gets you to the gorge's entrance by 10:30 a.m. The path into the gorge—descending for about one hour—is rough and steep enough to cause muscle strain on the legs, and you can either take it easy in order to arrive at Aghia Roumeli in ample time for the 5:30 p.m. boat (the last) or hurry and catch the 2:30 boat. Most people rush. There is fresh water from springs for the first and last portions of the gorge, cool water from the river for the final third, a spring at an abandoned village just past halfway. It isn't necessary to take food or drink, unless you plan a longer stay. You can stay overnight in the pension at Omalos or in rooms at Aghia Roumeli. But Chora Sfakion (with pebbly beach) is nicer and spots both hotels and pensions. The boat to Chora Sfakion costs around 95 drs, the bus to Chania (4 and 7 p.m.) about 80 drs.

BRIEFLY NOTED: **Horse-drawn surreys** will take you all around town in comfort. Bargain with the guy for a one-hour trip and you'll see all you need to. . . . Behind the Hotel Diktyna is a street of **shoe shops** where you can have shoes or sandals made to order. . . . The **covered market** (entrance opposite Hotel Kydon, where you can also inspect what's scheduled at the town's seven movies) is worth visiting before setting off for a picnic or your gorge trek. Spacious, clean and chock-a-block with fruit, vegetables, bread, cheeses, honey. . . . The bus to the beach—#21, marked "Nea Hora," leaves from outside the magazine store on Plateia 1866. Go to the end of the line. . . . Best ice cream (and fabulous pastries) in town can be found at **Kronos Patisserie** on Monsorou Street at Episkopol. . . . **Elafonissos** (Skaliki 24, tel: 23500) is a cheap car rental company, with small Fiats from $7 daily plus 10¢ per km. . . . **Canea Travel Bureau** (46 Karaiskaki St., tel: 24780) operates trips to Samaria Gorge for 400 drs but, of course, you can do it cheaper yourself. On Thursday nights they organize an excursion to the coastal village of **Kalives,** where there's dinner, wine, and Cretan folk dancing. . . . **Boats from Ag. Roumeli to Hora Sfakion** are at 9 a.m., 1:30, 2, 4:30 and 5 p.m. From Hora Sfakion to Ag. Roumeli, boats sail at 10, 10:30 a.m., and 3 and 5 p.m. . . . There are **flights to Athens** twice daily; flight takes 45 minutes; about $22 each way. Olympic Airways, 34 Stratigou Tzanaki St., tel: 27701 (Souda Airport: 2797).

BUSES FROM CHANIA: To Rethymnon and Iraklion: 5:30, 7:30, 8:30, 9:30, 10:30 a.m. and 12:30, 2:15, 3:30, 5:30, 7 p.m. All except the 8:30, 12:30, and 5:30 buses are expresses. They leave from 28 El Venizelou St. (tel: 23306); fare around 110 drs.

To Omalos: 5:15, 9 a.m., 4 p.m. Return at 6:45, 10:30 a.m., and 6 p.m. Departure from 15 Smirnis St. (tel: 23052); about 65 drs.

To Chora Sfakion: 9 a.m. and 2 p.m. Return at 6:30 a.m. and 6:30 p.m. From N. Episkon St. (tel: 23304); about 100 drs.

To Kastelli: 5, 7, 8:30, 10, 11 a.m., noon, 1, 2:30, 3:30, 4:30, 5:30, 6:30, 8 p.m. (Sundays: 7:30, 8:30, 9:30, 10:30 a.m., noon, 2, 4, 8, 9 p.m.). From 15 Smirnis St.; about 60 drs.

Buses run to Souda port every 15 minutes from in front of the Central Market. Buses to the beaches west of town (Kalamaki, Aptera, Glaros) depart from Plateia 1866.

BOATS FROM CHANIA: To Piraeus at 6 p.m. Sunday, 9 p.m. Monday and Tuesday, and 7 p.m. Wednesday through Saturday. (**Arek Shipping Co.,** Venizelou St., tel: 23636). It's about one hour by bus to Kastelli, at Crete's western end, from which the *Kanaris* sails at 10 a.m. (Sundays) to Kythera, Neapolis, Monemvassia, and Piraeus; and the *Cyclades* sails from here at 3:30 p.m. Wednesdays to Gythion, Ag. Pelagia, Neapolis, Monemvassia, and Piraeus. You can get tickets in Kastelli or buy them in Chania from **G. Nanadakis,** 3 Halidou St. (tel: 24352).

2. Rethymnon

The road along the coast, past Souda Bay and the naval base (Souda is internationally famous among the world's fleets because of its fine natural harbor), eventually turns inland, where there's nothing much of consequence to see beyond scrubby green countryside. (The construction of a new, high-speed road along the coast has uncovered some ancient caves, complete with prehistoric bones and stalactites, about four miles west of Rethymnon.)

After about 2½ hours, the road suddenly bends, and there stands Rethymnon in its full glory—a sprawling town on a headland jutting into the wave-flecked seashore.

The town itself is ancient and tumbledown; everything looks like it needs a coat of paint. But the harbor, lined with noisy tavernas, is charming and the broad seafront that leads into it is lined with restaurants and cafes. Best restaurant is nearest to Labrynth beach which is where you'll have to park if you're driving as cars aren't allowed further along.

Not surprisingly, fish can be seen everywhere in Rethymnon's harbor—on the cobblestone quay, hanging over motorcycle handlebars, drying outside the tavernas, and in the gleeful hands of boys with flaming torches who angle with nets off the rocks at night.

The tourists' best friend in Rethymnon is **Kostas,** amiable host of the spanking new tourist office on Koundourioti Street, only a couple of blocks from where the bus stops. Kostas speaks excellent English, knows everything and everybody, and keeps his office open every day of the week from 8 a.m. to 1 p.m. and again from 4 to 7 p.m.; phone: 29148.

On my recent visit Kostas gave me a charming book called *The Tale of a Town* (Doric Publications, Athens), written many years ago by a famous Greek novelist, Pandelis Prevelakis. It's a lovely story, all about life there in the old days and I can't do better than quote Angelos Sikelianos' tribute to its author: " . . . So today, thanks to you, deep in my mind's eye/I hold a town long lost, Rethemnos/Carved hard and clear out of pure speech/And lit serenely by your pain and your compassion."

Until that great Greek historian Sterghios G. Spanakis get around to covering Rethymnon (be sure to buy his excellent guide to eastern Crete), Prevelakis' little tale will do nicely.

WHERE TO STAY: The nearest hotel to where the bus pulls in is the pleasant **Acropol** (Plateia Agnostou, tel: 22344) most of whose bright rooms have balconies overlooking the square and the sea. Without bath, 185 drs single, 250 drs double; with bath, 250 drs single, 350 drs double.

Another cheap place—without frills, though adequate for budgeteers—is the **Hotel Minoa** (Arkadiou 62, tel: 22085), which has rooms with bath for 275 drs single, 385 drs double, and a few rooms without bath.

Newest hotels in town are the 70-room **Ideon** (Plastira Sq., tel: 22346), spacious, near the sea, and with restaurant and bar; and the **Minos** (on the Iraklion road, east end of town, tel: 28439), whose balconies overlook the sea. The Ideon costs about 550 drs double, the Minos about 500 drs double, both including breakfast. Next door to the Minos is the excellent **Famagusta** restaurant.

The **Valaris** (Koundouriotou 78, tel: 293-68), up the hill to the right, about 200 yards from the bus stop, and the ten-room **Park** (Igoumenou Gavriel 6, tel: 299-58) have rooms with bath for 400 drs double.

Best hotel in town is probably the **Xenia** (tel: 29111), right on the beach, and with an excellent restaurant. All rooms with bath and balcony, 600 drs double. Lunch or dinner, 175 drs.

A substantial number of Rethymnon's 4-5,000 weekly visitors end up in **private rooms,** which are numerous both along the harbor and the streets behind. About 150 drs single, 250 drs double.

Newly opened is an immense tourist resort called **Lavrys,** a few miles east of Rethymnon near the coastal village of Panormos. A 1,000-bed hotel with bungalows forms the heart of a self-contained facility which includes nightclub, swimming pools, tennis courts, golf course, volleyball courts, and even a hospital. There's a marina for private boats and facilities for aquatic sports such as skiing and water polo. Germans and Swedes seem to form the majority of the resort's patrons, attracted to a climate whose average temperature throughout the year is higher than that of Nice or Capri.

The coastline at both sides of Rethymnon is gradually getting snatched up by farsighted developers. Until recently there were mostly camping sites here— the elaborate **Camping Elizabeth** (three miles east at Missena, tel: 0831-28694), equipped with supermarket and showers; **Camping Arkadia** (4 kms east, tel: 28746), which describes itself as "a place full of trees flowers and shadow"; and now **Camping George** (15 kms east, tel: 61363)—but now hotels are springing up all along the coast.

Seven kilometers east of town is the 271-room **Rithymna Hotel** (tel: 29492) with tennis courts, mini-golf, an enormous swimming pool, and 90 bungalows in the adjoining "Cretan Village," with its shopping center, taverna, and church—and all of gleaming concrete. Expensive, of course: about 1000 drs single, 1600 drs double demi-pension. One kilometer further east is the somewhat similar (and slightly cheaper) **El Greco** hotel and bungalows (tel: 71281), with similar facilities but architecture described in the brochure as "unique split-level Knossos style."

WHERE TO EAT: The best way to eat in Rethymnon is to head for the **Chulubasis** area, which is the far eastern end of the beach (way around past the harbor), where you'll find several open-air tavernas. Preferred one here is the **Sakalis,** which sports a jukebox and features dancing on its smooth concrete floor on weekend nights. Usual dishes: liver, lamb, veal, meatballs, chops, etc., which will run you to about 60 drs each. Back in the central part of the beach, nearer to "midtown," is the **Pantheon** restaurant, also with a jukebox. And in the center of town, almost opposite the park entrance just back from the square, are several restaurants. The best one: **Apostolakis,** at Kallirois Paren Siganou Street. The chicken here is tops. The **Edelweiss** cafe (best in town) has good pastries and homemade ice cream.

WHAT TO SEE AND DO: The best time of the year to be in Rethymnon is the final week of July, when the **wine festival** is held in the park; upon payment of 50 drs you can go in and drink as much as you like.

    Nias Tours (Arkadion 116, tel: 23146) operate one-day tours to Samaria Gorge for 700 drs, departing at 6:30 a.m. and returning at 8:30 p.m. Another outing is on Thursday, this one visiting remote mountain villages, the monastery at Vrodissi, and the beach at Aghia Gallini. The cost is 500 drs, and the outing lasts from 8 a.m. to 6:30 p.m.

    On Saturday and Sunday nights various tavernas host **Cretan dancing.** Check with Kostas for specific details.

    Two popular excursions from Rethymnon are to the monasteries of **Arkadi,** in the mountains to the southeast (five kilometers east of town take the southern fork 24 more kilometers up the mountain), and **Preveli,** on the south coast of Crete, almost due south of Rethymnon. Both are well off the beaten track and both have heroic histories. When the Cretans revolted against Turkish rule in 1866, the head monk at Arkadi was appointed commander of the forces in the area. The gallant fight put up by the monks and other Cretans who took refuge in the monastery ended with them blowing themselves up—300 of them—by firing a pistol into the gunpowder room where all had gathered to commit mass suicide rather than be taken prisoner by the Turks. (There had been suggestions that those taken alive would be not only tortured but skinned alive.)

    Both Arkadi and Preveli earned a place in history for their help to the Greek Resistance movement during World War II. The Germans had taken possession of the island in 1941, but many British and Greek soldiers were still on the run for years afterwards. Despite the fact that anybody caught sheltering such refugees was shot on sight, both monasteries persistently sheltered and fed such wanted men. And in the summer of 1941, both helped organize a daring escape in which nearly 200 men were sneaked, with much danger, onto a British submarine which had cruised near shore by prearrangement.

    There are three buses daily from Rethymnon to Arkadi. Two (at 11 a.m. and 2:30 p.m.) stay at the monastery for about one hour and return to the town; the other, at 4 p.m., stays at the monastery overnight. Overnight visitors to Arkadi stay in a newly built tourist pavilion for 130 drs double and return the following morning. One bus each day leaves Rethymnon for Preveli on the south shore. This is a 2:30 p.m. The trip takes about two hours and the bus stays overnight (visitors are welcome—free), returning the next morning at 7 a.m. The buses, which cost 40 drs for each trip, leave from Agnostos Stratiotis Square in Rethymnon, opposite the Acropol hotel.

The road that connects **Xanea** and Iraklion, along the northern shore, is a broad highway that skirts the coast most of the way and affords many opportunities to **camp** right on the beach.

But if you have the time and your own transport (Crete is one place where car rentals are still reasonably priced), it's a gorgeous trip to drive from Rethymnon to Iraklion via the much-lengthier southern route. This could include a side trip to the famous and picturesque Preveli monastery (turn off to the right just before the charming mountainside village of **Spili**), on the way to which you'll pass through the majestic **Kourtaliotiko** ravine.

Maybe you'd prefer to save your time for two fabulous beaches: that of lovely **Aghia Galini** (details upcoming) and the even more remote **Matala** at the terminus of a dead-end road further south.

BUSES TO IRAKLION: 7:15, 9, 10:30, 11 a.m., noon, 3, 5, 8, 8:15 p.m. Express buses at 6:45 a.m. and 3:15 p.m.

BUSES TO CHANIA: 7:15, 9, 9:15, 11 a.m., noon, 3, 6, 8:15 p.m. Express buses at 9:15 a.m. and 6 p.m.

3. Aghia Galini

When I first visited Aghia Galini in the mid-sixties it was so primitive and unspoiled that there was no electricity and the man at the hotel where I stayed loaned his donkeys to guests when they wanted to go exploring in the mountains behind the town. Well, it's been "discovered" with a vengeance in recent years and a sign of the tourist times are the signs offering "Souvlaki & Chips" in local cafes. The road is being surfaced and five buses connect daily to Iraklion and two more to Rethymnon.

But Aghia Galini is still a lovely spot where wandering sheep and goats are apt to get entangled on the beach with the volley ball game, watched by people sitting under the trees at the edge of the adjoining harbor. More than 500 rooms are available in town—almost every house has at least one to rent—and there are a group of cheap hotels, the **Libya**, the **Acropol**, the **Pantheon**, and the **Aktaion**, overlooking the harbor.

Rooms in private homes cost about 150 drs per person, in the (C-class) hotels around 250 drs per person. There are plenty of places to eat, especially on the cafe-lined steps leading back from the harbor. Right by the town beach you'll see **Zorba's** "healthfood" cafe with a good selection of taped music and an 18-dr breakfast consisting of juice, toast, egg, and coffee.

For out-of-town activities, there are the beaches, stretching for miles around the coast but mostly rocky and hard to swim from (but fine for sunbathing), and the already mentioned mule trips into the hills. Just outside town on a hillside is a tiny church and graveyard, with cultivated gardens below, ingeniously irrigated by gasoline-powered water pumps and channels leading in all directions. The cliffs that frame both sides of town are riddled with caves, many enlarged and fitted out with interior staircases by the Germans whose gun emplacements guarded this part of Crete against invasion in World War II.

After Aghia Galini go back to the main road and through **Timbaki** before the sinuous climb up the hill to the magnificent **Phaistos,** once one of Minoan Crete's most important cities and devastated suddenly at the same time (about 1400 B.C.) as Knossos to the north. Phaistos, situated impressively on a ridge, was rediscovered early in this century by Greek and Italian archaeologists, who dated its early palaces to about 2000 B.C. It has been surmised that Phaistos, to which there are references in Homer's *Iliad* and *Odyssey,* was the seat of the wise king Radamanthis, brother of Minos. He may actually have lived at—or used as a seaside palace—the nearby royal villa of **Aghia Triada** of which impressive traces remain on the other side of the hill. It takes half an hour or so to walk between them so it might be advisable to pick up a soda from the tourist pavilion at Phaistos and take it with you.

The **Pension Olympic** in **Mires** is one of the places nearest to Phaistos to get an inexpensive room.

Yet a third interesting site, further east along the highway, is what remains of ancient **Gortys** which in pre-Roman times rivaled the other two for supremacy. The highlight of Gortys, now a sleepy ruin, is the Law Code—15,000 characters carved on a slab of rock and dealing with the legal administration and niceties of a community that existed 2,600 years ago. The ground around the site has been left as it was originally cut away and demonstrates how the ruins were preserved under solid feet of earth for so many centuries.

Before Gortys a side trip can be made about ten miles down to the seedy harbor of **Matala** framed by evil-smelling caves, which must have been living quarters for hundreds of years. Inside are bunks for sleeping carved out of the solid rock of the cliff face. Signs in English and Greek prohibit living in the caves today and periodically the police sweep out the young freaks who ignore the admonitions. Young people are all over the shabby town: eating in the numerous cafes, lying in tents and sleeping bags under the trees behind the beach, and squatting in front of blankets on the main street. The blankets are covered with jewelry, incense, and patchouli oil which they have brought from India and sometimes manage to sell to the unwary ladies alighting from the occasional tourist buses.

There are numerous signs offering rooms to rent (around 150 drs per person). There are buses from here to Iraklion at 5:30 a.m. and 2:30 p.m. each day.

4. Iraklion (Heraklion)

The city of Iraklion was one of the first communities to be built on Crete, its name dating back to the legendary hero, Heracles, who was given 12 tasks to perform, and who landed here at the request of King Minos to capture and remove the mad bull that was terrorizing the country.

At the time of Knossos' heyday, it served as a port for that splendid city, but first achieved stature in the ninth century when the Arabs built a fort there. Under the Venetians, the Arab name Chandax ("ditch") was corrupted to Candia and it was under this name that it withstood siege for 22 years, the "ditch", built for fortification, having been supplemented by a massive city wall that took a century to complete. It finally fell to the Turks in 1669 and was renamed Iraklion when Crete was absorbed into Greece just before World War I.

Today, with a population of around 100,000 it is an attractive city that serves as a pleasant base for excursions around the central part of the island. Some of the old city walls remain, mostly as ramparts around the four main gates, but the atmosphere is surprisingly cosmopolitan. Foreign newspapers and magazines on sale in Venizelou Square are one indication of the influx of tourists, most of whom are easily able to make themselves understood with only the barest smattering of Greek (and, in my case, none at all).

Several prominent names have been associated with Iraklion, among them the painter El Greco (1542-1614), whose real name was Domenikos Theotokopoulos. He was born in the village of Fodhele, about 15 miles from Iraklion, where he studied art before leaving for Venice to work under Titian.

Novelist Nikos Kazantzakis (1883-1957), author of *Zorba,* was born in the city, but is buried in unconsecrated ground in the city's wall, because the Greek church refused to bury him with full rites. The inscription on his grave is a quotation from one of his own works: "I hope for nothing. I fear nothing. I am free."

ORIENTATION: The tourist center of town is **Venizelou Square,** prominently in the center of which is a lovely 16th-century fountain gurgling deliciously. Four lions on the fountain are at least a century older.

There are several hotels just off the square, a small park only 100 yards away, and two good restaurants near the fountain. The main street leading downhill from the square, **25th of August Street,** leads straight to the harbor.

About one block up from the square, where the traffic policeman stands, is **N. Focas Square.** The wide street to the left is **King Constantine Avenue,** lined with the town's best shops, which leads to **Liberty Square**—a big open place known chiefly for cafe-sitting and the evening volta (promenade).

Off N. Focas Square to the right is **Kalokairinon Avenue,** a long, dull street where one of the ice cream sellers keeps his change in a tin box in the freezer compartment (cold cash); it leads to **Porta Khanion,** one of the main gates of the city when it was surrounded by the high walls that scarcely remain.

Just outside this gate is where the buses leave for **Phaestos.** The terminal is about a 15-minute walk from the traffic policeman.

Heading uphill from the policeman in N. Focas Square, there is a choice of **1821 Street**—not very interesting—or the parallel streets of **1866** or **Evans,** the latter presumably named after Sir Arthur Evans, who reconstructed Knossos. Evans Street is full of little restaurants, and 1866 Street is the town's official market, with numerous sidewalk stalls and shops, most of their wares outside. Both lead to **Kornarou Square,** where the buses leave for Knossos.

IRAKLION HOTELS: If you arrive by boat, walk from the harbor up 25th of August Street to Venizelou Square. Just below the square, on 25th of August Street (on which most of the shipping and tour agencies are located) is the attractive 20-room **Hotel Knossos** (right next to the tourist office, tel: 283247), with a bright, sunny air to it. Clean bathrooms down the hall, small balconies overlooking the busy street. Doubles here are 500 drs.

Just above the square and vying for the preferred position in the center of town is the **Hotel Cosmopolit** (44 Evans, tel: 283313), which has always been especially friendly to this book's readers. Comfortable lobby sitting room, elevators, more than half the rooms with balconies, and all with full-length mirrors. Rooms with bath cost 375 drs single, 450 drs double; there are a few bathless rooms.

There are two good choices located on the little park just below Venizelou Square. These are the comfortable **Park Hotel** (5 Koroneou, tel: 283934), with singles from 400 drs, doubles 500 drs; and the highly recommended (by readers) **Domenico** (14 Almyrou, tel: 288231) with similar rates. Also around this park are motor-scooter rentals (shop around before you commit yourself—prices vary widely) and the **New Dionysos** discotheque.

The 64-room **Hotel Dedalos** (Daedalou 15, tel: 224391) is a new addition just up the street opposite the fountain. Cool and attractive, its 62 rooms cost around 400 drs single, 500 drs double including breakfast. The classy **Mediterranean** (Smirnis St., tel: 289331) has a roof garden and TV lounge and—for 60 drs extra—air conditioning. Singles for 400 drs, doubles 530 drs including breakfast—but in midsummer you may have to take demi-pension.

Just down from Venizelou Square along Xandakos Street you'll come to the charming little **Hotel Xanea,** simply and tastefully decorated with figures and signs painted on the walls. A popular place with budget-conscious young nomads who can well afford the rooms at under 300 drs double. On this corner, amidst the sweet-smelling flamboyan which hangs over the walls, is the **Palladion** (16 Chandakos, tel: 282563) with similar rates, and just down the side street, Kydonias, comes a little square sheltering the relatively expensive **Kastro** (20 Theotokopoulou tel: 285020) at around 500 drs single, 700 drs double, and the pleasant **Pension Mirabelle** whose rates are a little over half of its neighbor.

On Kornarou Square, is the 73-room **Olympic Hotel** (tel: 288-861), which boasts a big-screen television set in the spacious lobby. All rooms are with bath and cost 400 drs single, 500 drs double. Breakfast is 40 drs. The owner's wife, Ely Ikonomy, is a guide, and weeknights she shows slides of Crete in the hotel's lobby.

The Olympic is actually on a pretty noisy corner but only a few yards away is a fascinating market, replete with marvelous smells and selling everything from gourds to leather belts.

Hotel El Greco, just on the square by the traffic lights, is one of the bigger hotels in town, its 90 rooms all with shower. Rates are 400 drs single, 500 drs double; breakfast is 40 drs.

Just off 25th of August Street, between the Morosini Fountain and the Park Greco, is the modern, marble **Selena Hotel** (Andro'geo St., tel: 287660), quiet and cool. All 25 rooms with bath; 420 drs single, 546 drs double, including breakfast.

If you are planning to spend a few days in Iraklion, you might find it nicest of all to stay in one of the hotels that have recently gone up down by the sea. They're a ten-minute bus ride from the center of town, but buses run very frequently all day. A taxi would cost about 15 drs.

The nicest choice is the sparkling **Hotel Poseidon** (tel: 285-859), which stands on a small headland above the beach (good view on both sides). It is owned and operated by amiable John Polychronides, my best friend in Crete, who also operates Viking Tours for Crete (office on Aug 25th St., tel: 282476) and has been a great help to this book's readers. In recent years the harbor has grown out to meet the Poseidon Hill, whose balconies offer a good view of ships arriving and departing. You can take the bus out to his place or walk along the docks and then up the hill. The Poseidon is one of Greece's brightest, most cheerful hotels, with usual C-class rates: around 400 drs single, 500 drs double. Adjoining it is the **Hotel Galini** (tel: 288223) and nearby is the slightly cheaper **Pension Alex** (Anthemiou 56, tel: 284413) with garden overlooking the sea.

The **youth hostel,** brightly painted and cheerful, is at 24 Chandakos Street (tel: 81063). Dormitory accommodations, separate for men and women, with bunks for only 50 drs per night. Hot and cold water are plentiful, and you can get breakfast for 30 drs, or a light, inexpensive dinner. You do not need to be a member to stay here. Emm Mavrogannis; who operates the youth hostel, speaks some English and is very friendly.

READERS' SELECTIONS: "Just a few minutes on the # 1 or # 5 bus to Poros beach will bring you to the **Pension Rania** (44 Koritsas) run by a pleasant and helpful woman" (A.J. Sinclair, Chigwell, Essex, U.K.). . . . "Showers are free at the **Pension Toupoyanni** (Malikouti 2, tel: 282548) and the proprietress is extremely hospitable and had many suggestions on things to do" (Virginia McKinley, Bristol, N.H.).

MEALS: Most tourists gather around Venizelou Square, whiling away their time in front of the beautiful Morosini fountain (which isn't turned on for the summer until there are enough tourists to appreciate it). There are two restaurants here, the **Knossos** and the **Caprice,** and both somewhat spoiled by their location. The Knossos is to be preferred, though not by much, and you'll probably have a better selection altogether if you eat elsewhere.

The narrow street at the side of the Knossos restaurant shelters two attractive tavernas, both with tables on the sidewalk and reasonable prices—nothing on the menu exceeding 90 drs, except steak. Imitation plastic vines and bunches of grapes hang overhead, and both the restaurants and the food are attractive. Take a look at the large selection of food in the kitchen before sitting down to order.

Just above Venizelou Square, at the point where the traffic policeman stands, is Evans Street, at the foot of which are a batch of restaurants, many of them on the narrow side street leading between Evans Street and Market Street. Sometimes the aggressive waiters on this block—known to locals as "dirty street"—literally grab customers as they go by and draw their attention to the day's specialties. The best of the bunch here is the **Ionia,** which, like the others, has an outdoor grill from which the aroma of roasting meat entices all who pass by. The Ionia has an unusually large selection at low prices.

There are numerous little pastry shops, which also offer a simple breakfast, along King Constantine Avenue.

Dinner at night is best taken in a taverna, with or without music. In town the most interesting spots are the **Kallithea** (Viglas Street, just past Liberty Square), which has a straw roof, plenty of trees, and space for dancing; the spacious **Glass House** (turn left at the foot of 25th of August Street and keep walking east), which also has a dance floor and live trio; and two tavernas you'll pass on the way, the **Akrogiali** and **Refina**, both by the waterfront.

There are a couple of tavernas with gardens along Zorgaphou Street, just off Odos Averoff from Liberty Square. These are the **Dionysos** and **To Asterosia**.

Near the center of town is the pleasant, brightly lit **Maxim** taverna; next to the Park Hotel, and way out of town at Florina Beach, right after the airport is **Zorba's** which has female singers, a bouzouki group, and 100-dr drinks. The liveliest tavernas are on Pedalou Street—**Minos, Klimateria,** and **Kostas**.

When you come out of the Archaeological Museum (see below), be sure to pay a call on my friend Lianna Finn (she was once married to an Irishman), who operates a discreet little **snack bar** in the square right opposite, among all the boutiques. Miami-born Lianna says she rarely tires of meeting people and she'll try to answer all your questions. "Fast Service. Snacks & Drinks. Stop"— so says her eye-catching sign.

READERS' SELECTIONS: "An excellent little restaurant, the **Triana**, is in the market less than five minutes' walk from Venizelou Square. Cheap and picturesque" (Idahlia and Gene Stanley, Cambridge, Mass.). . . . "Try the excellent **Kibelia** restaurant, a short walk from the Poseidon Hotel at Poros beach" (George Claghorn, West Chester, Pa.). . . . "Specializing in seafood is the **Stratos**, in the suburb of Poros on the road to the airport. Small, clean, gourmet cooking without the usually inevitable olive oil" (Jerry Yale, Closter, N.J.).

IRAKLION BY NIGHT: The sidewalk cafe-sitters are out in force in Venizelou Square, along busy King Constantine Avenue, and around Liberty Square where, especially on Sunday nights but also at other times, the volta takes place.

The *volta,* similar to Mexico's *paseo,* is the steady procession of people (mostly young) showing off themselves, their friends and lovers, and their clothes. Liberty Square is an amazing sight: thronged with people at tables 20 or 30 deep outside each cafe, the others walking to see and be seen.

An alternative walk is the one down by the harbor and then along the waterfront westwards (into the sunset) to the **Glass House**, previously mentioned, a fairly classy restaurant situated at a strategic point for watching the sunset, the mountains, and the sea, its waves beating at the foundation of the restaurant.

The brightly decorated **Blow Up** disco is just behind the museum.

MUSEUMS, ETC.: Iraklion's celebrated **Archaeological Museum** (turn left from King Constantine Ave. at Liberty Square) is famous for its relics of the Minoan culture, 4,000 years ago, many of them discovered in the ruins of Phaestos and Knossos. They include scores of tiny bronze votive figurines in the shape of wild horses and goats, a ring depicting a scene of the sacred tree cult, bronze double-headed axes. Upstairs are impressive frescoes, and the staircases are a maelstrom of students of all nationalities who have already stashed their backpacks and filled the seats beside the entrance long before opening time at 8:30 a.m. (Hikers have long ago taken over Iraklion, and the little park below Venizelou Square is filled every night with sleeping figures on blankets and bedrolls beneath the trees.)

The museum is well laid out with multilingual cards identifying all the exhibits. On the walls of each room are either photographs of the ruins today, or artists' conceptions of the way they looked in Minoan days, all of which help to relate the visitor to the bronze saws and cauldrons, the dried food (figs, barley, beans, and millet have been identified), and the double-edged axe he sees around.

Numerous vases, some bearing comical paintings of octopi, others with hieroglyphics not yet deciphered, fill room after room. Some of the vases have been patiently reconstructed from as many as hundreds of separate fragments. And there are unbroken statuettes—of men, owls, birds in a tree—which are as perfect as the day they were made.

One set of tiny mosaic squares forms a picture of a town when put together, some of the houses two and three stories, and this was used as a clue to reconstructing part of Knossos.

The delicacy of the seals, carved from ivory and various types of soft stone, are surprising. Presumably most Minoans carried seals to "sign" their documents, the way most people carry pens today. The seals were usually buried along with their bodies, which accounts for the survival of so many of them. Tiny plaster casts of the seals' imprints—swans, goats, dogs, humans—are displayed beside them in their glass cases.

Thin strips of beaten gold and silver take many decorative shapes: flowers, leaves, and masks. Tiny plaster heads, some no bigger than peach pits, show clearly the ancient hair styles. Helmets of boars' tusks, goddesses with bare breasts peeping over topless dresses, bronze mirrors, tweezers, razors, and necklaces—all help to delineate the fashions of a civilization as old as any we can trace in Europe.

Even some of the pastimes of these ancient days are revealed. Around the top of a sword, in thin gold leaf, is a picture of an acrobat rolled into a ball, his hands touching his toes.

And the heavy copper ingots, shaped like axe heads and now greenish black and corroded by time, were the famous "talents" which the various city states had to render to Athens each year as their contribution to the Maritime League.

Be sure to go upstairs where the paintings are, executed in most incredible blues. How they got the color exactly is still unknown. Look at the picture of the dolphins, or the acrobats on the bull.

The museum, open 9 a.m. to 1 p.m., 3 to 6 p.m. daily, except Sundays and Tuesdays (when it is open only mornings), costs 30 drs to enter.

Behind this museum is another, the **Historical Museum of Crete,** whose high spot is a reconstruction of the study in which the Cretan novelist, Kazantzakis, worked. His books (in various languages) are arranged pretty much the way he left them.

In the 13th-century **San Marco Church,** now used as an art gallery, are copies of Byzantine paintings. Open 10 a.m. to noon, 3 to 7 p.m., admission 6 drs. San Marco is right beside the Knossos Restaurant in Venizelou Square.

THE RUINS AT KNOSSOS: Organized tours to the ruins and museum at Knossos cost 370 drs. But regular buses run every 20 minutes (from Kornarou Square) and cost about 15 drs, while admission itself is 50 drs (students, 10 drs). Open 7 a.m. to 6 p.m.

As is the case with most ancient cities, the setting of Knossos is beautiful. Hills on two sides, bare of everything but scrub, cypresses, and olive trees, and a tranquility disturbed only by the chirping of crickets.

The ruins here, reconstructed beginning 1900 by the late British archaeologist Sir Arthur Evans, with funds from his own personal fortune, are mostly those of an immense palace from which a population of as many as 100,000 was ruled around 1600 B.C.

There's a slightly Egyptian flavor, typified by the colored murals. One of the most surprising discoveries is how complex and efficient the old drainage system was. In the main building of the palace, a stone throne stands—as it has in this place for at least 3,000 years.

CLIMBING MOUNT IOUKTAS: The mountain which overlooks Iraklion is Mount Iouktas, and it offers a pleasant 80-minute climb for the energetic. Take the bus to **Arkhanai,** about nine miles away, and start early if you want to go and return the same day. The outline of Mt. Iouktas, topped by a little chapel, is supposed to represent the profile of Zeus lying down.

BRIEFLY NOTED: The **post office** (open from 7:30 a.m. to 9:30 p.m. daily; 9 a.m. to 12:30 p.m. and 6:30 to 8 p.m. Sundays and holidays) is on Daskalogiani Square. . . . The **telegraph** and **telephone** office is at 10 Minotavrou Street, and doesn't close at all. . . . Motorcycles and bicycles can be rented from **Michael Logothetis** (Amissou St., tel: 4132). . . . Cars are for rent from **Polytravel** (tel: 282476), **Pan Europe** (tel: 286676), both on 25th of August Street, and from **Hercules** (16 Pediatos St., tel: 285879)—all around 250-300 drs daily plus mileage, or from $140 weekly with unlimited mileage. . . . There are numerous **movie theaters** in town, half of them in or beyond Liberty Square. . . . Most inspiring spot in town is beside the **grave of Kazantzakis,** up on the old town walls. A simple granite headstone, simpler wooden cross, and a view of the narrow, tangled streets of the old town (walk through them) stretching down to the harbor. . . . **Alexiou's Bookstore** near the fountain on Venizelou Square has an amazing collection of books, magazines, and newspapers, including airmail editions of New York and London papers the same night. They are also the publishers of two guidebooks about the Minoan civilization of Crete. . . . Speedboats can be rented for riding or water-skiing from **Pandelis Gaganis Ltd.** (62 Martyron St., tel: 283658); about $16 per hour or $50 per day. . . . Two colorful Iraklion parades and festivals are the **Flower Show** (the whole town is decorated, first week in June) and the **Grapes Festival** (free wine and national dance), about the middle of September. . . . Before you leave Iraklion, pick up the folder offered by **Creta Tours** (25th of August St., tel: 222763), which has good maps of both Iraklion itself and of Crete.

NEARBY BEACHES: The nicest beach is **EOT** beach (take # 1 bus marked "Amnissos" from Liberty Square), where 10 drs admission covers use of changing cubicle, storage for clothes, shower, snack bar, and seats on the beach. Take a mat or towel to lie on. Just before EOT is a free beach with none of these facilities, and further along is the expensive **Motel Ammissos.** The motel has a swimming pool and dancing at night. EOT beach is about four miles from town and the bus costs five drs.

BOATS FROM IRAKLION: Daily boats to Piraeus at 6:30 *(Ariadne)* and 7 p.m. *(Kandia)* (only 7 p.m. Thursday, only 6:30 p.m. Saturday). On Wednesdays, the *Elli* sails at midnight for Santorini, Ios, Mykonos, Tinos, Piraeus. On Wednesdays and Sundays, the *Limnos* sails at 10 p.m. to Santorini, Ia, Ios, Naxos, Paros, Syros, and Piraeus. Tickets for all these boats are available at **Paleologos Agency,** 25th of August St. #3 (tel: 283086). On Fridays at 7 a.m. the *Kanaris* sails for Santorini, Ios, Paros, and Piraeus; tickets from **Kronstanos Tours,** 25th of August St. #21 (tel: 280048).

BUSES FROM IRAKLION: To Malia: hourly from 7 a.m. to 7 p.m., and 8:30 p.m. About 50 drs.

To Ag. Nikolaos: 7 and 8:30, then hourly to 6:30 p.m., and 8:30 p.m. About 100 drs.

To Sitia: 7:30, 8:30, 10:30 a.m., 12:30, 2:30, and 5 p.m. About 200 drs.

To Lassithi Plateau and Psychro: 8:30 a.m., 12:30, and 2:30 p.m. (Sunday: 8 a.m. and 2:30 p.m.) About 100 drs.

All the above buses go from **Megaron Fitaki,** the bus station near the docks (tel: 282637).

To Ag. Galini: 6:30, 7:30, 8:30, 10 a.m., noon, 1, 2, and 5 p.m. (Sundays: Hourly from 7 a.m. to noon, then 2 and 4:30 p.m. About 100 drs.

To Phaistos: 6:30, 7:30, 8:30, 9:30, 10, 11 a.m., noon, 1, 2, 3, 4, 5, 6:30 p.m. (Sundays: hourly 7 a.m. to noon, then 2, 4:30, and 6 p.m.) About 90 drs.

To Matala: 7:30, 8:30, 10 a.m., noon, 3, and 5 p.m. (Sunday: 7:30, 8, 10 a.m., noon, 3, 4:30 p.m.) About 90 drs.

All these buses go from outside Chania Gate (tel: 283073).

PLANES FROM IRAKLION: To Athens: five times daily. Trip takes 55 minutes. Olympic Airways, Liberty Square, tel: 288866 (Iraklion Airport: 282025).

To Rhodes: one daily, in the afternoon; trip takes one hour.

BRANCHING OUT FROM TOWN: Big classy hotels are going up by the score to west and east of Iraklion on the coast. Eight kilometers west is the massive **Akti Zeus hotel** (tel: 081-223761), with pool, three bars, mini-golf, tennis, etc. To the east, 19 kms, is the equally lavish **Candia Beach** (tel: 0897-412141) with matching facilities. There are many others, and the prices are all around 900 drs single, 1400 drs double for demi-pension.

Amnissos, about nine kilometers east, has a beautiful beach which, says Crete's historian Sterghios G. Spanakis, has been "a good place for beaching boats from Minoan times until the Venetian occupation." Homer says Ulysses landed there and it's surmised that it was the disembarkation point for Theseus and the contingent of young boys and girls who came from Athens to be fed to the Minotaur.

Mallia

The bus to Mallia leaves every hour from the bus station in the port. (There's a line of crowded little cafes here equipped with jukeboxes, a good place to sit and watch the action. Shoe cleaners, nut vendors, and loafers crowd the scene, and although the jukebox selections are listed in Greek, one drachma, any choice will be a winner.)

The trip to Mallia takes about 1½ hours, stopping at a little cafe on the highway (the village of Mallia) before heading down a sandy road lined with the characteristic windmills which pump water to irrigate the region's crops. The ruins are about three miles from the village.

The beach is really beautiful—thoroughly unspoiled, with marvelously clear water and soft white sand.

On Mallia's main street the best place to sleep and eat is the friendly **Pension Stelios,** whose owner is cook at the restaurant and landlord of the pension across the street. The food's fine, and beds cost around 130 drs.

Mallia also has a **youth hostel.**

It is possible to get the bus onwards to Aghios Nikolaos from the main highway in Mallia. Last bus is at 6:15 p.m., but check with the tourist office in Iraklion before setting out. The trip to Aghios Nikolaos, the latter part of which is a series of hair-raising curves, takes about two hours. The major point of interest on the trip is a stop high in the mountains at the **Chapel of St. George Selinaris** (dedicated to travelers), where all the bus passengers alight and enter the chapel to light a candle.

5. East from Iraklion

Before you set off eastwards from Iraklion, it's worth considering what it is you want to see. Although the temptation in Greece (as anywhere) is to hang around the coast, there are many interesting places in the interior. One trip you might consider making is to the famous **Lassithi Plateau** with its scores of working windmills pulling up water for the fruit and vegetables that grow so richly in the region.

We'll deal with this diversion first and then continue onwards from **Neapolis** (birthplace of the 14th-century Pope Alexander V) to **Aghios Nikolaos.**

TO THE LASSITHI PLATEAU: If you are going by car, your turnoff will be six kilometers beyond **Gournia,** to the right. There's a bus stop here, clearly marked "Lassithi Plateau" and "Psychron."

Gournia was a thriving Minoan city with olive mills around 1600 B.C. when it was destroyed by fire and never rebuilt. Today its nest of houses cluster around a low-lying hill like topless boxes. It is only a few yards off the main highway.

The road up into Lassithi is populated more by horses and donkeys than by cars. A detour can be made to the sleepy village of **Krasi** with its enormous plane tree and running springs.

After the village of **Kera** the climb really begins, and at the top of the pass the hills sweep down to the road at both sides, guarded by a line of abandoned mills in which the warped and abandoned mesh wheels sit dusty and undisturbed. The view of the valley behind and the level plateau ahead is impressive. The road takes a clockwise circle around the plateau, passing through several tiny villages and among fertile fields of fruit and vegetables. There seem to be more abandoned windmills than working ones (which haul up water). At various places on the bus route rooms can be rented, notably **Ag. Giorgos.**

At the end of the line is **Psychron** (pop: 400), a 15th-century village named after the fountain of Psykhro, which still supplies the village.

One of the most famous caves in Greece—"the Bethlehem of the pre-Christians," Spanakis calls it—is the **Diktaean Cave** on a hill above the village. It is the legendary birthplace of Zeus, whose mother, Rhea, gave the baby to local shepherds to protect him from his father, Kronos. The cave, a place of worship in Minoan times, descends into the ground for about 300 feet and is cold and slippery. Guides (you don't need one, but take a flashlight) point out stalactites and stalagmites that they affect to see as sculptures of faces and "mama with baby." It takes about half an hour to climb the hill (there are donkeys for rent) and about the same time to descend into the cave. The climb will make you thirsty, so take some fruit or a can of juice.

At the foot of the hill are two restaurants, and in the village are various pensions and hotels named after Zeus and Rhea. All cheap.

Various artifacts discovered in the cave (women's jewelry, armored breastplates, etc.) are kept in Room 19 of Iraklion's Archaeological Museum, but for some reason the museum does not display them.

Leaving the plateau at its eastern end, via Mesa Lasithion, it's much more barren until you get over the mountains, where pear trees overhang the road and piles of wood atop houses indicate that winters around here must be prepared for well in advance.

It's possible to bypass Neapolis (which we will do) and head straight for Aghios Nikolaos.

AGHIOS NIKOLAOS: From being a quiet little fishing village a few years ago, Ag. Nikolaos has developed into a sleek, Riviera-type resort complete with smart boutiques and overpriced jewelry stores.

Eating and Sleeping

Both sides of the harbor boast very picturesque expensive tavernas, but there are plenty of cafes and cheaper eating places. In general, though, the ambience is a mixture of rich socialites and day-trippers with a handful of freaks thrown in for variety.

At the righthand side of the harbor (with your back to the sea) is a so-called "bottomless pond," **Lake Voulismeni,** said to be the outlet of an underground river. Two budget hotels overlook this lake, the 31-room **Acratos** (tel: 22721) and the 40-room **Hotel du Lac** (tel: 22711), both with rooms with bath for 345 drs single, 425 drs double. In the evening you can sit under the palm trees beside the lake and watch the sun set over the water—an odd experience considering you're at the seaside on the east coast.

At this end of town, round the bay, is another C-class hotel: the **Alkistis** (Koundourou 30, tel: 28170), with similar rates. There are two other cheap hotels: the **Rhea** (tel: 28321) and the aging **Lato** (tel: 22319), whose 22 rooms cost 190 drs single, 250 drs double without bath and are usually filled because not only are they cheap but the Lato—perched on the hill at the other end of the harbor—has the best location in town. There are rooms for rent in the side street almost opposite the Akratos.

At the top of the hill in the square with the war memorial (beneath which backpackers recline on the grass) is the gleaming new **Hotel Cronos** (tel: 0841-28761), whose 38 rooms cost around 400 drs single, 500 drs double including breakfast. Another new hotel, the 15-room **Dias** (Latus 2, tel: 28263) built of drab, gray stone, is pleasant and cool. It's on the road towards Sitia, at the bottom end of town, and costs about the same.

There's also a **youth hostel**—behind the square where the taxis park in the center of the harbor area.

If all the rooms in Ag. Nikolaos are filled, as is frequently the case in midsummer, it's well worth walking out of town in a northerly direction (i.e., with your back to the sea, go right) on the road past the expensive Hotels

Hermes and Coral, towards the smart **Minos Beach Colony** (bungalows with their own piece of rocky beach from $34 daily). Long before you get there, about half a mile from town, you'll come to the **Restaurant Ammoudi,** which takes its name from the beach opposite where you can stay at the **Dolphin** pension for about 300 drs double and eat under the trees right on the beach. Nearby is the pension **Polydoros,** with similar rates.

The main activity in Ag. Nikolaos is sitting at the cafes and watching the tourists, many of whom are into well-tailored casual wear; it's an unofficial fashion parade. There's a stylish coffee shop, the **Bousoulas,** with corny quotations on its walls and a menu that includes "goat's yoghurt with homemade honey," and next door a pizzeria cafe, the **Mermaid,** where you can get small pizzas as well as large—a boon to us single travelers. Try the cafe next to the bus station for cheap souvlaki and chips.

Nightlife

Several discos have sprung up—one out by the Dolphin pension and, among others, a gaudily painted spot called **Scorpios Dance Hall,** just off the harbor.

There are organized "Cretan Nights" to **Kritsa** on Sundays and Tuesdays, including food, wine, and dancing, for 450 drs. Kritsa, about six miles west, is where Jules Dassin filmed *He Who Must Die,* from the Kazantzakis novel, *Christ Recrucified.*

Buses from Aghios Nikolaos

To Iraklion: every hour or more from 6 a.m. to 3 p.m., then 4:30, 5, 6:30, 8:30 p.m.; about 100 drs.

To Elounda: 6:15, 7:15, 8:30, 10:30 a.m., 12:30, 1:30, 2:30, 5, 6, 7:30 p.m. (Sundays: every two hours from 6 a.m. to 6 p.m.); about 20 drs.

To Kritsa: 6, 7, 8, 9, 11 a.m., noon, 1, 2, 3, 4, 6, 7 p.m. (Sundays: 7, 9, 11 a.m., 1, 3, 5, 7 p.m.); about 20 drs.

To Gournia and Ierapetra: 6, 7, 9, 10 a.m., noon, 2, 4, 6:30, 8 p.m.; about 50 drs.

To Sitia: 6, 9, 10 a.m., noon, 2, 4, 6:30 p.m.; about 100 drs.

Check these schedules by telephoning 22234.

There's a cheap car rental, **Ilias** (Kon. Ephrakiamaki, tel: 28339) in Ag. Nikolaos, so if you're considering driving further east it might make sense to get a bus to this place and rent a car for the rest of the trip. Ilias has small cars from $8 daily plus mileage, or with unlimited mileage for $75 weekly.

Boats from Ag. Nikolaos

The *Kanaris* sails at 10 a.m. on Wednesdays to Santorini and Piraeus. On Tuesdays it sails, at 2:30 a.m. (as it has for years) to Sitia, Kassos, Karpathos, Diafani, Halki, and Rhodes.

NORTH TO ELOUNDA AND SOUTH TO SITIA: A pleasant excursion from Ag. Nikolaos is north to **Elounda,** with surprise vistas of oddly shaped islands swimming out to sea like a chain of porpoises. Crete's eastern shore has been sinking over the years and remains of more than one ancient village lie below the waters off the coast around here. Sometimes at low tide it is still possible to see the outlines of sunken houses.

Elounda itself is small, pretty, and fairly non-touristy although expensive bungalow colonies are starting to pop up in the surrounding area. The **Aristea** hotel on a hill at the entrance to town is about the only reasonably inexpensive spot to stay, and the chic **Taverna Delfini** is a good place to eat (although a "chic" taverna is pretty much a contradiction in terms).

Elounda Bay is charming. Elounda's salt lake—covered at dusk with millions of mosquitoes doing a mating dance—lies between the mainland and the island of **Spinalonga,** some of whose 16th-century castle walls are still standing. Spinalonga's fortress was so impregnable that not only did it remain under Venetian control for almost half a century after the Turks captured Crete, but it became a refuge for Turks hiding from the Christians thereafter. In 1903 it was turned into a leper colony but has now been deserted for many years.

Eastwards from Ag. Nikolaos, the road continues to skirt the sea, but beaches are few and far between and separated from the highway by olive groves much of the way. Just past Gournia, at **Pahia Ammos,** is the narrowest (12 kms) part of Crete. Here there is a pebble beach, a hotel complex in the process of being built, and the turnoff to **Ierapetra.**

Then the highway climbs again, offering lovely views of the sea and the nearby uninhabited island of **Mochlos.** Villages seem to be built across the highway from here onwards, but as you get close it's apparent that they are stretched out on ridges to left and right. From **Hamission,** a gleaming white city appears in the distance. It is **Sitia.**

The modern town of Sitia (pop: 5,800) is only about a century old, built on the site of a settlement that goes back to ancient times. It was destroyed by an earthquake in 1508, sacked by the famous Mediterranean pirate Barbarossa later in the same century, and finally destroyed and abandoned by its masters, the Venetians, in 1651 to prevent its capture by the Turks.

Sitia was the birthplace of Vincent Kornoros, author of a lengthy medieval drama called *Erotokritos,* almost untranslatable but quoted extensively by many Greeks.

Today Sitia is a pleasant, peaceful town with only once-weekly boat service to Piraeus.

Buses from Sitia

To Iraklion: 6, 9, 11 a.m., 1, 3, 4:30, 6:30 p.m.; about 190 drs.
To Ierapetra: 6 a.m., noon, and 5 p.m.; about 75 drs.
To Vai: 10 a.m., noon, 2 p.m.
Check these schedules (tel: 22272).

Places to Stay

As you enter town from Iraklion the first hotel you see, the **Minos** (tel: 28331), happens to be one of the biggest bargains, with bathless rooms for 200 drs single, 250 drs double. Just down the hill, about 100 yards away, the **Alice** (Papanastasiou 34, tel: 28450) is much more luxurious, with roof garden, basement bar called the Catacomb, and one of the most stylish cards ever seen. About 30 rooms, costing 325 drs single, 400 drs double. A bargain.

Preferred over all, however, is the amiable ambience of the **Pension Michel** (tel: 22875), run by hearty Giorgis Nikonarakis, who's the catalyst for an international crowd of beachcombers hanging around the tables on his terrace to eat, drink, and socialize. Simple rooms, beds with soft mattresses, and plenty of hot water—and the beach across the road. About 100 drs per person, 200 drs for a room with three beds. Pension Michel is on the seafront road to Paleokastron, about half a mile east of a town, where the beaches run unbroken for at least a mile. It's western neighbor is the colossal **Kappa Club** (tel: 28821). This 300-room complex, with interesting architecture, two swimming pools, and every kind of sporting diversion imaginable, is run by a French travel group, making it hard for outsiders to find space. Anyway, obligatory demi-pension costs around 850 drs single, 1300 drs double.

There are three hotels on Sitia's waterfront: the old 20-room **Flisbos** (tel: 22422) and the 20-room **Denis** (tel: 28356), in a nice location beside tree-shaded cafes, both under 400 drs double; and the classy 77-room **Hotel Itanos** (tel: 22146), with restaurant and bar, about 530 drs double including breakfast.

Running at right angles to the harbor behind the Hotel Denis is Kap. Siphi Street, on which there are three other hotels. In ascending price order these are: the smaller, older **Imison**, about 275 drs double without bath; the modern 42-room **Krystal** (tel: 22284), next door to a small supermarket; and the 37-room **Sitia** (tel: 28155), with lots of cactus and other plants lining the outside. These last two are five-story buildings, modern and cool, and both cost around 350 drs single, 425 drs double. The OTE office (phones and telegrams) is on the same block. Streets crossing it have rooms for rent.

READERS' SELECTION: "What made our stay in Sitia memorable was the hospitality extended to us by the Rosaki family at the **Star** pension, 37 Mihail Kolivaki St., tel: 22817, at the north end of the city and one block from the water. By the time we left we felt we were part of the family" (P.J. Milne, E.J. Crowley, M. Langer, University of Windsor, Ont., Canada).

EAST FROM SITIA:
It's highly recommended that from Sitia you keep heading east, if only to see the beautiful palm-fringed beach of **Vai**, where there's nothing but one taverna and hundreds of nomads from all over the world who camp under the trees in hammocks, bedrolls, blankets. They come in buses, cars, vans, by bicycle, motorcycle, and on foot. There's a bus from Sitia at 10 a.m., noon, and 2 p.m., with the last bus back at 3 p.m. You can rent a car cheaply in Sitia from **Apollon** (tel: 28446) for about six or seven dollars a day plus mileage, and as it's only about 20 miles from Sitia the cost should be low.

En route to Vai you'll pass through **Paleokastron** (pop: 700), which has a cheap hotel named after the ancient site of Itanos, six kilometers southeast. There used to be a temple to Zeus in Paleokastron and Minoan tombs have been found nearby. More ruins can be seen at **Zakros,** the extreme southeastern port of Crete, which was a thriving Minoan center about 1600 B.C.

IERAPETRA:
From Sitia you might like to head back via Ierapetra, a city that was minting coins with the head of the god Zeus on them well before the Romans came in 66 B.C. and destroyed the place after a long siege. Rebuilt, Ierapetra became rich through trade. It still has the remains of an ancient fort and the minaret of an abandoned mosque—but Ierapetra has obviously seen better days. Crete's historian, Sterghios G. Spanakis, sadly notes: "Although it is a maritime port the ships do not call there." Napoleon is said to have slept one night in Ierapetra on his way to Egypt, in June 1798.

A couple of miles east of town, with the beach across the road, is the 69-room **Hotel Atlantis** (tel: 28555), a standard, big, modern tourist hotel, with rooms for around 485 drs double including breakfast. Less than 200 yards away, on the beach, is the concrete-drab **youth hostel**, where a sign reads: "If there is nobody here, find a bed and sign the book." There are beds outside on the rear terrace, bunks indoors.

Overlooking Ierapetra's harbor is the **El Greco** (tel: 28472), over a furniture store. It's a slick, gray marble construction whose entrance is on the rear street—around 400 drs double. About the same price, above a bank on the main street into town, is the newly painted **Hotel Creta** (tel: 28550) with the cheaper, older **Hotel Liviton** a few doors away. Hidden away down an alley from the seafront is the **Hotel Ieraptyna** (tel: 28530) where doubles without bath cost 250 drs.

The shoreline to the east and west of Ierapetra is lined with hundreds of wood and plastic greenhouses in which tomatoes are grown. By midsummer, with the tomatoes harvested, the plastic has been torn away and litters the countryside, wrapping itself around telephone wires, trees, anything that harvests it from the winds.

The highway hugs the coast for many miles, but the shore is mostly rocky, with only occasional patches of beach. If you want to stay by the sea, better choose a place east of Ierapetra, because to the west there's nothing for miles (hotels are under construction, probably financed by tomato millionaires) until you reach **Mirtos,** the last coastal village before the road turns inland. The village beach is only passable, the villagers not overly friendly, and what few rooms are available go early in the day. Better, by far, to wait for the turnoff just past **Pefkos** which is marked "Aminos and Arvi Beach." From the highway here it's a hair-raising drive of about 14 kms down an unpaved road that doubles back on itself like a snake with itchy ribs.

But the drive is worth it, for **Arvi** is one of those places the tourist dreams of discovering but rarely does. The **Ariadne Hotel** greets you at the entrance to the village, which has one main street where almost every second house has rooms to rent, tavernas, and cafes, a grocery store—and that's it. The street is so narrow, the houses so small that intimate glimpses into people's lives—and sometimes their bedrooms, separated from the kitchen by only a sheet—are inevitable. There is a charming homeliness about the whole place. Stay at the Ariadne (about 350 drs single, 450 drs double) and try to get a room whose balcony overlooks the beach, and you'll fall asleep and wake to the lapping sound of the waves only a few feet away.

Inevitably, Arvi will be spoiled by more visitors. It is too small to cope with a tourist invasion. But this is it's first appearance in this book, which means it has a year or two left yet.

If you're driving, take the unpaved road towards **Ano Viano,** and long before you get there you'll see it sitting in a cleft of the hills, its houses mostly white but a spot of pink here, a splash of yellow there. Even on land, Greeks build their villages to look like islands.

Chapter XIV

RHODES AND THE DODECANESE

**1. Rhodes
2. Kos
3. Kalymnos
4. Patmos
5. Simi**

AFTER A STEADY DIET of small and relatively barren Greek islands, the island of Rhodes comes as a major shock. Who would suddenly expect to find, in this lonely sea, a cosmopolitan city with swanky hotels, French menus, and enough remnants of the chi-chi international set to make you believe that you've somehow strayed by mistake onto the Riviera?

Actually, it's not quite as posh as I've made it sound—just that it's such a contrast, after all those other little islands, that it almost seems as though it isn't Greek. And it hasn't always been. The major influence in this century has been the Italians, who captured Rhodes from Turkey (Rhodes being a few miles from the Turkish coast) and tried hard to make a show-spot resort out of it. In World War II, it suffered badly; it was a base used by the Germans and Italians for the capture of Crete, and was administered by the British for a brief period, before being handed back to Greece in 1948.

Lawrence Durrell ran a newspaper here for the British occupation forces in the mid-forties, and some of his experiences, together with a pleasantly painless history of Rhodes, are given in his *Reflections on a Marine Venus*.

In these uncertain times, of course, islands that are so near to Turkey are not considered to be the untroubled paradises they once were and tourism in this part of Greece has suffered considerably in the past year or two. Until times get more stable this situation will probably continue but meanwhile it does make islands such as Rhodes and Kos much less crowded.

1. Rhodes

The history of Rhodes has always been fascinating, and even its legendary birth (Zeus awarded one of the Dodecanese islands to each of the 12 gods, overlooking Apollo who was away; Apollo agreed to accept the next island that arose from the sea—Rhodes) has some basis in fact, because it suddenly appeared from the sea after a volcanic eruption thousands of years ago.

Because of its location, Rhodes was an important shipping power from early times, with considerable authority over the Mediterranean waters through which its captains sailed. Much of today's internationally acknowledged Maritime Law dates back to the days when Rhodes ruled the waves and nobody had heard of Britannia.

In 408 B.C., the island's three ancient cities—Ialysos, Kamiros, and Lindos—decided to create a new commercial capital at the northern end of the island. This is the present-day capital city, Rhodes. By the first century B.C., its influence was considerable, its population about 80,000 (just over a quarter of that today), and Pliny, the Roman historian, recorded the presence of several thousand statues, including at least 100 described as "colossal."

The original **Colossus of Rhodes,** an enormous bronze statue which stood astride the harbor (said to be where the two small statues of deer stand today), was one of the Seven Wonders of the Ancient World. It was a representation of the sun god, built by the sculptor Chares of Lindos, and carried a light to warn mariners. It had been built to commemorate the victory of Rhodes after an unsuccessful one-year siege of the city by an Alexandrian, Demetrios Poliorketes. The attacker was so impressed with the stability of the Rhodians that he presented them with the heavy assault machinery with which he'd been trying to batter down the walls, and this machinery was what the Colossus was made from.

After a mere 50 years of impressively guarding the entrance to the harbor, the statue was toppled in an earthquake and lay on the ground in ruins for a couple of centuries, until it was sold to a Syrian, who had it transported across to Asia Minor by boat and then loaded the metal onto 900 camels to be taken away and melted down.

In the 14th century, a semi-religious, semi-military group called the Knights of St. John (originally formed to take part in the Crusades) retreated from Jerusalem to Cyprus and from there to Rhodes, which they captured after a three-year siege. They built most of the impressive walls that still surround the old town, and they governed the island, beating off occasional attacks, until 1522, when they were finally ousted by the Turks.

The combination of lovely lush scenery, wooded mountains, gorgeous seacoast, and the medieval atmosphere of the old town itself, with its high walls and cobbled streets, makes Rhodes one of the world's most delightful islands, and it should not be missed.

ORIENTATION: Where you step off the boat at the pier, you'll be some distance from town. Even if you are heading into the old town area, behind the forbidding high walls nearest to you, you'll still be a ten- or 15-minute walk away.

In the old town, there are only small, very cheap, and very primitive hotels—ideal if you're on a really low budget, but not worth bothering about if you can afford, say, anything more than a couple of dollars per person for your room.

After walking around the harbor, you'll pass through two gates in the old stone wall—follow all the traffic—and you'll then be walking along the edge of **Mandraki,** the harbor of the new town.

The big white building on your left, with cafe tables scattered all along the front of it, is the market, an enclosed area filled with little shops and stalls of various kinds, but mostly devoted to tourist souvenirs.

Behind the market is most of the "downtown" shopping area. This is where buses go from, where travel agencies and airline and shipping offices are,

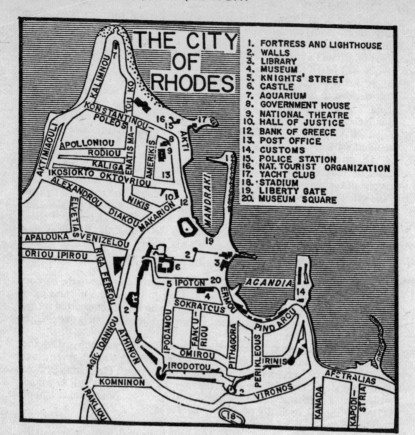

THE CITY
OF
RHODES

1. FORTRESS AND LIGHTHOUSE
2. WALLS
3. LIBRARY
4. MUSEUM
5. KNIGHTS' STREET
6. CASTLE
7. AQUARIUM
8. GOVERNMENT HOUSE
9. NATIONAL THEATRE
10. HALL OF JUSTICE
12. BANK OF GREECE
13. POST OFFICE
14. CUSTOMS
15. POLICE STATION
16. NAT. TOURIST ORGANIZATION
17. YACHT CLUB
18. STADIUM
19. LIBERTY GATE
20. MUSEUM SQUARE

where you'll be able to buy imported canned foods, have a hair set, or find a dry cleaner.

At the far end of Mandraki are big buildings: the county hall, a long oblong edifice on the right; the Court of Justice, the post office (open 7 a.m. to 8:30 p.m.), the town hall, and national theater to the left. Behind the court building, on the left corner of Makarios and Papagos Street, is the **tourist office.** Spyros Catechis is the Director for the Dodecanese.

The building sticking out on the point is the Aquarium, and from here onwards the coastline gets prettier and prettier, with numerous beaches and any number of plush hotels to share them.

The area up here, past the point I shall subsequently refer to as the **Grand Hotel Area,** because the Grand is the biggest and swankiest hotel of the bunch. It is also the site of the island's casino, where you can gamble for relatively low stakes (50 drs upwards), if you're prepared to dress up for the occasion, and pay the obligatory 120 drs for your first drink.

Most of the rest of the town is a rambling and rather monotonous residential suburb, pretty to drive through (elegant houses and lovely flowers) but hot and tiring to walk down (long, long streets, whose suffocating sameness is unrelieved even by the occasional store).

HOTELS IN RHODES: You'll have to make a choice right from the start. Do you want to take a hotel within a very short walk of the beaches? Or do you want to be about a 15- or 20-minute walk away in the downtown area near to the old town and the harbor cafes? There are a lot of newer hotels near the beach, but cheaper spots downtown. You can easily take a bus to the beach or bicycle or even walk. And if you're downtown, it's easier to while away your time sipping sodas in the main cafes in the harbor, admiring the passing parade, which closely resembles the scene outside American Express in Athens. But if you want to be nearer to the good restaurants and like to swim, then the beach is better. (Hotels in the old town are detailed later in this chapter.)

Downtown

Right on the harbor are the cafes where everybody sits and wastes time. Immediately behind these cafes is an open market with inexpensive restaurants, produce stores, and cheap souvlaki stands. And right behind the market is the downtown area whose major landmark is Cyprus Square.

Several of the best, and most convenient hotels are right off Cyprus Square, and if you can afford it you should certainly choose the **Tilos** (Makarios St., tel: 24591), which is very much like a chic, tasteful American motel in style, with a plush blue carpet in the lobby, elevators, and rooms with baths and balconies. The 21 rooms cost 140 drs single bathless, 255 drs double with bath.

Still in this general category, and if anything even more luxurious in its fittings, is the **Hotel Royal** (Queen Sophias 50, tel: 24601), which is a few blocks further away from the center of town—though still within easy walking distance—and therefore quieter. Here there's an attractive bar-lounge with TV off the lobby, a pretty little ground-floor restaurant half indoors and half on the vine-covered arbor off the sidewalk. Black tile bathrooms with a certain style, and an elevator. The Royal has 49 rooms, some without bath for 110 drs singles, 160 drs double; the others with bath for 165 drs single, 210 drs double.

The **Hotel Noufara** (35 Queen Sophias, tel: 24545) is near the Royal, but not as classy or expensive. There's an attractive terrace at the front of the hotel, at which you can have breakfast and watch the sidewalk strollers. Most rooms have balconies. No elevator, though. A clean hotel with 30 rooms which cost 110 drs single, 140 drs double without shower; 200 drs double with shower.

Also near Cyprus Square is the **Savoy Hotel** (Ethelondon 9, tel: 20721). A single with bath here costs 240 drs, 255 drs for a double. Most rooms have balconies and there is a roof garden where you can have breakfast for 30 drs.

Back in the Cyprus Square section, we come down a notch for the next hotel: still clean, tidy, cheap, and pleasant, but lacking that little extra bit of class. The **Hotel Laokoon** (Cyprus Square, tel: 24579) has pleasant rooms with balconies, and it has an elevator. Single rooms are 120 drs without bath; doubles with bath are 210 drs.

The **Colossos** (9 Haile Selassie St., tel: 243-31) is full of young Scandinavians and bright lights; the rooms are small, but they do have balconies opening onto the street—all 50 rooms bathless and costing 140 drs single, 195 drs double. Breakfast costs an additional 35 drs.

READERS' SELECTIONS: "Hotel Hermes, just around the corner from the Port Police, is clean and nice, costs about 400 drs double" (Greg Dyer, Mill Vall, Calif.). . . . "The modern **Hotel Silvia** (Xanthou & Kolokotroni 114) is on a quiet street outside the ancient walls of the old city. Its double rooms have private bathrooms with all the necessary facilities. The proprietor speaks English and is much concerned with the comfort of his guests. The hotel is about a 15-minute stroll to the Mandraki Pier and the center of the city's activities" (Mr. and Mrs. G. Walters, New York City).

Towards the Beach

If you can't decide whether to stay at the beach or downtown, stay in between. Just after you've passed the curve at the end of Mandraki and are heading out towards the beach area, you'll come across a quiet street called Casoulli. There are two modern hotels here, nothing special but popular with young Scandinavian students on a budget. The **Astron** (tel: 24651) has rooms without bath for 210 drs double, with bath for 255 drs; next door, the **Hotel International** (tel: 24595) is approximately the same price.

On another street, this one parallel to the Grand Hotel, is the more expensive **Hotel Carina** (Griva Street, tel: 22381), more in the style of a B-class hotel, what with its carpeted hallways, and bamboo chairs and wood tables (instead of the usual metal) on the balconies. Rooms are a little small, though, and cost 210 drs single, 255 drs double, but all have showers.

Hotels near the Beach

The extreme end of the peninsula, an inverted U, is bordered on both sides by wide sandy beaches. At the hollow end of the U stands a solitary building, the Aquarium, and coming down back towards town is a pleasant, grassy plaza called Place Roi Paul, bordered by many new hotels. The **Hotel Achillion** (tel: 24604) looks pretty classy, with lounge, elevator, balconies, etc., and has rooms with bath (210 drs single, 275 drs double).

Just down the street from the Achillion is **Hotel Al's** (Place Roi Paul; tel: 22481), its 32 rooms all with shower, music, and telephone; a really handsome place overlooking the palm trees on the square and the sea. With bath, singles are 220 drs; doubles, 275 drs (some rooms, cheaper, without bath). Breakfast costs an additional 24 drs.

But first choice for location and style is the **Hotel Marie** (Kos 7, tel: 22751), a few doors down from Clara Rhodos, next door to the Restaurant 13, quite near the beach. It has 50 rooms, all with shower, telephone, and music, plus carpeted hallways, plenty of light, and good-sized rooms. The price is 210 drs single, 275 drs double with bath.

The attractive C-class **Hotel Butterfly**, only ten minutes' walk from the beach, has rooms for 210 drs single, 255 drs double. Breakfast costs 30 drs.

RHODES' RESTAURANTS: Most of the town's best restaurants are not the easily visible ones downtown, but the attractive semi-outdoor places that have sprung up in the area of the beach to cater to the hordes of young Scandinavians that throng to the hotels around there. Naturally, their cuisine tends to be more northern European than Greek, and you can, in fact, eat better in Rhodes than anywhere else in Greece, including Athens.

The **Restaurant Oscar** (Kos Street 220 yards from the beach) is actually more French in style than anything else. It has a kind of tatami matting roof, cane and leather chairs, attractive lamps and contemporary chandeliers, bright red tablecloths on the sidewalk tables, and looks just like an intimate little spot lifted from St.-Germain-des-Prés. Entrees around 60-85 drs with set meals for 80 drs.

The **Restaurant 13** (surprisingly enough at 3 Kos Street) has one of the largest selections in town: a score of different hors d'oeuvres, including pâté, salmon, or sardines; six soups; fish; meats; moussaka; filet mignon; pastries and ice cream. Most entrees 50 to 80 drs. The restaurant is an attractive one, with most of its tables on a paved terrace adjoining the sidewalk.

The area around the Restaurant 13 is packed with attractive eating places whose style is best described as French-Greek-Scandinavian. All are fairly expensive with the exception of the **Snack Bar Hundred Palms** which faces a square lined with some pretty scraggly looking palm trees. It has similarly genteel airs (tablecloths, flowers) and may well be the cheapest restaurant in Rhodes with omelettes for around 18 drs, hamburgers 30 drs, etc.

Next to the Turkish Consulate on Vassilopedos Marias (this one is near Cyprus Square; the others were near the beach) is the **Scandia** restaurant, in an attractive vine garden, covered and decorated with fishnets, barrels, starfish, seashells. The Greek salad here comes with oil and vinegar separate—a nice change—and the rest of the food is equally well prepared. Omelettes (ham, bacon, cheese, potato, tomato), liver, veal, pork chops, chicken with fish a specialty. A nice outdoor atmosphere.

The **Circe** (Vassilopedos Marias Street 8) is situated in the center of the town, near the beach, between the Hotel Acandia and the Turkish Consulate. International kitchen, tasteful food, reasonable prices, excellent surroundings, quick service, flowers in the dining room and garden.

The **Dania**, across from the Circe, is a combination snack bar and restaurant with mainly Scandinavian clientele and menu—30 varieties of smorgasbord (open-face sandwiches) from 15 to 30 drs, all very tasty. Prices about the same as the other neighboring spots but much better food. It should be remembered that a Danish "hamburger" is an American meatball.

One of the best places in which to eat is the **market.** There are half a dozen cafes there, all interesting and cheerful to sit at in the evening. Try the **Butterfly** for example. There's also a souvlaki stand just inside the main gate that is one of the best I've ever encountered. A meal for a quarter!

Most of the big hotels have good dining rooms serving familiar Western cuisine, including bacon and eggs for breakfast, at reasonable prices. Lunch or dinner will usually cost over 100 drs, but the quality of the food is better than you'll get in most "native" restaurants, so you might want to splurge on one meal.

There are restaurants in the old town, too, and for these, read on.

READERS' SELECTIONS: "On Rhodes there is a restaurant called **Norden** at 13 Kos Street across the street from the Hotel Marie. Continental-style service—we had the works for two and it cost $10—very good for a splurge" (G. Dyer, Mill Valley, Calif.). . . . "**Langanis,** small with outdoor tables, is of gourmet calibre. We had swordfish steak broiled in a light egg batter that's the best I've ever tasted. Address is Solomou Alhedef 16" (Jerry Yale, Closter, N.J.). . . . "Four or five excellent restaurants are on **Vassilos Street**" (Murray MacDonald, Montreal, Canada).

THE OLD TOWN: The most memorable section of Rhodes, is, of course, the old town, much of it dating back to the 14th century, when it was built and administered by an international body of religious crusaders called the Knights of St. John of Jerusalem.

Apart from the massive walls, which defended the city from many attacks until the Turks finally captured Rhodes in 1522, the most enduring monument to the Knights is the majestic 300-room **Palace of the Knights,** as well as the narrow cobbled street leading up to it from the gate on the harbor.

The **Street of the Knights** (or Ippoton, as it reads today) starts from Plateia Mousion (Museum Square), and leads right up the hill. It is particularly fascinating at night, with its dim lanterns throwing just enough light to emphasize its medieval aspects.

People live off the mysterious alleyways and courtyards to each side, and it seems vaguely incongruous, somehow, to see gleaming white refrigerators and pink plastic toys when you peep through the shuttered windows.

The Knights comprised representatives of many countries, each with its own leader, and was directed by one Grand Master who was chosen for life. The Palace in which this big boss lived, and from where he administered the town, is open 9:30 a.m. to 1 p.m. and 3:30 to 6 p.m., Tuesday through Sunday and holidays; closed Mondays. Admission 10 drs.

The **Archaeological Museum** contains pottery, sculptures, cannonballs, and arms from the days of the Knights, many relics of a time at least 12 centuries before that, and a smooth, armless figure found at the bottom of the harbor by divers and mentioned by Lawrence Durrell in his book, *Reflections on a Marine Venus.* Is is open 8 a.m. to 1 p.m. and 3 to 6 p.m., Tuesday through Sundays; closed Mondays. Admission fee: 10 drs.

A tour of the walls can be made on Tuesdays and Saturdays at 5 p.m., when visitors are expected to assemble in the courtyard of the Palace to await a guide.

The old town is probably the best place in Rhodes to rent a bicycle or motor scooter, partly because the competition is so fierce. Many of the cheaper rental places are around Hippocrates Square, and your best bet is to do some comparison shopping. You'll find that the standard rate for a Vespa motor-scooter is 150 drs per day, but when business isn't too good, you can bargain down to about 100 drs.

Two Places to Eat in the Old Town

The old town is rife with such pensive street names as Sokratous, Pithagora, and Aristotelous, and should be thoroughly covered on foot without any plan or purpose. A stroll along Apellou Street, past the top side of the Museum, will bring you to a little square, where the cafe of **John Nitty** (20 Endimon) bears this sign: "Serves the most exotic food specialties steak, chicken omelette, grilled meat balls and sizkebab plus salad of different style. Most sanitary and inexpensive. Come one! Come all!"

It's a fine place for breakfast, at a table under the trees, and is also lively late at night when the radio is blaring and the most active of the old-town residents (plus a few low-living tourists) stop in for coffee on the way home.

Halfway up Sokratous, the old town's "main street," you'll spot **Niko's Bar** on your right. The food's so-so, but you should take a look inside, because there's an interesting garden at the rear with quite fantastic murals on the walls and a vine-covered patio in which to sit and sip a soda. Most of the usual dishes.

Where to Stay in the Old Town

On Panaitiou Street (walk up to the main street, Sokratous, to the top and turn right), is **Castello's Pension** (tel: 24042), a big old house whose rates are 165 drs double, 230 drs triple. Castello's is okay if you're not too fussy and want to eat breakfast late, sitting on the terrace at the front or in the shaded patio at the back.

Best of all is the **Pension Paul** (Aristotelous 42), an intimately small house with eight double rooms and a spiral staircase leading to a sunny rooftop. Considering how tiny the house is, the rooms seem amazingly spacious, and cost 190 drs double, 125 drs single (but you may have to share a two-bedded room with some other solitary transient if you're alone). There's a spotlessly clean bathroom with big tub and shower.

Both this pension and the nearby **Pension Nikos** (tel: 23423, Aristotelous 45) are just above Hippocrates Square in the downtown district of the old city, near St. Catherine's Gate leading into the harbor, and although their addresses appear to be the same, they're actually on parallel streets. Nikos has ten rooms, 23 beds in all, which cost 125 drs per person, including use of shower.

Any art student can stay in the **Knight's Castle** for 75 drs, but first you must have obtained in Athens a permit verifying that you really are an art student. To do this, go to the School of the Arts on Akadimias Street in Athens and see the general secretary. Have with you proof of your status.

NIGHTTIME: The castle, its ramparts and moats, are the scene of a nightly **Sound and Light** presentation, when a recorded commentary accompanies the subtle lighting from strategically placed spotlights. A batch of seats is set up inside the **Municipal Gardens** (just to left of market), but you can stand outside the railroad station and hear it all free. As far as the lighting is concerned, the best view is from the harbor, preferably on a boat. The performance lasts 55 minutes and is given in English at 8:15 p.m. on Monday and Tuesday, 9:15 on Wednesday, 10:15 on Thrusday, 9:15 on Friday, 9:15 on Saturday and Sunday. At various other times, it is given in French, German, and Swedish. Tickets are available at travel offices, the Rhodes tourist office, and at the entrance to the gardens itself. Admission is 50 drs, students 25 drs.

In summer there are nightly (except Saturday) performances of Greek **folk dancers** at 9 p.m. in the **"Old Town"** theater. In winter these are held in the **Rodin theater.**

There are additional concerts and recitals by national and international companies during the summer.

The **Aquarium,** good for nighttime sightseeing, is open 8 a.m. to 10 p.m. daily. Admission is 15 drs and it's the building out on the point going west, past the Hotel des Roses, at the outermost point of Rhodes. The ground floor is full of weird beasts—a one-eyed calf, an eight-legged lamb, very toothy sea animals—as well as the usual stuffed seals and skeletons and things, but in the basement, stone-walled tanks are imaginatively set into coral so that the illusion, even to the pebbled floors, is of being actually under the sea. There are octopi with tentacles pressed to the glass, eels standing on their tails, bright red starfish, and strange snail-like creatures that look like dark brown plastic bags.

A block or two eastwards, past where the walls of the old town end, is a batch of "nightclubs." They aren't too interesting and tend to try the standard nightclub fleecing of tourists, but if you go with this forewarning, you probably won't fare too badly.

There's an open-air movie theater, the **Rodon** (admission: 10 drs), at the far end of Mandraki, just left up a side street (behind the National Theater), and a discotheque called **33,** on Ploutarchou Plessou Street, which is the last little street on the left as you head past the downtown waterfront cafes. It directly adjoins the big pavilion cafe, where music is heard at night. In fact, there's quite a contrast—afternoon tea-type orchestrations at the cafe and pop and rock music in the minuscule discotheque (whose "members only" policy is actually interpreted so that once you pay the 50 drs admission you're a member). Drinks cost 50 drs, sodas 25 drs.

There are also the **Elli** and the **Nor,** restaurants with music for dancing, at the far end of Mandraki.   •

If you're in Rhodes from July through mid-September, you can go to the **Wine Festival** at **Rodini Park,** a real bargain. There's a 40-drachma entrance fee, but for this you get a free souvlaki plus all the wine you can drink, accompanied by the music of folk rock bands. It's only a ten-minute, 1½-dr ride (get off at Rodini Park) from any station. Nightly from 7 p.m. to 1 a.m.

THE ISLAND OF RHODES

AROUND THE ISLAND: Round about 100 B.C. there were three main towns on the island—but the town of Rhodes was not one of them. **Ialyse,** on a flat plateau of Mount Philerimos, was the nearest. Its site (nothing of the town remains) can be visited by taking a bus along the road to the west and south (past the Grand Hotel), and then turning off up the hill at the village of **Trianda.**

The view from **Philerimos** (900 feet) is impressive—the sea can be seen at both sides of the island. There are ruins of a chapel and Byzantine church, but the area here has been fortified and defended so much in the past that nothing remains of Ialyse.

About 22 miles from Rhodes, along the same (western) coastal road, is what remains of the ancient city of **Kamiros.** The elaborate water system, with tanks hewn out of rock and clay pipes for irrigating the fields, is the main item of interest here.

About halfway to Kamiros is a turnoff to **Petaloudes,** better known as the "Valley of the Butterflies." This is a delightful spot with a little restaurant (nothing over 30 drs) where you can sit in the open and commune with nature.

The valley extends about a mile, a path leading across bridges, beside a brook, and past waterfalls up through the woods. The butterflies, which look black and white when they are resting, suddenly become fluttering patches of bright red when they unfold their wings and fly about. During the summer, there are millions of them.

The road to Petaloudes, four miles from the main coastal road to the valley, peters out just above the valley, so it is necessary to go back to the main road to continue the journey.

Third of the ancient cities, **Lindos,** is about 35 miles down the east coast and is the island's major show spot. The remains of an **Acropolis** stand on a majestic hill high above the ancient town, and you can either walk up the path or pay 20 drs for a ride on a mule. The view from the top is fabulous and will certainly make you want to stay at least long enough to visit the town's magnificent beaches, one of which sits at the far end of an enclosed saltwater lake. The best restaurant, **Triton,** is also down there, but you can also get a fair meal (about 40 drs) in the restaurant adjoining where the buses stop. Incidentally, if you carry a bag of any sort, you'll be approached and offered a room (about 90 drs per night) as soon as you alight from the bus. All homes renting rooms are primitive but clean and comfortable. The **Triton** pension has rooms for 200 drs double.

The town is beautiful: narrow little alleyways not wide enough for cars and therefore always tranquil. Three worthwhile stops—the attractive art studio of **Willy & Dodo Hempel,** German painters of bright, geometric abstractions who've been here for some years; the oldest house in Lindos, a seventh-century home with painted ceilings, decorated pebble floors, and hidden safes 25 feet above ground to protect the valuables from pirates; and **Looms of Lindos,** a fabric store specializing in radiantly gay colored dresses, tablecloths and napkins, hats and ties, all produced in the village.

The buses to Lindos leave Rhodes at 9 a.m., 11:30 a.m., 3 p.m., and 5:30 p.m. daily: the trip takes about 1½ hours and costs 36 drs. There's just time to explore the town between 11 a.m. and 1 p.m., when the first bus returns. If you want to take a swim, be sure to be off the beach by 6 p.m. when the last bus returns to Rhodes.

Almost in the center of the island, but nearer to Kamiros, on the western side, is a wooded, mountainous region called **Prophitis Ilias.** Only one bus a day goes here, but it is easily accessible by car and motorcycle, and the tranquil atmosphere and lovely view (the mountains of Turkey can dimly be seen across the sea to the north) make it a pleasant stop to get away from it all. Tennis courts, but no other activity except walking.

The road that leads to the east coast is only a dirt track populated by occasional grazing goats with bells, but I have navigated it on a motorcycle without trouble. Be warned: at the village of **Eleonssa** (where a magnificent fountain suddenly appears in view), you must be careful to take the right road or you'll merely go by circular route back to the west coast where you started.

On the way to Prophitis Ilias is a village called **Salakos,** which might offer a resting place. An attractive pension there, the **Nymphis,** is very cheap (about 35 drs per person), and, as the village is halfway up the mountains, it is bracing and beautiful; in addition, it offers some activity by way of a couple of tavernas.

It is possible to drive to any of these places under your own steam, the coastal roads being particularly pleasant when you're on a motorcycle or in an open car. The circular route of the island is a lengthy trip, barely possible in a day if stops are to be made at Kamiros and Lindos, but a pleasant afternoon's motorcycle ride might be to drive out west through **Trianda** and **Paradissiou,** turn off for a side trip to Petaloudes, continue back down the main road to the turnoff for Prophitis Ilias, go up through the mountains and down the other side, and return along the east coast road. This excursion takes about four hours but, of course, eliminates Kamiros and Lindos.

These two ancient towns are both on the **Triton** tour excursions, leaving daily from the market downtown and calling, on request, at any of the main hotels.

The tour to Lindos leaves at 2 p.m. and costs about 330 drs. The tour to Kamiros also includes a visit to the Valley of Butterflies and to Philerimos. It leaves at 2 p.m. and costs 350 drs. In April and May and after mid-September, there aren't any butterflies around, so that portion of the tour is eliminated.

BEACHES: Numerous good ones are ranged along both coasts, in addition to the ones in town. Down the west coast, the lovely village of **Kritika,** with its brightly painted row of houses in different colors, is only a couple of miles out of town. There is a swanky hotel there, the **Poseidon** (tel: 24541), which offers only demi-pension rates (about 600 drs single, 700 drs double), all rooms with shower and veranda.

There is a tourist pavilion at the lovely beach of **Phaliraki,** about 40 minutes by bus. Buses go there about every half hour from 8:30 a.m. to 7:30 p.m. Fare 10 drs.

Bus #3 runs regularly to **Rodini,** a neat garden suburb on the way to **Kalithea.** It's cool and pleasant and the flowers and cypresses and oleanders and singing birds are beautiful and fragrant. There are cafes just outside the town at the port of **Konua,** and at Kalithea (seven miles from Rhodes), where there's also a good beach. Buses leave from the K.T.E.L. terminal behind the market.

TOURS, CAR RENTALS, ETC.: Cheapest car rental is **Nobel** (26 Eth. Dodecanision St., tel: 240-08), which offers Volkswagens for about $7 per day plus 9¢ per km, minimum of 80 kms per day. Most other car rentals start at 210 drs daily, with the same additional charges.

Triton Tours (Plastira St. 25, off Cyprus Square, tel: 249-49) is a relatively new local tour operator that has proved efficient. It offers a wide range of tours of the island and various other islands and has a boat operating between Rhodes and Lindos.

READERS' SELECTIONS AND SUGGESTIONS: "We rented motor bikes for 80 drs per day to get around the island, and the most interesting route is to Ialisos, Valley of the Butterflies, and Karmeros. . . . Free samples are offered after a tour of the **C.A.I.R. Winery** on Afstralias and only a few minutes' walk away is the **Erop Liquor Factory,** where they'll show you ouzo and Metaxa production. Around the island you can also stop in many potteries, wood carvers, silversmiths and hand-loom workshops" (Elaine Mura, Holte, Denmark). . . . "If you have not already booked a hotel, take a taxi to **Makarios Street;** it takes you right into the middle of the hotel area, and you can inquire at several while the driver waits (fare 100 drs). Some charge for luggage; some do not. Souvlaki joints are hard to find, but there's a good one in the middle of Averof in the Nea Agora, another on Aleandrou Papagou, close to Averof and the station for buses to Lindos and Faliraki" (I. E. Orton, Ottawa, Canada).

FLIGHTS: Olympic Airlines flies to Rhodes on a daily basis, leaving Athens three to six times daily. It's about 1080 drs one way for the 55-minute trip.

Flights also between Rhodes and Iraklion four times weekly.

BUS SCHEDULES: Buses to Lindos (60 drs) leave from Sound and Light Sq. at 9, 11:30 a.m., 1 and 3 p.m. Last bus back at 6 p.m. Regular buses to Faliraki (16 drs) depart from same place. From Averof Sq., get buses to

Kamiros (8:30 a.m., 12:30, 2:30, and 6 p.m.; 38 drs); to Koskinou (almost every 30 minutes until evening, then hourly, 12 drs); to Kalithea (10 a.m., 1:30 p.m., 12 drs); to Petaloudes (9 a.m. and noon, last bus back 1:50 p.m., 34 drs); to the airport at Maritsa (5:30, 6:30, 7:50, 11:30 a.m., 1:30, 2:15, 3, 4, 5, 6:30, 8:30, 9:30 p.m.).

BOATS FROM RHODES: Monday: 11 a.m., *Panormitis* to Symi, Tilos, Nissiros, Kos, Kalymnos, Lipsos, Patmos, Arkious, Agathonissi, Samos; 2:30 p.m., *Arion* to Leros and Piraeus.

Tuesday: 8 a.m., *Miaoulis* to Kastellorizon; 9 a.m., *Aegeon* to Kos, Kalymnos, Naxos, Paros, Piraeus; 8 p.m., *Miaoulis* to Simi, Tilos, Nissiros, Astypalea, Piraeus; 8:30 p.m., *Kanaris* to Halki, Karuathos, Kassos, Sitia, Ag. Nikolaos (Crete), Santorini, Piraeus.

Wednesday: 10 a.m., *Achilleus* to Symi, Tilos, Nissiros, Kos, Kalymnos, Astypalea, Amorgos, Folegandros, Piraeus; 11 a.m., *Panormitis* to Kastellorizon; noon, *Renetteta* to Kos, Kalymnos, Piraeus.

Thursday: 9 a.m., *Panormitis* to Kos, Kalymnos, Astypalea; 9 a.m., *Aegeon* to Kos, Kalymnos, Naxos, Paros. Piraeus; noon, *Mimika* to Kos, Kalymnos, Leros, Patmos, Mykonos, Piraeus.

Friday: noon, *Renetta* to Kos, Kalymnos, Piraeus; 3 p.m., *Arion* to Cyprus; 8 p.m., *Panormitis* to Halki, Diafana, Karpathos, Kassos.

Saturday: 6 p.m., *Achilleus* to Kos, Kalymnos, Leros, Patmos, Ikaria, Samos, Chios, Lesbos, Limnos, Thessaloniki.

Sunday: 9 a.m., *Aegeon* to Kos, Kalymnos, Leros, Mykonos, Tinos, Piraeus; noon, *Mimika* to Kos, Kalymnos, Leros, Patmos, Mykonos, Piraeus; 1 p.m., *Renetta* to Kos, Kalymnos, Piraeus; 6 p.m., *Panormitis* to Kastellorizon.

It is advisable to check these schedules by calling the **Kronos** agency (tel: 24000) about the *Mimika* and the *Renetta;* the **Kydon** agency (tel: 23000) about the *Achilleus* and *Miaoulis;* the **Red Sea** agency (tel: 22460) about the *Arion* and *Aegeon;* **Trans Maritimes Lines** (tel: 21636) about the *Kanaris;* and **Zervos** (tel: 22308) about the *Panormitis.*

2. Kos

Kos, one of Greece's most beautiful islands, is very popular among Greek vacationers, but so far, happily, it is not overly crowded with foreigners. It is an immensely lush and almost tropical place, with pomegranates, cactus, figs, bananas, mulberries, cherries, and even some coconuts growing, besides the more prosaic oranges, lemons, grapes, and tomatoes.

There's a winery on Kos (go right around the seashore to the right after you get off the boat—it's about a mile) whose products, while not as famous and sought after as Samos wine, are gaining in popularity throughout Greece.

WHERE TO STAY: As you get off the boat the town is straight ahead and then right. But off to the left, where you see the minaret, is where the nicer hotels are, including the expensive **Theoxenia;** the bargain-priced **Christina** (200 drs single, 275 drs double without bath; 400 drs double with); the **Zephyros** (250 drs single, 450 drs double with bath); and the highly recommended, relatively new **Hotel Hara** (6 Halkonos St.), which has a mere nine rooms in a tree-shaded old house and charges 400 drs double. Halkonos Street is second on your right past the Theoxenia; the other hotels are a couple of blocks further up where the promenade opens up into a square. Also near the Theoxenia, next to the Viking's office in fact, is a cheap pension which is comfortable and reliable. The new **Hotel Kos** offers 70 balconied rooms, bar, restaurant and taped music. Every room overlooks the sea, but rates are high and demi-pension is obligatory.

Back in the town itself, or on the streets behind it, are a couple of really cheap places, of which the **Dodecanesus** (2 Alexandrou Ypsilantou) and the **Helena** (5 Meg. Alexandrou) are probably the best examples: both have doubles without bath for about 250 drs and doubles with bath for about 400 drs. But, truth to tell, you're just as wise to take a private room, either from one of the women who approach you as you leave the boat or via the Viking's office. (Walk past the side of the Venetian fort that skirts the sea and then down the far side across the open plaza.)

RESTAURANTS ON KOS: The liveliest and best spot for dinner at night is along the harbor where there is a row of restaurants. A sea of tables forms, waiters run frantically through barbecue-smoke air. The menus (all in Greek) are approximately the same in all three: chicken, souvlaki, shishkebab, potatoes, salad. The best food to order on Kos is fresh fish. Vacationing Greeks from Athens come here expressly for that reason.

The best restaurant on the harbor is **Limnos,** near the bougainvillea and the flags of different countries. Menu in Greek and English is posted outside, but you're better off going into the kitchen to choose. Try the fresh fish and a bottle of Kos' own Glafkos wine—highly recommended by the natives.

If you stand in Liberty Square with your back to the market (the building with the painted grapes on it), you'll see a bougainvillea-covered stone archway over to your right, behind the mosque. The rows of tables under the pink and white flowering trees belong to the **Restaurant Drosia O Kassios** which is exceptionally good: reasonable prices, wide selection, and courteous and efficient service.

Excellent food is found at the **Miramare Restaurant,** which maintains a fine kitchen. Fish, caught the same day; vegetables, not overcooked; high-quality veal in tomato sauce, and spaghetti with meat sauce. Miramare is in a quiet part of town, just past the Xenia on Georgiou Street, with tables under the plane trees. Menu is in English and Greek, but again, walk in the kitchen to choose your fish or meat.

Adjoining the Miramare along the shore are the **Green Coast** and the **Ideal,** whose white-clothed tables line the sidewalk (two blocks before the Xenia Hotel, heading out of town). The cooking here is excellent and the range of dishes, too, is quite good. Everything looks so appetizing that if you go in the kitchen to look around, you'll probably want to try everything. The Ideal's moussaka is especially good; so is the Green Coast's lamb on a spit.

Another good place to eat is a taverna called **Erotokritos,** Aktikoyntouri-ot 17 (overlooking the port and fronted by a terrace shaded by mighty trees), notable for its fresh fish and charcoal-broiled hamburgers, roasted chicken, and steaks. It's an especially pleasant place to spend the evenings—a perfect outdoor restaurant, with a jukebox playing popular Greek songs.

For one year, the owners of the **Tsambala** saved all the bottles of Peroni beer their customers' drank. Then, in a burst of energy lasting one month, they made a four-walled enclosure out of 19,000 bottles set in plaster. Here and there a bottle has been inset with a colored light and the effect—when sitting at one of the tables in the patio-like enclosure—is rather remarkable. Other colored lights swing overhead in the gentle evening breeze and recorded music rounds the whole thing off. The food is all roasted or grilled, as befits an outdoor restaurant, and their cheese and potato omelette is fantastic. A large Greek salad with cheese, olives, tomato, cucumber and onion is a must, as are a few plates of the excellent french fries. Dinner altogether will probably cost you 90 drs. The restaurant is some way from town—15 minutes by bicycle or about 50 drs by taxi. Go straight along the road out of the harbor at the opposite end to the Xenia, and continue past all buildings for about one mile. Then take the first road to the left for about 200 yards and the Tsambala is on the right.

A good place for ice cream, cake, or coffee at night is the cafe in Liberty Square, or a place called the **Oasis** in the Vassileos Georgiou Hotel area. You can get a great sherbet drink, known as granita, for about nine drs.

READERS' SELECTIONS: "**O Bakchos,** corner of Martion and Ipsilantion, is the best fish restaurant around. Also try the inexpensive **Neon Faliron,** right on the beach near the power plant" (Joep and Paula van Gent, Echteld, Holland). . . . Susan Day of New York also recommends O Bakchos, for its low prices and personalized cooking: "The owner, a delightful man who wears a black beret, gives the taverna its pleasant atmosphere."

KOS' ASCLEPION: Located up on a hill about two miles to the east of the town, the famous **Asclepion of Hippocrates** is accessible to the hardy by walking or by bicycle, to the less-hardy by taxi (50 drs round trip).

The road winds out of town, past huts surrounded by scrambling donkeys and chickens and children, eventually leading up a verdant hillside lined on either side with sweetly scented fir trees. Hippocrates' choice of this site stemmed from his philosophy that health was the first condition for the equilibrium of man's soul; living in such magnificent natural surroundings was essential, giving the patient the inspiration to live and be cured. (According to Pausanias, it was even prohibited in this sacred ground for one to die, murder, or have a baby—and Hippocrates himself is said to have lived 104 years!)

On the side were many little springs; birds sang, and one had—and still has—a truly inspiring view of the sea and the mountains of Asia Minor.

Nobody's quite sure what's what up there. According to some reliable sources (e.g., Koan Iacob Zaraftis, the historian who dug up the site 40 years ago), you will come across the following: At the top of the second flight of steps are two temples, the Roman **Temple of Apollo** on the left, the Greek **Temple of Asclepion** on the right. Up another flight of stairs, you come to Hippocrates' lecture room, surrounded by wards for separate diseases and, supposedly, the stone seat where Hippocrates sat.

Some would have you believe (and I rather favor this version) that the group of rooms to the left of the first flight of steps was the surgical unit, the rooms in which anxious relatives awaited the verdict. Actually, it appears, these are the remains of a Greek swimming pool (Hippocrates thought this very good for the cure) and Roman baths atop the site where his surgery room *did* stand. At one time, there was also a stadium here for exercise—"physical therapy."

AGORA, THEATER, TEMPLES OF APOLLO AND VENUS: It's thrilling to walk through Greek ruins at sunset; in the case of Kos, with its profusions of flowering trees, it's particularly lovely, as well as nice and cool.

A pleasant tour might begin around 6 p.m. at the Agora. It's difficult to miss, being about three blocks up from the harbor and slightly to the left of Liberty Square. Urchins play among the stones, and old, black-kerchiefed women "shop" for scraps of food.

On the side furthest from Liberty Square, under a large tin roof, is a lovely Roman mosaic, entirely covered over with sand, containing figures of Paris and

Hermes. Greek, Roman, and Byzantine styles are so admixed that all three are sometimes combined in a single building; it's a good idea to nab a guard, who will point out (in perfectly comprehensible Italian) the various sections.

A short distance away, through a small square bordered with palm trees, are the Temples of Apollo and Venus, and next to them, the so-called **Casa Romani,** which, of course, is really Greek. (The area is off Leoforio Grigouriou.)

In this same general area is the theater, well-preserved and sometimes actually used for performances; it was in one of the niches underneath that the famous statue of Hippocrates (now in the Kos Museum) was found. Climb up to the very top tier of seats as the sky begins to redden—and a magnificent view of palm trees and oleander, lush fields, and misty mountains will take your breath away.

MUSEUM: A large, neat yellow building on Liberty Square houses Kos' museum. Its five rooms surround a court with a beautiful, large Roman mosaic floor containing figures of Hippocrates, Aesculapius, Aegea, Diana, and Dionysos.

The statues are not labeled, but the first room on the left contains Greek statues from about 300 B.C. There's one of Attalus flexing his muscles as you enter, a headless, armless Zeus, and a lot of nameless statues. In the next room, by itself, is the famous statue of Hippocrates, 400 B.C., which was found under the theater. Two vases dating back to 500 B.C. are on either side of him, with scenes of gods in chariots riding around the outside. The third room dates back to the Hellenic Period (300 B.C.). The lady in the glass case is Athena, a statue of Persephone on either side of her. Opposite Athena is Demeter, with Plato on the left. A very evil-looking Satan is on a pedestal further down, and is a bit fleshy. Opposite is a small figure of Heracles. The next room contains Roman statues dating back to 200 A.D. Hermes is sitting down, his eyes looking off into the distance, and there's a sheep looking up at him. You might note his winged sandals. There's a bust of Nero across the way, and next to him, that man hanging by his wrists from the tree is named Marsyas. He got involved in a musical contest with Apollo and lost, and that's how he had to pay. Back in the main room again, with the mosaic floor, you also can see 3 to 6 goddess of health. The serpent she is holding is a fertility symbol. To her left is a lifesize statue of Artemis, the huntress, with a dog looking up at her admiringly. The third, more complicated piece is Dionysos. Pan is on his shoulder playing him a tune. A satyr is on the other side and at his feet, a panther, his constant companion. That completes the small but interesting collection.

The museum is open daily except Monday, 8 a.m. to 1 p.m., and 3 to 6 p.m., and admission is 15 drs.

HIPPOCRATES' PLANE TREE: Mutter *"Platonos Ippocratos"* at several natives and you'll be directed up six palm-tree-lined steps to the left of the harbor. In a few hundred yards, you will find yourself alongside the gaping shell of a tree trunk, the weight of the tree's huge branches and of its years (a much-disputed 2,000) having nearly pried the trunk open (it's now several yards in diameter). The poor branches, albeit still verdant, are propped up by long forked supports, as many as nine on a single branch. It's cool and pleasant here, and you can stop for a drink of water in the tap that runs from the Turkish wall built around it. Though it's nice to think it's the very tree which Hippocrates planted and lectured under, botanists will assure you that rarely does such a tree live to be a few hundred years old. And as for living over two thousand years. . . .

CASTLE: Across a short bridge to the left of the tree, you'll find the sprawling remains of a 12th-century Venetian castle, used by the Knights of St. John in the 14th century. There are rarely any visitors, and you can play to your heart's content, crawling into the knights' rooms (six feet up, no stairways), looking for stalactites in the underground vaults, or walking the ramparts enjoying a splendid view of the harbor and sea and town. Little of artistic interest is on view here, but numerous plaques bearing the shield of the order of the Knights of St. John have been neatly leaned against the walls, along with old columns.

ELSEWHERE ON THE ISLAND: As the bus bounces happily along a dirt road en route to the first village, **Asfendiou,** you see the sea gleaming on the right, cows grazing against a background of hills on the left. After about two miles, the road curves further in from the coast, allowing, for most of the trip, momentary glimpses of the sea to either side, as the road winds snakily between the lovely hills. Patches of green fertile land contrast with the bare rocky hills. After about five miles, the bus begins the steep ascent up to Asfendiou, the road lined with firs and olive trees and, occasionally, the other-worldly tall stalks which I choose to call "yellow cauliflower trees." Then you are in Asfendiou, a tiny town of 2,500 inhabitants.

The bus arrives about 9 a.m. and stays 45 minutes. A quiet, lovely walk around the serene village takes you past a cow chomping next to the road, blandly watching you as she ruminates; fig trees, goats, millions of grasshoppers; and the sea far below to the left, dotted with small islands.

Generally, the best idea is to climb along with the rest of the passengers (almost exclusively Greek tourists) up **Mt. Dikeo,** a rocky but none-too-difficult ten-minute climb—not to the zenith but to the clear spring which runs down and provides water for the entire village. Just below the source, where it bubbles out into the open, women are squatting, washing small piles of laundry. Behind the source is the old church of **Ayia Maria.** The name of the area you climb to is **Kephakolrisi.** There is time, back at the cafe near the bus stop, to grab a cup of coffee to drink with the bag of plums you have bought for three drs from an old woman up on the hill.

The bus continues westward to **Pyli,** for a while on a smooth paved road lined with yellow blooming trees, arriving finally at **Cardemena,** where it stays for three or so hours while tourists fling themselves onto its lovely wide beach.

A trio of attractive hotels is located here, but your best bet is to make a few inquiries about lodgings in a private home. Rooms are clean and neat, though very plain, and priced around 50 drs per person.

Cardemena's beachfront boasts four or five restaurants, all with identical grass awnings and identical menus. The culinary fame of the area rests in its fresh fish: large red fish (sinagrida), and small black fish (lehtrini).

Going back up the main road after leaving Cardemena, the bus passes the **Castle of Antimachia,** built during the Venetian domination. The road is perched along the spine of the mountain ridge, the land is drier and rockier, and many shelters can be seen built right into the side of the rock. The island is quite narrow at its southern end and you can easily see the sea on both sides.

Kefalo, a quiet town, is reached a little after 4 p.m., and the bus stays for an hour. A lovely place, it is perched high on the cliffs at the far end of the island. A charming, sleepy spot with the remains of a castle and caves—they sheltered the inhabitants when pirates raided centuries ago—it gets few enough tourists that it's a moment of great amusement and curiosity for the villagers when the foreigners do arrive. The view is absolutely stupendous—the islands of **Kalymnos** and **Nisiros** a mile or two offshore, windmills on the ridge behind, and a magnificent sweeping bay below. There are not hotels, but one can find a private room in one of the cozy, yellow-shuttered cottages near the beach.

The bus returns to Kos at 6:30 p.m. If you wish to visit the smaller towns, buses used mostly by villagers run to **Marmari, Tingaki,** and **Mastichari** at 2 p.m., but you must wait till the next day for a return bus.

READER'S SELECTIONS: "A must is a trip to **Nisiros**, the small volcanic island that's 2½ hours by boat south of Kos. Departs 8:30 a.m., around 350 drs. A pickup truck takes you into the crater (50 drs roundtrip) where you feel the hot ground, smell the sulphur fumes and admire the boiling mud. Back in the harbor at **Mandraki**, eat fish at the taverna **Stauros**, visit the **old church** with its beautiful interior (the key is in the hole on the right of the door at shoulder level), take a swim on a beach further away from town (to avoid sewage) and catch the boat back at 4 p.m." (Joep van Gent, Echteld, Holland).

BRIEFLY NOTED: The most convenient beach is the one adjoining the Theoxenia Hotel, but better beaches (available by bus) are on the northwestern side of the island. Buses leave daily from the KTEL bus station; ask Viking's for schedules. . . . Museums are closed Mondays, open till sunset other days (but not in midafternoon). . . . The shipping offices are on the street that runs up from the harbor past the "elevated" cafe. . . . Movie times (four theaters) are 7:30, 9:30, and sometimes 11:30 p.m. There are billboards along the harbor showing what's playing.

BOATS: It's important to know that boat shcedules change from year to year and that the purpose of the following listing is to show the frequency of boats on this route, more than to list exact schedules.

Kos-Rhodes: Every day except Monday, 3-6 a.m.
Kos-Patmos: Monday, 9:30 p.m.; Friday, 6:30 p.m.
Kos-Mykonos: Tuesday, Thursday, and Sunday.
Kos-Kalymnos: Every day.
Kos-Piraeus: Every day but Monday, about 3 p.m.
Kos-Nisiros and Tilos: Tuesday, Thursday, and Friday.

FLIGHTS TO ATHENS: Once daily; trip takes 70 minutes; Olympic Airways, Vassileos Pavlou Ave., tel: 28331 (Antimachin Airport: 19).

3. Kalymnos

Kalymnos (pop: 14,000) is just across the water from Kos, a mere half hour's ride, and excursion boats run frequently. It's a tourist mecca in springtime, the time of the fishing fleet's departure for the Libyan shores for sponge fishing. Sponges are a fulltime occupation on Kalymnos and you can drop in at a workshop on the harbor at any time of the year and see great piles of them. They're dirty when first brought up, cleaned by soaking in a bath of hydrochloric acid.

The harbor of the main port is almost circular, very sheltered, and the town sits between two extremely barren mountain ranges. It's a sleepy little town. Being only 15 miles from Turkey, the sole **movie theater** has a tendency to screen Turkish movies most of the time (it's in a quiet square, just behind the harbor, adjoining the restaurant Paradisos).

A strangely popular trip is to take a taxi up the single-track road to the top of the hill behind the harbor (fantastic view) to the **convent,** where one of the dozen nuns will proudly show you the preserved skull of their founder St. Sabbas (died 1946), wrapped in robes in a glass-fronted coffin. Macabre.

Hotels in town are the **Thermae** (about 400 drs double with bath), the **Alma** (375 drs double with bath), and the cheaper **Chrystal** (300 drs double).

About five miles across the island at **Myrtes,** a beach resort, is the **Delfini** (about 400 drs double), plus two or three cheaper rooming houses at about half the price.

Apart from sponges, Kalymnos is also known for its mineral springs with curative properties. These are on the waterfront about one mile from town.

4. Patmos

Patmos could very well be the loveliest island of the Dodecanese, its smiling mouth the happy port of **Skala,** its crown the magnificent monastery near which St. John wrote the Apocalypse. It's a tiny island of about 2,500 inhabitants, with a magnificent coastline of bays and capes, a clear shimmering quality despite its nearly complete barrenness, and beautiful views from nearly any spot.

Since the new pier was built a spate of souvenir shops and boutiques have blossomed around the harbor but these tend to be open only when the cruise boats come in during most of the year. Boats from Piraeus (*Mimika* on Monday; *Renetta* on Thursday, Saturday) have a tendency to arrive very late at night.

WHERE TO STAY: The town has four hotels. You'll hit the **Hotel To Neon** as soon as you disembark from the small boat that shuttles you ashore. Its ground floor houses a cafe bar which attracts most of the visitors for late-evening snacks. The hotel's 17 rooms, many of them overlooking the harbor, cost 250 drs and 400 drs for single and double rooms with toilet.

Down the harbor to the right is the splendid **Hotel Patmion,** with 20 rooms. It's a nice hotel, with a large lobby, glossy marble floors, soft flower-printed chairs, and a wide veranda on which you can lounge, have coffee, and gaze out at the rest of the island and the sea. It charges 330 drs for the bathless rooms (either single or double), but most rooms have full facilities (toilet and hot showers—quite a luxury on an island where sinks are filled by small metal tanks over them) and cost 400 drs per room. You can get a breakfast of coffee, bread, butter, and marmalade for 40 drs, and the dining room serves moderately priced lunches and dinners. Every few nights, the lobby becomes the setting for a giant rock-and-roll mixer for the young people on the island.

The newest hotel, the 26-room **Chris** (tel: 403), right past the Patmion, costs 300 drs single, 450 drs double, all with shower.

On the harbor is the plush **Astoria** (about 400 drs double), but usually it insists on half-pension, which almost doubles this price. The smaller, 17-room **Rex** has rooms without bath for 250 drs double, with bath for 400 drs.

There's a row of large white houses to the right of the hotel, as you face the harbor, and nearly all offer several rooms from 60 drs per person; equally nice accommodations can be found in the pretty houses which spread up into the hills, in a somewhat quieter area. Just ask at the harbor; the larger places generally send emissaries to greet the ships. Don't rely too heavily on the tourist office behind the cafe-bar—there's seldom anyone there.

THINGS TO SEE AND DO: You will, of course, wish to go up to **Chora,** the promontory atop which are the 11th-century **Monastery of St. John Theologos,** and the **Holy Cave** where the *Apocalypse* was written. You may walk up (it's a steep exhausting climb), take the bus that leaves at 7:30, 9:30, and 11:30 a.m.; share a taxi or hire a mule for whatever price you can negotiate. The trip is spectacular at first: you ride along flat fields edged with pomegranate and citrus and fig trees (this is the area near the **Bay of Hochlaka**). You then begin the steep ascent, which reveals increasingly spectacular views of the barren but somehow electric landscape, with small sloping fields and sea-scalloped edges. Finally, you arrive at the pretty little settlement of Chora, with its white cube houses and cafe ("Welcome to all friends who seek the finest in popular music and entertainment, mineral water, snacks, octopus"), and the huge monastery.

Open 8:30 a.m. to noon and 3-5 p.m. (Sundays 8-12), the monastery charges 15 drs admission. Off its sunny courtyard are the tiny cells of the monks and a large chapel, and down its labyrinthine passageways are the treasury, library, and various other buildings. The amount you see will depend on your finding some nice, self-appointed guide who, for a small fee, will lead you to various nooks (e.g., the refectory, with long stone tables and frescoes of miracles involving food, where monks dine while someone reads inspiring passages aloud to them).

The monastery was founded in the late 11th century, when the Byzantine emperor Alexios I "granted to St. Christodoulos the privilege to found on the island of Patmos the Monastery of St. John" as a "school of virtue . . . always free from public rights and laws." The wise Christodoulos, quite aware of earthly perils, and using every privilege he could muster, carved on this heretofore barren island a nearly impregnable fortress-monastery, complete with a balcony over the main gate from which boiling oil could be poured on anyone aggressing the gate with an "unholy purpose." It flourished over the years, becoming a great center for learning, and, even during the Turkish occupation, managed to thrive and expand.

In the **museum** can be seen the original bull granting the island to Christodoulos, as well as the will of St. Christodoulos, outlining how the monastery was to be run after his death.

In a glass case in the center of the library are the 33 leaves of the *Codex Porphyzeus* (the Gospel of St. Mark), printed on purple parchment in silver ink ("Jesus" in gold). Next to it is a ninth-century illuminated parchment with vari-colored birds floating around it, and one of St. John and his student.

Lining the walls in glass cases is a fascinating collection (mostly in Greek) of 900 hand-written books and several thousand printed ones; most are theological, but I did spot codices containing the plays of Euripides and Sophocles, and several old editions of *Plutarch's Lives.* (For the historian, the numerous codices offer a fascinating study of the various periods through which the monastery passed.)

Down at the opposite end of the corridor from the library is the well-stocked treasury, actually containing only a small part of the monastery's gifts: gold- and silver-embroidered *sakos* (liturgical costumes) of the 17th and 18th centuries, benediction crosses and chalices, numerous ikons, and a striking 16th-century picture of a writhing Gothic mass of figures stretching their hands to heaven. And from the windows you get a nice, misty view of Chora and the harbor.

Once there were 250 monks here; now there are only about 25 and several of them spend most of their time in the public eye, even if they're not selling postcards, taking tickets, etc. Hardly conducive to meditation, one would imagine. But despite their paucity of numbers they exert a major influence on the island which, because of their presence, has no nightlife except a couple of movie theaters showing mostly Greek movies with an occasional American or Japanese kung fu epic. (A recent screening was "Fanny Hill Auf Swedish.")

Descending on your donkey (warning: hang on!), you may stop at the **Grotto** where St. John heard the voice of God through a crack in the ceiling and dictated the resulting Revelations to his student Prochorus. St. John, it is said, retreated here during a Christian persecution by the Roman emperor Domitianus, returning to Ephesus after the Emperor's death. A monk with a huge key will lead you down through the chapel of St. Ann to the cave, and will point out the cleft in the rock, as well as the spots where John laid his head, hoisted himself up, and wrote. It's an eerie place.

On the way down, ask somebody where the 17th-century house (it has no name) can be found. Still occupied, it's a fabulous treasure trove of folk art, furniture and greenery and well worth seeking.

There isn't much else to do in Skala except take a look at the distinctly unexciting distillation plant behind the town and buy incredibly cheap liquor in the duty-free stores.

OUT OF TOWN: Boats leave the harbor at infrequent intervals starting about 10 a.m. en route for **Grikou** or **Kambos** beaches, the latter sporting a solitary restaurant that does, however, stay open until pretty late. From Grikou you can take side trips to **Kallikatsou, Stavros,** and **Evangelismos,** all minuscule settlements—the last-mentioned interesting for its hand-made embroidery. **Kampos,** with its U-shaped bay, offers the better swimming, though.

The younger crowd seems to be favoring another beach, **Malloy,** these days and although a sign prohibits nude sunbathing it's not uncommon. (There are occasional arrests.) The taverna has a vine-covered porch overlooking both bay and tomato fields.

There are buses to Kambos at 8:15 and 10:30 a.m., also 4:30 p.m. Buses to Grikou run at 7:30 a.m. and 1:30 and 6:30 p.m., returning (via Chora) at 7:50 a.m. and 1:50 and 6:50 p.m. Buses direct to Chora run at 7:30, 9:30 and 11:30 a.m.; 1:30, 3:30, 5:30, and 7:30 p.m. Check these times.

Bicycles and motorcycles are for rent at a place in the port.

Highly recommended is a **tour** of the northern part of the island by boat—for the whole island is so gorgeous it's a shame to miss any of it. Talk ten other people into making the trip, and it will run about 35 drs each. The standard route takes you to the verdant **Hermitage of Apollou, Lambis Bay** (filled with pebbles), **Livadi Calogiron** and **Lefkes** (both with lovely gardens), and **Kouvari.** The trip takes several hours; you leave in the morning and return around sunset.

Some evening just before sunset, you might scramble up the deserted **Castello** (up to the right, your back to the harbor—keep yelling "Castello!" at people and you'll be pointed to the right track, and won't have to climb a vertical gorse-covered cliff, as I did). The barely visible sixth- and fourth-century B.C. walls give but a dim hint of an ancient town built over Skala, Hochlaka, and Mericha; the real joy is the magnificent view of the neighboring, smoky island, the fertile fields of Hochlaka, and a sea reddened by the setting sun.

RESTAURANTS: Skala has only three or four restaurants, with fresh fish, again, a good choice. The most varied menu is available at the one to the left and slightly back from the harbor, the **Avra,** its tables under a rare clump of trees. It offers boiled beef, meatballs, dolmati, fish, and roast beef. Right behind it, one street back, is another cozy place with a band and quite impressive dancer who polishes off some intricate folk steps while balancing a chair in his teeth.

The new bar/restaurant left of the port is the favored spot. Another "in" place is the **Arion coffee shop,** next door to the souvlaki and hot dog stand. Two tavernas put tables out on the beach and the **Astoria** also serves meals outside.

5. Simi

A tiny island (pop: about 3,000) that had hardly any tourists until a few years ago, Simi still has only one hotel, the **Nireus,** but now boasts numerous inexpensive pensions.

There are a couple of tourist boats that go there and back from Rhodes each day, as well as calls by regular boats (Monday, Tuesday, and Wednesday) on their northbound routes from Rhodes.

Chapter XV

HEADING NORTH

1. The Island of Evia and Mainland Volos
2. Meteora
3. Thessaloniki (Salonika)
4. Mount Athos
5. Kavala and Thassos

THERE ARE SEVERAL alternate routes north from Athens toward Turkey or Yugoslavia. You can fly to Thessaloniki or Istanbul: fast, expensive, no view of the country. You can go direct to Thessaloniki by bus or train: eight to nine hours of steady travel, compensated by some breathtaking scenery at Thermopylae, the Vale of Tempe, and the coastal road along the slopes of Mount Olympus.

Going more slowly still, you could island-hop: from Raphina, the port due east of Athens, to Karistos at the southern end of Euboea (pronounced—and spelled—on Greek maps, Evia), by bus to Kymi, and then by boat to Skopelos or Skiathos (detailed in Chapter XII) from which you can catch a boat back to the mainland at Volos. Evia is a relatively unexplored island (by foreign tourists) and once you get away from Halkis it can be rewarding.

The trip is best by car, however, and if you wanted a week-long drive for your rented car it would be hard to find an itinerary that would better combine beaches, scenery, and lack of crowds.

1. The Island of Evia and Mainland Volos

EVIA: Heading north up the National Road from Athens, you must watch carefully for the sign to **Halkis**. It comes up without warning (about 145 kms from Athens) just past the toll booth on the right and is in Greek only. There's another toll booth (10 drs) at the entrance to the swing bridge which joins the island to the mainland. In this narrow channel the tide changes every six hours and you can see the sudden increase in fishing-boat traffic.

Halkis and Politika

Halkis (pop: 36,000) is nothing special. A reminder of its strategic importance in the Middle Ages is provided by the remains of its medieval castle. Medieval relics are on display in a restored Turkish **mosque** which serves as a museum. There's a busy seafront cafe life and two C-class hotels (**Ethnikon** and **Hara**); but a more enticing place to stay might be at the little harbor of

Artaki (about 9 kms north), where the pleasant **Hotel Tele** (330 drs double without bath, 400 double with) sits on a headland with its own tiny patch of beach. Artaki itself has a somewhat shabby public beach and a movie theater.

Heading north again on the solitary main highway, you can make an interesting diversion to the sleepy village of **Politika**, the road winding through countryside studded with olive groves, corn fields, random goats, and an occasional horse-drawn cart piled high with yellow melons. Politika is not quite a dead end. Upwards the road meanders around mountain villages, downwards it leads to the sea, ending at a beautiful pebbled beach with cool clear waters and a trio of tavernas. No sound here except the occasional whirr of a farm tractor, wafted randomly on a refreshing breeze.

On Evia—named for Poseidon's mistress—you are never far from the sea; according to Greek legend the island was once joined to the mainland, being violently torn away by an earthquake.

Limni

Another worthwhile turnoff from the highway is westwards to Limni, a charming fishing harbor with lilac and purple sunsets and honeysuckle-filled gardens in narrow streets behind the port. Limni evenings see most of the population perambulating along the harbor, gorging themselves on the best selection of pastries outside Athens at the (nameless) cafe beside the big tree.

Homer mentioned Limni and so did Strabo, who referred to a temple to Poseidon which then existed on one of its cliffs.

Favored hotel in Limni is the 11-room **Plaza** (tel: 235), its balconies overlooking the sea and a cool arcade beneath. Singles are hard to get here, as at most small places, but doubles with bath go for 330 drs. Next door is the **Ilion,** its bathless rooms costing 165 drs single, 280 drs double; and around the corner, the **Avra** (tel: 220), with singles for 220 drs, doubles for 280 drs, all without bath. At the far (southern) end of the harbor is the bigger, modern **Adelphi,** all rooms with shower (but rarely hot water) and costing 275 drs single, 350 drs double. Ask for a room at the front or you may find yourself looking at somebody's back porch.

Just before the turnoff (west) to Limni is a turnoff (east) to the little resort of **Mantouthi** and the nearby harbor of **Kymasi,** where you can rent a motorboat to take you to **Skiathos.** But you'll get another (and more logical) opportunity to visit Skiathos later on this route.

On to Edipsos

Back on the main highway you'll find some unpaved stretches as the road careens round and round the tree-covered mountains. Evia is rich in trees—oleander, plane, mulberry and walnut.

Past **Ag. Anna,** the road descends again to the coast and more beaches appear just beyond **Vassilika. Artemision,** the site of a famous sea battle in 480 B.C. between the Greek and Persian fleets, is the last landmark before **Istiea,** biggest town of the region, with virtually nothing to intrigue the visitor except the **church** overlooking the dusty plaza.—It has an eye above the door and storks nesting on the roof. No hotels in Isteia; go further, to the sea at **Orei** or **Pyrgos,** beyond which is the little hideaway **Hotel Oasis.**

Ferry boats run back to the mainland from **Agiokabos** (to Glyfa) and from **Edipsos Baths** (to Arkitsa). If you plan to continue northwards, then the boat to **Glyfa** is best. It runs at 7:15, 9, and 11 a.m. and 1, 3, 5, 7, and 10:30 p.m. (Boats from Glyfa are each one hour earlier; last boat from Glyfa 8 p.m.) Check the ferry schedule; it may change. Passengers pay about 30 drs for the crossing; cars cost around 225 drs.

Edipsos Baths, famous as a spa since the Romans built there, comes as a surprise. It has something of the feel of a Riviera-type resort—there's even a **Riviera nightclub** on the bay outside town—with an almost unbroken line of cafes and tavernas along the waterfront. It tends to get an older crowd, though, of the type that favor some Florida resorts, and most of its hotels are expensive. (The **Knossos, Leto,** and **Anessis Batis** are among the bigger C-class places.)

Pleasantly located on a headland where the mountains join the sea, Edipsos was mentioned favorably by both Aristotle and Plutarch, and the emperor Hadrian was among its distinguished visitors. Many of its homes and hotels hang from the slopes which backstop the resort, and because of these cliffs there's no access to the sea except for one tiny cove. Beaches abound in the gently curving bay to the northwest, however, and there are so numerous (and so narrow) you can usually find one all for yourself.

There's a cafe conveniently close to the ferry dock—and from here boats run across to Arkitsa almost every hour between 5:30 a.m. and 10 p.m. The ferry (car and driver about 225 drs) takes about one hour.

ON THE WAY TO VOLOS: Once back on the mainland there's the **Hotel Panorama** in **Arkitsa** and then a series of relatively expensive resorts adjoining the National Highway. **Ag. Konstantinos** is typical with its trio of classy hotels—**Olga, Astir,** and **Amphytrion**—usually fully booked in summer. **Kamena Vourla** is another expensive resort, popular mainly with Greeks. (To the south there's even less: the grubby beach at **Skala** has one taverna and nowhere to stay, although there's lots of building going on; **Larimna** is on a bay totally filled with a smoke-belching factory.)

Glyfa, where the Evia ferry docks, has **rooms** (250 drs double) in a big house just beside the whitened tree (about five houses from the eastern end of the harbor), and a small hotel, the **Agriokali.** Ask about rooms at the Caravel boutique. The bay just before Glyfa, as you're driving from the turnoff at the main road, is lined with beaches and almost deserted.

Last spot to stay before Volos is **Ankhialos,** where a sign on the main road directs you to "Rooms by the Sea."

VOLOS AND VICINITY: Volos (pop: 70,000), from whence Jason set sail with his Argonauts in search of the Golden Fleece, is today a big industrial city that fills the (polluted) bay on which it sits. Although there are places to stay in the town itself (C-class hotels are **Alexandros, Kypseli,** and **Galaxias**), there are none along the shoreline just to the south, and a big cement factory dominates the bay to the north. It's not a place for lingering.

Watch for a turnoff at **Agria,** a few miles beyond. Here a small blue and white sign opposite the Mobil station directs you down an unpaved road to a taverna called **O Thomas,** whose huge red neon sign is the most noticeable thing for miles. Popular with visitors from the Volos at night, the taverna has some newly built hotel rooms—simple but with some style—which are fairly expensive, however, at 400 drs double, usually without hot water.

Boats from Volos

Volos, by the way, is the jumping-off point not only for the lovely little villages of **Mount Pelion** (of which the most beautiful and most photographed is **Makrynitsa**) but also for the **Sporades** islands (Chapter XII). Boats from

Volos usually stop at **Trikkeri** (southern end of the bay) before heading over to **Skiathos** and stopping at **Glossa** (on Skopelos) and **Skopelos port** itself, at the southern end of the island. The *Sporades* goes daily to all these places (7:30 a.m. and 5:30 p.m. on Monday; 1 p.m. on Tuesday, Wednesday, Thursday and Friday; 6 p.m. Saturday; 1 p.m. Sunday). The *Skyros* sails on Saturdays to Skiathos, Skopelos, Glossa, Alonissos, Kymi (on Evia), and Syros. The *Thira* sails 2:30 p.m. Saturdays to Skiathos, Skopelos, Glossa and Alonissos. North Aegean Lines runs boats to Ag. Konstantinou on the mainland and also to Skiathos, Skopelos, Kymi, Skyros, Limnos, and Kavala (beyond Thessaloniki). From Limnos you can catch connecting boats to Mytilini on Lesbos. Shipping offices for all these boats are down by the harbor in Volos (which is also where you'll find the 78-room **Alexandros** hotel).

Around the Peninsula

Heading eastwards from Volos and then southwards down the peninsula, you'll pass **Agria**, then **Lehonia**, and after that note a turnoff to **Platania**, where there are tavernas on a little beach. **Argalasti** is the last place of any size before you reach the turnoff for Platania, an utterly delightful port with sandy beach, shallow water, and flocks of lively swallows.

There's almost nothing to do in Platania except relax on the beach, eat at the harborside tavernas, and persuade **Stasos** to sail his caique across to Skiathos for the day. He leaves at 8 a.m., returns at 4 p.m., and charges 150 drs for the round trip if he can get a boat-load together. (Be sure not to miss his embarkation from the pier below the Xenia—across Koukounaries bay from where he docked—or you'll have to pay as much as 1000 drs to charter the yellow boat back.)

Stay at the **Villa of Roses** hotel (tel: 0423-54248) in Platania. The food's good, the tariff cheap (doubles 300 drs), and the owner, John Dovas, a friendly host. Alternatively, there's the **Agriokali** (same rates) on the harbor. Just around the rocks from the main beach is a smaller beach where bolder tourists go topless.

The road back up the peninsula's eastern side passes through some interesting places. You can go inland to the lovely little town of **Milies,** with its 18th-century church and rooms for rent in private homes. Or to tranquil **Tsangarada** with its ancient stately homes and 1,000-year-old plane tree. There's a luxurious **Xenia** hotel at Tsangarada (1100 drs double, demi-pension), and if you crave the luxury of total silence you might try sitting on the well-kept lawn there late at night. There are also **private rooms** to rent nearby.

The justly famous fine, sandy beach of **Mylopotamos** is seven kms away, the road ending on the top of the cliffs, with 130 steps leading down to the sea. Equally attractive is the tiny resort of **Ag. Ioaniss**, which is so popular that it has a **tourist office** with a multi-lingual lady who'll book you into a hotel room for about 400 drs double with bath or 350 drs double without. There are also **rooms** available in private homes for about 275 drs double. Turn left when you walk out of the tourist office and go beyond the main beach, right around the rocks to a nicer beach that's almost deserted.

Buses run from Volos to Ag. Ioannis at 8:15 a.m. and 1:30 and 5:15 p.m. Last bus to Volos from here is at 8 p.m.

Once back in Volos, the route north heads to **Larissa** (about which more under "Getting to Meteora," below), where a turnoff should be made westwards to **Trikkala** if you plan to visit the monasteries of Meteora.

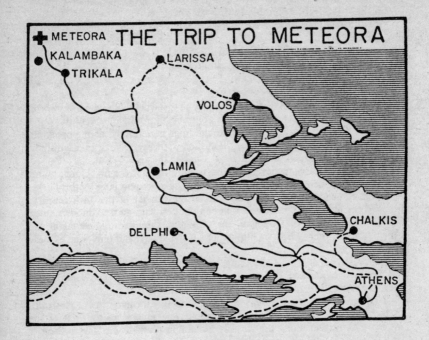

THE TRIP TO METEORA

+ METEORA
KALAMBAKA • LARISSA
TRIKALA
VOLOS
LAMIA
DELPHI
CHALKIS
ATHENS

2. Meteora

The word *meteora* means "rocks in mid-air," which is a little misleading because they are accessible from the ground—if you happen to be a monkey. The first sight of these incredible rocks, towering above the plain around them like gigantic, cavity-ridden teeth from the days before fluoride toothpaste, is impressive in itself, but when you spot the monasteries built precariously on their barren tops, you marvel at what people have done in the name of religion.

Actually, there was a major incentive: in the days when the monasteries were first built (14th century), this was wild, lawless country, repeatedly fought over and constantly at the mercy of whoever chose to impose force. A man named Neilos, who was abbot of a monastery at the foot of the rocks, built small churches atop some of them, and as the brigandry and persecution increased, monks retreated to them, isolating themselves from the world below by pulling up the ladders—the only means of access—behind them.

Rope baskets were lowered for supplies, and sometimes for people, and until late in the last century, this was still the only way to reach some of the monasteries. There must be travelers still alive who were hauled up in this way, despite the legend that the rope was never changed until it broke and had to be replaced.

Once there were a score of monasteries but only four exist today, scattered among the rocks of the gorge with faint traces remaining of the others. Even in the monasteries that can still be visited the rich treasures of Byzantine art have mostly disappeared leaving the visitor with only the buildings themselves and the fabulous views of and from the rocks. Of course, there are some artworks left, in particular the murals. The **Varlaam Monastery** has probably the most to offer having been rebuilt in the 16th century, and because strong rays of light have not been able to dim the paintings.

The nearest place from which access to the rocks is had is the sleepy town of **Kalambaka**. From there, you can hire a taxi for the three or four-mile trip (the narrow road winds ingeniously) around the four monasteries, all of which are now accessible from the road by stone steps.

HISTORY AND GEOLOGY: The weirdly shaped rocks—"rearing skywards in needles, in knife-edges, in enormous columns, in prodigious menhirs, some threatening like leaning towers or like buildings undermined at the base," as one authority puts it—were formed 50 million years ago, give or take a million years or so, when much of this area was under the sea.

The Meteora area, believed to have been settled for the first time around the 11th or 12th centuries, was conquered by the Serbs and later by the Turks. A monk named Athanasios, who came to the district in the 14th century, founded the first of the monasteries in conjunction with another monk named Varlaam. The abbot of Doupiani, the religious administrative center at the time, founded others. Only six altogether survive today, and only four of these are regularly visited.

Successive generations of looting, and abandonment, have not only caused the monasteries' decline, but also lost to the world much of the Byzantine art they are believed to have contained at one time.

The only hotel actually near to Meteora itself is the inexpensive **Kastraki,** in the tiny village of the same name about one mile from the first of the monasteries further along the steadily ascending road. If you have a camper or VW bus it is advisable to negotiate the road to its dead end, parking for the night opposite the cliff that accommodates the Grand Meteora monastery. (Its real name is Monastery of the Transfiguration and it is the highest, at 1,900 feet above sea level).

There are two camping sites along the road between Kalambaka and Meteora, both enclosed, the better one being the first you come to: a tree-shaded garden to the left of the road. Buses run occasionally from Kalambaka to Meteora but it's more likely you'll have to take a taxi (or thumb a ride) for this last stretch.

THE TOWN OF KALAMBAKA: The modern, cool 20-room **Hotel Odission** Kalambaka, tel: 22320), at the Meteora end of town, is the favored choice. Comfortable and attractive. Doubles without bath, around 350 drs; with bath 400 drs. Cheaper are the 16-room **Aeolikos Star** (tel: 22325) and the 22-room **Rex** (tel: 22372) both with rooms for 250 drs single, 300 drs double.

Kalambaka's a tiny place but it does have restaurants, a **movie theater,** and a **Byzantine church** on a hill at the eastern end of town (you'll find it locked; the woman in the house next door has the key).

Taxi rates to some of the monasteries: To St. Stephanos (the best), 100 drs one way, 175 drs round trip; to Metamorfoseos (Great Meteoron), 85 drs one way, 150 drs round trip; to Varlaam, 75 drs one way, 120 drs round trip. To this, add 12 drs per hour, or part of an hour, for waiting time.

The nearest of the monasteries will take at least one hour to reach on foot from town, but as there are always tourists from all countries rushing by in small cars, you can probably get a lift.

THE MONASTERIES: The monastery of **St. Stephanos,** built on the site of a 12th-century hermitage, was turned into a sizable monastery during the reign of Emperor Andronicos III Palaiologos in 1329, and was damaged by a bomb in World War II. No monks live there any more, only a group of solemn-faced nuns who never smile and who sit doing needlework, their faces almost obscured by black hoods covering all but eyes, nose, and mouths.

As you enter you'll be offered a jacket or sweater to cover your bare arms, and other nuns will sell you booklets or postcards in the souvenir shop. There's a small chapel with very minor treasures, including a saintly portrait so pocked with knife marks it appears to have been used as a dartboard. Apart from the view, which is fantastic, the visit is hardly worth the climb, but because this is the monastery that sits directly above the town of Kalambaka, perspective on the surrounding Pinios Valley is truly impressive.

Biggest of the monasteries, the Monastery of the Transfiguration, which is usually called **Great Meteoron,** is also the highest—613 meters above sea level. There's quite a lengthy climb from the road, and not too much to see when you get there, except for a batch of signs: Please Do Not Smoke; Please Do Not Enter; Please Do Not Take Photographs In the Church; Please Do Not Pass the Night In the Monastery; Please Drop Your Money in the Box. The man at the door is even more emphatic than most of the others in his insistence on men wearing a jacket and women wearing sweaters that cover their arms. The church shelters some fairly interesting portraits, including one of St. Athanasios, founder of this monastery.

Within walking distance (300 yards) of Great Meteoron is **Varlaam,** named after the monk who built the hermitage on the spot in the middle of the 14th century. A small museum (4 drs admission) contains old books, ikons, and chalices; the winch and equipment for hauling up supplies sits behind it, now driven by a small gas-powered engine.

One hundred and thirty steps lead up to the **Monastery of the Holy Trinity** (Moni Agia Triados), which is somewhat isolated between two ravines. It has some fairly interesting murals, painted by a monk in the 17th century. The **Roussanou Monastery,** founded by two brothers at the beginning of the 16th century, is now occupied by nuns. Its major interest lies in the fact that its walls are built right on the edge of the rock, with nothing outside them except a sheer drop of several hundred feet. Try not to fall out.

TRIKKALA: Trikkala is a pleasant town with a winding river, a street named after Lord Byron, and the remains of a high-walled fort, with clock tower, on a hill overlooking the town (you can hear the gunfire from the Western playing at the open-air theater below).

Some of the winding streets at the foot of the hill are rocky and potholed, and it's pleasant to wander through them at night, savoring the quietness, even though the main streets, and indeed the heart of town, are only a few blocks away. These streets are unlighted, which makes the occasional patches of illumination even more exciting: sudden flashes of white light—from a welding shop, as you turn a corner . . . the acetylene flares on a souvlaki stand . . . candles flickering in miniature shrines built in the shape of doll-sized Byzantine chapels, colored glass windows in the tiny dome . . . a procession of women carrying lighted tapers into a church at the foot of the hill.

Trikkala is one of those very special towns which, because it offers nothing "special," has incidents all around to offer if you have the perception and patience to see them: a youth rides past on a bicycle with four loaves tucked under his arm . . . girls glance out through the open door of a beauty shop, a captive audience under their aluminum hairdryers, as curious about you as you are about them . . . a man and his wife crush long blocks of ice with heavy mallets, showering nearby cafe-sitters with frozen chips, and tamping the frozen mush down around the containers of ice cream which await shipment on the blue station wagon purring nearby.

Where to Stay

Most of the hotels of Trikkala are in or around King George Square (Plateia Vassileos Georgiou) and on the adjoining side streets. This is the spot where most of the town's outdoor life is concentrated, and the river Lithaios loops around, necessitating three bridges across it in a short stretch. The river flooded just after the turn of the century and inundated the town, but these days it is quiet, lined with shady trees and a few cafes.

Best of the budget hotels is the **Rex** (Appollonos Street, tel: 28306), whose red and green sign can be spotted from the square only half a block away. Its lobby is modern, with brightly colored chairs and large unframed photographs of Greece on the walls. Its 58 rooms cost around 200 drs single, 275 drs double without bath; 300 drs single, 400 drs double with bath.

The bus from Kalambaka stops outside the **Hotel Palladion** (tel: 28091) on its way to the bus station (beside the river just past King George Square), and rooms here cost around 200 drs single, 300 drs double, all without bath. Almost next door is the 73-room **Achilion** (tel: 28192) that's expensive but has a sidewalk restaurant that's the town's best eating place. Cheaper are the 51-room **Dina** (tel: 27267), the attractive **Meteora** (tel: 27744), and the 21-room **Panhellinion** (tel: 27644) in the same building.

GETTING TO METEORA: The trip to Meteora can be made from Athens and back to Athens in about one and a half days. By rail, take the northbound Thessaloniki train and change at Paleopharsala for the Trikkala train.

At Trikkala, you can either stay on the train for one more stop—Kalambaka, near Meteora—or alight and take a bus for the final leg of the journey. Buses run between Trikkala and Kalambaka every hour.

One-way fare between Athens and Kalambaka is around 400 drs first class, 250 second. The S.E.K. ticket office is at 8 Omirou Street, Athens, tel: 633-005.

Even if you don't go by bus, it is better to come back that way. Buses for Trikkala leave Athens (260 Lissiou St., tel: 852-333) at 7:30, 9, 10:30 a.m., noon, 1:30, 3:30, 5, and 8:30 p.m. The trip takes just under six hours and costs 300 drs. Buses from Trikkala (bus station on Othonos Street) to Athens leave eight times each day. Buses run between Kalambaka and Trikkala about once every hour until 9:30 p.m.

It's almost impossible to avoid the bustling little town of **Larissa** on any trip to or from northern Greece, and it makes for a pleasant, untouristy stop. There isn't too much to see beyond the ancient citadel atop the hill and the urn from what is said to have been Hippocrates' tomb, discovered after a heavy flood in the last century. There are two big squares on both of which are cafes and hotels. Budget hotels are the **Pella** (Vass. Frederikis tel: 220031), the **Esperia** (Amalias 4, tel: 222106), and the **Olympion** (Megalou Alexandrou, tel: 226041). Places to eat are the **Xabah restaurant,** with sidewalk tables on narrow Kouma Street, or at any of the snack bars around the plushy Hotel Metropol.

The route between Trikkala and Thessaloniki passes through the famous **Vale of Tempe,** whose springs of Diana and Daphnia are signposted along the highway.

3. Thessaloniki (Salonika)

Thessaloniki, importantly situated at the crossroads of the main routes between Greece, Central and Western Europe, Turkey and Asia, has always been a prosperous city. It was founded in 315 B.C. and has known many masters, including Romans (146 B.C.), Saracens (904 A.D.), Normans (1185 A.D.), Latins (1204), Venetians (1300), and Turks (1430).

It was partly destroyed by fire three times in the past century. Nevertheless, many relics of its earlier history still survive: Byzantine churches, Roman monuments, impressive ramparts. Also, since it remained a part of the Ottoman empire until 1912, it displays relics of the Moslem culture, unlike southern Greece.

It has always been an intellectual town whose citizens wanted to know what was going on. Today, you commonly see passersby reading, and not necessarily buying, the local newspapers that a newsstand has thoughtfully hung on the nearby railings, or women under hairdryers on a second floor open balcony watching the action on Egnatia Street below.

It's also a very charming city; it sprawls for miles, glittering attractively in the sun. A tremendous amount of building is currently going on.

Warning: every September the city—Greece's biggest after Athens—is visited by thousands of visitors to its International Trade Fair. It is next to impossible to find rooms during this period, and the hotels are permitted to add 20% to their regular rate. Unless displays of heavy equipment are what turn you on, schedule your visit to Thessaloniki for some other time.

HOTELS: The railroad station is in a visually uninteresting section of town. If you absolutely must stay near the station—for a rest, say, because you don't want to go all the way to Istanbul in one jump—there's a semi-luxury hotel, the **Rotunda** (Monastirion 91, tel: 517121), about 200 yards up to the right of the station. The 80-room Rotunda is new, elegant, and well equipped, with roof-garden restaurant, and all-night snack bar. All rooms have bath and cost 375 drs single, 500 drs double. Breakfast is obligatory (42 drs), and sometimes so is demi-pension. Better check.

About eight blocks to the left of the station is a traffic circle, and the town—for all intents and purposes—begins here. A wide main street, which up to now has been called Monastirion, here begins again as **Egnatia.** Many new hotels, the biggest bargains in town, are located on or just off it, and it is traversed by buses #10 and #11.

There is an excellent luxury hotel here, the **Victoria,** within walking distance of both the railway station and town. At more than 600 drs double, it is out of this book's range.

Egnatia runs parallel to the harbor, about five blocks away. The main crosstown streets running between Egnatia and the waterfront are **Ermou, Alexandriou, Franklinou Rousvelt,** and—along the harbor—Konstantinou. Bus #1 from the station runs along Meg. Alexandrou.

The **Hotel Egnatia** (Leontos Sofou 11, tel: 536-321), is an eight-story marble edifice about a block below Egnatia Street, heading down towards the water. That makes it pretty central. But the Egnatia also has style: attractive ceramic plates listing the room number outside each door, enormous sunny balconies almost as big as the room, and a lovely first-floor restaurant and lounge with black leather armchairs. All 145 rooms have bath and (except for the period when the trade fair is on) cost 330 drs single, 475 drs double. Special bargain for families: the Egnatia has a few large comfortable four-bedded rooms. In addition to the standard continental breakfast (40 drs) there is an American breakfast with eggs for 50 drs.

About 3½ blocks from the Egnatia is the fully air-conditioned **Hotel Park** (Dragoumi 81, tel: 524121), which has all the characteristics of a first-class hotel. Right in front of the Ministry of Northern Greece, with a park across the way, it boasts a handsome spacious lobby with a beautiful ceramic mural covering part of one wall, professional English-speaking staff, large carpeted salon with TV, wall-to-wall carpeting in hallways and rooms(!), balconies from which you can see the harbor, music (three stations) in every room, and even little chairs to sit on in the showers. All single rooms have double-size beds and rent for around 330 drs single, 400 drs double; breakfast 40 drs.

On Dikastirion Square, diagonally across from the Hotel Park, is the equally pleasant **Hotel Esperia** (Olympou 44, tel: 268321) whose 70 spotless and airy rooms have tasteful furnishings, bathrooms, and (usually) balconies. Friendly management. Rooms cost around 400 drs double.

Another new budget hotel in this area is the **Delta** (Egnatia 13, tel: 516321), all of whose rooms have shower, telephone, music, mirror, and small balcony. Not as fancy as the Park, but less expensive: single 250 drs, double 400 and breakfast 40. The 113 rooms are clean and bright, and singles again have double-size beds. The English-speaking staff will be happy to assist you, and there is a restaurant on the premises.

Down the street, the 54-room **Hotel Olympic** (Egnatia 25, tel: 522131) is a high-grade place. Doubles only here: 475 drs with bath. Nice wooden floors in the rooms, French Provincial-type furniture, bar-lounge on first floor, roof garden, and large baths and bidets in the bathrooms.

Several cheaper hotels are also along Egnatia, of which the best is the **Hotel New York** (Egnatia 39, tel: 525062), whose manager, Anastasios Stamoulas, speaks excellent English. Rooms are very simple and primitive in furnishings, but spotless, and opening onto the hotel's major attraction: an indoor patio with sunlight streaming through an overhead skylight. All rooms without bath: 200 drs single, 275 drs double.

Another similar cheapie is the spartan but spotless **Hotel Kastoria** (Egnatia and Sofou, tel: 36-480), which charges 275 drs double. All rooms without bath.

The **XEN** (YWCA) is at 11 Ayias Sophia Street, two blocks up from the water and charges 100 drs for room. Full board is about 200 drs per day. Accommodation is in three-bed rooms and six- or eight-bed dormitories. The **XAN** (YMCA), by the White Tower Park (tel: 275026), charges 70 drs daily for a bed in six-bed rooms.

With prices rising so rapidly everywhere the big old-fashioned hotels are looking more and more of a bargain. The **Tourist Hotel** (Mitropoleos 21, tel: 276335) on the corner of Komninon and a couple of blocks up from the sea, is just such a place. Spacious, airy rooms off cool dark hallways cost a mere 175 drs single, 255 drs double without bath, and from some of the 40 rooms you can just catch a glimpse of the sea.

One block from Aristotelou Square and the waterfront is the **Hotel Rea** (Komninon 6, tel: 78449), simple and unostentatious, where bathless rooms cost 225 drs single, 400 drs double with bath.

If you have a few extra drachmas weighting you down, stay at the newly built **Hotel Palace** (12 Meg. Alexandrou, tel: 270505), two blocks from the harbor, at Venizelou Street near Aristotelou Square. Its 58 rooms are clean, with comfortable armchairs in each. Singles without bath are 265 drs, doubles 395 drs. Breakfast is 40 drs additional per person.

The best budget choice, conveniently central to both waterfront and Egnatia Street, is the charming **Hotel Amalia** (Hermou 33, tel: 268-321) whose 66 rooms all have decorated ceilings, lovely furnishings and pictures, balconies, and bathrooms. There's a delightful breakfast room and bar on the first floor, service and food are both first rate. The hotel is two blocks from the main square (Plateia Dikastirion) in one direction, three blocks from Plateia Aristotelou on the waterfront in the other direction. A fruit and flower market are among its neighbors offering local color. Rates: 325 drs single, 400 drs double.

Thessaloniki's **youth hostel** has closed down.

RESTAURANTS: Despite its size, Thessaloniki doesn't have much variety in places to eat. There are, so far as I was able to discover, no French or Italian or Chinese restaurants.

Most of the big squares have cafes rather than restaurants, which makes it impossible to get anything but pastries and snacks while sitting and watching the action. In common with the rest of Greece, though, nearly all the restaurants have at least a few of their tables outside on the sidewalk.

Especially to be considered are the restaurants up beside the old town ramparts, by the beaches at Aretsou to the east of town, and up in the village of Panorama, about five miles away. No specific restaurants are singled out in these areas, which are dealt with in later portions of this text, because you're not going there to get special cuisine but rather for the location of the eating place.

Well, maybe I'll mention one: A trip just past Aretsou Beach (bus #5) will bring you to the charming **Rembi** (Neakorni, tel: 41233), an open-air restaurant overlooking the sea; music and dancing at night. Most entrees about 40-60 drs. (Several other restaurants and cafes are also found along this stretch but, oddly, no hotels. Most consulates are stationed along the waterfront and it's a pity they don't rent rooms.)

Aristotelou Square in Thessaloniki proper you'd expect to be crowded, but the smarter cafes further east along the harbor seem to be more popular. A leisurely walk along to Pirgos (the White Tower) will take you past half a dozen of them, of which the **Tottis** and the **Corfin** (which even has an upper balcony) are the most chic, and the tiny **Salon** is the most cheerful (with an always-jumping jukebox).

There's another Tottis branch in the arcade off Ermou Street, very central, between Aristotelou and Komninon Street.

As for restaurants, the most popular is the enormous **Olympos Naonssa** (on Konstantinou, between Liberty Square and Komninon St.). It could accommodate, perhaps, three or four hundred people and feed them as fast as any place you could find. Service is excellent, so too the lighting, and the restaurant is popular with both tourists and Greeks. Menu is English, French, and Greek, and there's plenty of variety, ranging from soups to chocolate sundaes, with a few offbeat entrees such as chicken croquettes supplementing the more predictable fare. Most dishes about 50-70 drs.

Slightly further eastwards, along the water, is the popular **Stratis** (Konstantinou 19, tel: 79-353), partly on the sidewalk overlooking the water. Menu in German, French, and English.

The very pleasant **Bee Restaurant**, right next to Doucas Tours on Eleftherias Square, has outdoor tables and a vast menu clearly marked in English.

A good place to watch the action (look out for obstreperous lottery ticket sellers) and to eat a satisfying lunch for under 100 drs.

Until 2 p.m. the nicest place to eat is the fourth floor of the **OTE tower** just inside the entrance to the Trade Fair grounds, a couple of hundred yards from the White Tower. (The cafe in the White Tower is now closed but admission is free to those who want to climb the 70 winding steps). The OTE tower has a limited but surprisingly good menu ranging from various salads (the tuna fish salad is recommended) and cheeses, to a handful of hot dishes such as meatballs and veal cutlet. Besides the pastries, ice creams, and cold snacks there's a wide range of drinks including Irish coffee. All this and a revolving view!

In the little square beside the White Tower are a couple of inexpensive restaurants (the **Wistaria** is best) and a modern one called **Grill Chef**, attractively paneled with comfortable leather seats. Entrees mostly 70-80 drs with filet mignon topping the list. Also good salads including one of eggplant.

Navarino Square, with its intriguing sculpture fountain, kids' playground, and residential life is not too far away from the two towers, and just off the square is the **Spaghetteria** (Vyronos Street), spaghetti, and pizzas a specialty. An even better place for these dishes is **Ciao-Ciao** (Bongatsikon 6, tel: 25152), where the prices are higher but the Italian pop music and decor offer more ambience.

You can dance, drink, and admire the lovely view from the **Kastra**, up by the castle walls and known to most taxi drivers who'll ask anything from 65 drs upwards to take you there. Adjoining it is a tiny taverna, the **Argyros**, with terrace tables and entrees from a mere 65 drs.

The **Krikelas** restaurant (Grammou-Vitsi 32 Street, about three miles from town, tel: 41289) is a charming wood-paneled taverna on the main road, with tables at the front in a trellis-enclosed patio. Menu is all in Greek and nobody speaks English, but you can go into the spotless kitchen and point to all the usual favorites—moussaka, fish, veal, stuffed peppers, chicken, lamb, etc. Nothing on the menu costs more than about 80 drs. Try the baked quince-apple for dessert. The Krikelas, on the righthand side of the road, is identified by a big red and green neon sign atop a building on the left and is usually announced by the bus conductor. In any case, if you can, get up front on the bus and ask the driver to give you the word. Get the "Finix" bus from the corner of Alexandrou and Aristotelous Square. And get there after 9:30 p.m.—there's music.

ALONG THE WATERFRONT: Aristotelou Square is just about the center of the waterfront in the older part of town and it's the place where the action seems to be. This area doesn't look particularly old, because it's been rebuilt after various fires and earthquakes destroyed part of it. But if you walk along the waterfront, Konstantinou, to the ancient white tower built by the Venetians in the 15th century (**Pirgos Tower**), you'll see that it stands at the foot of what used to be the city's boundary wall. And if you don't see it now (because no vestiges of the wall are left down here at the harbor), you'll see it when you climb the hillside and see the whole place in perspective.

The White Tower, all that remains of the Venetian sea wall demolished a century ago, was repainted and renamed after being the "Bloody Tower," when that elite army the Janissaries were imprisoned and executed in it on the orders of the Sultan Mahmoud. A pleasant park with open-air cafes and a small zoo opens off from the tower. The zoo is free, specializing in "little" animals such as pelican, wolves, deer, monkeys, rabbits, owls, and peacocks (which screech disconcertingly from the trees overhead).

The **Archaeological Museum,** situated opposite the YMCA on White Tower Square, shelters a magnificent collection of gold jewelry, bronze and glass vases, and other treasures from ancient Thrace and Macedonia, as well as interesting floor mosaics from the Roman era. The Museum, closed Mondays, is open 7:30 a.m. to 7:30 p.m. Free admission Thursday and Sunday and 50 drs other days (students with IDs, 5 drs).

There are other attractive and valuable mosaics in the score of remaining Byzantine churches around town, particularly **Agios Dimitros** at Ag. Dimitriou and Aristotelos Streets.

Past the tower, to the east, the promenade widens and is separated from the towering, pastel-colored apartment buildings by a broad highway lined with grassy stretches and parks. Warships are moored along the quays, and altogether it's a section for driving along, because it lacks the cozy intimacy of little boats and old buildings that makes strolling so fascinating. The tourist office is on Aristotelou Sq., and it is usually very helpful with schedules, dates, prices, bus stops, etc. Olympic Airlines' office is here as well, along with the Mediterranean Palace Hotel on the waterfront at the foot of Komninon Street. This is also the part of town where you'll find the restaurants and nightclubs.

The **Folklore and Ethnology Museum of Macedonia** is housed in a century-old gabled mansion at the end of a long garden at Vassilissis Olgas 68 (take any of the downtown bus lines and get off at the "Flemming" stop), tel: 830591. Collections include costumes grouped by geographic area, jewelry, scale-model examples of Macedonian architecture, and a reconstruction of a typical Macedonian guest room. The collection here is constantly expanding, with fine examples of Macedonian arts and crafts—past and present—being added all the time. And Macedonian aficionados will particularly like browsing through the third-floor storeroom and study area.

TO THE BEACH: First of my do-it-yourself 25-cent tours is the 20-minute ride on the #6 bus out to the terminal. You can catch the #6 bus either in Dikastirion Square or on Egnatia St., east of the Pirgos Tower, and its route through a most attractive and active part of town will give you some idea of just how big Thessaloniki is. An alternative is to take the #5 bus from Liberty Square.

Past the new apartment blocks and the old quaint houses it goes. On the left, you'll catch a glimpse of the former mansion now occupied by regional NATO headquarters; to the right, a block away, is the sea. Very soon you're in a suburbia that is almost rural, with its greenery, sandy streets, and one-story houses with the wash spread over the garden fence. Horses and carts are delivering fruit and milk, just as they did in the England of my childhood, and women gather at the end of each block to fill buckets from the tap, although the neat stone houses appear comfortably middle-class.

The bus ends its route two blocks from the sea, and you can walk down to the shoreline where yachts bob in a man-made harbor between two piers. To the right is a beach called **Aretsou Beach,** and numerous tavernas are dotted along the road and the shore below.

You can either take the same bus back, by retracing your steps up the hill, or cross the main street opposite the Mpalkoni and catch bus #5 or #7.

You'll find even better beaches at **Agia Trias,** a mile or two further round the coast. To get there, you take either a #23 bus from Karolou Dil Street (25 minutes; nine drs) or one of the excursion boats leaving from opposite Pirgos

Tower. These run every hour, depending on the number of passengers, and charge ten drs. There are camping facilities at Agia Trias.

TO AND FROM THE RAMPARTS: High on the hills above town are the ancient city walls, said to have been impregnable in the fourth century A.D. when they were built. Today they offer a magnificent view of the city and its environs, as well as an actual sense of history that somehow I've never been able to derive from more famous ruins.

Bus #22 from Liberty Square will take you there. The precise spot you want is the **Convent of Vlatadou,** and the absorbing, tantalizing glimpses of the old town that you get on the way up will whet your appetite for the walk back down again, instructions for which will follow in due course.

Alight from the bus at the top of the hill called **Acropoleos** when you see the walls right ahead of you. Go right up the hill, following the path of the wall, and where it ends in a semi-ruined tower is the starting point for your climb up onto the ramparts.

The panoramic view is inspiring. The bay fills center stage; beyond it to the right (north) is the smoke of industry; nearer (left) are the University and Trade Fair, with a complex of new structures and a vast stadium. The tall, modern office and apartment buildings are mostly clustered around the harbor, and filling all the gaps in the great jigsaw puzzle are compact one- and two-story houses with red tile roofs, and adjoining soft, green cypresses, making it appear that the bigger buildings have been gently stuffed into a box with red and green packing to protect their fragility.

A line of white houses straggles up the ridge above Saison, to the left; below, within the walls of the city, donkey carts negotiate the sandy streets, offering fruit and vegetables as they undoubtedly did so many centuries ago when the walls were new.

You can walk atop the ruined walls, peering through the gun holes or from unprotected ledges, right down to the gate at which you left the bus, but the only other way down to the ground is about halfway along, opposite the open-air movie theater.

(The bus terminates its return ride in a central area of the old town, a small square shaded by trees and surrounded by tavernas, some on rooftops. Most of these aren't open at lunchtime, but one that is is the **Taverna Platona-teria.**)

Before you leave the tower, take a good look at the circular, sandstone building—obviously ancient—that follows the old line of the walls, now largely disappeared, down the hill. That is the **Rotunda,** a Roman building dating back more than 1600 years, which since the fifth century has been a church, **Agios Georgios.** It is closed on Tuesdays, open 7:30 a.m. to 7:30 p.m. on other days.

It's magnificently cool inside, with only what remains of a Byzantine mural just below the dome and a makeshift table covered with altar cloth and candle to remind visitors that it's a holy place. Holy or not, it would be a fine, spacious spot for a party; an echo reproduces even the softest tones as long as they are uttered while standing on the slab of white marble in the center of the room. Usually, the only sound is the purring of a pigeon, somehow trapped in the dome.

Outside, in the lovely, semi-tropical garden, is what remains of Thessaloniki's solitary minaret (once there were many), and it's considered unsafe to climb, although persistent visitors have been known to get permission from a higher authority than the custodians at the spot. Rotunda admission, 10 drs; hours are 9 a.m.-1 p.m., 4-7 p.m. daily, and 10 a.m.-1 p.m. Sundays.

The walk down through the old town vividly conveys Thessaloniki's former beauty. Even today, despite the incredible amount of building that is going on, care is obviously being taken not to disturb the picturesque streets.

In scores of spots, towering concrete buildings "nestle" cheek by jowl among the older houses, and in at least one place a narrow alley has been given even more character by a kind of concrete "bridge" built across its top; the bridge belongs to the tall, new structure which has gone up at one side.

About a block before the Rotunda is the charming, three-story **house** on St. Apostolu Paulo Street **in which Kemal Ataturk was born** in 1881. He is sometimes called the "father of modern Turkey." The house, under the wing of the Turkish Consulate General which it adjoins, has been preserved; the furniture and fittings (low divans, bed, sofas upholstered in dizzying Oriental patterns, kitchen with its old stone range) remain intact. A big black bust of the hero is in a room on the third floor. Another room on the top floor is lined with dozens of pictures of its former resident—looking like Lon Chaney sometimes, frowning, driving a tractor, delicately holding a coffee cup, in evening dress with youthful mustache, in fez and baggy britches, in Army uniform. The evening apparel, plus black silk topper, recline in a glass case.

The plaque outside reads: "C'est ici que vit le jour Gazi Moustapha Kemal, le grand renovateur de la Nation Turque et champion de l'Union Balcanique."

The house, set in a lovely garden in which dozens of cats peer slyly from behind bushes, is open 9 a.m. to 1 p.m., and 4 to 6 p.m., but you must obtain permission to enter from the adjoining consulate's office, where your identification will be demanded. Admission is free.

The block from the Rotunda down to the **Arch of Galerius** is lined with old, old houses, their overhanging balconies precariously supported by wooden beams—or maybe not so precariously, considering how long they must have stood. The Arch of Galerius, built by the Roman of that name in 303 A.D. to commemorate his victories over the Persians, depicts processions of soldiers, battles, and a feast, although 22 centuries have worn smooth many of the figures. Top of the arch is reconstructed from brick.

Behind the arch, a new church, the **Church of the Virgin,** is still being finished, but its incompleteness hasn't stopped the faithful. They are already swarming in, lighting candles, kissing ikons, and leaving money, even though the back of the altar is lined with rough wooden boards and much of the roof is still covered with straw mats.

You'll discover other ancient buildings in this neighborhood, but the most notable is the **Church of St. Sophia** (turn off Egnatia, just past the arch, and head down Ioaken Street), which is set in its own grounds blocking off the top of Iktinon Street. Built around 700 A.D., it was used as a mosque by the Turks from 1585 to 1912. Its dome bears a mosaic of Christ sitting on a rainbow with two angels clinging to his feet.

THE VIEW FROM PANORAMA: The Greeks had a word for it—a good view—and that word was *panorama,* so that's exactly what they called a little village on a hilltop eight miles from Thessaloniki.

Buses go every hour or so from outside a cafe on Dikastirion Square. The trip takes half an hour and costs 12 drs. As soon as the bus bumpily begins to climb the hill, you'll notice the lovely houses, all big and expensive, but with surprisingly few swimming pools. The village itself is set in a slight hollow and offers no view, but the climb up the road towards it, or up the hillside from it, will offer a sweeping vista for miles on every side.

Gently undulating slopes reach all the way down to the curve of Thessaloniki's wide bay, and although these appear at first glance to be merely bare hills, closer inspection reveals so much more: clusters of campers' tents, groves of cypress trees, heather, half a dozen horses choreographed randomly against a field, a patch of land covered with dark green shrubs, the yellow glint of a bulldozer at work on a road, some ploughed fields, some barren, and the whole patchwork in varying shades of green, brown, and red, with white and red houses spotted here and there.

There are a couple of tavernas where the bus stops in Panorama, better restaurants in the village itself, or on the way up the hill before it, a few minutes' walk.

A couple of luxury hotels have now gone up in Panorama, but if you want to stay here, choose the cheaper **Pefka** (tel: 22243), whose 54 rooms, all with bath, cost around 300 drs single, 400 drs double, breakfast 40 drs.

FURTHER AFIELD: The **Halkidiki Peninsula**, once isolated, is now an attractive and popular vacation area although still relatively unspoiled despite the increasing development taking place there. Old Macedonian customs (and architecture) still survive and the **Archaeological Museum** at the capital, **Poligiros**, merits attention. The five-room **Acropolis Hotel** (tel: 22342) charges about 350 drs double, but don't bank on finding a room empty on weekends.

The westernmost promontory, **Kassandra**, has fine beaches, especially around **Gerakini**, where the lavish **Gerakini Beach Hotel** (tel: 22474) offers luxurious living. There are cheaper rooms, of course, dotted along the coast. The central promontory, **Sithoria**, is still developing its road network from bumpy dirt tracks, but the scenic views of dozens of pine-clad inlets make the journey well worth the inconvenience. The village of **Arnea**, renowned for its wines and handwoven textiles—especially the famous flokati rugs—is also well worth a visit if you're en route to the easternmost peninsula. You'll also pass through **Staghira**, birthplace of Aristotle, before arriving at the coast, which (like the other two peninsulas) is riddled with lovely bays and beaches. **Ierissos** has a yacht harbor. The administrative center of this region is **Karie** from which visits can be made to the Holy Mountain region, **Mount Athos.**

Buses leave hourly for **Moudania**, and some go onwards to **Peliouri** to the south and **Marmaras** in the eastern leg. The trip to Moudania takes 1½ hours, to Peliouri about four hours. Peliouri has a **Xenia** hotel and good bathing.

Another spot you might want to check out is interesting only very early in the morning, but as it's exactly the place to park your handy VW bus for the night, you can fit it nicely into an outing to Kavala—or on the way back. The place is called **Ag. Vassilios** and it's on the shore of a lake about 23 kms outside Thessaloniki on the main road eastwards. Turn off the main road left at the village of Ag. Vassilios and make your way down a quarter mile of bumpy road to the lakeside. If you park there under the trees you'll be awoken by the sounds of a fish auction: the rhythmic chanting you'll hear is the sound of the man weighing and recording each fisherman's catch in the shed. After being weighed the shiny boxes of fish, fresh from the lake, are packed with ice and loaded onto trucks for the markets of Thessaloniki. In the chimneys and towers all around you are storks, and beside the lake donkeys graze. A lovely spot.

BRIEFLY NOTED: The buildings of the **International Trade Fair** are there permanently, the fair taking place in September each year. . . . Just opposite the trade fair entrance is a pleasant park in which there's an **open-air variety theater**. . . . The "Votsi" bus (#3), which heads east along Vassilissis Olgas Street, passes about half a dozen open-air **movie theaters**. . . . English-speaking **lawyer** who'll defend Americans: Mike Panagiokopoulis (Konstantinou, tel: 21-852), a very busy man but always gracious to those with problems. . . . Self-service laundromat, **Canadian,** can be found in Navarino Square. . . . Where to get fruit, delicatessen items for train ride to Istanbul: **Komninon Street** between Irakleon and Alexandriou streets, just across from the American Express office. There are also three terrific pastry shops in the same block as Amex, the best one around the corner on Komninon. . . . The **statue** in front of the white tower is of N. Botsis, a Greek officer who fought the Turks in a naval battle in 1912. . . . The **post office** (45 M. Alexandrou) is open until 11 p.m. . . . **Tourist Police** are at 10 Egnatia Street, tel: 522587. . . . The **U.S. Consulate General** is at 59 King Constantine, tel: 273941, the **British Consulate** a few doors away at #11 (tel: 78006). . . . There is a **tennis club** at 16 Kypron Street, tel: 411569. . . . English-speaking **doctor:** George Pandoulas, 99 Egnatia Street, tel: 277596. . . . **Dentists:** Demetrios Syrris, 8 Aghias Theodoras Street, tel: 275868; and Lazaros Koufas, 85 Egnatia Street, tel: 277747. . . . The minimum charge for a **taxi** is 10 drs, even if the meter reads less.

CARS, TOURS, BOATS: **Doucas Tours** (8 Venizelou St, tel: 224-100) is one of half a dozen car rental agencies offering VW's for around 300 drs daily, plus 8 drs per km, with a 100 km daily minimum. Doucas also operates numerous local tours: a sightseeing tour around town from 10 a.m. to 12:30 p.m.; a one-day coach and boat tour to Mount Athos (6:30 a.m. to 9 p.m.), during which the women stay on board and the men go to visit one of the monasteries; and to such other tourist attractions as the ancient city of Pella, to Meteora, Kavala/Thassos, and the peninsula of Halkidiki.

Twice weekly there's a boat from Thessaloniki to Iraklion in Crete, with stops at Thera, Ios, Mykonos, Tinos, Skopelos, Skiros, and Skiathos along the way. The entire trip, one way, takes 33 hours.

BUSES: Local: #22 from Eleftherias Square goes to the Monastery of Vlatadou and wanders around the old town streets. Take #15 from Pavlou Melas to the end of the line, up past the university to Saison—then go for a walk in the woods (tourist pavilion planned here). Numbers 5, 6, and 3, among others, will take you along Egnatia and to Pirgos Tower (on the waterfront), which separates the old town from the new, and where the theaters are.

Regular buses run out to Pella (from Andigonidon St.) every half hour until 7:30 p.m. The trip takes 45 minutes, costs 40 drs.

To Kastoria: three times daily, from Andigonidou Street 23. The trip takes four hours and costs about 200 drs one way.

To Panorama: Buses go the seven-mile distance in 25 minutes; depart from Filippi St., near Aristotelou Square; cost 22 drs.

To Aretsou: Bus #5 or #6 goes to this area, with its tavernas and little restaurants on the harbor and good swimming. Departures every ten minutes from Liberty Square; 30-minute ride; 15 drs.

To Kavala: Every hour on the hour (starting at 6 a.m.), from 61 Dragoumi Street. Trip takes 3½ hours and costs around 150 drs. Last bus at 7 p.m.

TRAINS TO THE EAST: Trains leave Thessaloniki at 7:59 daily for Drama (four hours) and Istanbul (26 hours). From Thessaloniki to Istanbul is a long and boring ride, not to mention an uncomfortable way to spend the night if you can't afford a compartment. I recommend taking a bus to Kavala (see above), another to Alexandropoulos, then the train for the last leg of the journey.

GETTING TO THE YUGOSLAV BORDER: The Yugoslav border in the attractive Lake Ohrid section is a sensitive military area in Greece and travel is not permitted beyond Florina without a special military pass. Yugoslavia-bound tourists, therefore, are recommended to head directly for **Skopje**—a journey that, by train, takes four hours and costs about 300 drs second class. Trains leave Thessaloniki three or four times daily.

4. Mount Athos

The best-known fact about Mount Athos, a self-governing community of monks—a monastic state, in effect—off the coast about 80 miles southeast of Thessaloniki, is that no women have been allowed there for 900 years.

In fact, this interesting piece of male supremacy is compounded even further by a provision against female animals! The supposed attraction of the community, although how any place without women could be worth visiting is beyond me, is the wealth of old manuscripts, frescoes, and paintings to be seen in the score of monasteries.

The scenery, of course, is spectacular, with mountains rising quite suddenly to six or seven thousand feet.

Formalities required to proceed to Mount Athos are that you first go to the American Embassy in Athens with your passport and ask for a letter of recommendation, which you must then take personally to the office of the Ministry of Foreign Affairs (2 Zallocosta Street) between 10 a.m. and 12:30 p.m. on Monday, Wednesday or Friday. The permit gives access to the monasteries and their libraries for up to one week. Photographs are allowed but tape recorders and movie cameras are not. Mount Athos regulations include the following: "Your appearance in general, both in regard to clothing as well as hair, should be appropriately restrained." It doesn't say whether wearing your hair as long as that of the monks is acceptable or not.

A permit can also be obtained by taking the letter from your embassy to the Ministry of Northern Greece (Direction of Politique Affairs) in Thessaloniki. The office, open 9 a.m. to 2 p.m., is at Dikastirion Square. Permits are not issued to women or to men under 21.

The bus to Ouranoupolis, from where the boat sails to the peninsula, leaves from 3 Platonas Street. One-way fare is about 75 drs. Check ahead, but at this writing there were six daily bus departures from Thessaloniki to Ouranoupolis via Ierissos, starting at 6 a.m.; it's a four-hour trip. From Ierissos to Tripiti (the starting point of the sea trip to Mount Athos), there are six buses daily charging three drs for the seven-km drive. There are also "motor sailing boats" from Ouranoupolis to Dafni (the entrance port of Mount Athos) which take three hours and cost 56 drs one way. If you take the first morning bus out of Thessaloniki you can make the connecting boat from Ouranoupolis.

If you would like to spend the night in **Ierissos**, there are private houses renting rooms as well as four hotels, the **Oros Athens**, the **Akanthos**, the **Athos**, and the **Akroyali**, all charging about 250 drs single, 350 drs double. At 5 a.m., a bus leaves Ierissos, arriving at Tripiti in time for the 6 a.m. boat. Check all these times carefully: they change.

Consult the **State Tourist Office** in Thessaloniki, 8 Aristotelous Square (tel: 71-888), for final pre-departure information.

Once on the peninsula, it is a two-hour walk to **Karyiae,** the capital. A mule can be rented for the ride for around 100 drs or 400 drs for the day.

The permit is presented at the office in Karyiae; in return for 150 drs, another permit, called "Diamonistirion," is issued, entitling the bearer to stay at any of the monasteries on the peninsula for up to three days.

There are about 20 monasteries on the peninsula, all of which have accommodations for visitors (free) and meals. Both rooms and meals get mixed reviews from readers.

Doucas Tours (Venizelou 8, tel: 24100) conducts one-day private tours to Mount Athos (men only) for about 150 drs per person in groups of four or more. They'll acquire the necessary permits for you to stay at the monasteries.

5. Kavala and Thassos

Since the train doesn't go to Kavala, you'll be traveling by car or bus. The trip takes three to four hours and includes some very nice scenery. Once out of Thessaloniki, you turn east for a 40-mile run through cotton and tobacco fields. The low mountains of Halkidike are on the right, and on the left the beautiful lakes Koronia and Volvi perfectly mirror the hills and villages on the far shores.

After Rentina, the road climbs through the hills, suddenly revealing the sea, with Mount Athos stretching away to the right into hazy distance. Before Asprovalta there's a well-cared-for camping ground on the shore, set in a poplar grove: full facilities and a formal flower garden, but only two lonely campers last time I looked! Asprovalta itself is a rather unsightly cluster of summer bungalows on a pebbly beach. Not far beyond is a restaurant/gas station/tourist court where the buses stop. Three-mile stretch of sand beach here, with a restaurant pavilion under huge poplars. In September, the big breakers are still warm . . . and the beach is completely deserted.

About ten miles further on, the road bends suddenly to cross the Strimon River—and there stands the big stone Lion of Amphipolis, guarding the crossing as he has since Alexander's time. On the other side of the river, the road runs for 35 miles between a coastal range and the fantastic peaks of Mount Pangeon, whose gold mines financed Philip and Alexander's expeditions. Then it snakes up to a narrow pass, and down to Kavala, cupped in an amphitheater of hills on a natural harbor.

KAVALA: It is a surprisingly large place . . . but so tucked away in little bays and folds of hills that it gives the impression of a large village. Kavala is a very pretty town, with clean streets, grassy parks, bright houses, and colorful fishing boats moored along the harbor wall. To the east is a well-preserved medieval aqueduct leading to the ramparts of a Byzantine fortress on the hill that protects that harbor. Just below it you'll see the domes of the Imaret: the largest Moslem architectural complex in Greece.

Inhabited since 3000 B.C., Kavala became an important port during the fifth century B.C., and even minted its own coins. St. Paul landed here, to preach his first sermons in Europe—this memorialized by the huge cross atop the mountain behind the town. Important to Alexander (his name does keep cropping up in this region!), the Byzantine emperors, the Franks, the Venetians, and the Turks, Kavala was the favorite home of Mohammed Ali, who refused to give it up to Greece until 1913.

Where to Stay and Eat

The **Hotel Philippi** (Filellinon and Venizelou, tel: 22856) is a modern semi-luxury hotel with some bathless rooms for around 300 drs double. Doubles with bath run to about 400 drs. Whether you stay there or not, visit the fourth-floor bar for a panoramic view of the harbor area.

Another bar-with-a-view is atop the **Hotel Panorama** (32c Venizelou, tel: 24205), where bathless rooms cost 250 drs single, 300 drs double; 400 drs for doubles with bath. The rooms are just as nice, and the Panorama is a big (52 room), rather flashy American-style place.

Also on Venizelou, west of the expensive Hotel Galaxy, is the cheap **Hotel Acropolis** (tel: 23543) with bathless rooms for 200 drs single, 300 drs double. And right behind Venizelou, on Palama Street, is the cheaper **Astoria** (tel: 22355).

Another hotel for penny-savers is the **Parthenon** (Spetson 14, tel: 23205), with its cute wooden balconies and minuscule rooms on a back street off Omonia Square, right across from the National Bank. Very simple and old-fashioned.

What to Do

Your two or three days in Kavala and Thassos will probably be restful ones, full of lolling in the sun, but there are some interesting trips for the energetic. Buses leave every half hour for **Drama,** 23 miles to the north, but since the most interesting thing about Drama is its name, get off at **Philippi** just 15 minutes away. Spend an hour wandering through the ruins of this fourth century B.C. city built by Philip of Macedon. This is also the place where Brutus met Caesar's ghost, and subsequently lost the Roman Empire . . . not to mention his life.

During the last week of July through the middle of August, the **State Theater of Northern Greece** presents classic plays at the ancient theaters of Philippi and Thassos. You'll be sure to see the schedule around town, or stop by the National Tourist Office at the corner of Venizelou and Dragoumi.

They can also give you advice on the route to follow if you decide to climb the hills back of town to the **Church of Prophet Elias** for a sensational view of the whole area. Unfortunately, one of the beautiful churches atop the mountain (another favorite walk, and view) was just recently destroyed in a forest fire.

A shorter and more rewarding climb will take you to the **Panagia** area on the fortress hill. From Plateia Nikotsara (the large intersection just in front of the aqueduct), head straight toward the fortress, then right on Kapsali and left on Pavliou. This will take you past the **Imaret,** with its peculiar domes and spires topped by bronze crescents. It would be fun to wander around inside, but the Greeks use it as a warehouse. A little further on and you'll come to the tip of the peninsula and the **statue of Mohammed Ali** which faces his house, now a museum—if a completely empty house can be a museum. There is no admission charge, but the doorkeeper will be glad to give you a complete tour and describe the peculiar housekeeping arrangements required by a man with seven wives and a houseful of bodyguards. Three or four drs is the customary tip for the tour.

If you backtrack to the Imaret and then take the wide ramp heading uphill, you will eventually come to the **fortress** gate (open 8 a.m. to 1 p.m., 3 to 6 p.m.; no admission, but again, you're expected to tip the gatekeeper). You can explore the dungeon or walk along the well-preserved battlements for a series of splendid views. On some evenings, musical programs are presented in the courtyard. Turn left when you leave, and you'll return to town by a different route, with a view of the hidden eastern harbor.

Panagia itself is completely different in character from Kavala, with tiny twisting streets that become stairs, pastel houses overgrown with flowers, and a pomegranate tree in every yard. Near the aqueduct on your way back, you'll pass several fascinating shops where bronze and copper items are made and sold.

Kavala has an **archaeological museum** in a park at the west end of the quay, with finds from Amphipolis and Philippi. Five drs admission, except Thursdays and Sundays.

Cheapest restaurants are to be found along **Phetaivias Street,** the one behind the brightly lit Verona Pizza place and which leads to the bus station. At the other side of the harbor is the glittery **Stathis** restaurant with tables outdoors and inside. Plenty of cafes along the harbor for sitting and watching the action, but an even better view is from the rooftop bar atop the **Hotel Galaxy.**

For nighttime activity Kavala has several "snack bars," oldest and most central of which is the **American Snack Bar** at the corner of Venizelou and Azerof. Good pizza, tasty hamburgers and sandwiches. There are similar snack bars on **Omonias Street,** which runs up from the Eleftherias Square more or less parallel with the harbor and contains three **movie theaters** (one, the **Victor,** is actually in a cobbled alleyway just off Omonias beside the Yamaha shop). Last movie show is usually 10:15 p.m. There's a discotheque, **N.O.K.,** on the pier and others on the road towards the beach.

The Beaches

Beaches extend for several miles on both sides of town, with the best one to the west, starting at Kalamitsa (the little town at the west end of the harbor). The beautiful **N.T.O.** camping site (5 km), **Kara-Orman, Kraklitsa,** and **Nea Peramos** (20 km) are all reached by regular bus service.

If you're taking the boat to Thassos, it might be wise (and it will certainly be fun) to wander through the **market area** between Plateia Eleftherias and the aqueduct, and buy a picnic lunch—food is rather expensive on the island. The market offers colossal mounds of colorful fruit and vegetables very cheaply, and there are shops with a wide variety of cheeses and salamis. Try Vitseris, a local cheese like a mild Swiss. And you might take an empty bottle to the shop full of casks, where you can fill it with ouzo or retsina at ridiculously low prices.

THASSOS: Thassos is a big island with a very respectable mountain, but somehow it manages to appear cozy and charming. It also has plenty of hotels and restaurants without seeming touristy. One of the greener islands, with pines, poplars, willows, and sycamores, it is quite a contrast to the Cyclades. There are 23 villages on it, but most have never seen a tourist and wouldn't know what to do with one if he came along. Only in the past year has the road been completed, so now the bus can make a full circuit of the island. Some of the daily boats from Kavala touch at the tiny port of **Ormos Prinon** before continuing around Pahi headland to **Limin.**

In the sixth century B.C., Thassos was very prosperous, and a little later Herodotus wrote that he'd seen gold on the island—but nowadays only cadmium is mined at Limenaria in the south, and all that remains of the good old days are a few ruins and some statues in the museum. Hippocrates (the only man to be remembered for his oath) lived here for three years, but apparently

Thassos has always been a bit off the beaten track, and has kept its delightful calm intact.

Where to Stay

In Limin—a small wedge of soft white stone and red tiles set into a dark green landscape—you'll find all you need for a couple of delightful days. The pleasant ten-room **Hotel Theano** (tel: 21209) right opposite the dock is probably the most convenient place to stay, especially since the manager speaks English. Single rooms go for around 250 drs, doubles about 320 drs, and there are views of the sea. Classier is the almost adjoining **Hotel Timoleon** (tel: 21277), whose 30 rooms come with breakfast, in season, for about 400 drs single, 500 drs double. But there are many cheaper places of which the **Angelica** (tel: 21387) at the southeast corner is probably the best. Behind Thassos Tours at this end of the harbor are the budget-priced **Astir** and **Gallini,** both with simple rooms for 230 drs single, 300 drs double.

What to Do

The main street behind the harbor leads to several things:

(1) The **Archaeological Museum** (open 8 a.m. to 1 p.m. 3 to 7 p.m.; admission five drs), with a collection of carved stones and chips of painted ceramic, all found on the island.

(2) A quiet, sheltered harbor, concealed from view in town, with cafes aplenty.

(3) A path leading up the hillside behind the Hotel Angelica to the remains of an **ancient theater,** in a clearing in the woods, with a pretty view of the town. Old-fashioned stone benches have been supplemented with low wooden ones, and dramas are performed here on some July and August weekends. (Ask for the schedule at the tourist office in Thessaloniki.)

Boats, Buses, Beaches . . . and Movies

There are half a dozen boats daily between 8:30 a.m. and 4:30 p.m. from Kavala to Thassos, but some go to **Limin** and some to **Skala Prinas**—different parts of the island and 20 minutes apart by bus—so make sure you know which is which. Limin is the most interesting part; **Limenaria,** on the south coast, is depressingly arid and industrial. You can make a circuit of the island by bus visiting the pleasant village of **Potami,** or rent a bicycle or motor scooter in Limin behind the Hotel Theano. There's a good beach not far from Potami. Ferry between Kavala and Thassos takes about 1½ hours.

A tip, don't continue to **Makriamos** for a swim, despite the beautiful photo in the brochure, unless you're willing to shell out 50 drs to enter, share the beach with the rich crowd that rents bungalows there, and eat at the expensive restaurant.

There's a beach at the museum end of the town, and another one outside the Hotel Xenia, but the best beach is further around the bay past the Xenia, and launches run there constantly from the harbor.

Thassos has two movie theaters, one an open-air theater.

THE DRACHMA AND THE DOLLAR

AS THIS BOOK goes to press, one U.S. dollar will buy 35.33 Greek drachmas—making each drachma worth precisely 2.83 U.S. cents. The currency conversion table below was prepared at this rate of exchange—but don't use it as an *exact* guide: rates of exchange tend to vary, slightly, from day to day. The relationship between the dollar and the drachma is not expected to change substantially in the near future, but it is always good to double-check these things before you go. In any case, the chart below ought to give you a relative idea of how many of your hard-earned dollars you'll be spending.

Drs	Dollars	Drs	Dollars
1	.03	150	4.25
2	.06	175	4.95
3	.09	200	5.66
4	.11	300	8.49
5	.14	350	9.91
10	.28	400	11.32
15	.42	450	12.74
25	.71	500	14.15
35	.99	600	16.98
50	1.42	700	19.81
60	1.70	800	22.64
75	2.12	900	25.47
100	2.83	1000	28.30

ARTHUR FROMMER, INC.
380 MADISON AVE., NEW YORK, N.Y. 10017   Date_____

Friends, please send me (postpaid) the books checked below:

$10-A-DAY GUIDES

(In-depth guides to low-cost tourist accommodations and facilities.)

- ☐ Europe on $10 a Day $4.95
- ☐ Australia on $15 a Day $4.95
- ☐ England on $15 a Day $4.95
- ☐ Greece on $10 & $15 a Day $4.50
- ☐ Hawaii on $15 & $20 a Day $4.50
- ☐ Ireland on $10 a Day $4.50
- ☐ Israel on $15 a Day $4.50
- ☐ Mexico and Guatemala on $10 a Day $4.95
- ☐ New Zealand on $10 & $15 a Day $4.50
- ☐ New York on $15 & $20 a Day $4.50
- ☐ Scandinavia on $15 & $20 a Day $4.50
- ☐ South America on $10 & $15 a Day $4.50
- ☐ Spain and Morocco (plus the Canary Is.) on $10 & $15 a Day $4.50
- ☐ Turkey on $10 & $15 a Day $4.50
- ☐ Washington, D.C. on $15 a Day $4.50

DOLLAR-WISE GUIDES

(Guides to tourist accommodations and facilities from budget to deluxe, with emphasis on the medium-priced.)

- ☐ England $4.50
- ☐ France $4.50
- ☐ Germany $4.50
- ☐ Italy $4.50
- ☐ Portugal $4.50
- ☐ California & Las Vegas $4.50
- ☐ New England $4.50
- ☐ Southeast & New Orleans..$4.50

THE ARTHUR FROMMER GUIDES

(Pocket-size guides to tourist accommodations and facilities in all price ranges.)

- ☐ Athens $1.95
- ☐ Boston $1.95
- ☐ Honolulu $1.95
- ☐ Ireland/Dublin/Shannon ...$1.95
- ☐ Las Vegas $1.95
- ☐ Lisbon/Madrid/Costa del Sol $1.95
- ☐ London $1.95
- ☐ Los Angeles $1.95
- ☐ New York $1.95
- ☐ Paris $1.95
- ☐ Rome $1.95
- ☐ San Francisco $1.95
- ☐ Washington, D.C. $1.95

By the Council on International Educational Exchange

☐ Whole World Handbook $3.95
(A student guide to work, study and travel worldwide.)

☐ Where to Stay USA $3.95
(A guide to accommodations in all 50 states costing from 50¢ to $12 per night.)

Enclosed is my check or money order for $_____

NAME_____

ADDRESS_____

CITY_____STATE_____ZIP_____